MASTERING SAP R/3®
FI : Transactions Made Easy

V. Narayanan

BPB PUBLICATIONS
B-14, CONNAUGHT PLACE, NEW DELHI-110001

FIRST EDITION 2007

Distributors:

MICRO BOOK CENTRE
2, City Centre, CG Road,
Near Swastic Char Rasta,
AHMEDABAD-380009 Phone: 26421611

COMPUTER BOOK CENTRE
12, Shrungar Shopping Centre, M.G. Road,
BANGALORE-560001 Phone: 25587923, 25584641

MICRO BOOKS
Shanti Niketan Building, 8, Camac Street,
KOLKATTA-700017 Phone: 22826518, 22826519

BUSINESS PROMOTION BUREAU
8/1, Ritchie Street, Mount Road,
CHENNAI-600002 Phone: 28410796, 28550491

DECCAN AGENCIES
4-3-329, Bank Street,
HYDERABAD-500195 Phone: 24756400, 24756967

MICRO MEDIA
Shop No. 5, Mahendra Chambers, 150 D.N. Road,

Next to Capital Cinema V.T. (C.S.T.) Station,
MUMBAI-400001 Ph.: 22078296, 22078297

BPB PUBLICATIONS
B-14, Connaught Place, **NEW DELHI-110001**
Phone: 23325760, 23723393, 23737742

INFO TECH
G-2, Sidhartha Building, 96 Nehru Place,
NEW DELHI-110019
Phone: 26438245, 26415092, 26234208

INFO TECH
Shop No. 2, F-38, South Extension Part-1
NEW DELHI-110049
Phone: 24691288

BPB BOOK CENTRE
376, Old Lajpat Rai Market,
DELHI-110006 PHONE: 23861747

Price : Rs. 450/-

ISBN 81-8333-131-9

Published by Manish Jain for BPB Publications, B-14, Connaught Place, New Delhi-110 001 and Printed by him at Akash Press, New Delhi.

Dedication

To my father, C.V. Veeriah....

Acknowledgments

Many, many thanks to my beloved wife, Meena, for all her support through out the mission of writing this book, right from conception of the idea. In fact, she has been the catalyst behind this work.

Special thanks to my boys, Sidhu and Kaushik, for putting up with me; without bothering me during this task. They had been intelligent enough in adjusting without any complaint, of me not spending time with them!

Thanks also to other members of my family, my friends and colleagues for all the encouragement I got through out.

And, thanks to Hariharan, and his staff at Maagnus Infotech (www.maagnus.com) for allowing me to use their SAP system for configuring / developing the screen shots for use in the book.

Trademark Acknowledgment

SAP R/3® is the registered trademark of SAP, AG. SAP's trademark and copyrights are duly acknowledged.

Disclaimer

Introduction

With not many books available in the market on SAP R/3 FI (Financial Accounting), there has been a long felt need among the users, trainers, consultants etc for a book which is simple and authentic to understand SAP's Financial Accounting (FI). True, there have been books on the configuration side of FI but none on the transaction side. The proof of configuration is when one is able to complete successfully the business transactions using the SAP system. This book aims at providing that proof to ensure that transactions are made correctly & intelligently in the system.

It is true that over a period, by practice, you would have known how to put through transactions. But, it is also true that you have been doing that as rote without understanding the nuances and repercussions a particular transaction would result in. This is where this book is going to add value by providing the necessary insight into the transactions. At the end of this book, I am sure you would certainly understand what you had been missing all these days by not knowing the innards of a transaction.

All the materials available with SAP are excellent, informative and exhaustive. It is so exhaustive that you may find it difficult to zero-in on the relevant area of information. Any text and narration becomes boring and exhausting after some time and you feel wanting for a 'seeing-is-believing' experience in learning. That is exactly this book aims at:

1. Providing a concise 'ready-reckoner' source of information, arranged transaction-wise which is easy to follow and understand.
2. Providing the necessary screen-user interface relying heavily on transaction-oriented, actual screen-shots from SAP R/3 system.
3. Easy learning which is fun as well. You can read the book in any way you want: there is no compulsion that you should start at the 1st chapter and end at the last. Since the focus is on a single transaction, which is a self-contained study unit replete with information, tips and ideas, you will never need to cross reference, most of the time!

All said, the book is a modest attempt to bring some of the important, and basic sometimes, transactions under various functional areas of:

- FI-G/L (General Ledger)
- FI-AP (Accounts Payable)
- FI-AR (Accounts Receivable)
- FI-AA (Asset Accounting)

In each of these areas, transactions have been included to reflect;

- Master records
- Document entry
- Account management
- Periodic processing
- Reporting

As you will agree, it is next to impossible to cover each and every transaction in a book like this, because the transactions in any of these functional areas will easily run into hundreds and hundreds. However, a fair attempt has been made to include the most vital transactions, and difficult as well, so as to give the reader a whole view of the transactions of the module as such. An attempt has been made to unravel the mysteries and complexities of transactions like *dunning program*, *automatic payment program*, *depreciation run* etc. which you will agree that most of us got it wrong on many occasions (may be even now!)

An interesting aspect you would notice through out the book is, that the author does not stop with a particular transaction while explaining the same; in most of the cases, you are taken much beyond the transaction highlighting how a particular transaction has updated the document(s), accounts(s), master(s) etc providing you the insight of what happens after a transaction has been posted into the system.

A 'miscellaneous' chapter is also thrown in which provides some of the configuration related transactions like maintaining payment terms, exchange rates, number range administration for documents etc. It also deals with the 'Schedule Manager' which you can use across modules for managing periodic operations.

All the screen shots used in the book relate to SAP R/3® version 4.6c.

How to use this book?

Make no mistake that this is not the regular book in the sense that you are not required to follow the conventional way of reading from cover to cover (shall we say chapter-by-chapter!). As mentioned elsewhere, you are free to jump to any of the transactions across the book and still complete that unit without the fear that you might miss something if you have not read the earlier ones.

The book is organized in five sections:

1. FI-G/L (General Ledger)
2. FI-AP (Accounts Payable)
3. FI-AR (Accounts Receivable)
4. FI-AA (Asset Accounting)
5. Miscellaneous

Under each of the sections the various transactions are logically arranged starting from:

- Document entry
- Document
- Account
- Master records
- Periodic processing
- Information system
- Environment

A typical transaction starts with (a) business process overview or transactions overview. This is followed by the (b) actual transaction, explained in steps. At the end of the transaction, there may be another section which acts like (c) verifying the transaction explained earlier in (b).

1. The chapter heading explains what the transaction is, with the transaction code at the end of the sentence

Example:

AR / AP – Dunning Program: F150

2. Followed by the chapter heading, there is table indicating how to access the transaction. The table contains the transaction code, menu path and some times, the name of the program.

Example:

Transaction Code	F150
Menu	**Accounting > Financial Accounting > Accounts Receivable > Periodic processing > Dunning**

Example:

Transaction Code	S_ALR_87100205
Program	RFHABU00
Menu	Accounting > Financial Accounting > General Ledger > Periodic Processing > Closing > Document > Balance Audit Trail > All Accounts > General Ledger from Document File

3. The section which follows is the ***business process or transaction overview*** which, besides giving you the glimpse of that particular transaction, gives much more information related to that process or transaction.

Example:

Business Process Overview

The SAP System allows you to dun ("remind") business partners automatically. The system duns the open items from business partner accounts. The dunning program selects the overdue open items, determines the dunning level of the account in question, and creates a dunning notice. It then saves the dunning data determined for the items and accounts affected. You can use the dunning program to dun both customers and vendors. It may be necessary to dun a vendor in case of debit balance as a result of a credit memo.

Dunning is administered through a ***Dunning Program,*** which uses Dunning Key (to limit the dunning level per item), Dunning Procedure and Dunning Area (if dunning is not done at company code level)

Dunning Procedure controls:
- Dunning Interval / frequency.
- Grace days / minimum days in arrear.
- Number of Dunning levels (at least one level) —one level dunning procedures are known as 'payment reminders'.
- Transactions to be dunned.
- Interest to be calculated on the overdue items.
- Known or negotiated leave, if any, which needs to be considered in selecting the overdue items.
- Company code data like (a) Is dunning per dunning area? (b) Is dunning per dunning level? (c) reference company code (d) dunning company code etc.
- Dunning forms / media to be selected for the dunning run.
  .....
  ......

4. After the business process / transaction overview, you get into the ***transaction steps***. Each transaction step is numbered as **Step-1**, **Step-2** etc. The explanation below the step number has also the screen identifier shown as **"xxxxxxxxxx"** ("Dunning" , in the example below).

Example:

Transaction Steps
Step-1
Access the transaction either by the transaction code or menu, and you will be taken to **"Dunning"** screen (Figure: **F150-1**).

5. At each step you are shown a screen-shot; each screen is numbered as (Figure: **F150-1**) wherein **F150** denotes the transaction and the number following indicates the screen-shot number in that transaction. Hence, Figure: **F150-1** represents the first screen-shot relating to the **transaction code F150**.

6. At each step you are shown the fields for data entry with a small explanation. It is also shown whether the data entry is mandatory (**M**) or optional (**O**). Within a screen, the fields are identified by serial number even though they may be grouped under various data entry blocks.

> 1. **Dunning date (M):** Enter the date of dunning, which needs to be updated on the documents, including the dunning notices.
> 2. **Docmnts posted up to(M):** Enter the date up to which the system will look for the overdue and dunnable items.
> 3. **Company code (M):** Enter the company code (s) for which the dunning is done.
> Under, Account restrictions:
> 4. **Customer (O):** Enter the customers to whom the dunning is relevant. For all the customers to be considered, leave the field(s) blank.

7. **Additional information or 'tips'** is shown as under:

Example:

> The payment difference can be treated the way it is configured in the system. If the difference is within the tolerance limit, defined in the system using the *tolerance groups* (defined at the company code level), the cash discount is adjusted or the system automatically posts the difference to a gain/loss account. When the payment difference exceeds the limits of defined tolerance, then the incoming amount may be processed as a *partial payment* (the original open item is not cleared, but the incoming payment is posted with a reference to that invoice) or the difference is posted as the *residual item* (the original open item is cleared and a new open item created by the system for the difference amount) in the system.

8. There are situations or areas where you need to be extra careful. These areas or instances are denoted by **'warning'** icon and a text, which will appear as under:

Example:

> The total debit amount must equal the total credit amount and the indicator light must be green ⬤⬤⬤. Correct any warning or error messages displayed at the bottom left of the screen (Status bar) Warning messages appear in yellow ⬤⬤⬤ and must be noted, corrected if necessary. To ignore the warning and to proceed further, press the 'enter' key. Error messages appear in red ⬤⬤⬤ and must be corrected before the document can be posted.

9. The system generated messages can be displayed as pop-up (if configured that way) or will be shown at the bottom of the screen on the status bar. So, do not be alarmed if you do not get the pop-up screen. The same information/warning message should be shown in the status bar.

Example:

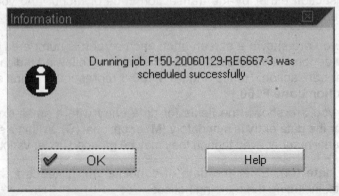

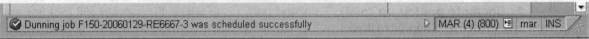

10. At the end of the transaction, if you see the following 'End of Transaction' sign, then this means that you are now going to be shown how the transaction has updated the system as to the document or master or account etc.

Example:

―――――――――――――| End of Transaction |―――――――――――――

11. Now, you will see a different convention in transaction step numbering. The steps will start as **Step-A**, **Step-B** etc.

Example:

> **Step-A**
>
> Use *Transaction Code: FD03* to view the customer master record. When you enter the code, system pops up **"Display Customer: Initial Screen"** (Figure: **F150-FD03-1**).

12. Note that the numbering for screen shot now shows two transactions namely **F150** & **FD03** meaning that you are in the chapter relating to **transaction code F150**, but actually 'verifying' that completed transaction using the **transaction code FD03**.

13. Almost in all the places the steps are shown using SAP's standard icons like , etc. However, you may also see function keys mentioned along with the buttons like **"F8"**, **"F6"** etc.

14. Throughout the book, you will find mention of either "SAP or "SAP R/3". Both mean the same and refer to "SAP R/3" only.

Table of Contents

FI - G/L
General
Ledger

1

G/L - Easy Access: FSMN

Transaction Code	FSMN

Transaction Overview

Transaction Code FSMN provides you the easy access to all the transactions you need in General Ledger. As you will be seeing in the following pages, the various transactions are neatly arranged into various top-level folders for easy access within a particular functionality. The transactions are grouped under:

1. Document entry
2. Document
3. Account
4. Master records
5. Periodic processing
6. Reporting
7. Information system
8. Environment

As a ready reckoner, the entire tree of transactions is shown in a convenient table at the end of this transaction.

Transaction Steps

Step-1

Access the transaction either by the transaction code or by the menu, and you will be taken to **"SAP Easy Access General Ledger"** Screen (Figure: **FSMN**-1).

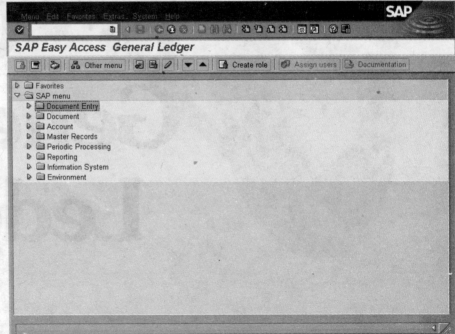

Figure: **FSMN**-1

Step-2

Expand "***Document Entry***" folder to view the transaction codes/menu for (a) ***Document entry*** (b) ***Reference documents*** and (c) ***Others*** (Figure: **FSMN**-2).

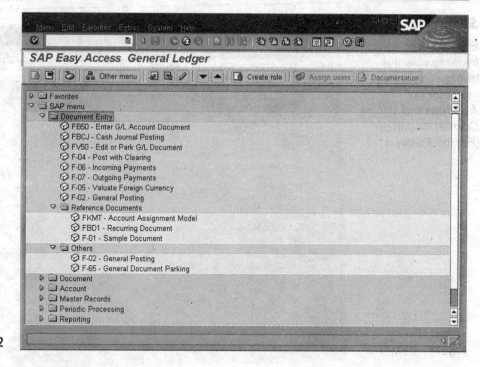

Figure: **FSMN**-2

Step-3

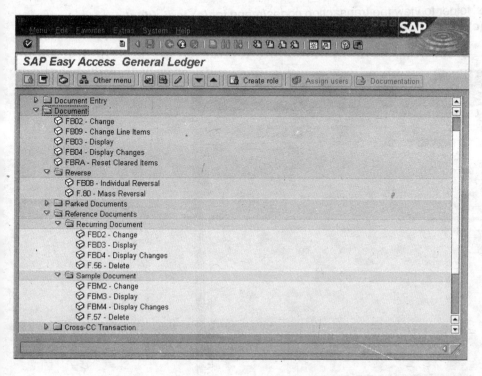

Expand "***Document***" folder to view the transaction codes/ menu for (a) ***Document*** (b) ***Reverse documents***, (c) ***Parked documents***, (d) ***Reference documents – Recurring / Sample document*** and (e) ***Cross company code transactions*** (Figure: **FSMN**-3).

Figure: **FSMN**-3

Step-4

Expand "*Account*"
folder to view the
transaction codes/
menu for (a)
Account and (b)
*Correspondenc*e
(Figure: **FSMN**-4).

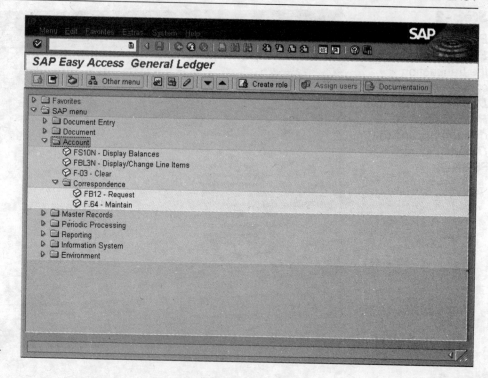

Figure: **FSMN**-4

Step-5

Expand '*Master Records*' folder to view the transaction codes/menu for (a) *Individual processing* (b)
Collective processing, (c) *Display changes,* (d) *Compare company code* and (e) *Sample account*
(Figure: **FSMN**-5).

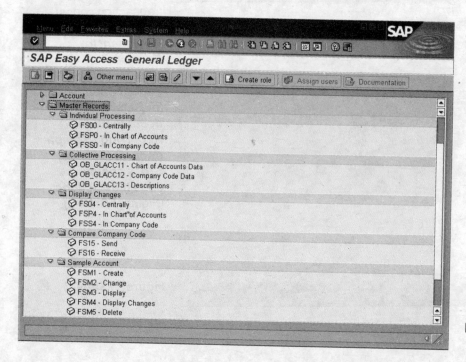

Figure: **FSMN**-5

Step-6

Expand '*Periodic Processing*' folder to view the transaction codes/menu for (a) *Schedule manager,*

(b) *Interest calculation*, (c) *Automatic clearing*, (d) *Print correspondence*, (e) *Recurring entries*, (f) *Archiving,* (g) *Planning* and (h) *Closing* (Figure: FSMN-6).

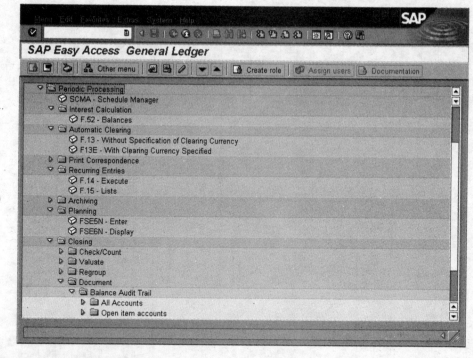

Figure: **FSMN**-6

All the transaction codes under *FSMN* are shown on the following pages:

Document Entry
- FB50 - Enter G/L Account Document
- FBCJ - Cash Journal Posting
- FV50 - Edit or Park G/L Document
- F-04 - Post with Clearing
- F-06 - Incoming Payments
- F-07 - Outgoing Payments
- F-05 - Valuate Foreign Currency
- F-02 - General Posting

Reference Documents
- FKMT - Account Assignment Model
- FBD1 - Recurring Document
- F-01 - Sample Document

Others
- F-02 - General Posting
- F-65 - General Document Parking

Document
- FB02 - Change
- FB09 - Change Line Items
- FB03 - Display
- FB04 - Display Changes
- FBRA - Reset Cleared Items

Reverse
- FB08 - Individual Reversal
- F.80 - Mass Reversal
- FBV0 - Post/Delete

Parked Documents
- FV50 - One-Screen Transaction for Posting/Deleting
- FBV2 - Change
- FV50 - One-Screen Transaction for Changes

- FBV3 - Display
- FBV4 - Change Header
- FBV5 - Display Changes
- FBV6 - Refuse

Reference Documents

- Recurring Document
  - FBD2 - Change
  - FBD3 - Display
  - FBD4 - Display Changes
  - F.56 - Delete
- Sample Document
  - FBM2 - Change
  - FBM3 - Display
  - FBM4 - Display Changes
  - F.57 - Delete

Cross-CC Transaction

- FBU2 - Change
- FBU3 - Display
- FBU8 - Reverse

Account

- FS10N - Display Balances
- FBL3N - Display/Change Line Items
- F-03 - Clear
- Correspondence
  - FB12 - Request
  - F.64 - Maintain
- Individual Processing
  - FS00 - Centrally

Master Records

Periodic Processing		
		FSP0 - In Chart of Accounts
		FSS0 - In Company Code
	Collective Processing	OB_GLACC11 - Chart of Accounts Data
		OB_GLACC12 - Company Code Data
		OB_GLACC13 - Descriptions
	Display Changes	FS04 - Centrally
		FSP4 - In Chart of Accounts
		FSS4 - In Company Code
	Compare Company Code	FS15 - Send
		FS16 - Receive
	Sample Account	FSM1 - Create
		FSM2 - Change
		FSM3 - Display
		FSM4 - Display Changes
		FSM5 - Delete
	SCMA - Schedule Manager	
	Interest Calculation	F.52 - Balances
	Automatic Clearing	F.13 - Without Specification of Clearing Currency

- F13E - With Clearing Currency Specified
- **Print Correspondence**
  - F.61 - As per Requests
  - F.63 - Delete Requests
  - F.62 - Internal Documents
- **Recurring Entries**
  - F.14 - Execute
  - F.15 - Lists
- **Archiving**
  - F48A - Documents
  - F64A - Transaction Figures
  - FCAA - Checks
  - F53A - G/L Accounts
  - F61A - Banks
- **Planning**
  - FSE5N - Enter
  - FSE6N - Display
- **Closing**
  - **Check/Count**
    - F.03 - Comparison
  - **Valuate**
    - F.05 - Foreign Currency Valuation
    - FBS1 - Enter Accrual/Deferral Doc.
    - F.81 - Reverse Accrual/Deferral Document
    - FJA1 - Inflation Adjustment of G/L Accounts
    - FJA2 - Reset Inflation Data
  - **Regroup**
    - F.19 - GR/IR Clearing
    - F.50 - Profit and Loss Adjustment
  - **Balance**
    - F.5D - Calculate

Report			
Document	**Balance Audit Trail**	**All Accounts**	S_ALR_87100205 - General Ledger from the Document File
			S_ALR_87012313 - General Ledger Corresponding Accounts (Russia)
		From Balance Audit Trail	S_ALR_87012314 - Extract for the Accumulated Historical Balance Audit Trail
			S_ALR_87012315 - Account Balance from Accumulated Historical Balance Audit Trail
			S_ALR_87012316 - Historical Balance Audit Trail by Alternative Account N
		Open item accounts	S_ALR_87012317 - Open Item Account Balance Audit Trail from the Document
		From Balance Audit Trail	S_ALR_87012318 - Extract for Accumulated Open Item Balance Audit Trail
			S_ALR_87012319 - Acct Balance from Accumulated Open Item Balance Audit Trail
			S_ALR_87012320 - Open Item Balance Audit Trail by Alternative Account Number
	Sheet Adjustment		F.5E - Post
			F.5F - Display Log
			F.5G - Special Functions
General Ledger Reports	**Balance Sheet/ Profit and Loss Statement / Cash Flow**	**General**	S_ALR_87012269 - Balance Sheet Using Cost of Sales Approach (German Trade)
			S_ALR_87012270 - Profit and Loss Statement Using Cost of Goods Sold (Germany)
		Actual/Actual Comparisons	S_ALR_87012249 - Actual/Actual Comparison for Year
			S_ALR_87012250 - Half-Year Actual/Actual Comparison
			S_ALR_87012251 - Quarterly Actual/Actual Comparison
			S_ALR_87012252 - Periodic Actual/Actual Comparison

- **Plan / Actual Comparisons**
  - S_ALR_87012284 - Balance Sheet / Profit and Loss Statement
  - S_P00_07000329 - SAP Minimal Variant
  - S_ALR_87012253 - Annual Plan/Actual Comparison
  - S_ALR_87012254 - Half-Year Plan/Actual Comparison
  - S_ALR_87012255 - Quarterly Plan/Actual Comparison
  - S_ALR_87012256 - Periodic Plan/Actual Comparison
- **Time Series**
  - S_ALR_87012257 - 10-Year Actual/Actual Comparison
- **Cash Flow**
  - S_ALR_87012271 - Cash Flow (Direct Method)
  - S_ALR_87012272 - Cash Flow (Indirect Method) Variant 1
  - S_ALR_87012273 - Cash Flow (Indirect Method) Variant 2
- **Account Balances**
  - **Background Processing**
    - FSIB - Background Processing
  - **General**
    - **G / L Account Balances**
      - S_ALR_87012277 - G/L Account Balances
      - S_ALR_87012276 - SAP Minimal Variant
      - S_ALR_87100198 - Offsetting Account Program
    - **Totals and Balances**
      - S_ALR_87012301 - Totals and Balances
      - S_ALR_87012300 - SAP Minimal Variant
    - **Structured Account Balances**
      - S_ALR_87012279 - Structured Account Balances
      - S_ALR_87012278 - SAP Minimal Variant
    - **Average Balances**
      - S_ALR_87012334 - Local Currency, Period Version
      - S_ALR_87012335 - Period Version - Transaction Currency
      - S_ALR_87012336 - Posting Date, Daily Version
      - S_ALR_87012337 - Value Date Daily Version
      - S_ALR_87012338 - Period Version - Local Currency Year-to-Date

Line Items	General Ledger, Line Items		S_ALR_87012339 - Period Version - Transaction Currency Year-to-Date
			S_ALR_87012282 - G/L Line Items, List for Printing
			S_ALR_87012280 - SAP Minimal Variant
			S_ALR_87012304 - SAP Minimal Variant - Open Items
	G/L Account Statements		S_ALR_87012332 - G/L Account Statements
			S_ALR_87012331 - SAP Minimal Variant
Document	General	Document Journal	S_ALR_87012287 - Document Journal
			S_ALR_87012286 - SAP Minimal Variant
		Compact Document Journal	S_ALR_87012289 - Compact Document Journal
			S_ALR_87012288 - SAP Minimal Variant
		Line Item Journal	S_ALR_87012291 - Line Item Journal
			S_ALR_87012290 - SAP Minimal Variant
		Display of Changed Documents	S_ALR_87012293 - Display of Changed Documents
			S_ALR_87012292 - SAP Minimal Variant
		Invoice Numbers Allocated Twice	S_ALR_87012342 - Gaps in Document Number Assignment
		Posting Totals	S_ALR_87012344 - Posting Totals
			S_ALR_87012343 - SAP Minimal Variant
		Recurring Entry Documents	S_ALR_87012346 - Recurring Entry Documents
			S_ALR_87012345 - SAP Minimal Variant
			S_ALR_87012347 - Document Items Extract
Master Data	Chart of Accounts		S_ALR_87012326 - Chart of Accounts
			S_ALR_87012325 - SAP Minimal Variant
	G/L Account List		S_ALR_87012328 - G/L Account List

- Information System
  - General Ledger Reports
    - Balance Carrying Forward
      - Carrying Forward
        - F.16 - Balance Carry Forward
    - Balance Sheet/ Profit and Loss Statement / Cash Flow
      - General
        - Actual/ Actual Comparisons
          - S_ALR_87012249 - Actual / Actual Comparison for Year
          - S_ALR_87012250 - Half-Year Actual/Actual Comparison
          - S_ALR_87012251 - Quarterly Actual/Actual Comparison
          - S_ALR_87012252 - Periodic Actual/Actual Comparison
          - S_ALR_87012269 - Balance Sheet Using Cost of Sales Approach (German Trade)
          - S_ALR_87012270 - Profit and Loss Statement Using Cost of Goods Sold (Germany)
          - S_ALR_87012284 - Balance Sheet / Profit and Loss Statement
          - S_P00_07000329 - SAP Minimal Variant
        - Plan/ Actual
          - S_ALR_87012253 - Annual Plan/Actual Comparison

- Account Assignment Manual
  - S_ALR_87012327 - SAP Minimal Variant
  - S_ALR_87012330 - Account assignment manual
  - S_ALR_87012329 - SAP Minimal Variant
- Display Changes to G/L Accounts
  - S_ALR_87012308 - Display Changes to G/L Accounts
  - S_ALR_87012307 - SAP Minimal Variant
- S_ALR_87012333 - G/L Accounts List
- FB41 - Post Tax Payable
- F.38 - Transfer Deferred Tax
- GC44 - Send Data to Consolidation

- **Comparisons**
  - S_ALR_87012254 - Half-Year Plan/Actual Comparison
  - S_ALR_87012255 - Quarterly Plan/Actual Comparison
  - S_ALR_87012256 - Periodic Plan/Actual Comparison
- **Time Series**
  - S_ALR_87012257 - 10-Year Actual/Actual Comparison
- **Cash Flow**
  - S_ALR_87012271 - Cash Flow (Direct Method)
  - S_ALR_87012272 - Cash Flow (Indirect Method) Variant 1
  - S_ALR_87012273 - Cash Flow (Indirect Method) Variant 2
- **Background Processing**
  - FSIB - Background Processing
- **Account Balances**
  - **General**
    - **G/L Account Balances**
      - S_ALR_87012277 - G/L Account Balances
      - S_ALR_87012276 - SAP Minimal Variant
      - S_ALR_87100198 - Offsetting Account Program
    - **Totals and Balances**
      - S_ALR_87012301 - Totals and Balances
      - S_ALR_87012300 - SAP Minimal Variant
    - **Structured Account Balances**
      - S_ALR_87012279 - Structured Account Balances
      - S_ALR_87012278 - SAP Minimal Variant
    - **Average Balances**
      - S_ALR_87012334 - Local Currency, Period Version
      - S_ALR_87012335 - Period Version - Transaction Currency
      - S_ALR_87012336 - Posting Date, Daily Version

Line Items	**General Ledger, Line Items**	S_ALR_87012337 - Value Date Daily Version
		S_ALR_87012338 - Period Version - Local Currency Year-to-Date
		S_ALR_87012339 - Period Version - Transaction Currency Year-to-Date
		S_ALR_87012282 - G/L Line Items, List for Printing
		S_ALR_87012280 - SAP Minimal Variant
		S_ALR_87012304 - SAP Minimal Variant - Open Items
		S_ALR_87012281 - Poland: With Account Balances
	G/L Account Statement	S_ALR_87012332 - G/L Account Statements
		S_ALR_87012331 - SAP Minimal Variant
Document	**General**	**Document Journal** — S_ALR_87012287 - Document Journal
		S_ALR_87012286 - SAP Minimal Variant
		Compact Document Journal — S_ALR_87012289 - Compact Document
		S_ALR_87012288 - SAP Minimal Variant
		Line Item Journal — S_ALR_87012291 - Line Item Journal
		S_ALR_87012290 - SAP Minimal Variant
		Display of Changed Documents — S_ALR_87012293 - Display of Changed Documents
		S_ALR_87012292 - SAP Minimal Variant
		Invoice Numbers Allocated Twice — S_ALR_87012341 - Invoice Numbers Allocated Twice
		S_ALR_87012340 - SAP Minimal Variant

S_ALR_87012342 - Gaps in Document Number Assignment

Posting Totals
- S_ALR_87012344 - Posting Totals
- S_ALR_87012343 - SAP Minimal Variant

Recurring Entry Documents
- S_ALR_87012346 - Recurring Entry Documents
- S_ALR_87012345 - SAP Minimal Variant

S_ALR_87012347 - Document Items Extract

Chart of Accounts
- S_ALR_87012326 - Chart of Accounts
- S_ALR_87012325 - SAP Minimal Variant

G/L Account List
- S_ALR_87012328 - G/L Account List
- S_ALR_87012327 - SAP Minimal Variant

Account Assignment Manual
- S_ALR_87012330 - Account assignment manual
- S_ALR_87012329 - SAP Minimal Variant

Display Changes to G/L Accounts
- S_ALR_87012308 - Display Changes to G/L Accounts
- S_ALR_87012307 - SAP Minimal Variant
- S_ALR_87012333 - G/L Accounts List

Master Data

Tools

User Parameters
- FQUS - General Ledger Query
- FB07 - Control Totals
- FB00 - Editing Options

Environment

Current Settings	S_BCE_68000174 - Enter Translation Rates	S_ALR_87003642 - Open and Close Posting Periods	S_ALR_87002678 - Enter Reference Interest Values	S_ALR_87005102 - Maintain Worklist for Processing Open Items	S_ALR_87005192 - Maintain Worklist for Displaying Line Items	S_ALR_87005056 - Maintain Worklist for Displaying Balances

2

G/L- User Parameters (Editing Options): FB00

Transaction Code	FB00
Menu	Accounting > Financial Accounting > General Ledger > Environment > User Parameters > Editing Options

Business Process Overview

SAP provides a way of lessening your day-to-day data entry operations by facilitating default entries for fields, and bringing out the most suitable **display variant** for document display, document entry, open / line item processing etc. The **Editing Options** (a) saves time and (b) results in more accuracy, as data entry errors are eliminated with the default values. Depending upon the role you are assigned, you can parameterize so that the next time you are in that particular transaction SAP 'intelligently' brings up the values on your behalf!

You can, among many alternatives, set that:

- System to default the "**exchange rate**" from the first line item.
- You do not process any "**special GL transactions** or **foreign currency transactions**".
- The document needs to be complete before it is '**parked**'.
- System always calculates the tax component on '**net**' invoice and not on '**gross**'.
- Your document currency either as the "**local currency**" or the one used in the last document.
- System needs to make a currency conversion if documents are to be fetched from "**archives**".
- Documents needs to be displayed using "**reference number**".
- Open items are processed using '**commands**'.
- Open items are sorted using +/- signs.
- "**Payment reference**" is used as a selection item in open item processing.
- Activate branch/head office '**dialog**' while processing line items.
- System enables open item selection by '**due date**'.

Transaction Steps

Step-1

Access the transaction either by the transaction code or by the menu, and you are taken to "**Accounting Editing Options**" (Figure: **FB00**-1).

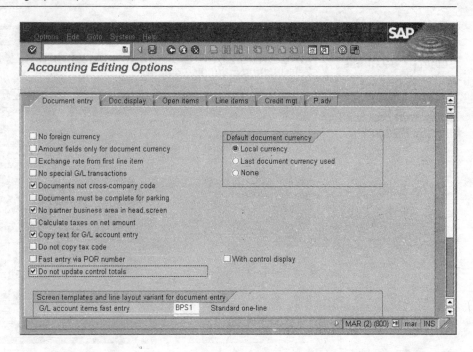

Figure: **FB00**-1

Select your *options* by checking the check boxes or by selecting the screen template for *G/L account items fast entry*.

Step-2

Select | Doc.display | tab and maintain your preferences for the document display parameters (Figure: **FB00**-2)

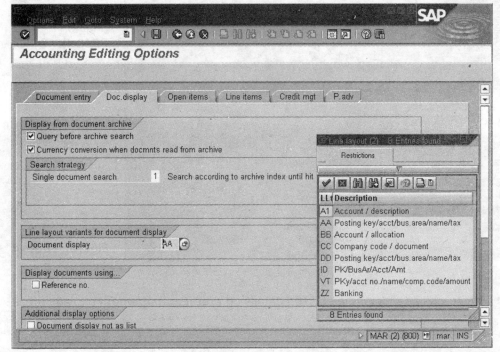

Figure: **FB00**-2

Step-3

Select [Open items] tab and maintain your *preferences* for the *open item processing* (Figure: **FB00**-3).

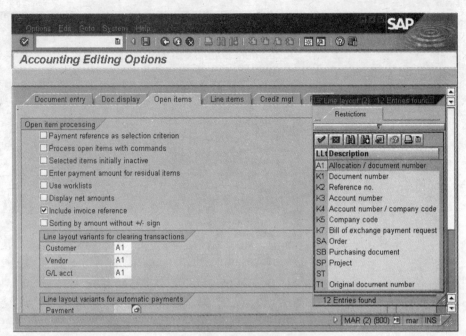

Figure: **FB00**-3

Step-4

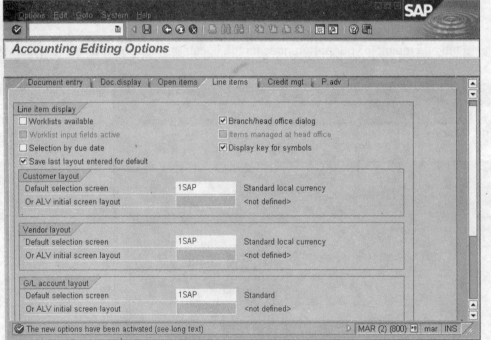

Select [Line items] tab to maintain your preferences for the *line item processing* (Figure: **FB00**-4).

Figure: **FB00**-4

Step-5

Likewise, select the other tabs as well for maintaining details on *credit management* etc. and press 💾 to save the parameters entered.

3

G/L – Account Assignment Model: FKMT

Transaction Code	FKMT
Menu	Accounting > Financial Accounting > General Ledger > Document Entry > Reference Documents > Account Assignment Model

Business Process Overview

SAP recommends, "***Reference methods***" as a document entry tool to facilitate faster and easier document entry into the system, when it is required to enter the same data time and again. Besides making the document entry process less time consuming, this also helps in error-free document entry.

Types of Reference Methods

1. Reference Documents
2. Account Assignment Models
3. Sample Documents
4. Recurring Entries

Account Assignment Model

Account Assignment Model is a reference method used in document entry when the same distribution of amounts to several company codes, cost centers, accounts etc is frequently used. The account assignment model is valid only for G/L account items. Unlike a ***Sample Account***, an Account Assignment Model may be incomplete which can be completed during document entry, by adding or deleting or changing the data already saved in the model.

Instead of manually distributing the amount among accounts or company codes, you may use ***equivalence numbers*** for distributing both the credit and debit amounts. A cross company code account assignment model can also be created.

Transaction Steps

Step-1

Access the transaction either by the transaction code or by the menu, and you will be taken to "***Account Assignment Model: Create Header***" Screen (Figure: **FKMT**-1).

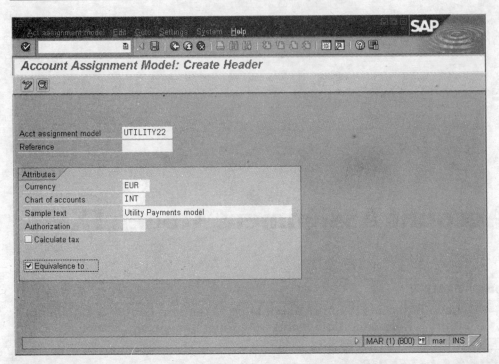

Figure: **FKMT**-1

Enter the details as under:

1. **Acct. assignment model (M):** Give a suitable identification for the account assignment model.
2. **Reference (O):** If you need to create the new model referring to a model already available in the system, enter the reference model.

In <u>Attributes</u>:

3. **Currency (O):** Enter the currency in which the model is to be created.
4. **Chart of accounts (O):** Enter the chart of accounts.
5. **Sample text (O):** Enter a text.
6. **Calculate tax (O):** Check, if applicable.
7. **Equivalence to (O):** Check if the amounts need to be distributed is based on equivalence numbers.

Step-2

Press ⊘ to check if there are errors. If not, press ☒ to create the line items, and you will be taken to "***Account Assignment Model: Change Line Items***" Screen (Figure: **FKMT**-2).

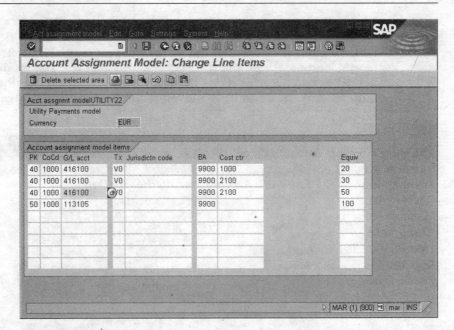

Figure: **FKMT**-2

Under Account assignment model items,

1. **PK (O):** Enter Posting Key.
2. **CoCd (O):** Enter Company Code.
3. **G/L account (O):** Enter a G/L account.
4. **Tx (O):** Enter a tax category, if applicable.
5. **Jurisdiction code (O):** Enter the code, if relevant.
6. **BA (O):** Enter a business area.
7. **Cost ctr (O):** Enter a cost center.
8. **Equiv (O):** Enter an equivalence number.(Note to distribute the numbers in such a way that all the debit items' equivalence numbers add up to 100, similarly for credit entries as well).

Step-3

Press 💾 to save the model (Figure: **FKMT**-3).

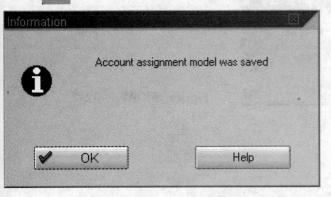

Figure: **FKMT**-3

End of Transaction

How to use the account assignment model?

While making a document entry, in G/L, you may call upon an account assignment model, and complete the transaction. You may use the model as such or change the details or add additional line items etc before posting the document. The steps below indicate how this can be achieved using Transaction Code: F-02.

Step-A

Enter the transaction using **Transaction Code: F-02**. Maintain the '*Document Header*' details (Figure: **FKMT-F-02**-1).

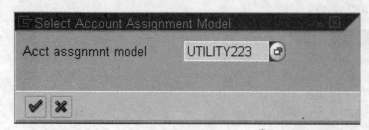

Enter G/L Account Posting: Header Data

| Held document | Act assgnmt model... | G/L item fast entry | Post with reference |

Document date	28.01.2006	Type	SA	Company code	1000
Posting date	28.01.2006	Period	1	Currency/rate	EUR
Document number				Translation dte	
Reference				Cross-CC no.	
Doc.header text					
Trading part.BA					

                                                          MAR (1) (800) mar INS

Figure: **FKMT-F-02**-1

Step-B

Press Act assgnmt model... . On the pop-up "*Select Account Assignment Model*" screen (Figure: **FKMT-F-02**-2), select the appropriate model.

Select Account Assignment Model

Acct assgnmnt model   UTILITY223

Figure: **FKMT-F-02**-2

Step-C

Press 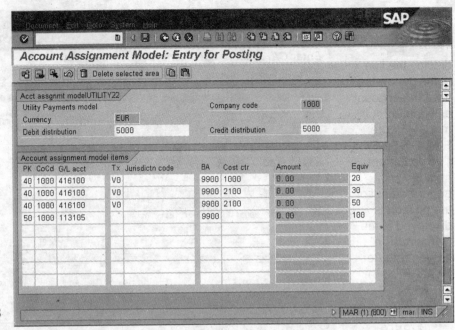 on the pop-up after selecting the model. The system brings up "***Account Assignment Model: Entry for Posting***" screen (Figure: **FKMT-F-02**-3).

Figure: **FKMT-F-02**-3

Enter:

1. **Debit distribution (M):** Enter the debit amount which needs to be distributed, according to the equivalence maintained in the assignment model.
2. **Credit distribution (M):** Enter the Credit amount which needs to be distributed, according to the equivalence maintained in the assignment model.

Step-D

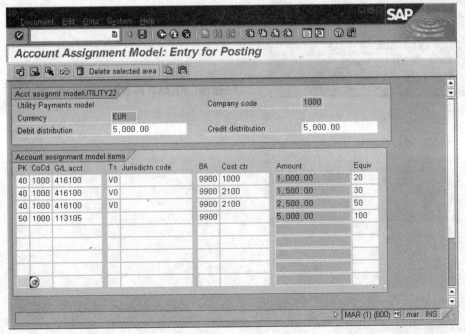

Press . The system brings up "***Account Assignment Model: Entry for Posting***" screen (Figure: **FKMT-F-02**-4), with the debit and credit amounts distributed to the various line items defined in the model.

Figure: **FKMT-F-02**-4

Step-D

Press 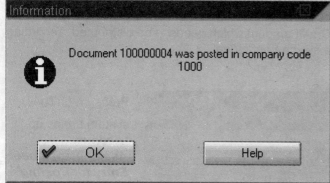 to display the line items generated from the account assignment model (Figure: **FKMT-F-02**-5). The document number generated out of the posting is displayed in the "***Information***" screen (Figure: **FKMT-F-02**-6).

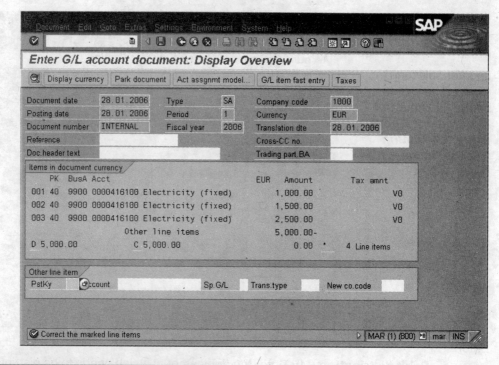

Figure:
FKMT-F-02-5

Figure: **FKMT-F-02**-6

4

G/L – Document Entry: FB50

Transaction Code	FB50
Menu	Accounting > Financial Accounting > General Ledger > Document Entry > G/L account posting

Business Process Overview

A *document* is the result of a posting in accounting in SAP, and is the connecting link between various business operations. The document created out of financial accounting postings is referred to as the *'original document'* as against a *'processing or special document'* like a sample or recurring document, which are used to simplify transaction entry.

Every document consists of:

1. A document header, and
2. Two or more line items (SAP allows a maximum of 999 line items in a single document).

The *Document Header* contains information that is valid for the whole document such as:

- Document date
- Document type
- Document number
- Posting date
- Posting period
- Company code

Besides the above, the document header also has information (editable, later on) like (a) trading partner, (b) document header text, (c) reference, (d) cross company code number etc.

The *Line Items* only contain information on the particular item in question: for instance, the account number, amount, debit/credit, tax code, amount etc.

Before attempting to enter a document, note to call up the relevant **document entry function** as the system provides a variety of ready made document entry templates suited to different transactions like regular G/L entry, customer invoice posting etc. The details entered in a document can be simulated and displayed before it is actually posted in the system. You may also choose to "park" the document and post it later.

Transaction Steps

Step-1

Access the transaction either by the transaction code or by the menu, and you will be taken to *"Enter G/L account document"* Screen (Figure: **FB50**-1).

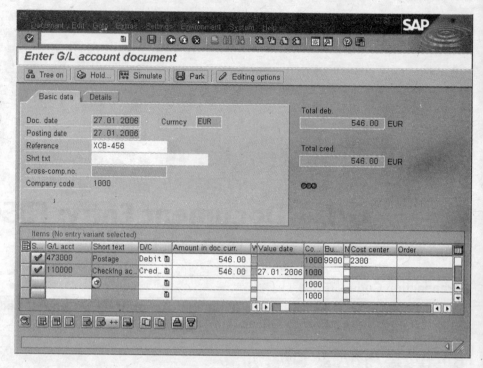

Figure: **FB50**-1

In Basic data tab:

1. **Doc. Date (M):** Enter the document date.
2. **Posting date (M):** Enter the posting date; default date can be changed.

> Document date can be different than that of the posting date. The system derives the *posting period* from the posting date and you will have the option of changing this period as well, from the initial screen. SAP provides you with the concept of normal and special posting periods; contrary to the normal posting periods, *special periods* are those which you will require at the end of the fiscal year to adjust and close your books. You may have a maximum of 16 posting periods (normal 12 + special 4) in case of G/L accounting and 366 in case of special purpose ledgers.

3. **Currency (M):** Enter or change the currency.

> For the first time during the day, the currency needs to be entered: for all the subsequent transactions, the system defaults the currency entered for the first time. Currency in SAP is identified using a 3-character identifier and comes with the almost all the currencies already defined in the system. However, you may also define your's, should you require one!

4. **Reference (O):** Enter a reference, if any.
5. **Shrt Txt (O):** Enter or change the currency.
6. **Company code (M):** Enter or change the company code.

> **Company code,** (the smallest organization unit with in SAP FI, with self contained set of accounts, for which legal/external reporting (financial statements like balance sheet / profit & loss statement) can be made) is defaulted from the user settings. Also, the company code entered for the first transaction will always be defaulted for the subsequent transactions for the day. You can also change the defaulted company code. Use the Menu: Edit > Change the company code or Press 'F7".

In <u>Items</u>:

7. **G/L acct (M):** Enter the relevant G/L account number.
8. **D/C (M):** Select either 'Debit' or 'Credit' as the case may be.
9. **Amount in doc. curr (M):** Enter the amount to be posted.
10. **Tax (O):** Enter the tax code; for all tax relevant accounts, Tax code is mandatory.
11. **Value date (O):** Enter a date if the value date is different from the posting date.
12. **Cost Centre (O):** If the G/L account requires a cost center or CO object assignment, then this filed becomes mandatory.

Step-2

Select ⎡ Details ⎤ tab in the document header and enter relevant information if any (For example "***Partner BA***") (Figure: **FB50**-2).

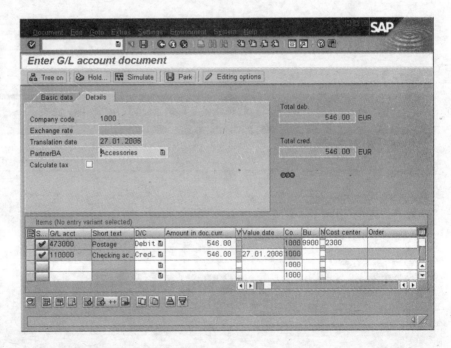

Figure: **FB50**-2

Step-3

When all the line items have been entered, press .

> The total debit amount must equal the total credit amount and the indicator light must be green ⚫⚫⚫. Correct any warning or error messages displayed at the bottom left of the screen (Status bar). Warning messages appear in yellow ⚫⚫⚫ and must be noted, corrected if necessary. To ignore the warning and to proceed further, press the enter key. Error messages appear in red ⚫⚫⚫ and must be corrected before the document can be posted.

Step-4

Click on 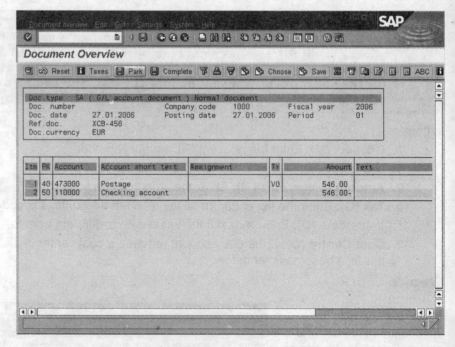 Simulate to view how the document will look like, in respect of all the entries. At this point, the system also displays the system-generated postings (like tax etc) and displays the same along with the line items entered by you, in the **"Document Overview"** screen (Figure: **FB50**-3).

Figure: **FB50**-3

Step-5

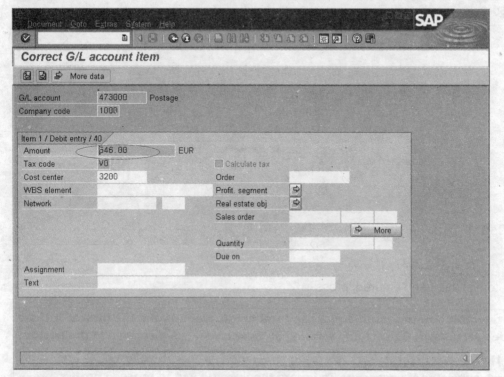

Double click any of the line items or select a line and press icon, to go to **"Correct G/L account item"** screen (Figure: **FB50**-4).

Figure: **FB50**-4

Step-6

Press ◀ to go back to the "***Document Overview***" screen (Figure: **FB50**-3) and press 💾 to post the document (Figure: **FB50**-5).

Information

Document 100000000 was posted in company code 1000

OK   Help

Figure: **FB50**-5

5

G/L – Cash Journal Posting: FBCJ

Transaction Code	FBCJ
Menu	Accounting > Financial Accounting > General Ledger > Document Entry> Cash Journal Posting

Business Process Overview

Cash Journal helps to maintain the cash transactions, both the cash receipts and cash payments. It also keeps track of check receipts. The cash journal has the provision to display the cash position for:

- Today
- This week
- Current period

The transaction facilitates: ·

- Changing to another cash journal with in the transaction
- Enables printing of receipts
- Print the entire cash journal
- Saving and or posting the entries

The 'balance display for the display period' displays the:

Opening balance

_____

+ Total cash receipts (displays number of receipts as well)

+ Total check receipts (displays number of receipts as well)

- Total cash payments (displays number of receipts as well)

_____

= Closing balance

The transaction also provides the functionality to display the FI documents overview of all the associated line items in the cash journal; and from there you may also drill down to the original documents.

Transaction Steps

Step-1

Access the transaction either by the transaction code or by the menu, and the system takes you to the pop-up screen "*Cash Journal: Initial*", Screen (Figure: **FBCJ**-1).

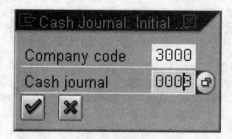

Figure: **FBCJ**-1

Enter:

    1. **Company Code (M):** Enter the company code.
    2. **Cash Journal (M):** Enter the cash journal name.

Step-2

Press ✔ and you will be taken to "**Cash Journal**" Screen (Figure: **FBCJ**-2).

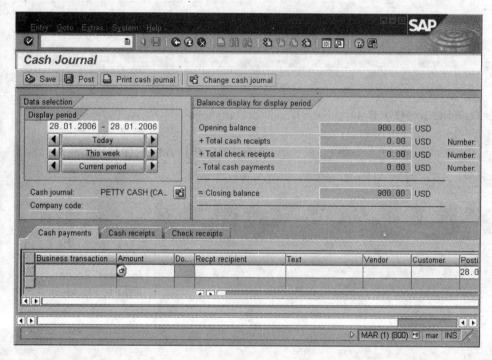

Figure: **FBCJ**-2

Step-3

On Cash receipts tab enter all the cash receipts, "***Cash Journal***" Screen (Figure: **FBCJ**-2).

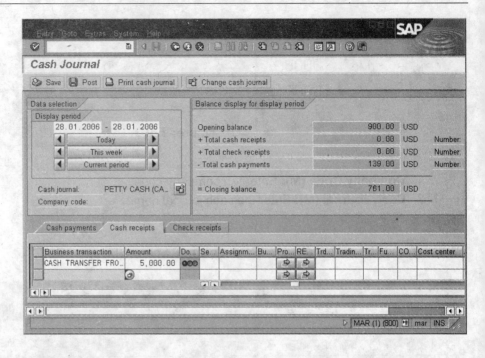

Figure: **FBCJ**-2

Enter:

1. **Business Transaction (M):** Enter the cash receipt transactions.
2. **Amount (M):** Enter the transaction amount.
3. Enter any other details for that particular transaction (like tax code, CO object assignment etc).

Step-4

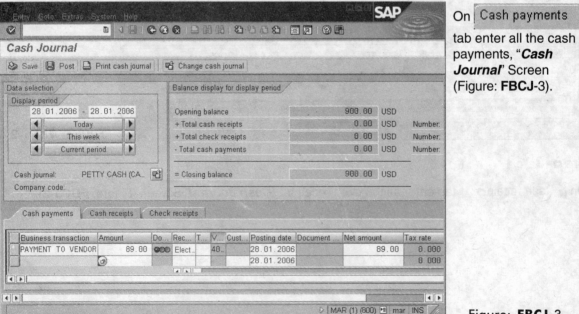

On Cash payments tab enter all the cash payments, "*Cash Journal*" Screen (Figure: **FBCJ**-3).

Figure: **FBCJ**-3

Enter:

1. **Business Transaction (M):** Enter the relevant payment transactions.
2. **Amount (M):** Enter the transaction amount.
3. Enter any other details for that particular transaction (like tax code, CO object assignment etc).

Step-5

Press [💾 Post] to post the transactions, and the cash journal is updated with the receipts and payments, **"Cash Journal"** Screen (Figure: FBCJ-4).

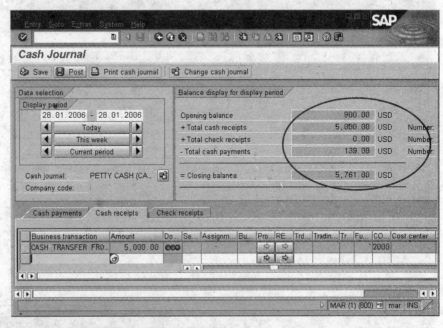

Figure: **FBCJ**-4

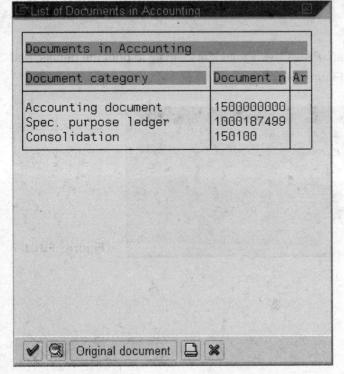

Step-6

Press *"F2"* or use *Menu: Go to* >FI – **follow-on documents** to view the documents generated by the system. The pop-up screen *"List of Documents in Accounting"* displays all the relevant documents (Figure: **FBCJ**-5).

Figure: **FBCJ**-5

Step-7

Select a FI document to view the details and press 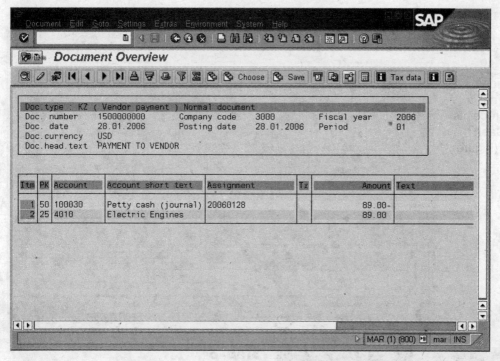, to display "***Document Overview***" screen (Figure: **FBCJ**-6). You may drill down further to the line items, as well.

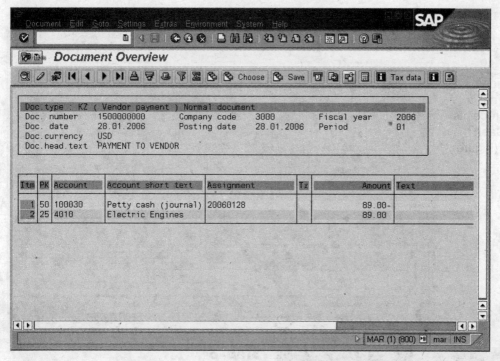

Figure: **FBCJ**-6

Step-7

Go back by pressing to the initial screen. Press Print cash journal to print the details, and the system pops up "*Information*" screen (Figure: **FBCJ**-7).

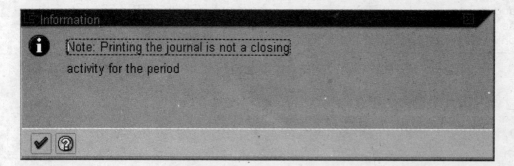

Figure: **FBCJ**-7

Step-8

Press 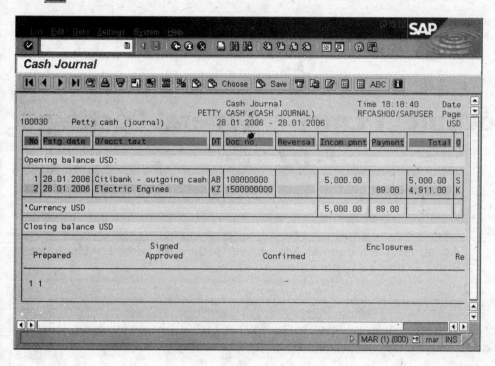 and you are taken to "*Cash Journal*" screen (Figure: **FBCJ**-8).

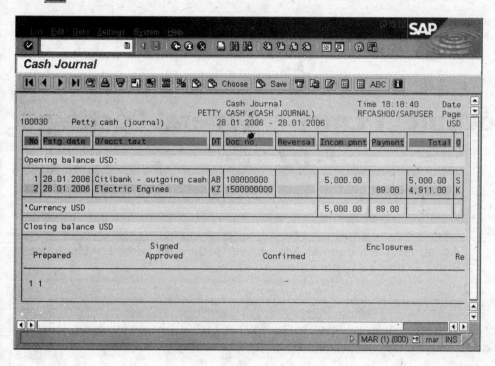

Figure: **FBCJ**-8

6

G/L Document Entry – General Posting: F-02

Transaction Code	F-02
Menu	Accounting > Financial Accounting > General Ledger > Document Entry > Others >General Posting

Business Process Overview

The *classic way* of entering a standard document in General Ledger involves the following steps:

1. Entering the details in the Document Header:
   a. Posting date
   b. Document date
   c. Company code
   d. Currency
   e. Other details like Reference, Document header text, Trading Partner BA etc
2. Entering Line Items:
   a. Enter the posting key and the account. Before the next screen is brought up, when "enter" key is pressed, system checks for (i) whether the posting period is open, (ii) whether document number range is available for the type of posting, (iii) whether the number range is valid for the posting year etc. The system also checks whether the account entered is defined for the company code and is not blocked for posting etc.
   b. Depending upon the posting key, and the account number entered in the initial screen, the system brings up the next screen for data entry.
   c. The details are maintained and again the posting key and the account number are entered for the 2nd line item.
   d. The steps (a) to (c) are repeated till all the line items have been entered.

When completed, upon pressing the "Post" icon, system **checks for consistency**; checks whether debits equal credits and posts only when the document is complete. If not, the document is not posted and the system proposes the corrections, which needs to be carried out before the same is again posted to.

Upon successful posting, system updates the relevant account balances.

Transaction Steps

Step-1

Access the transaction either by the transaction code or by the menu, and you will be taken to **"Enter G/L Account Posting: Header Data "** Screen (Figure: **F-02**-1). (Scroll down to see the '**first line item'** details, if necessary).

Figure: **F-02**-1

Enter G/L Account Posting: Header Data

| Held document | Act assgnmt model... | G/L item fast entry | Post with reference |

Document date		Type SA
Posting date 28.01.2006	Period 1	
Document number		
Reference		
Doc.header text		
Trading part.BA		

Company code 1000
Currency/rate EUR
Translation dte
Cross-CC no.

First line item
PstKy 40 Account 110009 G/L Trans.type

MAR (1) (800) mar INS

Enter the details:

1. **Document Date (M):** Enter the date of the document. (This can never be later than the 'Posting Date') This is the date when an invoice, payment etc. was issued.

2. **Posting Date (M):** Enter the posting date. This date can differ from the document date.

3. **Company Code (M):** If this is the first occasion, a particular company is posted to, then you may need to enter the company Code. For all the subsequent transactions of the day, the same Company Code is defaulted.

4. **(Document) Type (M):** Defaulted to "**SA**" when we selected the **Transaction: F-02** which relates to G/L account posting (general postings).

Remember SAP comes delivered with a multitude of *document types,* used in various postings, like:

   AB General Documents

   SA All G/L documents

   DR Customer Invoice

   DG Customer Cr memo

   DZ Customer Payment

   KG Vendor Cr memo

   KZ Vendor Payment

   KR Vendor Invoice

The *document type* helps to classify an accounting transaction with in the system, and is used to control the entire transaction determining what are all the account types a particular document type can post to. Every document type is assigned to a number range.

You may use *Transaction: OBA7* to define a new document type, or use *Transaction: OBAB* to rename an existing document type.

5. **Posting Period (M)** is defaulted from the posting date entered in the document. You may need to change this if you want the posting period correspond to any other period like a 'special period'.

6. **Currency/rate (M):** The Company Code currency is defaulted; if required you may enter another currency to post the document.

In First line item:

7. **PstKy (M):** Enter the posting key.

A *posting key* in SAP is a 2-digit alphanumeric key, which controls the entry of line items. The posting key determines (a) what account can be posted to (b) which side of the account (debit or credit) to be posted to and (c) what is the 'layout' screen to be used for that particular transaction.

SAP comes with many posting keys for meeting the different business transaction requirements: 40 (G/L debit), 50 (G/L credit), 01 (customer invoice), 11 (customer credit memo), 21 (vendor credit memo), 31 (vendor payment) etc.

Use *Transaction Code: OB41* to define posting keys.

---

8. **Account (M):** Enter the relevant G/L account.

Step-2

Press 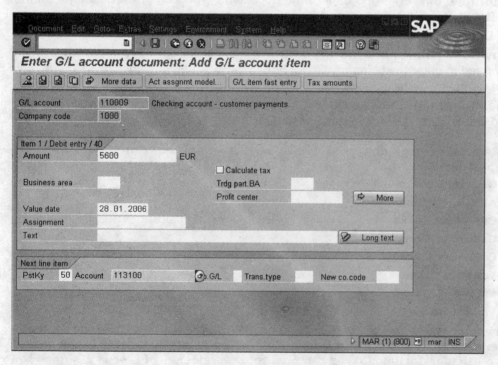, and you will be taken to "**Enter G/L Account Posting: Add G/L line item** " Screen (Figure: **F-02**-2).

Figure: **F-02**-2

Enter the details, in <u>Item 1 / Debit Entry / 40</u>

    1. **Amount (M):** Enter the amount to be posted.

    2. **Value date (O):** Enter a date, if it is different from that of the posting date.

In the <u>Next line item:</u>

    3. **PstKy (M):** Enter the posting key.

    4. **Account (M):** Enter the account.

Step-3

Press, to display to "**Enter G/L Account Posting: Add G/L account item** " Screen (Figure: **F-02**-3).

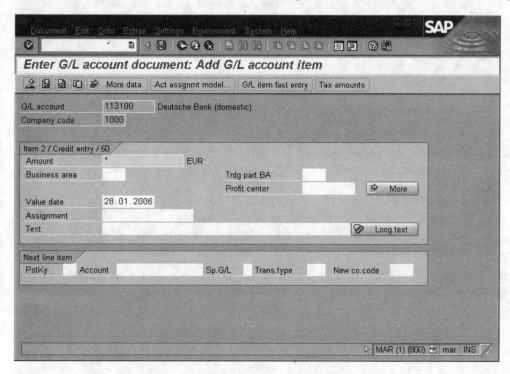

Figure: **F-02**-3

Enter the details as under, in <u>Item 2/ Credit Entry / 50</u>:

    1. **Account (M):** Enter the account or just enter *

A *line item* is composed of an account, a posting key, amount to be posted, and some additional details like tax category, account assignment etc.. Besides the one entered by you during an document entry, the system may also create its own line items called 'system generated line items', like tax deductions etc.

Any number of *line items* (maximum, 999!) can be added by following the above steps. Irrespective of number of line items entered, it needs to be ensured that the total of these are always zero (that is total debits should equal total credits). Else, the system will not allow you to post the document.

Step-4

Press 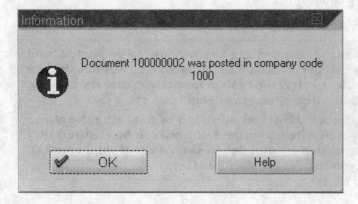, to display to "**Enter G/L Account Posting: Display Overview** " Screen (Figure: **F-02**-4).

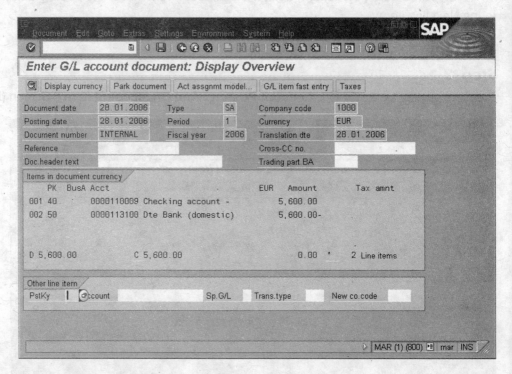

Figure: **F-02**-4

At this point, system displays all the line items, including the ones generated automatically by the system (like, tax postings).

Step-5

Press 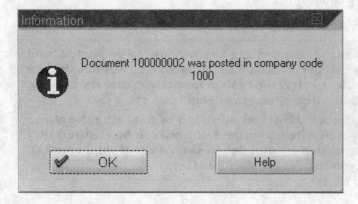, to post the document. The document is posted in the system and a document number generated (Figure: **F-02**-5).

Figure: **F-02**-5

7

G/L - Post Incoming Payments: F-06

Transaction Code	F-06
Menu	Accounting > Financial Accounting > G/L > Document entry > Incoming payment > Post

Business Process Overview

SAP supports processing of *incoming payments* from the business partners. Incoming payments, from customers, are usually for clearing their invoices as against the incoming payments from vendors, which could be for a business transaction like refund from vendor.

The clearing can be done (1) manually or (2) automatically using SAP's **clearing program**.

Under **manual** clearing, you will select the open items, based on the incoming payment, so that the selected open items are cleared. In cases like refunds from a vendor or transactions involving bank sub accounts and clearing accounts etc, you will resort to manual clearing. When cleared, the system flags these line items as 'cleared', creates a clearing document and enters the clearing document number and clearing date in these open items. Besides the clearing document, the system may also generate additional documents in cases like partial or residual processing, and for posting the loss / gain to the assigned G/L account.

The transaction is same as *Transaction Code: F-28, Menu: Accounting > Financial Accounting > Account Receivable > Document entry > Incoming payment > Post*

Transaction Steps

Step-1

Access the transaction either by the transaction code or menu, and you will be taken to "**Post Incoming Payments: Header Data**" screen (Figure: **F-06**-1).

Figure: **F-06**-1

Enter the details as outlined below:

1. **Document Date (M):** Enter the date of the document. (This can never be later than the 'Posting Date') This is the date of an original document like invoice.

2. **Posting Date (M):** Enter the posting date. This date can differ from the document date.

3. **Company Code (M):** If this is the first occasion, a particular company is posted to, and then you may need to enter the company Code. For all the subsequent transactions of the day, the same Company Code is defaulted.

4. **(Document) Type (M)** is defaulted to "**DZ**" when we selected the *Transaction: F-06* which relates to manual incoming payments.

5. **Currency/rate (M):** The Company Code currency is defaulted; if required you may enter another currency to post the document.

In the Bank data area:

6. **Account (M):** Select the G/L account (Bank) to which the incoming payment is to be posted

7. **Amount (M):** Enter the amount to be paid.

8. You may also enter the **Value date (O)**, if it is going to be different from that of the posting date.

9. **Text (O):** Maintain some explanatory text which will possibly identify this payment.

10. **Business Area (O):** if business area accounting is active, enter the relevant business area to where this payment should be updated.

In the Open Item Selection block of the screen:

11. **Account (M):** Enter the Customer account from whom the payment is being received.

12. **Account type (M):** Select 'D' from the drop-down list.

13. **Standard O/Is (M):** Select the check-box so that the system considers the standard open items only.

14. **Automatic Search (O):** If this check box is selected, the system is going to search for open items which will match the payment amount entered in (7).

Step-2

Press button or | Process open items | , and the system pops-up the **"Proposal for Clearing"** screen (Figure: **F-06**-2).

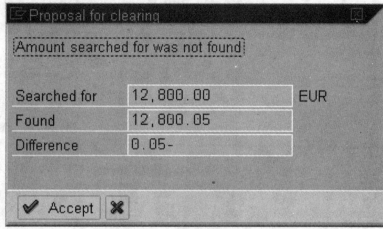

Figure: **F-06**-2

Note that the system was unable to find an exact match to clear the open item with the incoming payment amount entered, and is proposing to you to accept it for further processing. Either you can accept or go back to **Step-1** and change the amount to match the open item amount selected by the system.

Step-3

Press | ✔ Accept | , and the system takes you to the **Post Incoming Payments: Process Open Items"** screen (Figure: **F-06**-3).You can see from the screen that the system has actually clubbed two open items (12345 & 455.05) and has assigned the payment as 12800.05 which is 0.05 less than the incoming payment amount 12800 entered in the initial screen. So, the 'Not assigned' amount is shown as 0.05, which needs to be effectively dealt with for putting through the transaction. If this has been due to an error, you may correct it by entering the correct amount by going back to screen Figure: **F-06**-1.

> The payment difference is treated the way it is configured in the system. If the difference is within the tolerance limit, defined in the system using the *tolerance groups* (defined at the company code level), the cash discount is adjusted or the system automatically posts the difference to a gain/loss account. When the payment difference exceeds the limits of defined tolerance, then the incoming amount may be processed as a *partial payment* (the original open item is not cleared, but the incoming payment is posted with a reference to that invoice) or the difference is posted as the *residual item* (the original open item is cleared and a new open item created by the system for the difference amount) in the system.

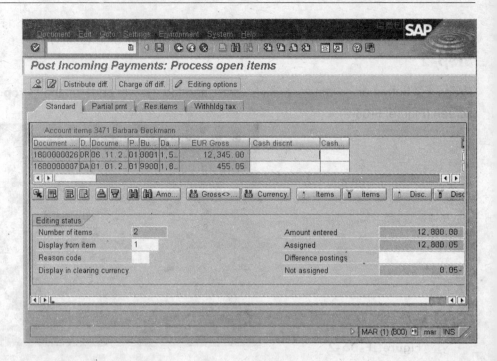

Figure: **F-06**-3

Step-4

Activate 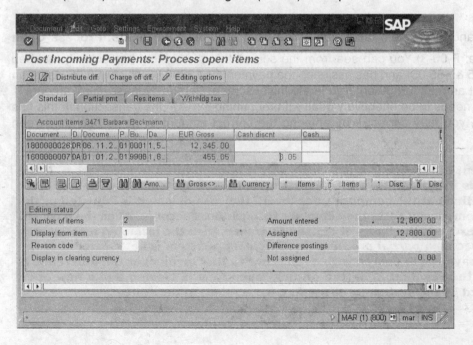 Disc. and enter the cash discount (0.05) **Post Incoming Payments: Process Open Items**" screen (Figure: **F-06**-4) where the difference is now shown as the discount and both the amount entered (12800) and the amount assigned (12800) are equal.

Figure: **F-06**-4

Step-5

Press 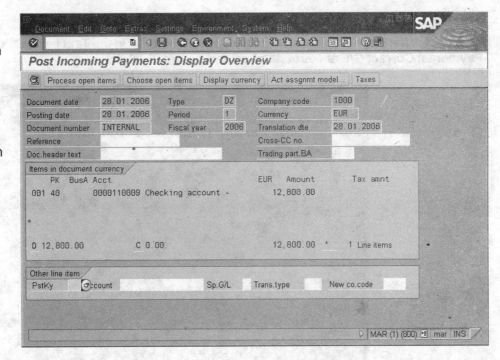 button and you are taken to "**Post Incoming Payments: Display Overview**" screen (Figure: **F-06**-5).

Figure: **F-06**-5

Step-6

Press 💾 button to post; you are required to correct <u>marked item(s)</u> (if, any) while displaying "**Post Incoming Payments: Display Overview**" screen (Figure: **F-06**-6).

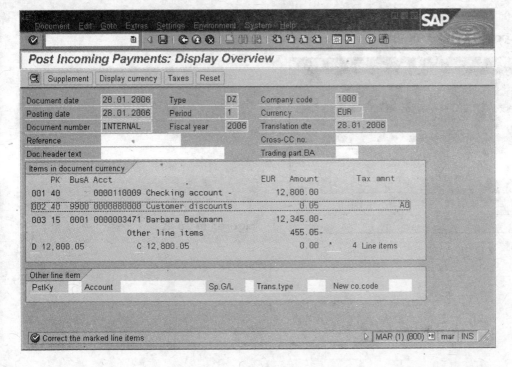

Figure: **F-06**-6

Step-7

Double-click the marked line (shown in blue) and enter a text in the **Text** field in "**Post Incoming Payments: Correct G/L account item**" screen (Figure: **F-06**-7).

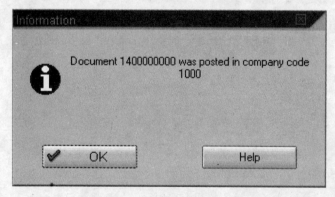

Figure: **F-06**-7

Step-8

Press button to post (Figure: **F-06**-8).

Figure: **F-06**-8

8

G/L - Edit or Park Document: FV50

Transaction Code	FV50
Menu	Accounting > Financial Accounting > General Ledger > Document Entry > Edit or Park G/L Document

Business Process Overview

SAP provides a functionality called "*Parking of Documents*" which can store incomplete documents in the system. These can later on be called upon for completion and posting. While doing so, the system does not carry out the mandatory validity checking (no automatic postings or no balance checks) as in other cases when a document is entered. As a result, the transaction figures (account balances) are not updated. This is true in case of all financial transactions except in the area of TR-CM (Cash management) where parked documents will update the transactions.

The data entered, even if not posted, in a parked document can be used for evaluations (unlike in '*hold documents*'). However, it is to be noted that *substitution* functionality cannot be used with document parking, as substitution is activated only upon transaction processing.

Parking of documents can be used to park data relating to customers, vendors or assets (acquisition only). When a cross company code document is parked, only one document is created in the initial company code; when this parked document is posted all other documents relevant for all other company codes will be created.

The added advantage is that a document parked by an accounting clerk can be called upon for completion by some one else. The parked documents can be displayed individually or as a list from where the required document can be selected for completion and posting. The number of the parked document is transferred to the posted document.

The original parked document, if necessary, can be displayed even after the same has been posted to.

Transaction Steps

Step-1

Access the transaction either by the transaction code by the menu, and you will be taken to "**Park G/L account document / edit parked G/L account document**" Screen (Figure: **FV50**-1). The system brings up the last parked document.

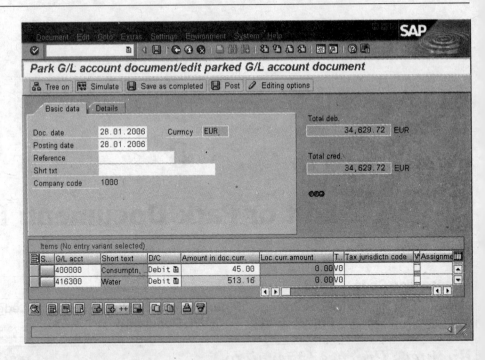

Figure: **FV50**-1

Step-3

Press 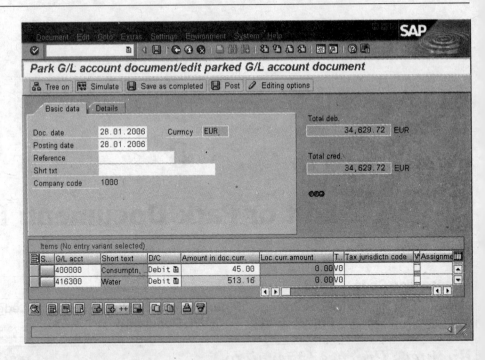 Simulate to view the document, with system generated line items, in **"Document Overview"** screen (Figure: **FV50**-2)

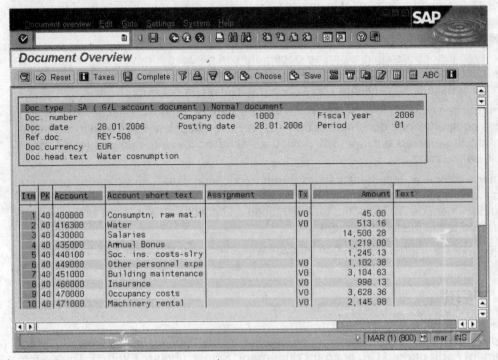

Figure: **FV50**-2)

Step-3

Make changes, if necessary. You may also save the same as 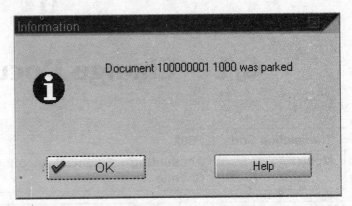 Complete instead of posting. Post the document by pressing 💾 . (Figure: **FV50**-3).

Figure: **FV50**-3

9

G/L – Change Document: FB02

Transaction Code	FB02
Menu	Accounting > Financial Accounting > General Ledger > Document > Change

Business Process Overview

Change document function helps you to look at the already posted documents to find out the details of that transaction, and to change certain information. Remember, SAP will NOT allow you to change all the data, which have already been posted to: for example you can change the 'document header text'. All the "greyed-out" fields cannot be changed

Transaction Steps

Step-1

Access the transaction either by the transaction code or by the menu, and you will be taken to **"Change Document: Initial Screen"** Screen (Figure: **FB02**-1) and enter the details as outlined below:

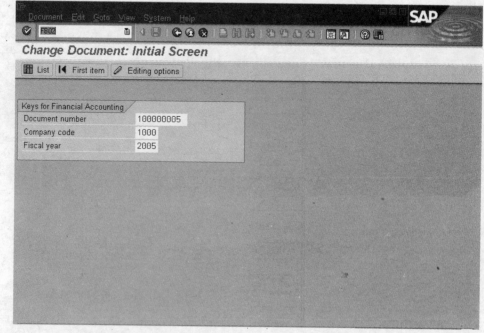

Figure: **FB02**-1

1. **Document no. (M):** Enter the document number, which needs to be changed.

If document number is not known, use *"List"* option to find the relevant document (See Step-1a).

2. **Company code (M):** Enter the relevant company code.
3. **Fiscal year (M):** Enter the relevant fiscal year to which the document has been posted to.

Step-1a

Use the **List** option to search for a document, if you are not sure of the document number. Enter the necessary search details on the "***Document List***" screen (Figure: **FB02**-2) to retrieve the particular document(s).

Figure: **FB02**-2

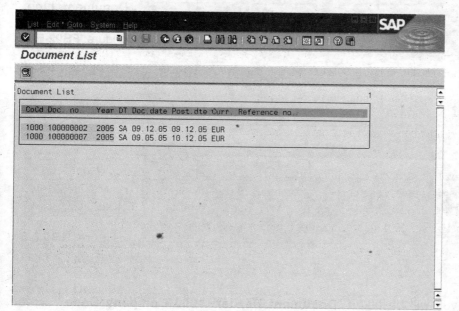

Step-1b

From the "***Document List***" screen (Figure: **FB02**-3) select the one, which needs to be changed.

Figure: **FB02**-3

Step-2

After entering the details in **Step-1**, press 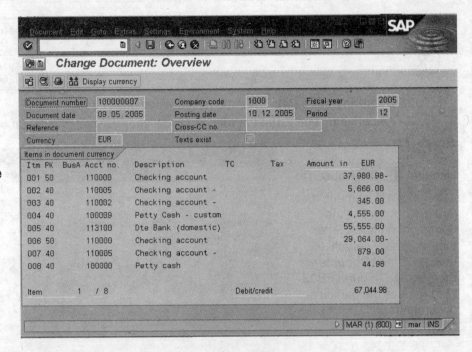 to see the document to be changed (or at the end of **Step-1b**, select the document from the list and double click or use the icon) and you will be taken to **"Change Document: Overview"** screen (Figure: **FB02**-4).

Figure: **FB02**-4

Step-3

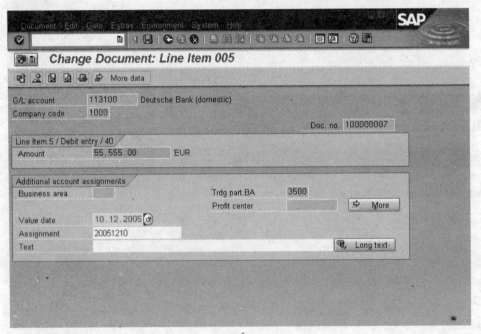

Select a *line item* and double-click on the same to change some details, in "**Change Document: Line Item 005**" screen (Figure: **FB02**-5).

Figure: **FB02**-5

Step-4

Click on the icon and you will be taken "**Document Header: 1000 Company Code**" screen (Figure: **FB02**-6).

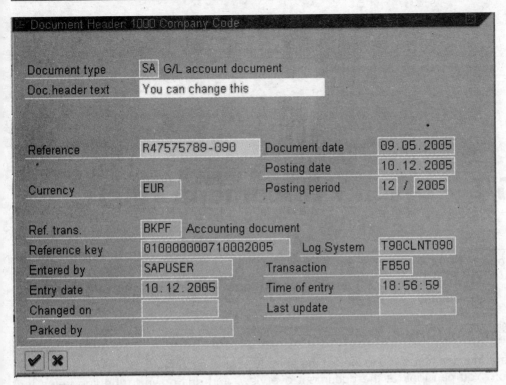

Figure: **FB02**-6

Step-5

Click on 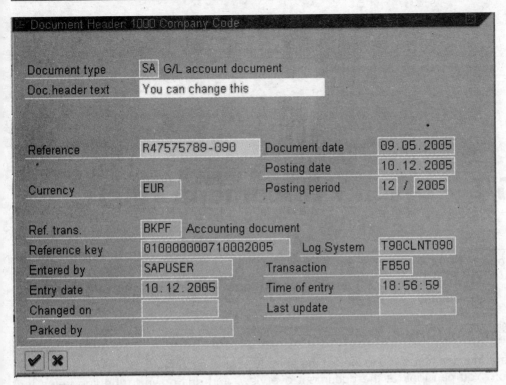 to save and exit.

10

G/L – Display Document: FB03

Transaction Code	FB03
Menu	Accounting > Financial Accounting > General Ledger > Document > Display

Business Process Overview

Display document function helps you to look at the already posted documents to find out the details of that transaction. You can look at the document overview, and drill down to the line items for displaying the line item details. You also have option of switching to editing to change the document.

Transaction Steps

Step-1

Access the transaction either by the transaction code or by the menu, and you will be taken to **"Display Document: Initial Screen"** Screen (Figure: **FB03**-1) and enter the details as outlined below:

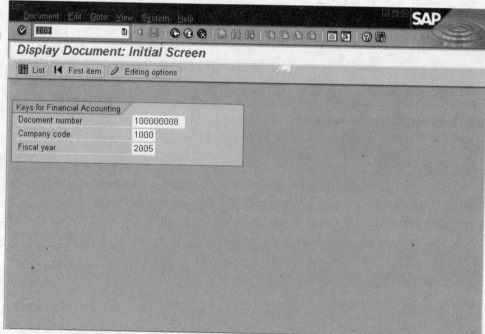

Figure: **FB03**-1

1. **Document no. (M):** Enter the document number, which needs to be displayed.

> **If document number is not known, use "List" option to find the relevant document (See Step-1a & 1b of Transaction FB02).**

2. **Company code (M):** Enter the relevant company code.
3. **Fiscal year (M):** Enter the relevant fiscal year to which the document has been posted to.

> *Fiscal year* **is the period for which your company creates the financial statements, and is usually for a period of 12 months. This fiscal year may be of a (1)** *calendar year* **(January to December) or (2)** *non-calendar year* **(say, April to March). A fiscal year can also be less than 12 months, and this kind of fiscal years are known as** *shortened fiscal years* **which will be used in case of switching from one type of fiscal year to the other or during initial company formation wherein you may like to draw the financial statements for the interim period before start of the regular fiscal year.**

Step-2

Press ✅ to see the document to be reversed and you will be taken to "**Display Document: Overview**" screen (Figure: **FB03**-2).

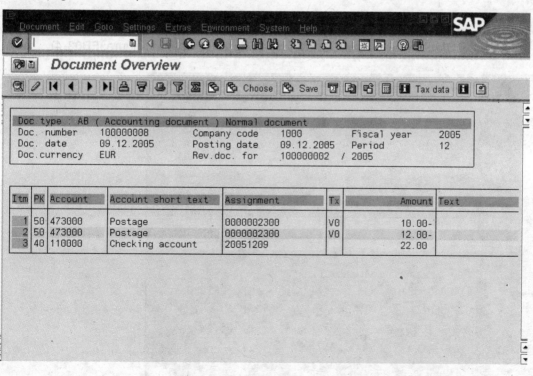

Figure:
FB03-2

Step-3

Select a line item
and double-click

or press 🔍 to

go to, in "**Display
Document: Line
Item 003**" screen
(Figure: **FB03**-3).

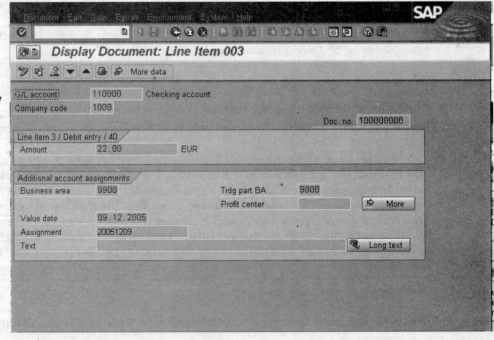

Figure: **FB03**-3

Step-4

Click 🖥 icon to view "**Document Header: Company Code 1000**" screen (Figure: **FB03**-4).

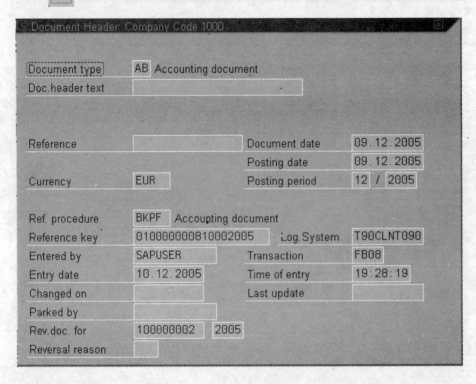

Figure: **FB03**-4

11

G/L – Reverse Document: FB08

Transaction Code	FB08
Menu	Accounting > Financial Accounting > General Ledger > Document > Reverse > Individual reversal

Business Process Overview

Reversal of a document is necessary when you want to correct a document, which has already been posted to in the system. As SAP does not allow you to change the document once it is posted, any corrections need to be made by reversing the original posting and posting a new document or by making additional postings. Upon reversal, the system creates a new reversal document and the reversal date/information are written to the corresponding line items.

In case of documents with internal number assignment, if you have not defined a separate number range for reversal documents, the system uses the same document type that has the internal number assignment for reversal as well. But, in case of document types where you are using external number assignment, make sure that you have defined an internal document number range for reversal of those documents.

Transaction Steps

Step-1

Access the transaction either by the transaction code or by the menu, and you will be taken to **"Reverse Document: Header"** Screen (Figure: **FB08**-1).

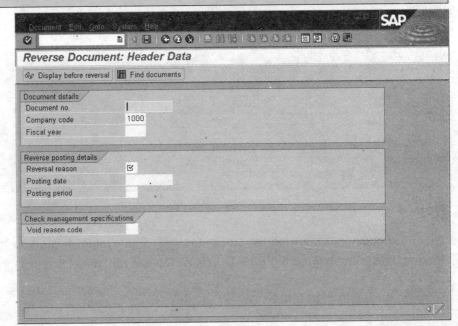

Figure: **FB08**-1

Step-2

Enter the Document details, if the document number to be reversed is known. Else, use

⊞ Find documents to list the documents from which you can select one and reverse the same. Let us use

⊞ Find documents route.

Press ⊞ Find documents button and you will be taken to **"Document List"** screen (Figure: **FB08**-2).

Figure: **FB08**-2

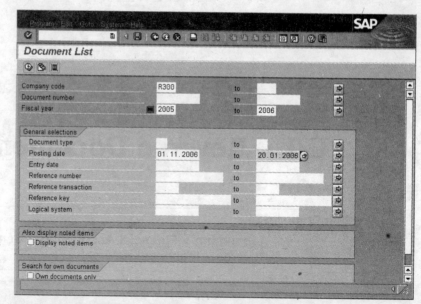

Step-3

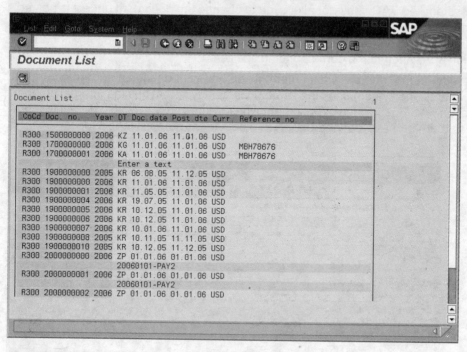

Press '**F8**' or , and the system will bring up the documents in **"Document List"** screen (Figure: **FB08**-3).

Figure: **FB08**-3

Step-4

Select the document from the list and press ⌖. The system takes you to **"Reverse Document: Header Data"** screen (Figure: **FB08**-4), with all the relevant data filled in 'Document details' block:

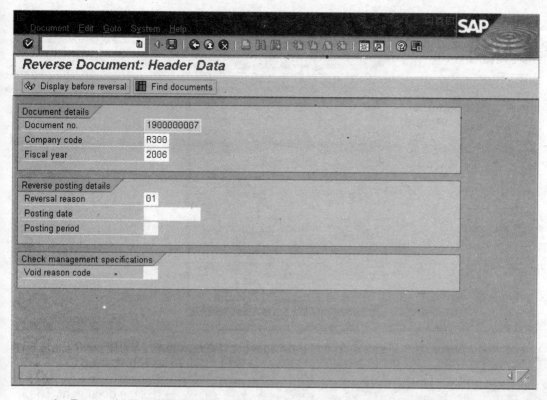

Figure:
FB08-4

1. **Reversal Reason (M):** Enter a reversal reason, by selecting from the drop-down list.

Reversal reason is stored in the reversed document, which helps to identify why the reversal was carried out. Depending upon the reason for the reversal, the system determines (a) whether the reversed document can have different posting date than that of the original and (b) whether the reverse document will result in in the transaction figures already posted to the account(s).

The examples of reversal reason are shown in "Reason for Reversal" screen under 'Restrictions' tab (Figure: FB08-4A).

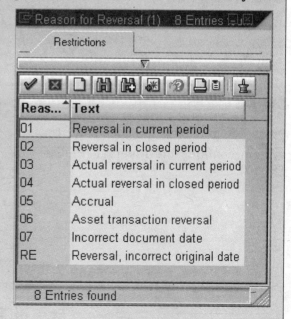

(Figure: **FB08**-4A)

Step-5

It is a good practice to look at the document before reversing.

Press   Display before reversal   and you are taken to "**Document Overview**" screen (Figure: **FB08**-5).

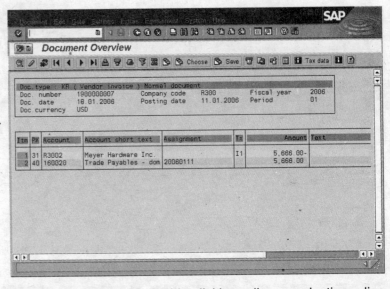

Figure: FB08-5

You can also drill down further to look at the line items, by double clicking a line or selecting a line and pressing .

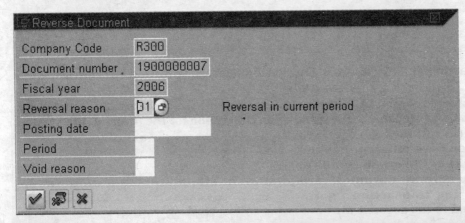

Step-5

Press to reverse the document. The system pops-up the "**Reverse document**" screen to confirm the reversal (Figure: **FB08**-6).

Figure: FB08-6

Step-5

Press to reverse the document. The system confirms the reversal (Figure: **FB08**-7).

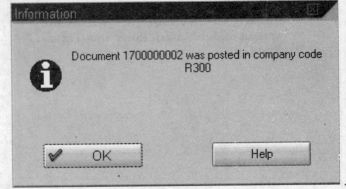

Figure: FB08-7

End of Transaction

You may now check the reversal by displaying the document:

Step-A

Use *Transaction Code: FB03* to check the reversed document (Figure-**FB08-FB03**-1).

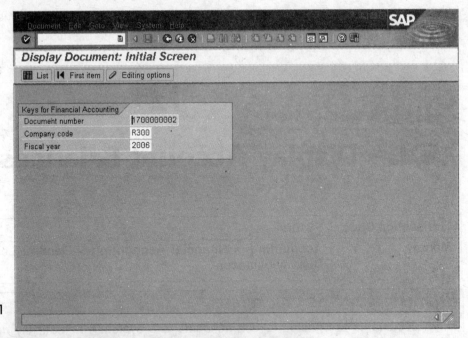

Figure-**FB08-FB03**-1

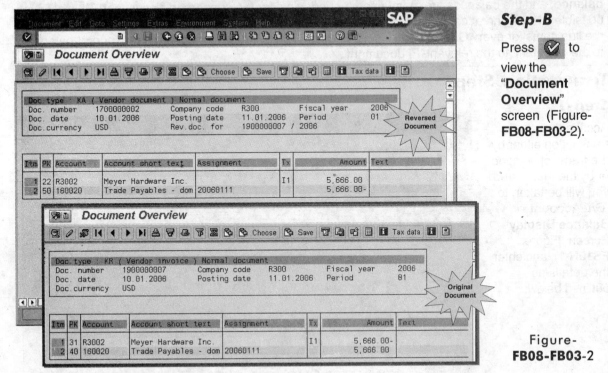

Step-B

Press 🗸 to view the **"Document Overview"** screen (Figure-**FB08-FB03**-2).

Figure-
FB08-FB03-2

12

G/L – Display Account Balances: FS10N

Transaction Code	FS10N
Menu	Accounting > Financial Accounting > General Ledger > Account > Display balances

Business Process Overview

When documents are posted to G/L accounts, the system automatically updates the **account balance**, and the balances are maintained 'period-wise' for the concerned 'fiscal year'. It is always possible to view the account balances and (depending on the specifications in the master record) the line items for every G/L account. The 'drill-down' facility helps to move from the 'period-balance' to the 'line-item' to the relevant 'FI document'.

Transaction Steps

Step-1

Access the transaction either by the transaction code or by the menu, and you will be taken to **"G/L Account Balance Display"** Screen (Figure: **FS10N**-1), and enter the details as outlined below:

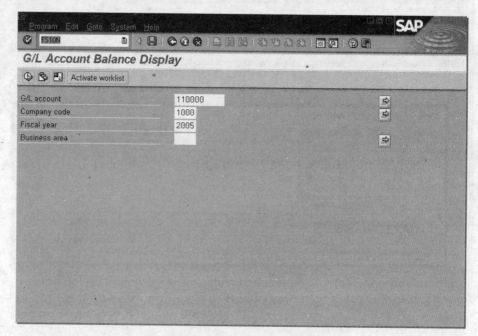

Figure: **FS10N**-1

1. **G/L account (M):** Enter the G/L A/c number for which you want to display the balances.
2. **Company code (M):** Enter the company code.
3. **Fiscal year (M):** Enter the fiscal year.

Step-2

Press ⊕ or '*F8*', and the '**G/L Account Balance Display**' screen (Figure: **FS10N**-2) will be shown, relating to the G/L account entered in **Step-1** above.

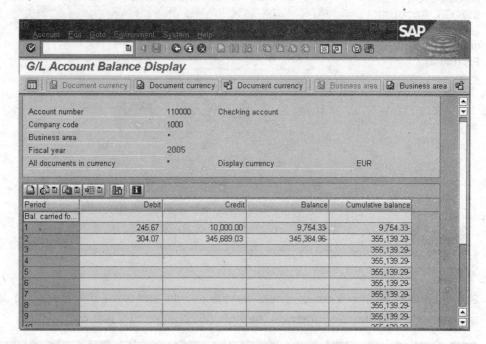

Figure: **FS10N**-2

Step-3

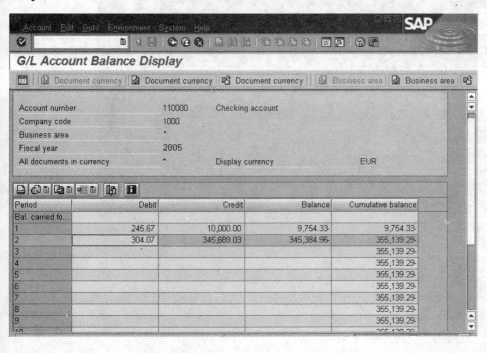

Now, select a row (1, 2 etc) to see the details. Once selected, the row will be highlighted. For example, the '**Period-2**' row has been selected as shown in the screen (Figure: **FS10N**-3).

Figure-FS10N-3

Step-3

'*Double-click*' on the selected row to see the "**G/L Account Line Item Display**" screen (Figure: **FS10N**-4).

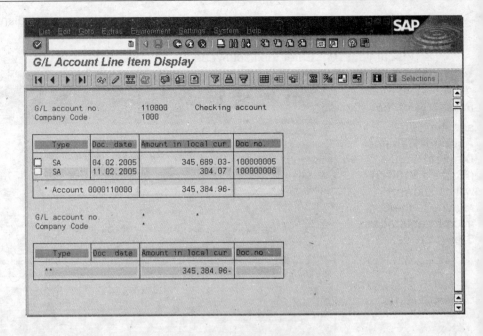

Figure: **FS10N**-4

Step-4

Select any of the 'Check boxes' displaying the details, and press 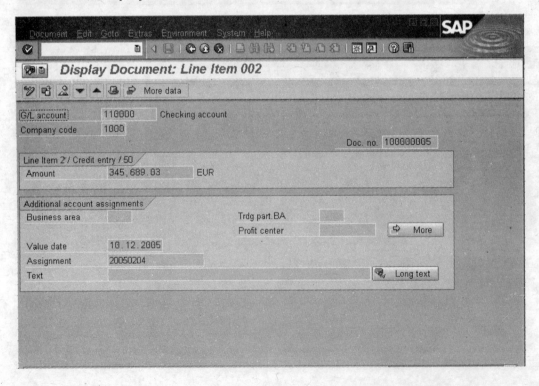 to see the document relating to the line item, "**Display Document: Line item 002**" (Figure: **FS10N**-5).

Figure: **FS10N**-5

13

G/L - Master Record, Create Centrally: FS00

Transaction Code	FS00
Menu	Accounting > Financial Accounting > General Ledger > Master records > Individual processing > Centrally

Business Process Overview

The *G/L master record* contains information that is required to control the posting and processing of transactions to G/L, and is consisting of two areas:

1. Chart of accounts area
2. Company code area

The **chart of accounts** area consists of information, which is valid across the company codes. These include:

- G/L account number
- Short text of the account
- Chart of accounts
- P&L or Balance Sheet indicator
- Account group

The **company code area** of a G/L master record contains information that is valid only for that particular company code. These include:

- Account currency
- Reconciliation account
- Open item management?
- Line item display?
- Sort key
- Field status group

The G/L master record can be created / edited in two different ways:

1. **Centrally:** both the chart of accounts area and the company code area information are created at one-go. This also known as 'one-step' G/L account creation.
2. **Individually for the Chart of accounts area and company code area**: this is known as step-by-step or 2-step G/L master creation wherein the G/L master information is created at the chart of account area (*Transaction code: FSPQ*) initially, the company code (*Transaction code: FSSQ*) specific information is done after wards.

It is also possible that in a centralized environment, where the chart of accounts is uniform across company codes, the G/L master record for the company code area is created centrally and the company code specific information added to this later on. On the contrary, in a decentralized set-up the G/L master record is created separately by each of the company codes in both the areas simultaneously.

The G/L master record can be created by different methods of creation:

1. **Using SAP's Data Transfer Workbench:** you can transfer the G/L master records from legacy / existing system and create the same in SAP.

2. **By Reference**: If G/L master records have already been defined for a company code, you can use them as reference and create these records for other company codes. The advantage of this method is that you will be able to create all account assignment logic as well, while creating the master records.

   Use the **Menu Path: Financial Accounting > Customizing under General Ledger Accounting > G/L Accounts > Master Data > G/L Account Creation > Create G/L Accounts with Reference.**

   You copy the G/L master records from a reference company code to a target company code, and edit the same before accepting the copied records. While doing so, you have the flexibility of limiting the account numbers which needs to be copied, and looking and editing the accounts before accepting the same in the target company code. SAP provides the functionality of displaying the details in a 'table' format where you can change the account numbers and names. It is also possible that you save only the 'table' for further changes or rework before actually creating these copied accounts in the target company code.

The reference method of G/L master creation is to be used only:

a.   When you want to use the chart of accounts provided in the standard system.
or
b.   When an existing chart of accounts is to be used as reference

---

3. **By Copy:** You copy the G/L master record; first in the chart of accounts area and then in the company code area.

Use 'Copy' method of G/L master creation only when you are sure that the chart of accounts available in the system, from where you are going to copy, meets your exact requirements; else you should prefer creating the master records using 'reference' method.

---

4. **By manual creation:** This is the most time consuming method where G/L master records are created, manually, one-by-one in the system. Normally, you will resort to this laborious method only when you feel that neither the standard SAP system nor your existing system has a chart of accounts, which can be used for referencing or copying.

Transaction Steps

Step-1

Access the transaction either by the transaction code or by the menu, and you will be taken to **"Enter G/L account document'** Screen (Figure: **FS00**-1).

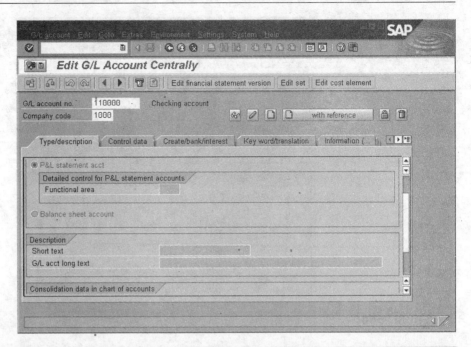

Figure: **FS00**-1

This is a composite maintenance screen from where you can:

1. **Display the account details.**

2. **Change an existing account.**

3. **Create new account.**

4. **with reference** **Create new account with reference.**

5. **Block an account.**

6. **Delete an account.**

Enter the details as outlined below:

1. **G/L account number (M):** Enter the number which needs to be created / changed / displayed / blocked /deleted.
2. **Company code (M):** Enter the relevant company code.

The company code in SAP is an organization unit, within financial accounting, for which independent balance sheet and financial statements are drawn. Each company code in SAP is identified by a 4-letter alphanumeric key. A company can contain many company codes.

Step-2

Click on the desired icon (for example, press [pencil icon] and you will be taken to "**Change G/L account centrally**" Screen (Figure: **FS00**-2).

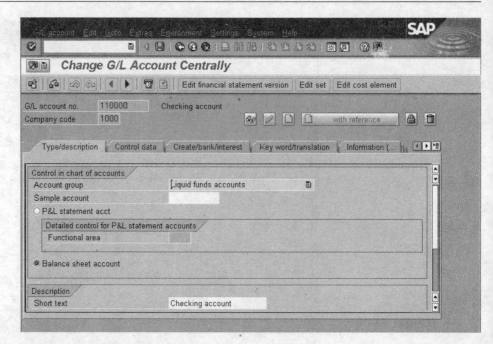

Figure: **FS00**-2

The screen contains various tabs, arranged for **chart of accounts area** and **company code area**:

1. **Chart of accounts area**
   a. Type/description
   b. Key word/translation
   c. Information C/A
2. **Company code area**
   a. Control data
   b. Create/bank/interest
   c. Information (CoCd)

Step-3

Enter the following under <u>Control in chart of accounts</u> block in | Type/description | tab:

1. **Account group (M):** Select the relevant account group from the drop down list.

> ***Account Group* (four digit alphanumeric key) attached to a chart of accounts, is an important control parameter, which decides, in conjunction with activity type: the account control, the account management and the document control. It, thus, sets the *field status* for creating / changing / displaying the master records. A number range interval is added for each of the account groups, which controls the numbering of G/L master records.**
>
> **SAP comes with a number of standard account groups like: SAKO (G/L accounts general), MAT. (Materials management accounts), FIN. (Liquid funds accounts) etc. Account group is mandatory for creating a master record. The same account groups can be used by one or more company codes if they all use the same chart of accounts. Each G/L account is assigned to only one account group.**
>
> **Use *Transaction Code: OBD4* to change an existing account group or to create your own.**

2. **Sample Account (O):** Select the relevant sample account from the drop down list.

A *Sample Account* is a master record, which is used to create a G/L account master record in the company code area. Use of sample accounts simplifies creation of master records, as these accounts contain all the relevant data for a particular account group, which can easily be copied. Sample accounts are dependent upon the chart of counts under which they are created. Sample accounts cannot be posted to.

3. **P&L statement acct (M):** Select the radio button, if the account is classified under Profit & Loss account (either 3 or 4 is selected).

4. **Balance sheet account (M):** Select the radio button, if this is a Balance Sheet account (either 3 or 4 is selected.

By default all the accounts are having the radio button 'P&L statement acct' selected. Note to change this correctly, other wise you will have a lot of problems when you are preparing the balance sheet and profit & loss account.

Under Description:

5. **Short text (M):** Enter the short text which identifies the account.

6. **G/L acct long text (M):** Enter the description of the account.

Step-4

Press ⌈ Control data ⌋ tab (Figure: **FS00**-3).

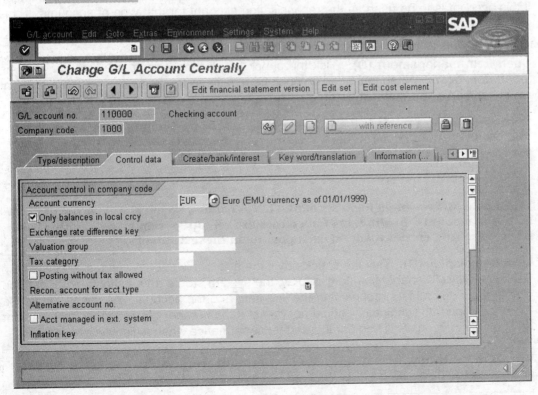

Figure: **FS00**-3

Enter the following under <u>Account control in company code</u> block

1. **Account currency (M):** Enter the currency in which the account needs to be maintained.
2. **Only balances in local crcy (O):** Check this check box to maintain the balance only in local currency.

> If an account is maintained as *'open item basis'*, then checking this check-box will affect the clearing. This needs to be checked for (a) all balance sheet items including accounts which are not kept in foreign currency and accounts which are not maintained on 'open item basis', (b) cash discount clearing accounts, and (c) GR/IR accounts. Do not tick this indicator for Customer / Vendor reconciliation accounts.

3. **Tax category (O):** Select from the drop down list.
   a. – Denotes 'only input tax is allowed'.
   b. + Denotes 'only output tax is allowed'.
   c. * Denotes 'all tax types allowed'.
   d. An entry in this field determines:
      i. Whether the account is tax relevant?
      ii. Whether the account is a tax account?
4. **Posting without tax allowed (O):** If the account needs to be posted both with taxable or non-taxable transactions, then checking this box will allow to post the account even with out a tax code.
5. **Recon account for acct type (O):** Select the account type (vendor or customer or assets), if this account is to be used as the reconciliation account for that type of accounts. If this is not to be denoted as a reconciliation account, then leave the field as blank.

Enter the following under <u>Account management in company code</u> block:

6. **Open Item management (O):** Tick the check box if the account is to be managed as *'open item basis'*. When managed on open item basis all the items posted to the account are either marked as 'open' or 'cleared'.

> Accounts that are to be managed as *'open item basis'* include clearing accounts like: GR/IR clearing account, Bank clearing account, Cash discount clearing account etc.

> You should NOT maintain bank accounts, tax accounts, reconciliation accounts, raw material accounts, profit & loss accounts etc on 'open item basis', as there will be no offsetting entries made to each posting in these accounts.

7. **Line item display (O):** Tick the check-box if the account is to be managed with 'line item display' facility. To enable line item display, the system stores an additional entry per line item in the index table(s) connecting the line item and the account. As this will increase the system load, this indicator should not be set if the number of postings to this account is to be very large that will hamper the system performance when a display is called upon.

> Do NOT activate 'line item display' for tax accounts, receivables accounts, payables accounts etc.

8. **Sort key (O):** An entry here will indicate what <u>layout rule</u> should be used for the <u>allocation field</u> in the document line item.

Step-5

Press

Create/bank/interest

tab (Figure: **FS00**-4).

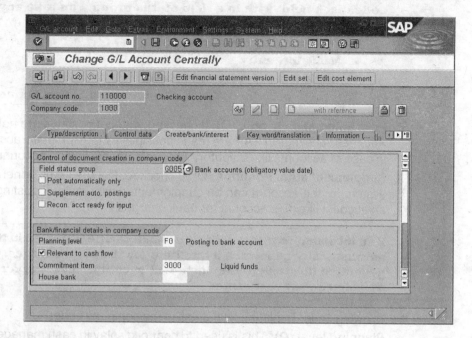

Figure: **FS00**-4

Enter the following under <u>Control of document creation in company code</u>:

1. **Field status group** (M): Select the field status group from the drop-down list. (Sample list is shown in Figure: **FS00**-5).

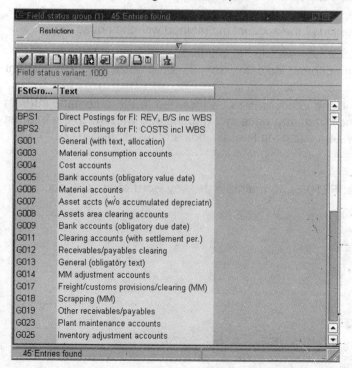

Figure: **FS00**-5

Field Status Group determines the screen layout for a document entry. The field status groups are assigned to a Field Status Variant, which is assigned to a Company Code. Each field, with in a field status group, can take any one of the following status:

- Optional entry (mandatory)
- Mandatory entry
- Hidden or suppressed for entry

Use *Transaction Code: OBC4* to maintain Field Status Variant / Group.

2. **Post automatically only** (O): If checked, manual postings are not possible to the account. Automatic postings in SAP are made possible via the automatic account determination. Used in case of accounts like inventory accounts, reconciliation accounts etc.

3. **Supplement auto. Postings** (O): If checked, the line items generated automatically by the system for the account can be supplemented with manual postings. This is usually set for an account like 'G/L account for bank charges'.

If an incoming payment with some bank charge is posted in the system, the system automatically generates a line item for the bank charges. You view the system-generated line item in the document overview, and *supplement* the same with an assignment, say cost center.

Enter the following under <u>Bank/financial detail in the company code:</u>

4. **Planning level (O):** This is used to control display in cash management. SAP recommends to use **F** level for bank accounts, customers, and vendors, and **B** level for bank clearing accounts.

5. **House Bank (O):** Select a house bank from the drop down list. This is to be entered if it is a bank account.

6. **Account ID (O):** Enter the account id of the account maintained with the house bank.

Enter the following under <u>Interest calculation information in the company code:</u>

7. **Interest indicator (O):** Select the interest indicator, from the drop down list, if the account is to be included in automatic interest calculation.

8. **Interest calc. Frequency (O):** If the account is to be included in the automatic interest calculation, mention the frequency (monthly, once in 2 months etc) with which the interest needs to be calculated by the system using the interest indicator mentioned in (7).

Step-6

Press   Key word/translation   tab (Figure: **FS00**-5), to maintain the key word of the G/L account in other languages.

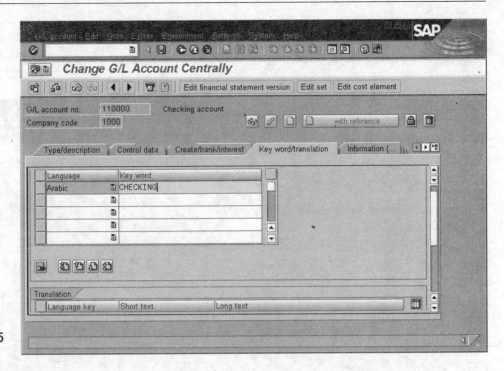

Figure: **FS00**-5

Step-7

Press Information (C... tab (Figure: **FS00**-6), to maintain the key word of the G/L text in chart of accounts.

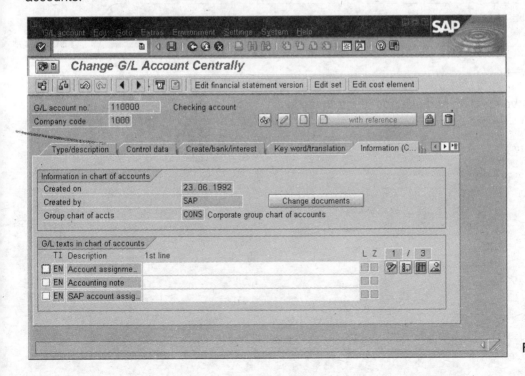

Figure: **FS00**-6

Step-8

Press Information (CoCd)   tab (Figure: **FS00**-7), to maintain the key word of the G/L text in company code area.

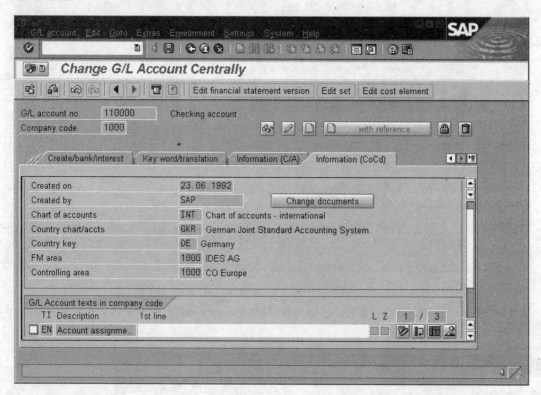

Figure:
FS00-7

Step-9

Press 🖫 to save the data and exit from the transaction.

14

G/L - Create G/L Account (mass maintenance) – Chart of Accounts Area: OB_GLACC11

Transaction Code	OB_GLACC11
Menu	Accounting > Financial Accounting > General Ledger > Master records > Collective processing > Chart of accounts area

Business Process Overview

The master record, in General Ledger, contains information that is required to control the posting and processing of transactions to G/L, and is consisting of two areas:

1. Chart of accounts area
2. Company code area

The **chart of accounts** area consists of information, which is valid across the company codes. These include:

- G/L account number
- Short text of the account
- Chart of accounts
- P&L or Balance Sheet indicator
- Account group

Mass maintenance helps you to maintain the changes to multiple G/L accounts from a single transaction, as against the individual processing. You can change:

- Balance Sheet / Profit & Loss indicator
- Account Group

You can choose to display both the original and the changed values from the same screen.

Transaction Steps

Step-1

Access the transaction either by the transaction code or by the menu and you will be taken to "*Mass Maintenance: G/L accounts*" Screen (Figure: **OB_GLACC11**-1).

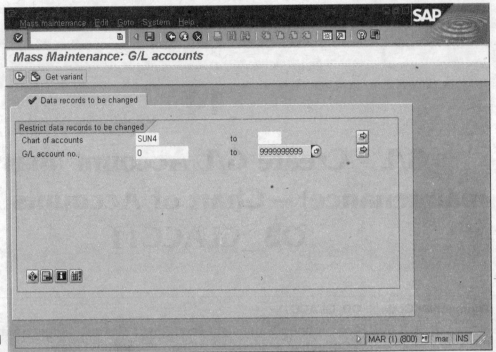

Figure:
OB_GLACC11-1

Step-2

Press "**F8**" or , the system takes you to the "***Processing mode***" screen (Figure: **OB_GLACC11**-2).

Figure:
OB_GLACC11-2

Step-3

Press [Display all records] and you are taken to "***Mass Maintenance: G/L accounts***" screen (Figure: **OB_GLACC11**-3).

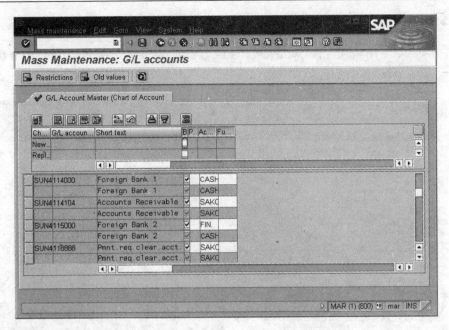

Figure: **OB_GLACC11**-3

Select the row(s), change the required fields:

1. **B(alance Sheet Indicator) (M):** Tick the check box if it is a Balance Sheet account. Else, un-tick.
2. **P(rofit & Loss account indicator (O):** Put an 'X' in the field, if the account is a P&L account.
3. **Ac(count group) (M):** Select the appropriate account group for the account.

Step-4

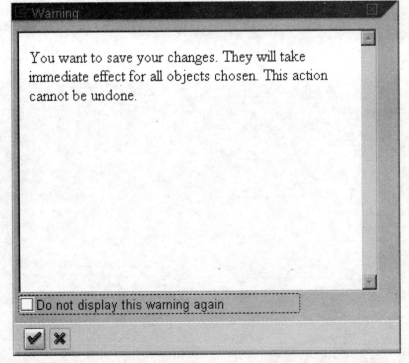

Press and you are taken to "**Warning**" screen (Figure: **OB_GLACC11**-4).

Figure: **OB_GLACC11**-4

Step-5

Press 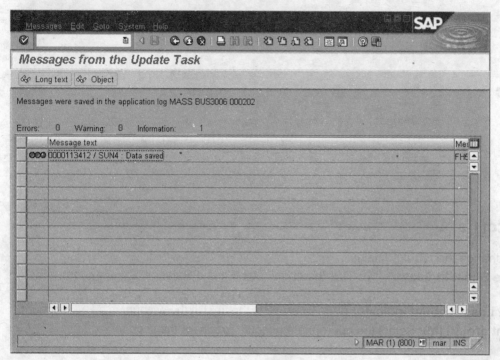.The changes, you just made, are displayed in "***Messages from the Update Task***" screen (Figure: **OB_GLACC11**-5).

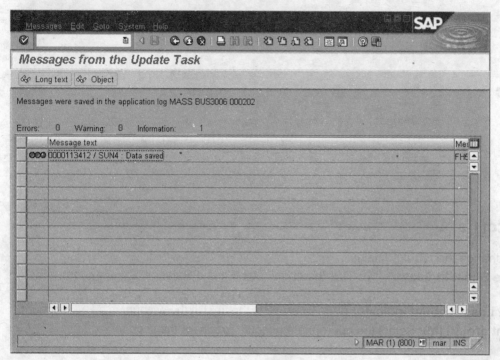

Figure:
OB_GLACC11-5

15

G/L - Create G/L Account (mass maintenance) – Company Code Data: OB_GLACC12

Transaction Code	OB_GLACC12
Menu	Accounting > Financial Accounting > General Ledger > Master records > Collective processing > company code data

Business Process Overview

The master record, in General Ledger, contains information that is required to control the posting and processing of transactions to G/L, and is consisting of two areas:

1. Chart of accounts area
2. Company code area

The **company code area** of a G/L master record contains information that is valid only for that particular company code. These include:

- Account currency
- Reconciliation account
- Open item management?
- Line item display?
- Sort key
- Field status group

Mass maintenance helps you to maintain the changes to multiple G/L accounts from a single transaction, as against the individual processing. You can change:

- Field Status Group
- Account currency
- Only balances in local currency
- Tax category
- Posting w/o tax allowed
- Line item display
- Open item management
- Sort key

You can choose to display both the original and the changed values from the same screen.

Transaction Steps

Step-1

Access the
transaction either by
the transaction code
or by the menu and
you will be taken to
"***Mass Maintenance:
G/L accounts***"
Screen (Figure:
OB_GLACC12-1).

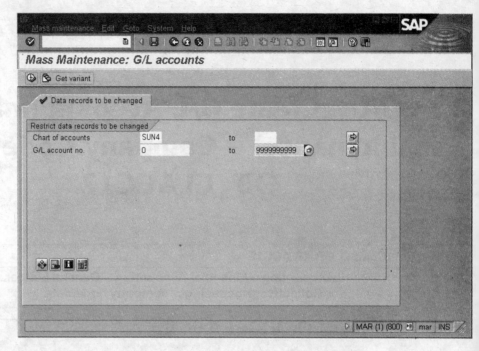

Figure:
OB_GLACC12-1

Step-2

Press "**F8**" or 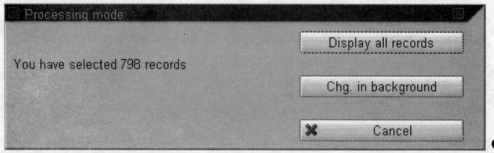, the system takes you to the "***Processing mode***" screen (Figure: **OB_GLACC12**-2).

Figure:
OB_GLACC12-2

Step-3

Press [Display all records] and you are taken to "***Mass Maintenance: G/L accounts***" screen
(Figure: **OB_GLACC12**-3).

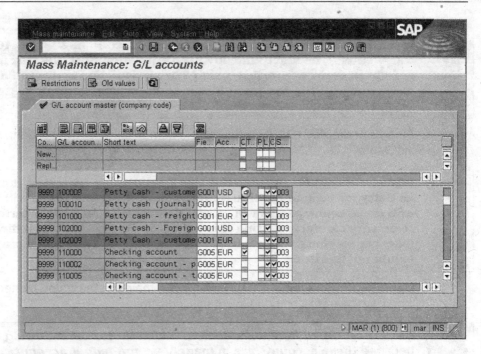

Figure:
OB_GLACC12-3

Select the row(s), change the required fields:

1. **Field status (M):** Change the field status group, wherever required.

2. **Account currency (O):** Change the account currency.

3. **Only balances in local currency (O):** Select this if you want to update the balances of this account only in local currency.

> Set this indicator for accounts, the balance of which need not be maintained per currency. If you set this indicator for accounts managed on open item basis, then this setting will interfere with the clearing of the open items. The indicator needs to be set for accounts like cash clearing & GR/IR clearing account. You cannot set this indicator for any reconciliation account. The normal rule is that you set this indicator for accounts, which are maintained on open item basis but, not maintained in foreign currencies.

4. **Tax category (O):** To determine whether this account is tax relevant or is it a tax account or is it a tax relevant G/L account?

> If the account in question is NOT tax relevant, then leave this field blank. Alternatively, if you want this account to be used for posting taxes only, then you need to decide whether you want to use this for input tax (tax on purchases) or output tax (tax on sales). The third option available is making use of this account as a G/L account to which tax relevant postings (using the appropriate tax codes) will be posted to.

5. **Posting w/o tax allowed (O):** Indicates whether it is possible to post to the account even if a tax code is not entered.

There could be instances where you want to post without specifying a tax code (even though you would have set up a tax code like V0 or A0 for non-taxable transactions). Instances like invoice verification postings (tax information would have been derived from PO), using a tax jurisdiction code (you may not be able to come out with the tax jurisdiction code for your foreign customers) etc would demand posting be allowed without entering a valid tax code.

6. **Line item display (O):** If you need line item display for the account, you need to set this indicator.

When an account is set with the 'line item display' indicator, the system will store an entry for each of the line items in an index table, which will link the line item with the account; as this will greatly compromise on system performance you need to be very careful in setting this indicator. Do NOT set this indicator for accounts (like, tax accounts, receivable/payable account etc) where you are foreseeing a large number of line items.

7. **Open item management (O):** If you want maintain the items posted to this account as 'open' or 'cleared', you need to set this indicator.

Do *NOT* set *'open item management'* indicator for the following type of accounts, because these accounts are managed as *'sub-ledger accounts'*:

- ● **Bank accounts**
- ● **Tax accounts**
- ● **Raw material accounts**
- ● **Reconciliation accounts**

Do *NOT* also set this indicator for P/L accounts and also for some of the material management accounts where the posting is done with a posting key with the account type "M".

8. **Sort key (O):** To indicate to the system what layout rule is to be used for the allocation field in the document line item.

Step-4

Press 🔲 Old values to display the old values as well, so as to check and compare with the new values entered (Figure: **OB_GLACC12**-4).

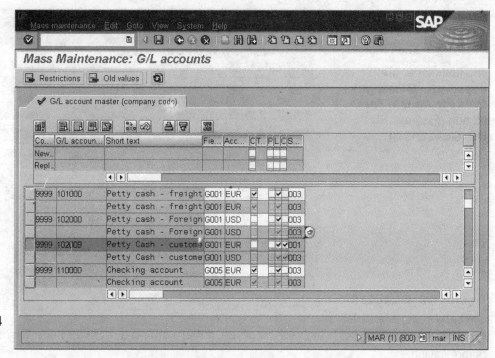

Figure:
OB_GLACC12-4

Step-4

Press 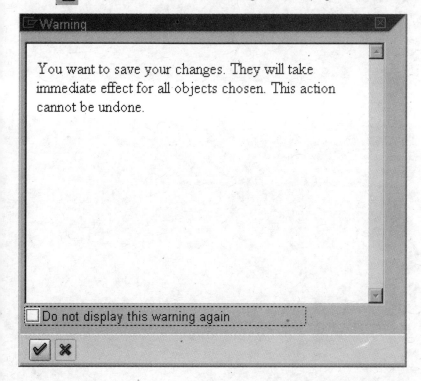and you are taken to "**Warning**" screen (Figure: **OB_GLACC12**-4).

You want to save your changes. They will take immediate effect for all objects chosen. This action cannot be undone.

☐ Do not display this warning again

Figure: **OB_GLACC12**-4

Step-5

Press 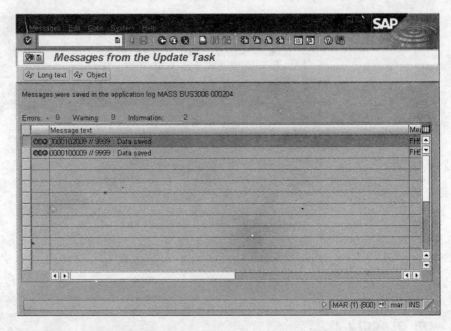.The changes, you just made, are displayed in "***Messages from the Update Task***" screen (Figure: **OB_GLACC12**-5).

Figure: **OB_GLACC12**-5

Pay attention to the ⊙⊙⊙ which will be green, if there are no errors/warnings. Else, correct the same before saving.

16

G/L - Maintain G/L Account Description (mass maintenance): OB_GLACC13

Transaction Code	OB_GLACC13
Menu	Accounting > Financial Accounting > General Ledger > Master records > Collective processing > Descriptions

Business Process Overview

The master record, in General Ledger, contains information that is required to control the posting and processing of transactions to G/L, and is consisting of two areas:

- Chart of accounts area
- Company code area

When G/L accounts are created by reference, it is necessary to change, in the **chart of accounts area**, the **short text** as well as the **G/L account long text** to customize for the copied environment. When you have hundreds and hundreds of G/L accounts (most common, right!), it would be tedious to change these individually. The mass change functionality through this transaction will make the task simple and fast.

You can change:

- Short text
- G/L account long text

You can choose to display both the original and the changed values from the same screen.

Transaction Steps

Step-1

Access the transaction either by the transaction code or by the menu and you will be taken to "**Mass Maintenance: G/L accounts**" Screen (Figure: **OB_GLACC13**-1).

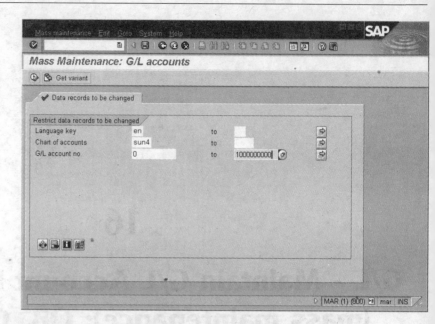

Figure: **OB_GLACC13**-1

In 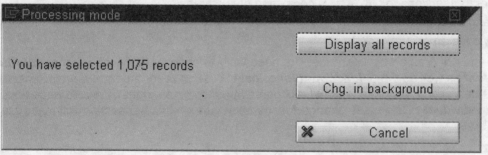 tab, under <u>Restrict data records to be changed</u>:

1. **Language key (O)**: Enter the language key.
2. **Chart of accounts (O):** Enter the chart of accounts, wherein the G/L records are listed.
3. **G/L account no. (O):** Enter the G/L account numbers or maintain complex selections using ⇨ button.

Step-2

Press "**F8**" or 🔽, the system takes you to the "***Processing mode***" screen (Figure: **OB_GLACC13**-2).

Figure:
OB_GLACC13-2

Step-3

Press [Display all records] and you are taken to "***Mass Maintenance: G/L accounts***" screen (Figure: **OB_GLACC13**-3).

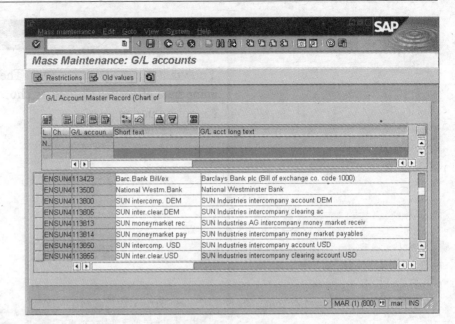

Figure: **OB_GLACC13**-3

    1. Select the row(s), change the text(s) for (1) ***Short text*** and/or (2) ***G/L account long text***.

Step-4

Press 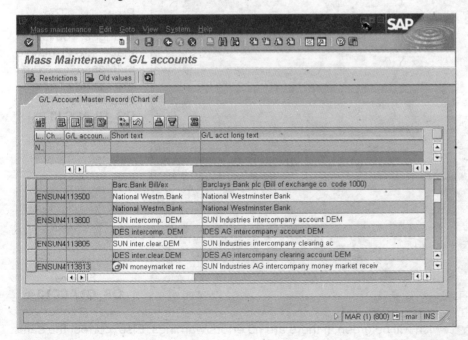 **Old values** to display the old values as well, so as to check and compare with the new values entered (Figure: **OB_GLACC13**-4).

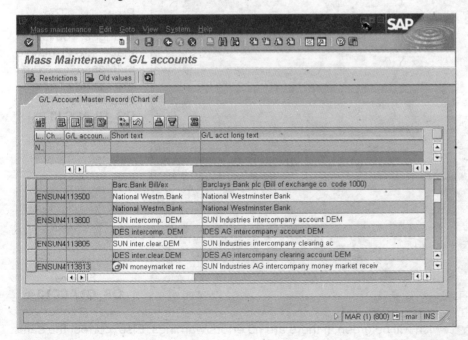

Figure:
OB_GLACC13-4

Step-4

Press   and you are taken to "***Warning***" screen (Figure: **OB_GLACC13**-5).

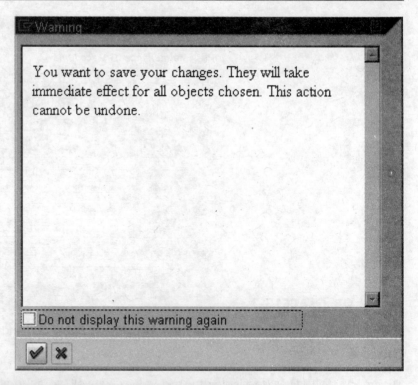

Figure: **OB_GLACC13**-5

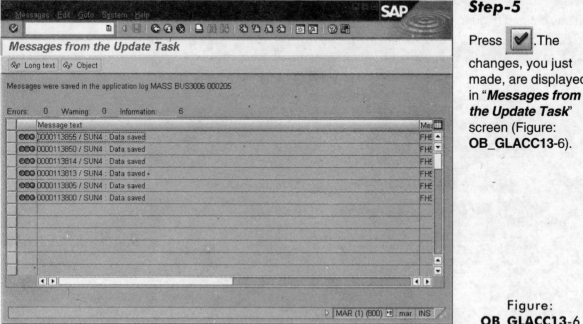

Step-5

Press .The changes, you just made, are displayed in "***Messages from the Update Task***" screen (Figure: **OB_GLACC13**-6).

Figure:
OB_GLACC13-6

Pay attention to the ⊙⊙⊙ which will be green, if there are no errors/warnings. Else, correct the same before saving.

Step-6

You can check the changes by going into the selected account. Select a row, press 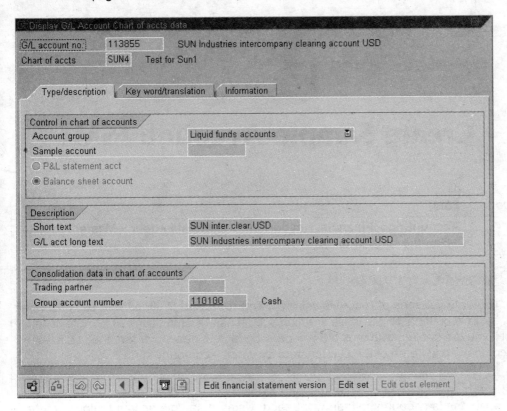 Object ,
and you will be taken to the respective master data display "***Display G/L Account Chart of accts
data***" screen (Figure: **OB_GLACC13**-7).

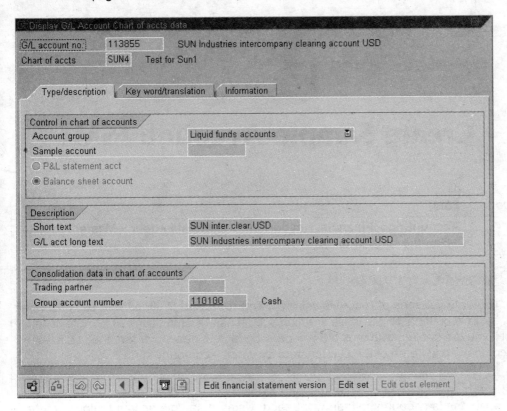

Figure:
OB_GLACC13-7

17

G/L - Create Sample Account: FSM1

Transaction Code	FSM1
Menu	Accounting > Financial Accounting > General Ledger > Master records > Sample Accounts

Business Process Overview

One of the ways to create G/L master record is using a **Sample Account**. Along with **data transfer rule**s, sample account is optional to use while creating such masters. But, usage of sample account would be helpful if you are dealing with multiple company codes but need to create the G/L masters centrally, in the company code area of the G/L masters for various company codes.

A **sample account** is a G/L master record, containing some data, which is transferred when a new G/L account master is created. The sample account is dependent on chart of accounts; and you can create as many sample accounts as you want/need. Using a sample account, along with the data transfer rules, you will be controlling the creation of the G/L account like:

- Whether the data transferred from the sample account can be over written or not:
  - a. The data transfer rule may be:
    - i. Field value can be not changed, if it has already been <u>set</u> in the sample account.
      1. For example, you set the value "INR" in the currency field. When the data transfer rule is set to (i) above, you will not be able to change this currency code to any other, when a new G/L master is created using this sample account.
    - ii. Field value can be not changed, if it has already been <u>set</u> as 'blank' in the sample account.
    - iii. Field value can be changed, when it is <u>transferred </u>from the sample account.
      1. Under this rule, you will be able to change the field's contents, even if there is an initial value (like the text, sort criterion etc) transferred from the sample account.

The **reference** method of G/L account creation is different from the sample account way of G/L creation, because in reference method you can copy and change the data from an existing master record as against the sample record where the field value changes are constrained and controlled by the data transfer rules.

Remember, a sample account is used only for creation of a G/L account, and this can never be posted to.

Transaction Steps

Step-1

Access the transaction either by the transaction code or by the menu and you will be taken to "***Create Sample Account: Initial Screen***" Screen (Figure: **FSM1**-1).

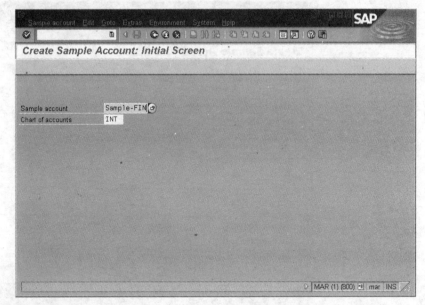

Figure: **FSM1**-1

Enter the details as outlined below:

1. **Sample account (M):** Give a meaningful name for the sample account you are creating.
2. **Chart of account (M):** Enter chart of account for which you are creating the sample account.

 The sample account is dependent upon the *chart of account* where it is created. Sample accounts are used to create the G/L master record in the *company code area*. You may create any number of sample accounts!

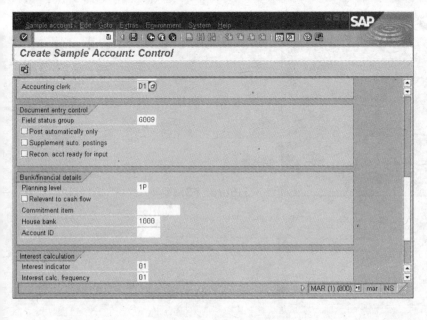

Step-2

Press and you will be taken to "**Create Sample Account: Control**" Screen (Figure: **FSM1**-2).

Figure: **FSM1**-2

Step-3

Scroll down and maintain other values "**Create Sample Account: Control**" Screen (Figure: **FSM1**-3).

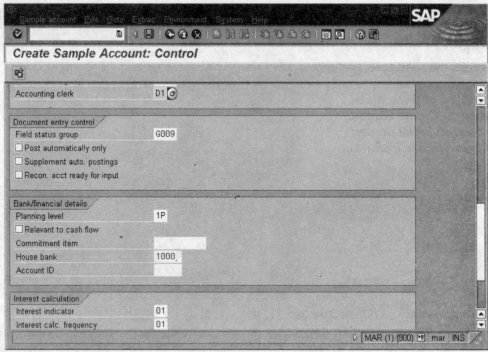

Figure: **FSM1**-3

Step-4

Press 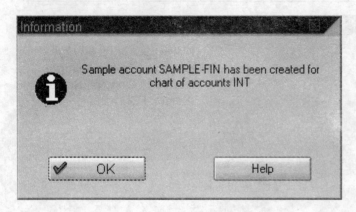 save, when completed, and the sample account will be created in the chart of accounts mentioned (Figure: **FSM1**-4).

Figure: **FSM1**-4

18

G/L – Automatic Clearing Program: F.13

Transaction Code	F.13
Menu	Accounting > Financial Accounting > G/L > Periodic Processing > Automatic Clearing

Business Process Overview

The clearing functions, in SAP, support processing of incoming payments from the business partners. Incoming payments, for example, from customers, are usually for clearing customer open items as against the incoming payments from vendors, which could be for a business transaction like refund from vendor. It is also possible to create a transfer posting with clearing.

The clearing can be done (1) manually or (2) automatically using SAP's clearing program.

Under **manual clearing**, you will select the open items, based on the incoming payment, so that the selected open items are cleared. In cases like refunds from a vendor or transactions involving bank sub accounts and clearing accounts etc, you will resort to manual clearing. When cleared, the system flags these line items as 'cleared', creates a clearing document and enters the clearing document number and clearing date in these open items. Besides the clearing document, the system may also generate additional documents in cases like partial or residual processing, and for posting the loss / gain to the assigned G/L account.

Under **automatic clearing**, the program groups the open items per account (of vendor or customer or G/L) based on certain pre-defined criteria, and clears the group of items (in local/parallel/foreign currency) if they balance to zero. The grouping is done by selecting all the items belonging to the same (1) business area or (2) reconciliation account number or (3) trading partner etc.

However, all these are possible provided you have already taken the pre-requisites that all the customer/vendor accounts have been managed on **open item basis,** and you have manually managed some of the G/L accounts like payroll clearing account(s), check (bank) clearing accounts etc. And, you have also defined, in customizing, that the accounts can be cleared automatically.

Transaction Steps

Step-1

Access the transaction either by the transaction code or menu, and you will be taken to "**Automatic Clearing without Definition of Clearing Currency (SAPF124)**" screen (Figure: **F.13**-1).

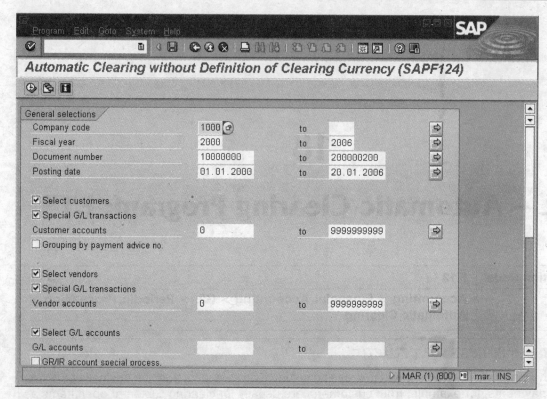

Figure: **F.13**-1

Under <u>General selections</u>:

1. **Company code (M):** Mention the company code(s).
2. **Fiscal year (O):** Enter the fiscal year (s).
3. **Document number (O):** Enter the document number(s).
4. **Posting date (M):** Enter the posting date (s).
5. **Select customers (O):** Tick the check box, to select customer accounts.
6. **Special G/L transactions (O):** Tick the check box to select special G/L transactions as well.
7. **Customer accounts (O):** Enter the customer account number or a range to restrict the selection.
8. **Select vendors (O):** Tick the check box, to select vendor accounts.
9. **Special G/L transactions (O):** Tick the check box to select special G/L transactions as well.
10. **Vendor accounts (O):** Enter the vendor account number or a range to restrict the selection.
11. **Select G/L accounts (O):** Tick the check box, to select G/L accounts.
12. **G/L accounts (O):** Enter the G/L account number or a range to restrict the selection.

Step-2

Scroll down to the remaining portion of "**Automatic Clearing without Definition of Clearing Currency (SAPF124)**" screen (Figure: **F.13**-2) and maintain additional details.

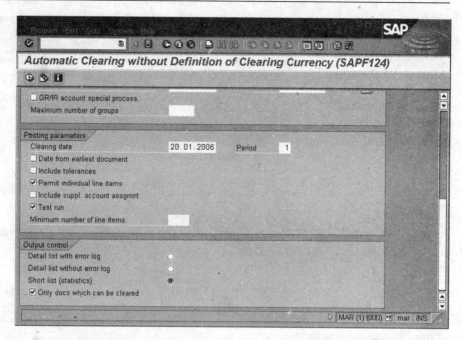

Figure: **F.13**-2

Under Posting parameters:

    13. Clearing date (M): enter the clearing date, and the **period** (O).

    14. Permit individual line items (O): Tick this check box to allow individual line items.

    15. Test run (O): Tick this, to do a test run before final postings.

Under Output control:

    1. Maintain the required parameters to limit the display and log.

Step-3

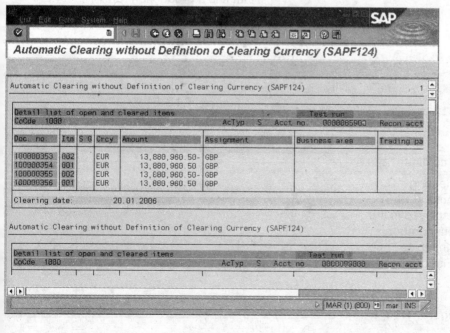

Press ⊕ and you are taken to the *test run* display at "**Automatic Clearing without Definition of Clearing Currency (SAPF124)**" screen (Figure: **F.13**-3). Pay attention to the "test run" display in red background.

Figure: **F.13**-3

Step-4

Press ⊙ to go back to "**Automatic Clearing without Definition of Clearing Currency (SAPF124)**" screen (Figure: **F.13**-4).

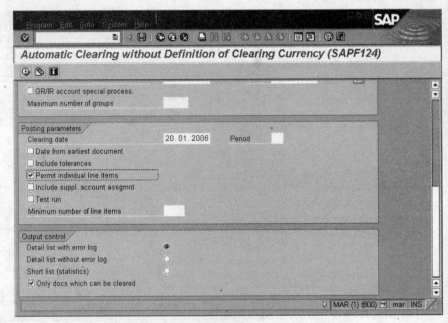

Figure: **F.13**-4

Under Posting parameters:

    1. Test run (O): Remove the tick in the check box for enabling the production run.

Under Output control:

    2. Change the parameters, if necessary to suit the requirement.

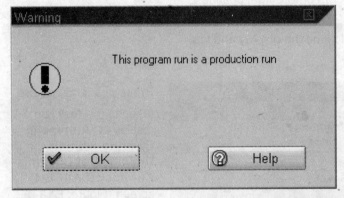

Step-5

Press ⊙ and the system pops up a "**Warning**" screen (Figure: **F.13**-5) to alert that it is a production run.

Figure: **F.13**-5

Step-6

Press ✔ OK to continue, and the system displays the clearing document information (Figure: **F.13**-6). (The document number displayed in the pop up is the last document number posted by the system during this automatic clearing run.) Else, close the warning up and go back.

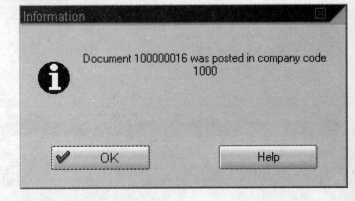

Figure: **F.13**-6

Step-7

Press to continue, and the system displays the clearing details (Figure: F.13-7). Scroll down to see all the clearing documents created and posted by the system.

Note the display 'update run' in red background.

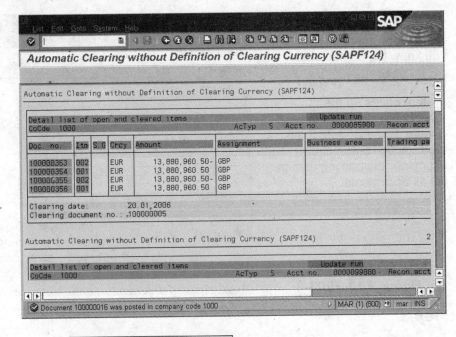

Figure-F.13-7

End of Transaction

As usual, let us find out how the clearing program has updated the documents, automatically.

Step-A

Use *Transaction Code: FB03* to go to *"Display Document: Initial Screen"* (Figure: F.13-FB03-1).

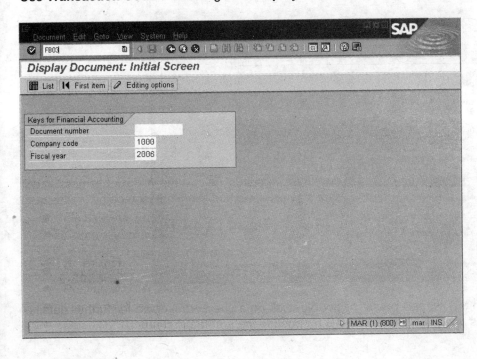

Figure: F.13-FB03-1

Step-B

Enter a document number, if you know the number. Else, press [List] and the system brings up the *"Document List"* screen (Figure: **F.13-FB03**-2). Enter the selection parameters, especially the posting date to list all documents.

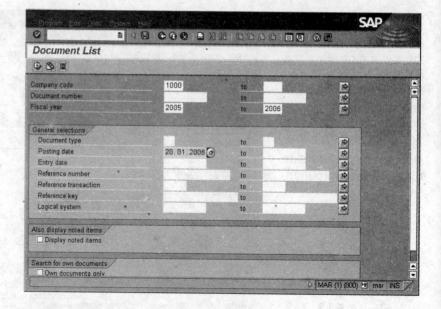

Figure: **F.13-FB03**-2

Step-C

Press [⊕] and the system brings up "**Document List** screen (Figure: **F.13-FB03**-3).

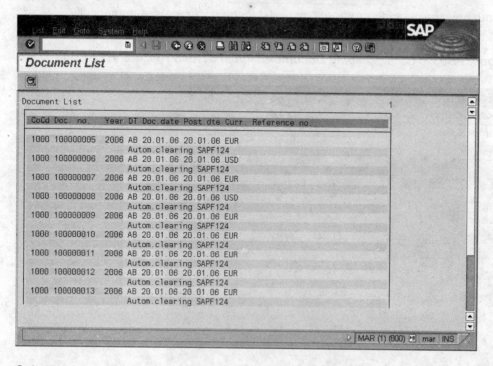

Figure: **F.13-FB03**-2

Select a document from the list and press or double-click on a line to drill-down for further details. Note that the system has used document type **AB** for posting the automatic clearing.

19

G/L - Balance Audit Trail: S_ALR_87100205

Transaction Code	S_ALR_87100205
Program	RFHABU00
Menu	Accounting > Financial Accounting > General Ledger > Periodic Processing > Closing > Document > Balance Audit Trail > All Accounts > General Ledger from Document File

Business Process Overview

There are several programs, in SAP R/3, recording all the postings made to an account (even if some of the documents relating to the transactions in these accounts are archived) so as to substantiate, at a later date, the balance in that account on the basis of the corresponding line items from those archived documents. The reports from these programs are called as the **Balance Audit Trails**.

Essentially, these programs:

1. Evaluate the documents and master data.
2. List postings made to each of the accounts.
3. Take into account the balances carried forward in each of the accounts.
4. Take into account the balances for the periods.
5. Sort the line items of an account automatically and add up all the line items of an account.
6. Compare the total of (5) with that of the total account balance.
7. Throw appropriate messages if the totals are different.

The balance audit trail programs can be grouped according to the **sorting method**:

1. **Chronological (Program: RFHABU00)**

   Line items are sorted chronologically by the posting date and document number.

2. **Open item basis (Program: RFKKBU00)**

   In case of accounts that are maintained on Open Item basis, the line items are sorted:

   1. All the clearing items by the clearing date.
   2. All the open items by the posting date.

You may also group the balance audit trail programs, based on the **data origin**:

1. Balance audit trail from the **online** system

> The system documents only the current data, and is useful for producing reports during a fiscal year, like monthly balance audit trail.
>
> 2. Balance audit trail from as ***extract***
>
> This is the ***accumulated audit trail.*** Transfer the balance extract to a file, and update the same whenever new data is available online. This is useful to create the report, say, at the end of the fiscal year.

Transaction Steps

Step-1

Access the transaction either by the transaction code or by executing the ***program*** or by the menu, and you will be taken to "**General Ledger from the Document File**" Screen (Figure: **S_ALR_87 100205**-1) and enter the details as outlined below:

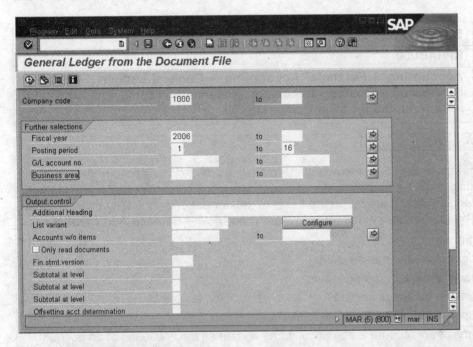

Figure:
S_ALR_87100205 -1

Enter the following details:

    1. **Company code (O):** Enter the company code(s).

Under <u>further selections</u> block:

    2. **Fiscal year (O):** Enter the fiscal year for which you want the balance audit trail.

    3. **Posting period (O):** Enter the posting period, from & to.

    4. **G/L account no. (O):** Enter the number range, from & to, if you want to restrict.

Under <u>Output control</u> block:

    5. Make any further selections, as you feel necessary.

> Almost all the fields, in the data input screen, are optional. However, it is a good practice, always, to restrict the values so as to improve the system performance. Especially, the values for company code & fiscal year needs to be restrictive enough.

Step-2

Press and you will be taken to "**General Ledger from the Document File**" Screen (Figure: **S_ALR_87100205** -2):

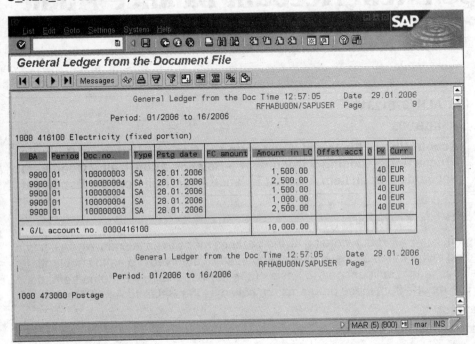

Figure:
S_ALR_87100205 -2

> The General Ledger balance audit trail lists the transactions in the G/L accounts selected, chronologically. Scroll down the list and look at the details. As in any other transactions, you may select a line on the display and drill down further to see the details.

20

G/L - Open Item Account Balance Audit Trail: S_ALR_87012317

Transaction Code	S_ALR_87012317
Program	RFKKBU00
Menu	Accounting > Financial Accounting > General Ledger > Periodic Processing > Closing > Document > Balance Audit Trail > Open Item Accounts > Open Item Account Balance Audit Trail from the Document

Business Process Overview

There are several programs, in SAP R/3, recording all the postings made to an account (even if some of the documents relating to the transactions in these accounts are archived) so as to substantiate, at a later date, the balance in that account on the basis of the corresponding line items from those archived documents. The reports from these programs are called as the *Balance Audit Trails*.

Essentially, these programs:

1. Evaluate the documents and master data.
2. List postings made to each of the accounts.
3. Take into account the balances carried forward in each of the accounts.
4. Take into account the balances for the periods.
5. Sort the line items of an account automatically and adds up all the line items of an account.
6. Compare the total of (5) with that of the total account balance.
7. Throw appropriate messages if the totals are different.

The balance audit trail programs can be grouped according to the *sorting method*:

1. **Chronological (Program: RFHABU00)**

   Line items are sorted chronologically by the posting date and document number.

2. **Open item basis (Program: RFKKBU00)**

   In case of accounts that are maintained on Open Item basis, the line items are sorted:

   1. All the clearing items by the clearing date.
   2. All the open items by the posting date.

You may also group the balance audit trail programs, based on the *data origin*:

1. Balance audit trail from the *online* system

> The system documents only the current data, and is useful for producing reports during a fiscal year, like monthly balance audit trail.
>
> 2. Balance audit trail from as **extract**
>
> This is the <u>accumulated</u> audit trail. Transfer the balance extract to a file, and update the same whenever new data is available online. This is useful to create the report, say, at the end of the fiscal year.

Transaction Steps

Step-1

Access the transaction either by the transaction code or by executing the **program** or by the menu, and you will be taken to **"Open Item Account Balance from the Document File"** Screen (Figure: **S_ALR_87012317** -1) and enter the details as outlined below:

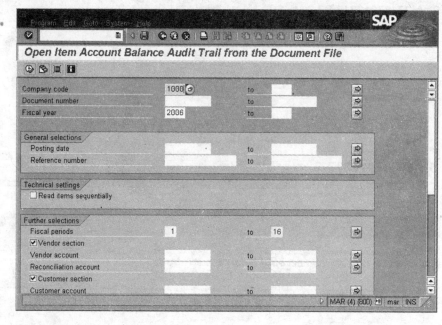

Figure:
S_ALR_87012317-1

Enter the following details:

1. **Company code (O):** Enter the company code(s).
2. **Document number (O):** Enter the document number(s).
3. **Fiscal year (O):** Enter the fiscal year for which you want the balance audit trail.

Under <u>General selections</u> block:

4. **Posting period (O):** Enter the posting period, from & to.
5. **G/L account no. (O):** Enter the number range, from & to, if you want to restrict.

Under <u>Further selections</u> block:

6. **Fiscal Period (O):** Enter the fiscal period(s) for which you want the audit trail.
7. **Vendor Selection (O):** Check the check box, to select the vendor accounts for the report.
8. **Vendor account (O):** Enter the vendor account number or a range.
9. **Customer Selection (O):** Check the check box, to select the customer accounts for the report.
10. **Customer account (O):** Enter the customer account number or a range.

Almost all the fields, in the data input screen, are optional. However, it is a good practice, always, to restrict the values so as to improve the system performance. Especially, the values for company code & fiscal year needs to be restrictive enough. Make a practice to enter at least three parameters.

Step-2

Press 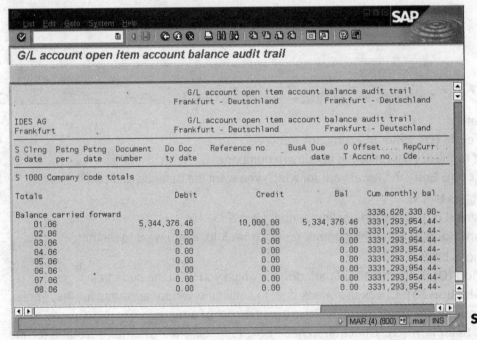 and you will be taken to "**G/L account open item account balance audit trail**" Screen (Figure: **S_ALR_87012317**-2 & 3):

Figure:
S_ALR_87012317-2

Figure:
S_ALR_87012317-3

21

G/L - Account List: S_ALR_87012327

Transaction Code	S_ALR_87012327
Program	RFSKVZ00
Menu	Accounting > Financial Accounting > General Ledger > Periodic Processing > Closing > Report > General Ledger Reports > Master Data > G/L Account List > S_ALR_87012327 SAP Minimal Variant

Business Process Overview

The **G/L Account List** provides you with the details of all the G/L accounts in a company code or company codes. The listing helps you to display, for each of the accounts:

1. **Status in chart of accounts**
   a. Creation block?
   b. Posting block?
   c. Planning block?
2. **Account control**
   a. Tax category
   b. Balances in local currency
   c. Reconciliation Id
3. **Account management**
   a. Line item management?
   b. Open item management?
   c. Sort key
4. **Document entry control**
   a. Field Status

Transaction Steps

Step-1

Access the transaction either by the transaction code or by executing the **program** or by the menu, and you will be taken to "**G/L Account List**" Screen (Figure: **S_ALR_87012327**-1) and enter the details as outlined:

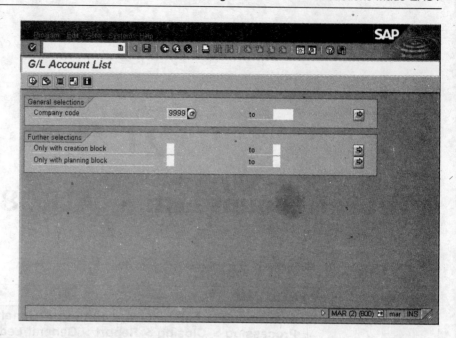

Figure:
S_ALR_87012327-1

Under <u>General selections</u>:

    1. **Company code (O):** Enter the company code(s).

Under <u>Further selections</u>

    2. **Only with creation block (O):** Select a value.

    3. **Only with planning block (O):** Select a value.

 Almost all the fields, in the data input screen, are optional. However, it is a good practice, always, to restrict the values so as to improve the system performance. Especially, the values for company code needs to be restrictive enough.

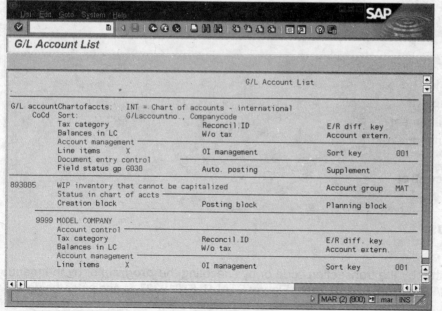

Figure:
S_ALR_87012327-2

Step-2

Press ⊕ and you will be taken to "**G/L Account List**" Screen (Figure: **S_ALR_87012327**-2).

22

G/L - Cash Flow Report – Direct Method: S_ALR_87012271

Transaction Code	S_ALR_87012271
Menu	Accounting > Financial Accounting > General Ledger > Periodic Processing > Closing > Report > General Ledger Reports > Balance Sheet / Profit & Loss / Cash Flow > General > Cash Flow > Cash Flow (Direct Method)

Business Process Overview

SAP R/3 provides multitude of reports for analyzing the business performance. Under General Ledger, the various reports are grouped into tree like structure as detailed under:

1. General edger Reports
    a. *Balance Sheet / Profit & Loss / Cash Flow*
        i. *General*
            1. Actual / actual comparisons
            2. *Plan / actual comparison*
            3. Time series
            4. Cash Flow
                a. Cash Flow (Direct Method)
                b. Cash Flow (Indirect Method) Variant 1 (S_ALR_87012272)
                c. Cash Flow (Indirect Method) Variant 2 (S_ALR_87012273)

Transaction Steps

Step-1

Access the transaction either by the transaction code or by executing the *program* or by the menu, and you will be taken to "**Selection: Cash flow (direct method)**" Screen (Figure: **S_ALR_87012271** -1) and enter the details as outlined:

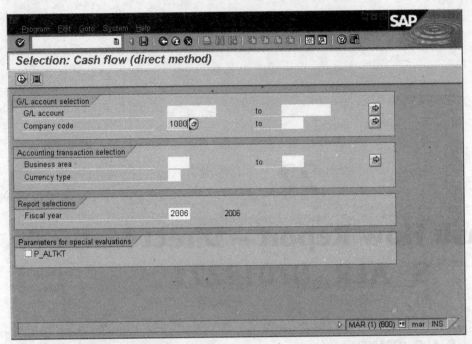

Figure:
S_ALR_87012271-1

Under <u>G/L account selection</u>:
1. **G/L account (O):** Enter the G/L account or range of accounts.
2. **Company code (O):** Enter the company code(s).

Under <u>Accounting transaction selection</u> block:
3. **Business area (O):** Enter the business area(s).
4. **Currency type (O):** Enter currency type.

Under <u>Report selection</u> block:
5. **Fiscal year (O):** Enter the fiscal year.

 Almost all the fields, in the data input screen, are optional. However, it is a good practice, always, to restrict the values so as to improve the system performance. Especially, the values for company code & fiscal year needs to be restrictive enough. Make a practice to enter at least three parameters.

Step-2

Press ⊕ and you will be taken to "**Execute Drilldown Report Cash flow (direct method)**" Screen (Figure: **S_ALR_87012271**-2):

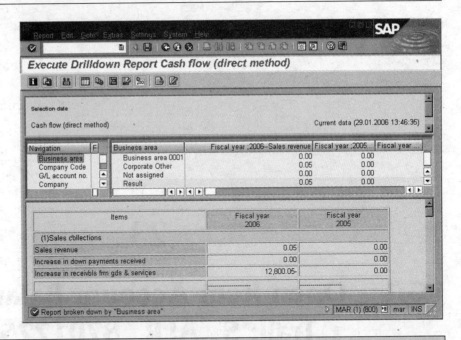

Figure:
S_ALR_87012271-2

 Use *Menu: Settings* to manipulate the display in number format / currency / characteristics display / totals row / column display etc.

Step-3

Scroll down to display more (Figure: **S_ALR_87012271**-3).

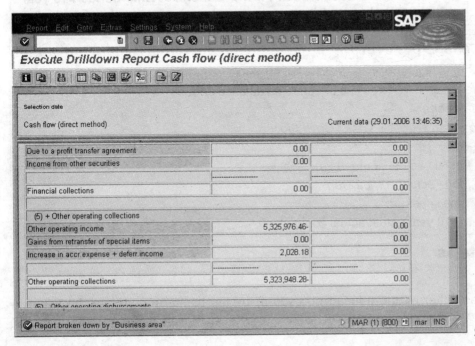

Figure:
S_ALR_87012271-3

23

G/L - Open Item Account Balance Audit Trail: S_ALR_87012257

Transaction Code	S_ALR_87012257
Menu	Accounting > Financial Accounting > General Ledger > Periodic Processing > Closing > Report > General Ledger Reports > Balance Sheet / Profit & Loss / Cash Flow > General > Time Series >10 year actual / actual comparison

Business Process Overview

SAP R/3 provides multitude of reports for analyzing the business performance. Under General Ledger, the various reports are grouped into tree like structure as detailed under:

1. General edger Reports
   a. Balance Sheet / Profit & Loss / Cash Flow
      i. General
         1. Actual / actual comparisons
         2. Plan / actual comparison
         3. Time series
            a. 10 year actual/actual comparison

Transaction Steps

Step-1

Access the transaction either by the transaction code or by the menu, and you will be taken to **"Selection: 10-year actual/actual comparison"** Screen (Figure: **S_ALR_87012257** -1) and enter the details as outlined:

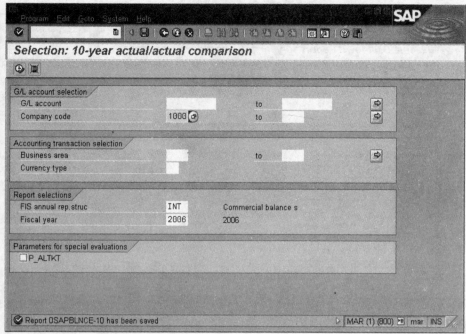

Figure:
S_ALR_87012257-1

Under <u>G/L account selection</u>:

1. **G/L account (O):** Enter the G/L account or range of accounts.
2. **Company code (O):** Enter the company code(s).

Under <u>Accounting transaction selection</u> block:

3. **Business area (O):** Enter the business area(s).
4. **Currency type (O):** Enter currency type.

Under <u>Report selection</u> block:

5. **FIS annual rep stru (O):** Select from the drop own values.
6. **Fiscal year (O):** Enter the fiscal year.

 Almost all the fields, in the data input screen, are optional. However, it is a good practice, always, to restrict the values so as to improve the system performance. Especially, the values for company code & fiscal year needs to be restrictive enough. Make a practice to enter at least three parameters.

Step-2

Press and you will be taken to "**Execute Drilldown Report 10-year actual/actual comparison**" Screen (Figure: **S_ALR_87012257**-2):

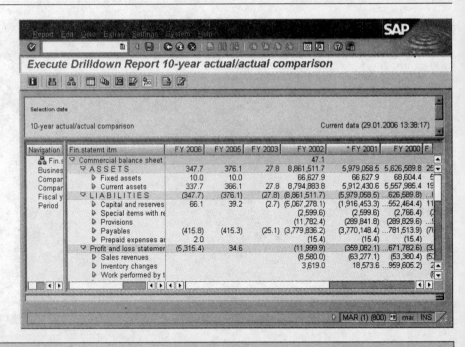

Figure:
S_ALR_87012257-2

Use *Menu: Settings* to manipulate the display in number format / currency / characteristics display / totals row / column display etc.

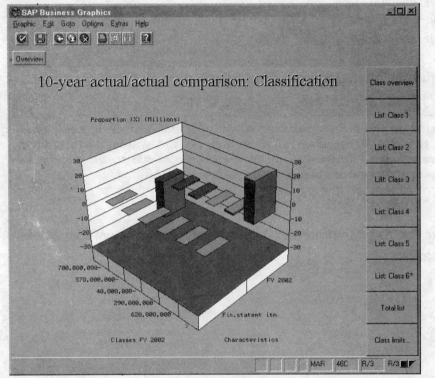

Figure:
S_ALR_87012257-3

Step-3

*Go to **Menu: Edit > Analysis > Classification*** to display the details in a graphical format (Figure: **S_ALR_87012257**-3).

24

G/L - Balance Sheet / Profit and Loss Statement : S_ALR_87012284

Transaction Code	S_ALR_87012284
Program	RFBILA00
Menu	Accounting > Financial Accounting > General Ledger > Periodic Processing > Closing > Report > General Ledger Reports > Balance Sheet / Profit & Loss / Cash Flow > General > Actual/Actual Comparison >S_ALR_87012284 - Balance Sheet / Profit and Loss Statement

Business Process Overview

Financial statements, **Balance Sheet and Profit & Loss Account**, needs to be generated as a part of the year end operations to meet the country specific statutory requirements. Financial statements can be created:

- For various **organizational units** defined by you (like the company, company code, business area etc).
- In different **languages.**
- In different **types** (opening or closing) with varying degrees of **detail and summarizations.**
- In various **currencies** (local currency, group currency etc).

However, to create the financial statements:

1. You should have already defined (**IMG: Financial Accounting > General Ledger Accounting > Business Transactions > Closing > Documenting > Define Financial Statement Versions**) the **Financial Statement Version** (s), which takes care of the lay out(s).
2. You should have completed all the **preparatory postings**:
   a. **Sales & Distribution**
      - Completed posting of goods issues and invoices for the delivery notes.
      - Completed creation of rebate settlements and the credit notes.
      - Excluded all the preliminary invoices.
   b. **Material Management**
      - Completed physical inventory.
      - Completed material valuation.

c. **Asset Accounting**
   ➤ Posted depreciation for the relevant fiscal year.
   ➤ Completed creating Asset History.

d. **Human Resources**
   ➤ Posted (and transferred to FI) salaries/wages for the last accounting period.

The other preparations include:

- Balance confirmation exercise.
- Analyze GR/IR Clearing account.
- Complete Value Adjustments (like bad debt reserve).
- Foreign currency valuation.
- Transferring and sorting receivables and payables.

Transaction Steps

Step-1

Access the transaction either by the transaction code or by executing the **program** or by the menu, and you will be taken to "**Selection: Annual plan/actual comparison**" Screen (Figure: **S_ALR_87012284**-1) and enter the details as outlined below:

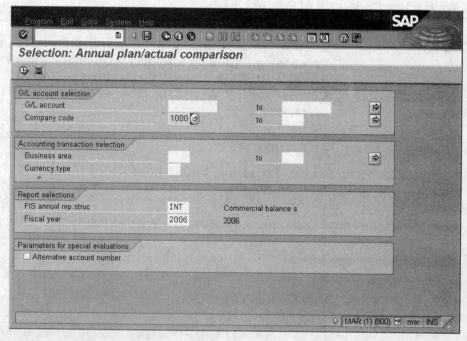

Figure:
S_ALR_87012284-1

Under G/L account selection:
1. **G/L account (O):** Enter the G/L account or range of accounts.
2. **Company code (O):** Enter the company code(s).

Under Accounting transaction selection block:
3. **Business area (O):** Enter the business area(s).
4. **Currency type (O):** Enter currency type.

Under Report selection block:
5. **FIS annual rep stru (O):** Select from the drop own values.
6. **Fiscal year (O):** Enter the fiscal year.

Almost all the fields, in the data input screen, are optional. However, it is a good practice, always, to restrict the values so as to improve the system performance. Especially, the values for company code & fiscal year needs to be restrictive enough. Make a practice to enter at least three parameters.

Step-2

Press and you will be taken to "**Execute Drilldown Report Annual plan/actual comparison**" Screen (Figure: **S_ALR_87012284**-2):

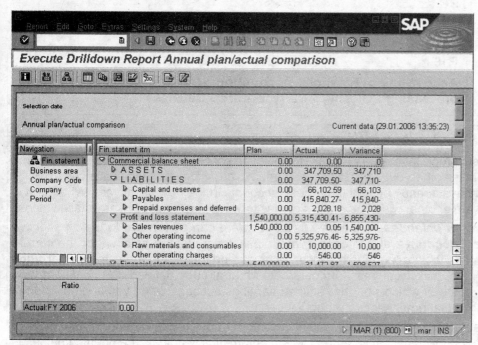

Figure: **S_ALR_87012284**-2

📖 Use *Menu: Settings* to manipulate the display in number format / currency / characteristics display / totals row / column display etc.

25

G/L – Balance Carry Forward: F.16

Transaction Code	F.16
Menu	Accounting > Financial accounting >General Ledger > Periodic processing > Closing > Carry forward > Balances

Business Process Overview

SAP R/3 uses different programs to carry forward the balances of G/L, customer or vendor accounts from one fiscal year to the other. But, you do not even need to carry forward these balances explicitly and manually, if you have already posted to of these accounts in the new fiscal year. Whether it is by manual carry forward or other wise, the system carries forward these balances as detailed below:

1. The **G/L account balances**, to the new fiscal year, are carried forward to their respective **balance sheet accounts**; and in case of profit loss accounts, the balance for the current year will be made to zero, and the balance will be carried forward to the **retained earnings** account(s) to the next fiscal year (of course, you had already defined and configured the system in such a way which was the retained earnings account, when you first defined the master record of that profit & loss account).

   When the balances have been carried forward, and if postings are made to any of these accounts in the previous fiscal year, the system automatically adjusts the opening balances carried forward. Hence, it is never required to carry forward more than once as the system takes care of the adjustments.

2. The balances in **customer / vendor accounts** will be carried forward to their respective accounts for the next fiscal year. The point to be noted is, unlike G/L accounts where all the accounts can be carried forward, in case of customer or vendor accounts you can carry forward only for individual accounts.

   ● Use menu: **Accounting > Financial accounting >Accounts receivable/Accounts payable > Periodic processing > Closing > Carry forward > Balances**

3. You can also carry forward the balances in **Special Purpose Ledgers** using **Menu: Accounting > Financial accounting > Special purpose ledger > Periodic processing > Balance carry forward**

Transaction Steps

Step-1

Access the transaction either by the transaction code or by the menu and you will be taken to "**Balance carryforward**" Screen (Figure: **F.16**-1) .

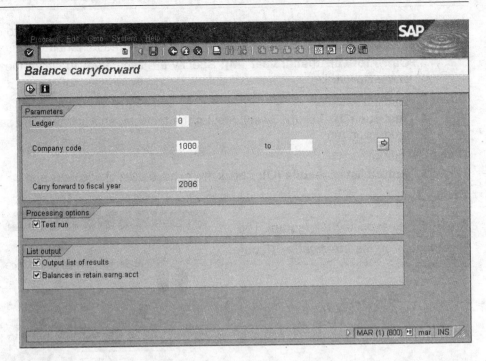

Figure: **F.16**-1

Under <u>Parameters</u>:

   1. **Ledger (M)**: Select the appropriate ledger (Table: **GLT0**) from the drop down list (Figure: **F.16**-2).

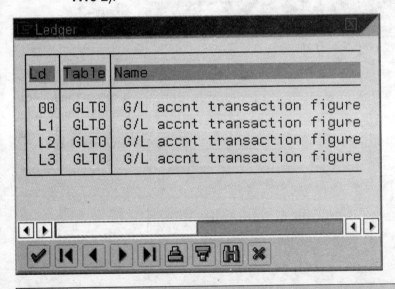

Figure: **F.16**-2

 In cases where you are using parallel currencies in the general ledger, if your second or third currency is the group currency, then balances will be carried forward in this group currency in *ledger 00*. If you maintain additional general ledgers, other than 00, and if you run the parallel currencies in these additional ledgers, then you need to carry forward the balances for each of these additional ledgers like L1, L2 etc.

2. **Company code (M):** Enter the company code for which you want to carry forward the G/L account balances. Maintain the range if it is required for a number of company codes.

3. **Carry forward fiscal year (M):** Specify the fiscal year to which the balances need to be carried forward.

Under <u>Processing options</u>:

4. **Test run (O):** Tick the check box for the test run, and uncheck the same when you do the production run.

Under <u>List output</u>:

5. **Output list of results (O):** Check this to have a list of accounts and balances carried forward.

Step-2

Press 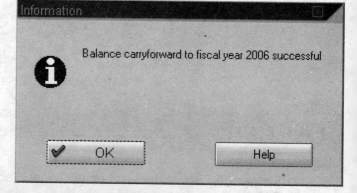 to execute the program. The system pops up the *information* (Figure: **F.16**-3).

Figure: **F.16**-3

Step-3

Press

and the system displays the log for the test run of the balance carry forward (Figure: **F.16**-4).

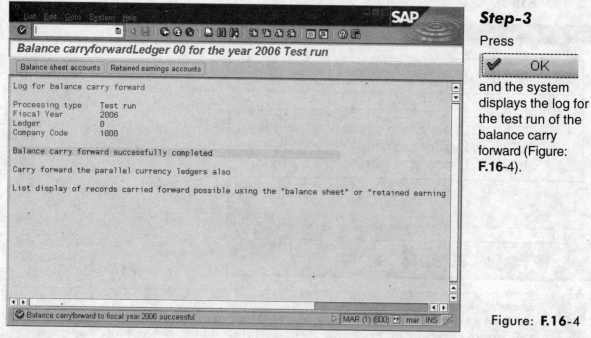

Figure: **F.16**-4

Step-5

Press   Balance sheet accounts   to look at the balances which will be carried forward, in the *balance sheet accounts* (Figure: **F.16**-5).

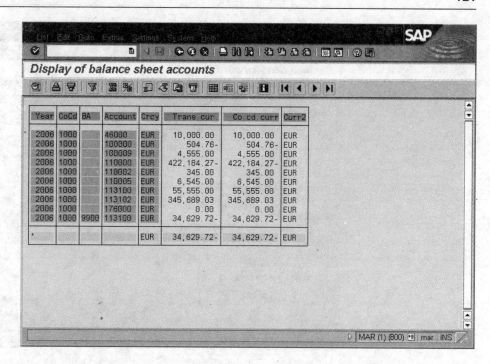

Figure: **F.16**-5

Step-6

Go back by pressing . Press Retained earnings accounts to view the details for ***retained earnings accounts*** (Figure: **F.16**-6).

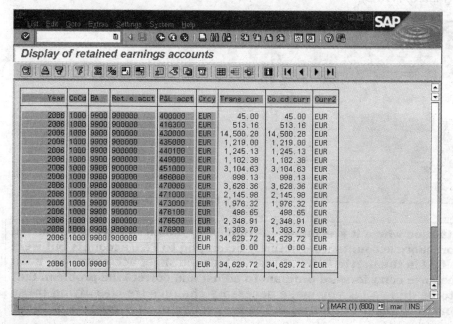

Figure: **F.16**-6

Step-7

Press and you will be taken to "**Balance carryforward**" Screen. Uncheck "Test run" check box. (Figure: **F.16**-7).

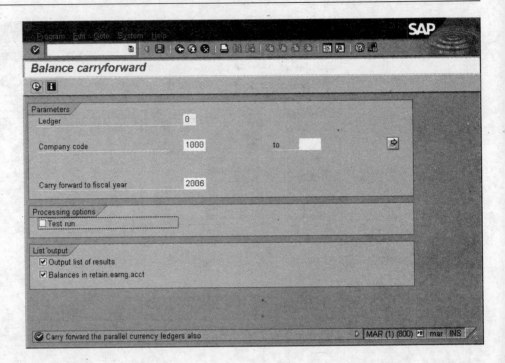

Figure: **F.16**-7

Step-8

Press 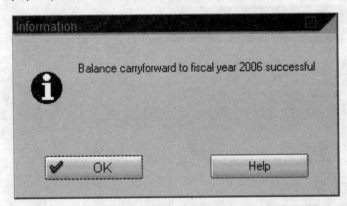 for the production run. When balances have been carried forward successfully, the system pops up the ***information*** (Figure: **F.16**-8).

Figure: **F.16**-8

 In case of a situation where it was found out that, after balances have been carried forward, one ore more accounts were actually belonging to P&L accounts but were wrongly classified in the previous fiscal year as balance sheet accounts, you need to re-run the balance carry forward program to adjust and correct the problem. But, these needs to be done after you make necessary changes (re-classifying these accounts as balance sheet accounts) in the respective master records of these accounts.

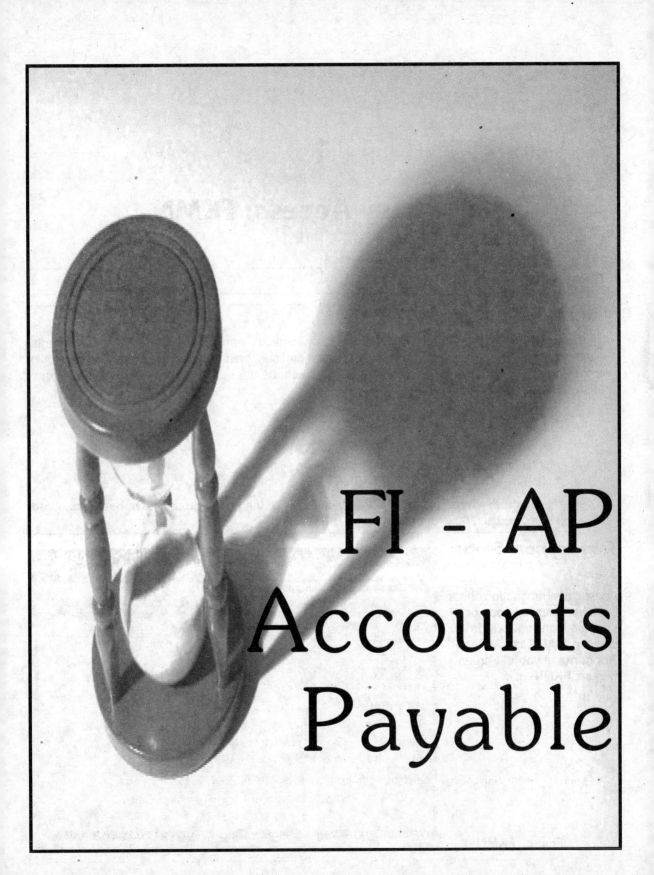

FI - AP
Accounts
Payable

1

AP - Easy Access: FKMN

Transaction Code	FKMN

Transaction Overview

The **Transaction FKMN** provides you with all the necessary transactions under FI-AP (Accounts Payable) for document entry, account analysis, master creation, credit management, archiving, periodic processing and reporting. As in any other 'Easy Access' menu, this menu also groups these transactions conveniently into:

- Document entry
- Account
- Periodic processing
- Withholding tax
- Environment
- Document
- Master records
- Reporting
- Information system

As a single point ready reference, all the transactions in all the above groups have been expanded and nicely arranged in a table at the end of this transaction.

Transaction Steps

Step-1

Access the transaction either by the transaction code or by the menu, and you will be taken to "**SAP Easy Access Accounts payable**" Screen (Figure: **FKMN**-1).

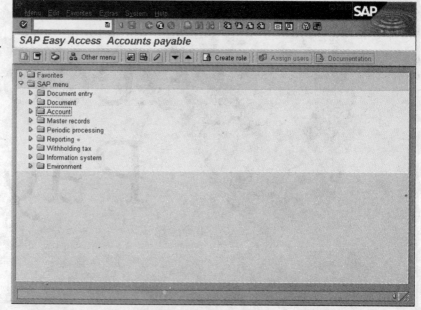

Figure: **FKMN**-1

Step-2

Expand '**Document Entry**" folder to view the transaction codes/ menu for (a) **Document entry** (b) **Reference documents** and (c) **Others** (Figure: FKMN-2).

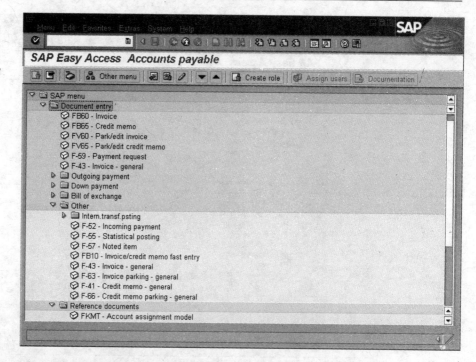

Figure: **FKMN**-2

Step-3

Expand '**Document**" folder to view the transaction codes/ menu for (a) **Document** (b) **Reverse**, (c) **Special G/L transactions**, (d) **Parked documents**, (e) **Reference documents – Recurring / Sample document**, (f) **Cross company code transactions** and (g) **More functions** (Figure: FKMN-3).

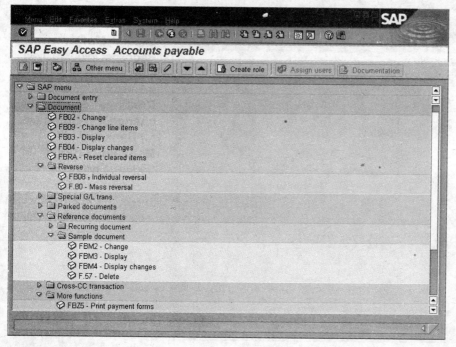

Figure: **FKMN**-3

Step-4

Expand "**Account**" folder to view the transaction codes/menu for (a) **Account** and (b) **Correspondence** (Figure: FKMN-4).

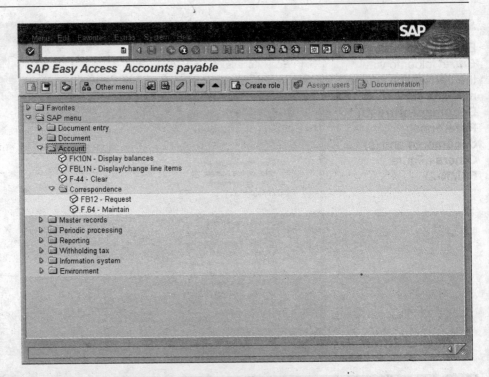

Figure: **FKMN**-4

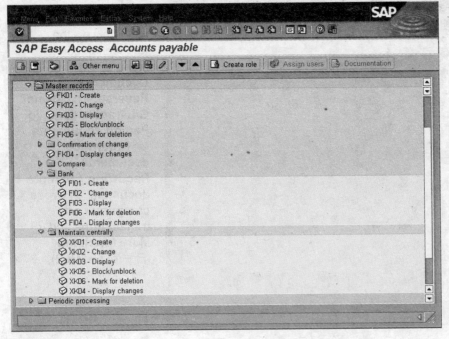

Step-5

Expand '**Master Records**' folder to view the transaction codes/menu for (a) **Confirmation of change**, (b) **Compare**, (c) **Bank** and (d) **Maintain centrally** (Figure: **FKMN**-5).

Figure: **FKMN**-5

Step-6

Expand '**Periodic Processing**' folder to view the transaction codes/menu for **(a) Schedule manager (b) Interest calculation, (c) Print correspondence, (d) Recurring entries, (e) Bill of exchange processing, (f) Archiving and (g) Closing** (Figure: **FKMN**-6).

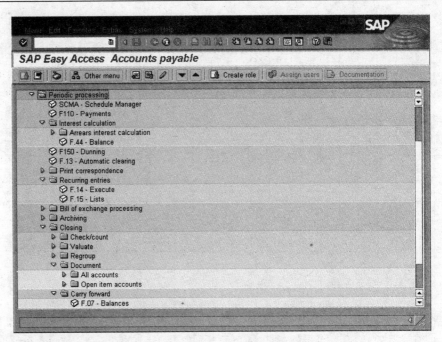

Figure: **FKMN**-6

The entire transactions under *FKMN* are tabulated in the next page(s) for your ready reference:

Document entry		
	FB60 - Invoice	
	FB65 - Credit memo	
	FV60 - Park/edit invoice	
	FV65 - Park/edit credit memo	
	F-59 - Payment request	
	F-43 - Invoice - general	
Outgoing payment	F-53 - Post	
	F-58 - Post + print forms	
Down payment	F-47 - Request	
	F-48 - Down payment	
	F-54 - Clearing	
Bill of exchange	F-40 - Payment	
	FBW6 - Check/bill of exchange	
Intern.transf.psting	F-42 - Without clearing	
	F-51 - With clearing	
Other	F-52 - Incoming payment	
	F-55 - Statistical posting	
	F-57 - Noted item	
	FB10 - Invoice/credit memo fast entry	
	F-43 - Invoice - general	
	F-63 - Invoice parking - general	
	F-41 - Credit memo - general	
	F-66 - Credit memo parking - general	

Document

- Reference documents
  - FKMT - Account assignment model
  - FBD1 - Recurring document
  - F-01 - Sample document
- FB02 - Change
- FB09 - Change line items
- FB03 - Display
- FB04 - Display changes
- FBRA - Reset cleared items
- Reverse
  - FB08 - Individual reversal
  - F.80 - Mass reversal
- Special G/L trans.
  - F-56 - Reverse statistical posting
  - F-46 - Reverse check/bill of exchange
  - FBWD - Edit b/exch. payable
- Parked documents
  - FBV0 - Post/delete
  - FV60 - One-Screen Transaction for Posting/Deleting
  - FBV2 - Change
  - FV60 - One-Screen Transaction for Changes
  - FBV3 - Display
  - FBV4 - Change header
  - FBV5 - Display changes
  - FBV6 - Reject
- Reference documents
  - Recurring document
    - FBD2 - Change
    - FBD3 - Display
    - FBD4 - Display changes

Master records
- FK01 - Create
- FK02 - Change
- FK03 - Display
- FK04 - Display changes
- FK05 - Block/unblock
- FK06 - Mark for deletion
- Confirmation of change
  - FK08 - Single
  - FK09 - List
- Compare
  - Company codes
    - FK15 - Send
    - FK16 - Receive
  - F.48 - Purchasing - accounting
- Bank
  - FI01 - Create
  - FI02 - Change
  - FI03 - Display

Account
- FK10N - Display balances
- FBL1N - Display/change line items
- F-44 - Clear
- Cross-CC transaction
  - FBU2 - Change
  - FBU3 - Display
  - FBU8 - Reverse
  - Sample document
    - F.56 - Delete
    - FBM2 - Change
    - FBM3 - Display
    - FBM4 - Display changes
    - F.57 - Delete
- More functions
  - FBZ5 - Print payment forms
  - Correspondence
    - FB12 - Request
    - F.64 - Maintain

- FI06 - Mark for deletion
- FI04 - Display changes
- XK01 - Create
- XK02 - Change
- XK03 - Display
- XK05 - Block/unblock
- XK06 - Mark for deletion
- XK04 - Display changes

Maintain centrally

- SCMA - Schedule Manager
- F110 - Payments
- F.4A - Without open items
- F.4B - With open items
- F.4C - Without postings
- F.47 - Free selections

Arrears interest

- F.44 - Balance interest

Interest Calculation

- F150 - Dunning
- F.13 - Automatic clearing
- F.61 - As per requests
- F.63 - Delete requests
- F.27 - Periodic account statements

Print correspondence

Periodic processing

Category	Subcategory	Transaction
		F.62 - Internal documents
Standard letters		SO10 - Enter text
		F.66 - Issue letters
		F.18 - Print letters
Balance confirmation		F.1B - Create index
		F.1A - Group vendors
Recurring entries		F.14 - Execute
		F.15 - Lists
Bill of exchange processing	General	S_ALR_87012208 - Bill of exchange list
		S_ALR_87012115 - Extended bill of exchange list with Listviewer
	Korea	
Archiving		F48A - Documents
		F64A - Transaction figures
		FCAA - Checks
		F56A - Vendors
		F61A - Banks
	Check/count	F.03 - Comparison
		F.2E - Reconcile affiliated companies
		F.18 - Balance confirmation: Print
		F.1B - Balance confirmation: Create index
		F.1A - Balance confirmation: Group vendors
Closing	Valuate	F.05 - Open items in foreign currency
		FJA4 - Inflation adjustment of open items in foreign currency
		FJA5 - Inflation adjustment of open payables in local currency
	Regroup	F101 - Receivables/payables
	Document	All accounts — From balance audit trail data
		S_ALR_87012095 - Extract for the accumulated historical balance audit trail

	Open item accounts	S_ALR_87012098 - Open item account balance audit trail from the document	
			S_ALR_87012096 - Account balance from accumulated historical balance audit trail
			S_ALR_87012097 - Historical balance audit trail by alternative account number
		From balance audit trail	S_ALR_87012099 - Extract for accumulated open item balance audit trail
			S_ALR_87012100 - Acct balance from accumulated open item balance audit trail
			S_ALR_87012101 - Open item balance audit trail by alternative account number
	Carry forward	F.07 - Balances	
Withholding Tax		S_P00_07000134 - Generic withholding tax reporting	
		S_ALR_87012122 - Withholding tax report for the vendor	
Information system	Reports for accounts payable accounting	Vendor Balances	S_ALR_87012077 - Vendor Information System
			S_ALR_87012082 - Vendor Balances in Local Currency
			S_ALR_87012093 - Vendor Business
			S_ALR_87012079 - Transaction Figures: Account Balance
			S_ALR_87012080 - Transaction Figures: Special Sales
			S_ALR_87012081 - Transaction Figures: Sales
		Vendors: Items	S_ALR_87012078 - Due Date Analysis for Open Items
			S_ALR_87012083 - List of Vendor Open Items for Printing
			S_ALR_87012084 - Open Items - Vendor Due Date Forecast
			S_ALR_87012085 - Vendor Payment History with OI Sorted List
			S_ALR_87012104 - List of Cleared Vendor Items for Printing

	Master Data	S_ALR_87012105 - List of Down Payments Open On Key Date - Vendors
		S_ALR_87012086 - Vendor List
		S_ALR_87012087 - Address List
		S_ALR_87012089 - Display Changes to Vendors
		S_ALR_87012090 - Display/Confirm Critical Vendor Changes
	Payment Transactions	S_P99_41000099 - Payment List
		S_P99_41000101 - Check Register
		S_ALR_87012119 - Cashed Checks
		S_P99_41000102 - Number Ranges for Checks
	Configure	OBAO - Specify data volume
		OBAK - Select evaluations
		F.45 - Create evaluations
Environment	Tools	F.46 - Display evaluations
		FQUK - Query for accounts payable
		FB07 - Control totals
	User parameters	FB00 - Editing options
	Current settings	S_BCE_68000174 - Enter exchange rates
		S_ALR_87003642 - Open and close posting periods
		S_ALR_87001486 - Available amounts for the payment program
		S_ALR_87001320 - Enter interest rates
		S_ALR_87001487 - Bank selection for payment program
		S_ALR_87002510 - Enter time interest terms
		S_ALR_87002678 - Enter reference interest values
		S_ALR_87002894 - Maintain worklist for processing open items
		S_ALR_87002940 - Maintain worklist for displaying line items

S_ALR_87003060 - Maintain worklist for displaying balances

- **Check information**
  - **Display**
    - FCH1 - For check
    - FCH2 - For payment document
    - FCHN - Check register
  - **Change**
    - FCH4 - Renumber
    - FCH7 - Reprint check
    - FCH6 - Additional info/cash
    - FCHR - Online cashed checks
    - FCHT - Assignment to payment
  - **Create**
    - FCH5 - Manual checks
  - **Void**
    - FCH3 - Unused checks
    - FCH9 - Issued checks
    - FCH8 - Cancel payment
  - **Delete**
    - FCHD - For payment run
    - FCHF - Manual checks
    - FCHE - Voided checks
    - FCHG - Reset data
  - FCHX - External data transfer
- **Internet functions**
  - FBWAPI0EA - FI Internet: Vendor line items
  - FNETSVA2 - Vendor: Change address
  - FNETSVB1 - Vendor: Create bank details
  - FNETSVB2 - Vendor: Change bank details
  - FNETSVB6 - Vendor: Delete bank details

2

AP– Post Vendor Invoice: FB60

Transaction Code	FB60
Menu	Accounting > Financial Accounting > Accounts Payable > Document entry > Invoice

Business Process Overview

When integrated with materials management module, most of the postings into FI, by way of vendor invoice relating to material purchases, takes place though logistics invoice verification. However, there will be situations where you are required to post some of other invoices and credit memo directly using the G/L invoice entry screens.

As in any document posting, you need to make sure that the amount posted goes to the correct G/L / Vendor accounts, tax are properly calculated by selecting the appropriate tax codes suggested by the system or correcting the same when necessary, ensuring that the posting is done to the relevant posting period. These precautions will obviate the needs for a correction at a later stage by posting a reversal or additional document.

The document needs to be entered using the correct "document entry template" by selecting the same form the initial screen.

Transaction Steps

Step-1

Access the transaction either by the transaction code or menu, and you will be taken to "**Enter Vendor Invoice**" screen (Figure: **FB60**-1).

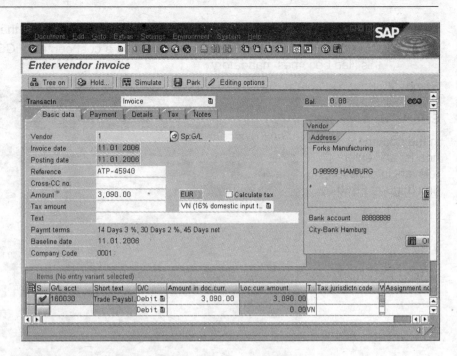

Figure: **FB60**-1

Under | Basic data | tab, enter the details as outlined below:

1. **Vendor (M):** Enter the vendor number.
2. **Document Date (M):** Enter the date of the document. (This can never be later than the 'Posting Date') This is the date of the original document like invoice.
3. **Posting Date (M):** Enter the posting date. This can differ from the document date.
4. **Currency/rate (M):** The Company Code currency is defaulted; if required you may enter another currency to post the document.
5. **Reference (O):** Enter a reference, if any.
6. **Tax amount (O):** Enter the tax, if it is manually calculated or select from the drop down the applicable tax rate.
7. **Text (O):** Enter an explanatory text.
8. **Company code (M):** Enter or change the company code.

Company code, (the smallest organization unit within SAP FI, with self contained set of accounts, for which legal/external reporting (financial statements like balance sheet / profit & loss statement) can be made) is defaulted from the user settings. Also, the company code entered for the first transaction will always be defaulted for the subsequent transactions for the day. You can also change the defaulted company code: use the **Menu: Edit > Change the company code** or Press **'F7"**.

In Items:

9. **G/L acct (M):** Enter the relevant G/L account number.
10. **D/C (M):** Select either 'Debit' or 'Credit' as the case may be.
11. **Amount in doc. curr (M):** Enter the amount to be posted.
12. **Tax (O):** Enter the tax code; for all tax relevant accounts, tax code is mandatory.

13. **Value date (O):** Enter a date if the value date is different from the posting date.

14. **Cost Centre (O):** If the G/L account requires a cost center or CO object assignment, then this filed becomes mandatory.

Step-2

Select [Details] tab in the document header and enter relevant information, if any (Figure: **FB60**-2).

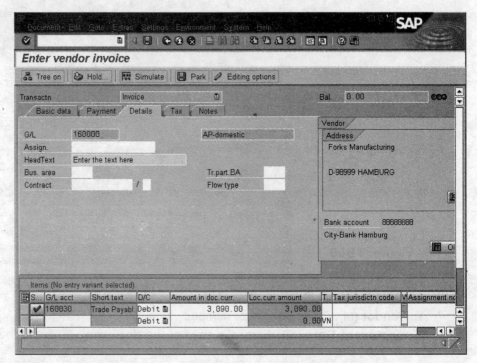

Figure: **FB60**-2

1. **Assign. (O):** Enter an assignment, if necessary.
2. **HeadText (O):** Enter a document header text.
3. **Bus. Area (O):** Enter the relevant business are, if required.

> **Use the other tabs like *"Payment"*, *"Tax"* or *"Notes"* to maintain the relevant information or to change the default entries proposed by the system like the payment terms or tax code etc.**

Step-3

When all the line items have been entered, press [✓].

> **The total debit amount must equal the total credit amount and the indicator light must be green ●○○. Correct any warning or error messages displayed at the bottom left of the screen (Status bar). Warning messages appear in yellow ○○○ and must be noted, and corrected if necessary. To ignore the warning and to proceed further, press the 'enter' key. Error messages appear in red ○○○ and must be corrected before the document can be posted.**

Step-4

Click on 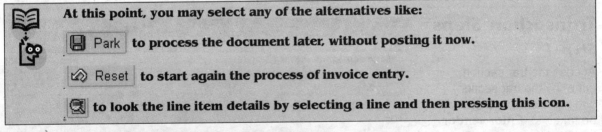 Simulate to view how the document will look like, in respect of all the entries. At this point, the system also displays the system-generated postings (like tax etc) and displays the same along with the line items entered by you, in the "**Document Overview**" screen (Figure: **FB60**-4).

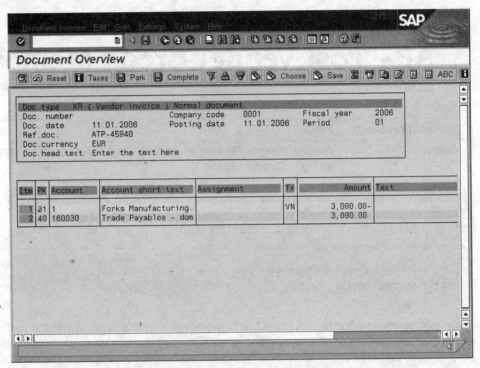

Figure: **FB60**-4

📖
👁️ At this point, you may select any of the alternatives like:

💾 Park to process the document later, without posting it now.

↩ Reset to start again the process of invoice entry.

🔍 to look the line item details by selecting a line and then pressing this icon.

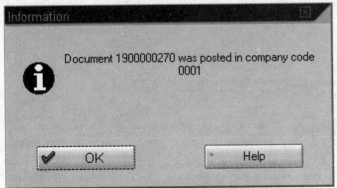

Step-5

When completed, Press 💾 to post the document (Figure: **FB60**-5).

Figure: **FB60**-5

3

AP – Post Vendor Credit Memo: FB65

Transaction Code	FB65
Menu	Accounting > Financial Accounting > Accounts Payable > Document entry > Credit Memo

Business Process Overview

You request a vendor to issue you a **credit memo** for various reasons such as:

- Inappropriate delivery of goods
- Damaged goods during delivery
- Returned goods
- Overpayment

The vendor will respond by issuing a credit memo which when posted will bring down his (AP) account balance. The system uses a document type **"KR"** for processing vendor credit memo. When posted, the system updates the transaction figures: the account balance of the vendor (and also the A/P ledger balance) comes down.

Transaction Steps

Step-1

Access the transaction either by the transaction code or menu, and you will be taken to "**Enter vendor credit memo**" screen (Figure: **FB65**-1).

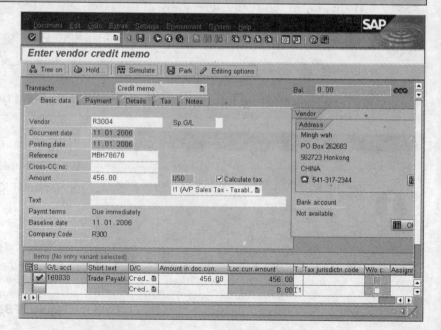

Figure: **FB65**-1

Under ⎡ Basic data ⎤ tab, enter the details as outlined below:

1. **Vendor (M):** Enter the vendor number.
2. **Document Date (M):** Enter the date of the document. This is the date of the original document like invoice.
3. **Posting Date (M):** Enter the posting date. This can differ from the date of document.
4. **Currency/rate (M):** The Company Code currency is defaulted; if required you may enter another currency to post the document.
5. **Reference (O):** Enter a reference, if any (Vendor's credit memo number).
6. **Tax amount (O):** Enter the tax, if it is manually calculated or select from the drop down the applicable tax rate.
7. **Text (O):** Enter an explanatory text.
8. **Company code (M):** Enter or change the company code.

> **Company code is defaulted from the user settings. Also, the company code entered for the first transaction will always be defaulted for the subsequent transactions for the day. You can change the defaulted company code: use the Menu: Edit > Change the company code or Press 'F7".**

In <u>Items</u>:

9. **G/L acct (M):** Enter the relevant G/L account number.
10. **D/C (M):** Select either 'Debit' or 'Credit' as the case may be.
11. **Amount in doc. curr (M):** Enter the amount to be posted.
12. **Tax (O):** Enter the tax code; for all tax relevant accounts, tax code is mandatory.
13. **Value date (O):** Enter a date if the value date is different from the posting date.
14. **Cost Centre (O):** If the G/L account requires a cost center or CO object assignment, then this filed becomes mandatory.

> **Use the other tabs like *"Details, Payment", "Tax" or "Notes"* to maintain the relevant information or to change the default entries proposed by the system like the payment terms or tax code etc.**

Step-2

When all the line items have been entered, press .

> **The total debit amount must equal the total credit amount and the indicator light must be green ⚬⚬⚬. Correct any warning or error messages displayed at the bottom left of the screen (Status bar). Warning messages appear in yellow ⚬⚬⚬ and must be noted, and corrected if necessary. To ignore the warning and to proceed further, press the 'enter' key. Error messages appear in red ⚬⚬⚬ and must be corrected before the document can be posted.**

Step-3

Click on 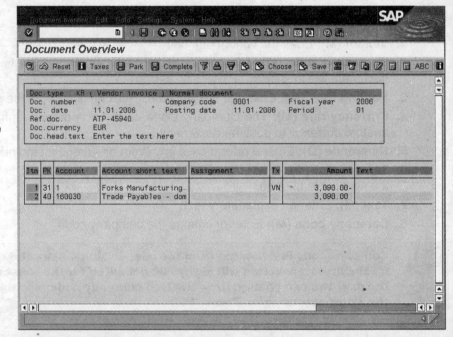 Simulate
to view how the
document will look like,
in respect of all the
entries. At this point, the
system also displays the
system-generated
postings (if any, like tax
etc) and displays the
same along with the line
items entered by you, in
the "**Document
Overview**" screen
(Figure: **FB65**-2).

Figure: **FB65**-2

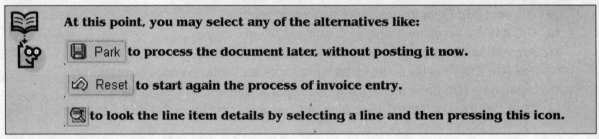

At this point, you may select any of the alternatives like:

     💾 Park to process the document later, without posting it now.

     ↩ Reset to start again the process of invoice entry.

     🔳 to look the line item details by selecting a line and then pressing this icon.

Step-4

When completed, Press 💾 to post the document (Figure: **FB65**-3).

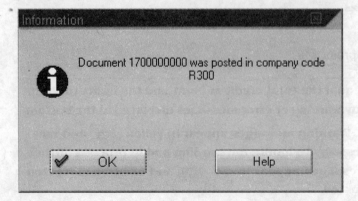

Figure: **FB65**-3

4

AP - Post Vendor Invoice, using Purchase Reference: MIRO

Transaction Code	MIRO

Business Process Overview

When integrated with materials management module, most of the postings into FI, by way of vendor invoice relating to material purchases, takes place though invoice verification. Using this transaction you can post the vendor invoice with reference to the purchasing documents in the system, for that vendor. Essentially, you would have already created the purchasing order or a scheduling agreement, from which the material line items will be copied and the invoice generated in the system. Invoice verification, thus serves to:

- Complete procurement process - from purchase requisition (PR), to purchasing, to goods receipt (GR) and with invoice receipt (IR).
- Process the invoices that do not originate in materials procurement (liker service costs.) to be processed.
- Process credit memos.

A typical **invoice verification** task includes:

1. Entering the invoice/credit memo in the system.
2. Ascertaining the accuracy of the invoice by checking the content, price etc.
3. Posting the invoice in the system.

Since you can use the same transaction for posting, invoice, credit memo etc., take care to select the suitable transaction while on the initial screen:

- An invoice
- A credit memo

As in any document posting, you need to make sure that the amount posted goes to the correct G/L / Vendor accounts, tax are properly calculated by selecting the appropriate tax codes suggested by the system or correcting the same when necessary, ensuring that the posting is done to the relevant posting period. These precautions will obviate the needs for a correction at a later stage by posting a reversal or additional document.

Transaction Steps

Step-1

Access the transaction either by the transaction code or menu, and you will be taken to "**Enter Invoice**" screen (Figure: **MIRO**-1).

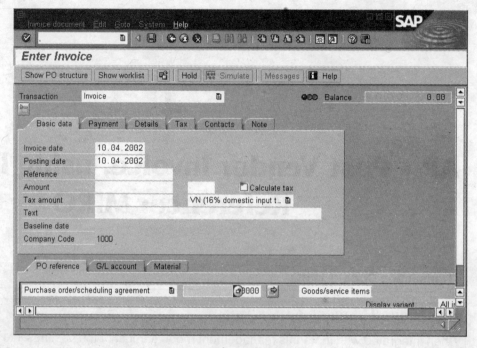

Figure: **MIRO**-1

Ensure that you have selected "*Invoice*" under the *Transaction* drop down list.

Under | Basic data | tab, enter the details as outlined below:

1. **Invoice Date (M):** Enter the date of the document.
2. **Posting Date (M):** Enter the posting date.
3. **Reference (O):** Enter a reference, like Vendor's reference number, if any.
4. **Tax amount (O):** Enter the tax, if it is manually calculated or select from the drop down the applicable tax rate.
5. **Text (O):** Enter an explanatory text.
6. **Company code (M):** Enter or change the company code.

> **Company code is defaulted from the user settings. Also, the company code entered for the first transaction will always be defaulted for the subsequent transactions for the day. You can change the defaulted company code: use the Menu: Edit > Change the company code or Press 'F7".**

Under Other selections:

1. **Invoice expected (O):** Check this check box to enable the system to propose the items for which invoice is to be generated.
2. **Cred memo expected (O):** Uncheck this check box.

Step-2

Under ▢ PO reference ▢ tab, Select **"Purchase order/scheduling agreement" (M),** enter the number, if known. Else, press ⊞. You will be taken to "**Possible Entries for Purchasing Document**" screen (Figure: **MIRO**-2).

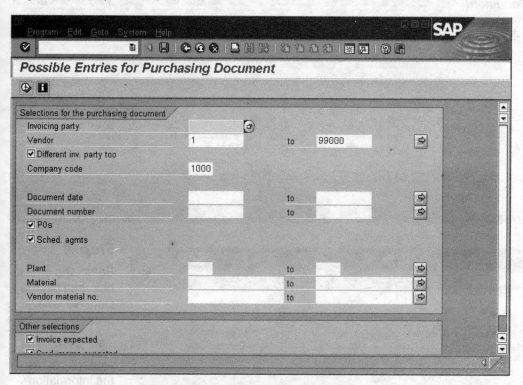

Figure:
MIRO-2

Under "Selections for the purchasing document":

1. **Invoicing party (O):** Enter if the invoicing party is different from that of the vendor.
2. **Vendor (O):** Enter the vendor(s).
3. **Company code (O):** Enter the company code.
4. **Document date (O):** Enter the document date, if known, to narrow the search.
5. **Document number (O):** Enter the document number, if known.
6. **POs (O):** Check the check box to select the Purchase Orders.
7. **Sched. Agmts. (O):** Check, to include all the scheduling agreements in the search.

> **Since we are searching for purchase related documents, take note to check at least one as detailed above in 6 & 7. Also, make it a point to enter as much information as possible by entering the values in these fields, so as to narrow down the search and to get the documents selected faster!**

Step-3

Press 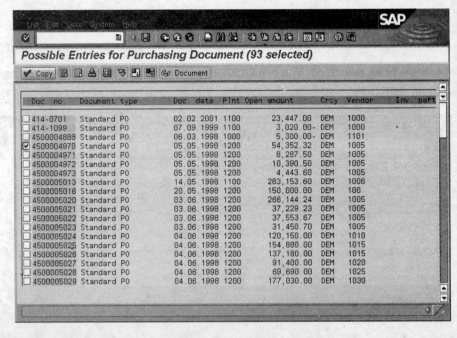 and the system displays *"Possible Entries for Purchasing Document (93 selected)"* screen (Figure: **MIRO**-3).

Figure: **MIRO**-3

Step-4

Select the check-box, against the Doc. No. and press

✔ **Copy**. The system copies the information from the selected document(s) and you are taken back to the initial screen *"Enter Invoice"* (Figure: **MIRO**-4).

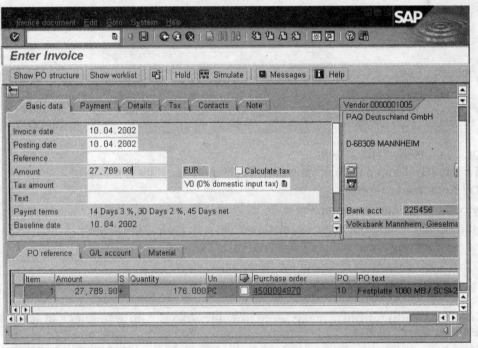

Figure: **MIRO**-4

1. **Amount (M)**: Enter the invoice amount matching the amount copied under PO reference .

Step-5

Under PO reference tab, select the required rows and press 🎲 Simulate to simulate the postings and look for errors/warnings, if any (Figure: **MIRO**-5).

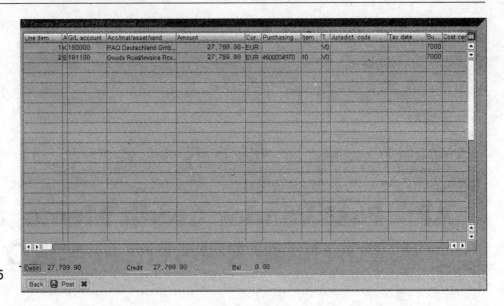

Figure: **MIRO**-5

Step-6

When **Debit = Credit**, (i.e., when **Balance is zero**), press [💾 Post] to complete the transaction

(Figure: **MIRO**-6). Else, press [Back] to make corrections.

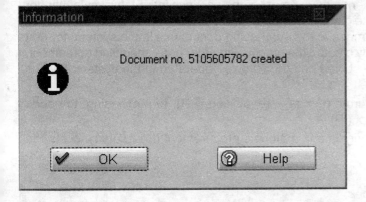

Figure: **MIRO**-6

5

AP - Post Vendor Credit Memo, using Purchase Reference: MIRO

Transaction Code	MIRO

Business Process Overview

When integrated with materials management module, most of the postings into FI, by way of vendor invoice relating to material purchases, take place though invoice verification. Using this transaction you can post the vendor invoice with reference to the purchasing documents in the system, for that vendor. Essentially, you would have already created the purchasing order or a scheduling agreement, from which the material line items will be copied and the invoice generated in the system. Invoice verification, thus serves to:

- Complete procurement process - from purchase requisition (PR), to purchasing, to goods receipt (GR) and with invoice receipt (IR).
- Process the invoices that do not originate in materials procurement (liker service costs.) to be processed.
- Process credit memos.

A typical **invoice verification task** includes:

1. Entering the invoice/credit memo in the system.
2. Ascertaining the accuracy of the invoice by checking the content, price etc.
3. Posting the invoice in the system.

Since you can use the same transaction for posting various transactions, take care to select the suitable transaction while on the initial screen:

- An invoice
- A credit memo

As in any document posting, you need to make sure that the amount posted goes to the correct G/L / Vendor accounts, tax are properly calculated by selecting the appropriate tax codes suggested by the system or correcting the same when necessary, ensuring that the posting is done to the relevant posting period. These precautions will obviate the needs for a correction at a later stage by posting a reversal or additional document.

Transaction Steps

Step-1

Access the transaction either by the transaction code or menu, and you will be taken to **"Enter Invoice"** screen (Figure: **MIRO**-1).

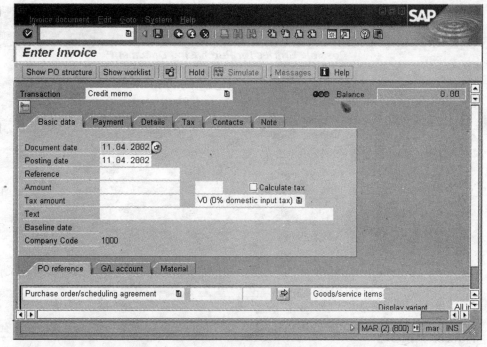

Figure: **MIRO**-1

Ensure that you have selected **"*Credit memo*"** under the **Transaction** drop down list.

Under Basic data tab, enter the details as outlined below:

1. **Invoice Date (M):** Enter the date of the document.
2. **Posting Date (M):** Enter the posting date.
3. **Reference (O):** Enter a reference, like Vendor's reference number, if any.
4. **Tax amount (O):** Enter the tax, if it is manually calculated or select from the drop down the applicable tax rate.
5. **Text (O):** Enter an explanatory text.
6. **Company code (M):** Enter or change the company code.

> **Company code is defaulted from the user settings. Also, the company code entered for the first transaction will always be defaulted for the subsequent transactions for the day. You can change the defaulted company code: use the Menu: Edit > Change the company code or Press 'F7'.**

Step-2

Under PO reference tab, Select **"*Purchase order/scheduling agreement*" (M):** enter the number, if known. Else, press . You will be taken to **"*Possible Entries for Purchasing Document*"** screen (Figure: **MIRO**-2).

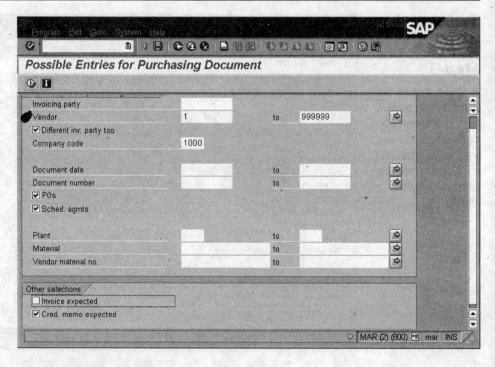

Figure: **MIRO**-2

Under "Selections for the purchasing document":

1. **Invoicing party (O):** Enter if the invoicing party is different from that of the vendor.
2. **Vendor (O):** Enter the vendor(s).
3. **Company code (O)**: Enter the company code.
4. **Document date (O)**: Enter the document date, if known, to narrow the search.
5. **Document number (O):** Enter the document number, if known.
6. **POs (O)**: Check the check box to select the Purchase Orders.
7. **Sched. Agmts. (O):** Check, to include all the scheduling agreements in the search.

> Since we are searching for purchase related documents, take note to check <u>at least one</u> as detailed above in 6 & 7. Also, make it a point to enter as much information as possible by entering the values in these fields, so as to narrow down the search and to get the documents selected faster!

Under Other selections:

1. **Invoice expected (O):** Uncheck this check box.
2. **Cred memo expected (O):** check this check box to enable the system to propose the items for which credit memo is expected.

Step-3

Press and the system displays "***Possible Entries for Purchasing Document (1 selected)***" screen (Figure: **MIRO**-3).

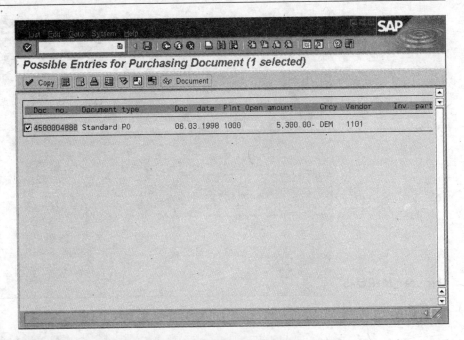

Figure: **MIRO**-3

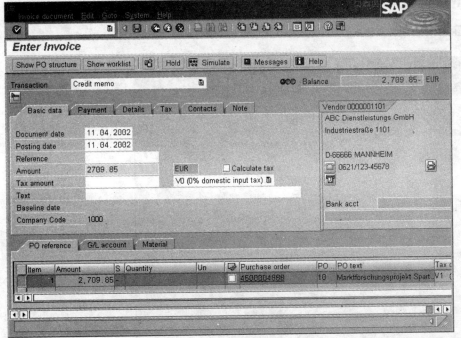

Figure: **MIRO**-4

Step-4

Select the check-box, against the Doc. No. and press

Copy . The system copies the information from the selected document(s) and you are taken back to the initial screen *"Enter Invoice"* (Figure: **MIRO**-4).

1. **Amount (M)**: Enter the credit memo amount matching the amount copied under PO reference .

Step-5

Under PO reference tab, select the required rows and press Simulate to simulate the postings and look for errors/warnings, if any (Figure: **MIRO**-5).

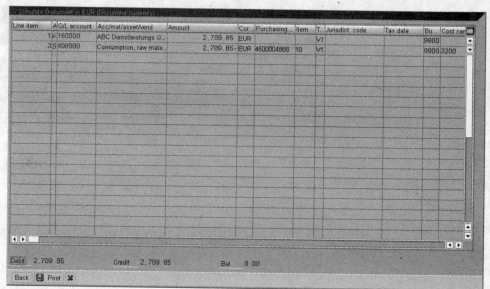

Figure: **MIRO**-5

Step-6

When **Debit = Credit**, (when the **Balance is zero**), you can press 💾 Post to complete the

transaction or press Back to go to the initial screen (Figure: **MIRO**-6).

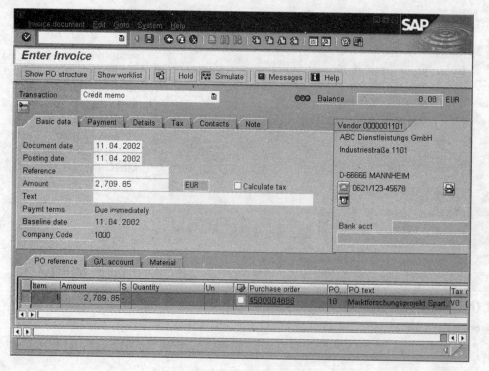

Figure: **MIRO**-6

Step-7

Press  to post the credit memo document (Figure: **MIRO**-7).

Note that the traffic icon is green now, with the balance=0

◎◎◎   Balance   0.00   EUR .

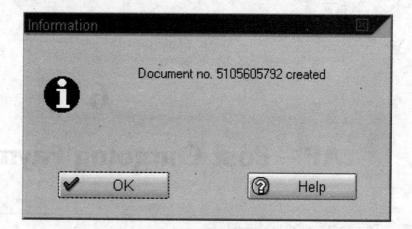

Figure: **MIRO**-7

6

AP – Post Outgoing Payments: F-53

Transaction Code	F-53
Menu	Accounting > Financial Accounting > Accounts Payable > Document entry > Outgoing payment > Post

Business Process Overview

SAP provides two ways of making payment:

- **Automatic Payments**
- **Manual payments**

Automatic payments are used when you want to make a large number of payments without any manual intervention. Automatic payment program is executed by using the **Transaction Code F110 or via Menu "Accounting > Financial Accounting > Accounts Payable > Periodic Processing >Payments"**.

When automatic open item selection is not desired, or where it is required to make a fewer payments you can use SAP's **manual payment** postings where clearing is done manually and the account posted accordingly.

This transaction is same as that of **Transaction Code: F-07, Menu: Accounting > Financial Accounting > General Ledger > Document entry > Outgoing payment**.

Use the **Transaction Code: F-58 Menu: Accounting > Financial Accounting > Accounts Payable > Document entry > Outgoing payment > Post + print forms**, for printing the forms (check, payment advice etc) besides posting the outgoing payment document.

Transaction Steps

Step-1

Access the transaction either by the transaction code or menu, and you will be taken to "**Post Outgoing Payments: Header Data**" screen (Figure: **F-53**-1).

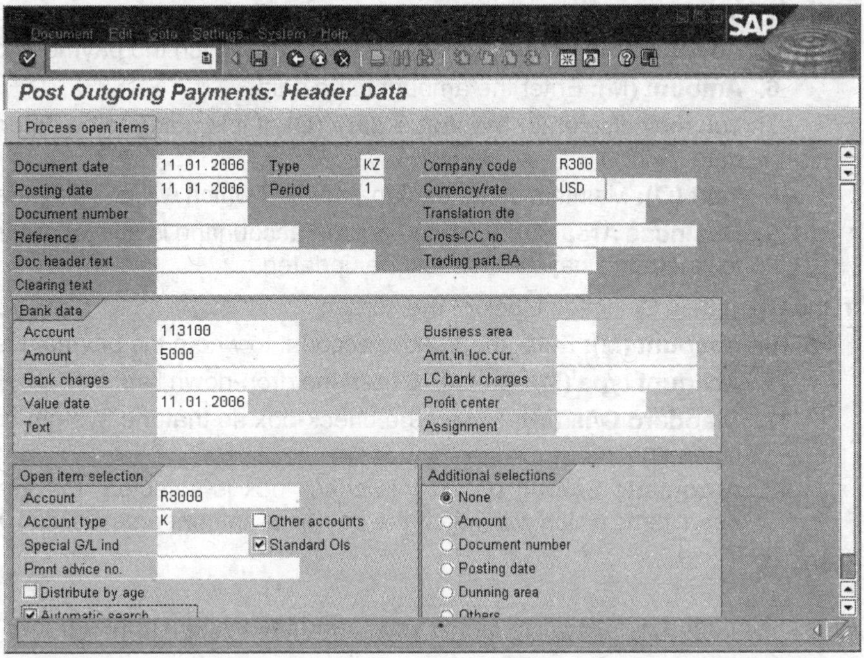

Figure: **F-53**-1

Enter the details as outlined below:

1. **Document Date (M):** Enter the date of the document.
2. **Posting Date (M):** Enter the posting date. (This can differ from the 'Document Date').
3. **Company Code (M):** If this is the first occasion, a particular company is posted to, then you may need to enter the company Code. For all the subsequent transactions of the day, the same Company Code is defaulted.

The (Document) Type (M) is defaulted to "KZ" when we selected the *Transaction: F-53,* **which relates to manual outgoing payments.**

Remember SAP comes delivered with a multitude of document types, used in vendor postings, like:

> **KG Vendor Cr memo**
>
> **KZ Vendor Payment**
>
> **KR Vendor Invoice**
>
> **KN Vendor net invoice and credit memo**

You may use *Transaction: OBA7* **to define a new document type, or use** *Transaction: OBAB* **to rename an existing document type.**

Posting Period (M) is defaulted from the posting date entered in the document. You may need to change this if you want the posting period correspond to any other period like a 'special period'.

4. **Currency/rate (M):** The Company Code currency is defaulted; if required you may enter another currency to post the document.

In the <u>Bank data</u> area:

5. **Account (M):** Select the G/L account from which the payment to be made.

6. **Amount (M):** Enter the amount to be paid.

7. You may also enter the **Value date (O)**, if it is going to be different from that of the posting date.

8. **Text (O):** Maintain some explanatory text which will possibly identify this payment.

9. **Business Area (O):** If business area accounting is active, enter the relevant business area to where this payment should be updated.

In the <u>Open Item Selection</u> block of the screen:

10. **Account (M):** Enter the Vendor account to whom the payment is being considered.

11. **Account type (M):** Select 'K' from the drop-down list.

12. **Standard O/Is (M):** Select the check-box so that the system considers the standard open items only.

13. **Automatic Search (O):** If this check box is selected, the system is going to search for open items which will match the payment amount entered in (10).

Step-2

Press ✅ button or ⬜ Process open items , and the system pops-up the **"Proposal for Clearing"** screen (Figure: **F-53**-2).

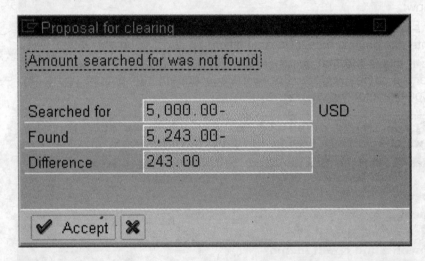

Figure: **F-53**-2

Note that the system was unable to find an exact match to clear the open item with the payment amount entered, and is proposing you to accept it for further processing. Either you can accept or go back to **Step-1** and change the amount to match the open item amount selected by the system.

Step-3

Press ⬜ ✔ Accept , and the system takes you to the **"Post Outgoing Payments: Process Open Items"** screen (Figure: **F-53**-3).

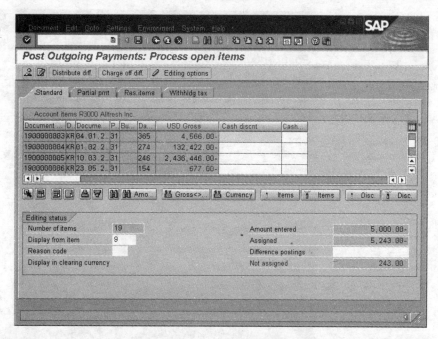

Figure: **F-53**-3

You can see from the screen that the system has actually clubbed two open items (4566 & 677) and has assigned the payment as 5243, which is 243 less than the payment amount 5000 entered in the initial screen. So, the 'Not assigned' amount is shown as 243, which need to be effectively dealt with for putting through the transaction. If this has been due to an error, you may correct it by entering the correct amount by going back to screen **F-53**-1.

If you do not want to adjust the amount, as proposed by the system, there is an option to make the payment as 'partial payment'. Select the Partial pmt **tab, and make the partial payment as may be required. Each partial payment will require a reason code assigned. Note that the system saves the partial payment information and both the original items and this partial payment are kept 'open' in the system. When the remaining amount is posted, both the original open item and the partial payment are cleared.**

Instead of 'partial payments', you may also do a residual posting, when the amount posted is less than the amount of the open item. In this case, you can post the details in Res.items **tab. The system clears the original open item, but creates a new open item for the amount, which is equal to the original open amount minus the current payment. For the residual item you can make the system to assign the same terms of payment as that of the original open item or you may assign pre-determined terms of payment.**

Step-4

Press Charge off diff. , to reach "**Post Outgoing Payments: Display Overview**" screen (Figure: **F-53**-4), where the difference can now be posted as shown below:

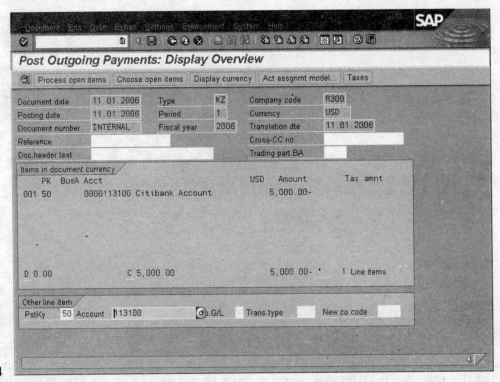

Figure: **F-53**-4

In <u>Other line item</u> block, enter:

    1. **PstKy (M):** Enter '50' as the posting key.

    2. **Account (M):** Enter the G/L account (which you initially used in **F-53**-1 screen).

Step-5

Press ✓ button and you are taken to "**Post Outgoing Payments: Add G/L account item**" screen (Figure: **F-53**-5).

Figure: **F-53**-5

In <u>Item 2 / Credit entry / 50</u> block:

1. **Amount (M):** Enter the "not assigned" amount.
2. **Value Date (O):** Enter a date.
3. **Text (O):** Enter some explanation for this posting.

Step-5

Press 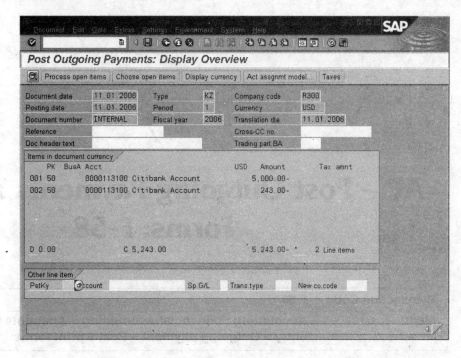 button and you are taken to **"Post Outgoing Payments: Display Overview"** screen (Figure: **F-53**-6), where you can see that the two line items now total to the amount proposed by the system earlier.

Figure: **F-53**-6

Step-6

Press 🖫 button to post and you can see the **"Information"** screen (Figure: **F-53**-6) displaying the document number posted.

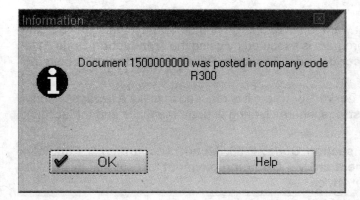

Figure: **F-53**-6

7

AP – Post Outgoing Payments and Print Forms: F-58

Transaction Code	F-58
Menu	Accounting > Financial Accounting > Accounts Payable > Document entry > Outgoing payment > Post + print forms

Business Process Overview

SAP provides two ways of making payment:

- **Automatic Payments**
- **Manual payments**

Automatic payments are used when you want to make a large number of payments with out any manual intervention. Automatic payment program is executed by using the **Transaction Code F110 or via Menu "Accounting > Financial Accounting > Accounts Payable > Periodic Processing >Payments"**.

When automatic open item selection is not desired, or where it is required to make a fewer payments you can use SAP's **manual payment postings** where clearing is done manually and the account posted accordingly.

This transaction is same as that of **Transaction Code: F-58, Menu: Accounting > Financial Accounting > General Ledger > Document entry > Outgoing payment**, except that this allows for printing the payment forms and payment advice.

Transaction Steps

Step-1

Access the transaction either by the transaction code or menu, and you will be taken to **"Payment with Printout: Header Data"** screen (Figure: **F-58**-1).

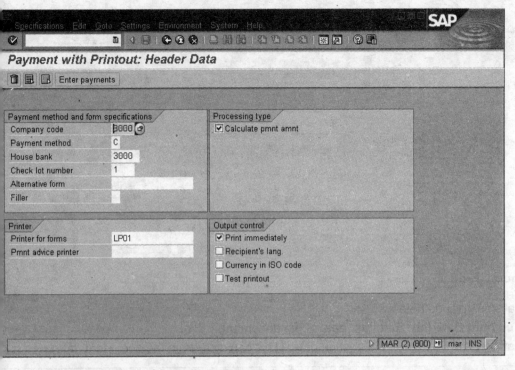

Figure:
F-58-1

Under <u>Payment method and form specifications</u>:

1. **Company Code (M):** Enter the paying company code.
2. **Payment method (M):** Enter the payment method with which you can create/print checks for payments.
3. **House bank (M):** Select the house bank from which the payment needs to be processed.
4. **Check lot number (M):** Provide the check lot number for payment method "*C*".

Under <u>Printer:</u>

5. **Printer for forms (M):** Select the suitable printer.
6. **Payment advice printer (O):** Select the suitable printer.

Under <u>Processing type:</u>

7. **Calculate pmt amt** (O): Select the check box if the payment amount is not known. The outgoing payment amount will be determined by the system based upon the open items.

Under <u>Output control:</u>

8. **Print immediately** (O): Select the check box if the printing needs to be immediate.
9. **Test printout (O):** Check this to see how the printout will be. Take care to uncheck before actually printing the check/oayment advice.

Step-2

Press Enter payments and you are taken to "**Payment with Printout: Header data**" screen (Figure: F-58-2).

Document date	08.02.2006	Type	KZ	Company code	3000
Posting date	08.02.2006	Period	2	Currency/rate	USD
Document number				Translation dte	

Payment with Printout: Header Data

Process open items

Document date	08.02.2006	Type	KZ	Company code	3000
Posting date	08.02.2006	Period	2	Currency/rate	USD
Document number				Translation dte	
Reference					
Doc.header text					
Clearing text					

Bank posting details
Amount	38970		Business area	
Value date	08.02.2006		Assignment	
Text				

Payee
Vendor	3000		Company Code	3000
Customer			Payee	
☐ Payment on acct	Pmnt on acct			

Paid items
☑ Standard OIs

Additional selections
⦿ None

MAR (2) (800) mar INS

Figure: **F-58**-2

Enter the details as outlined below:

1. **Document Date (M):** Enter the date of the document.
2. **Posting Date (M):** Enter the posting date. (This can differ from the document date).

> The (Document) Type (M) is defaulted to "KZ" when we selected the
> *Transaction: F-58,* which relates to manual outgoing payments.
>
> Remember SAP comes delivered with a multitude of documents, used in vendor
> postings, like:
>
>   **KG** Vendor Cr memo
>
>   **KZ** Vendor Payment
>
>   **KR** Vendor Invoice
>
>   **KN** Vendor net invoice and credit memo
>
> You may use *Transaction: OBA7* to define a new document type, or use
> *Transaction: OBAB* to rename an existing document type.

> Posting Period (M) is defaulted from the posting date entered in the document.
> You may need to change this if you want the posting period correspond to any other
> period like a 'special period'.

3. **Currency/rate (M):** The Company Code currency is defaulted; if required you may enter another currency to post the document.

In the Bank posting details area:

4. **Amount (M):** Enter the amount to be paid.
5. You may also enter the **Value date (O)**, if it is going to be different from that of the posting date.
6. **Text (O):** Maintain some explanatory text which will possibly identify this payment.
7. **Business Area (O):** If business area accounting is active, enter the relevant business area to where this payment should be updated.

In the Payee:

8. **Vendor / Customer (M):** Enter the Vendor/Customer account to whom the payment is being considered.

Under Paid items:

9. **Standard O/Is (O):** Select the check-box so that the system considers the standard open items only.

Step-3

Press 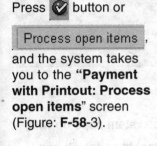 button or

Process open items ,

and the system takes you to the **"Payment with Printout: Process open items"** screen (Figure: **F-58**-3).

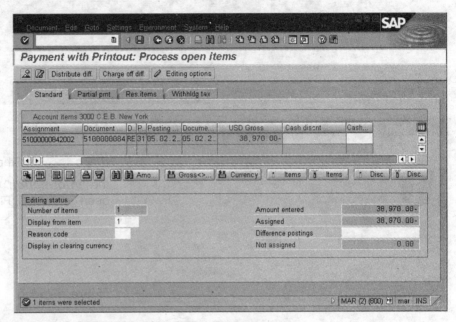

Figure: **F-58**-3

The matching open item(s) is/are determined and shown on the screen.

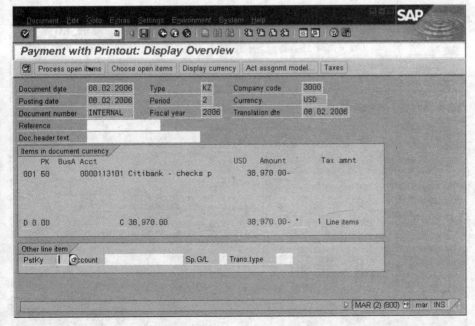

Figure: **F-58**-4

Step-4

Press 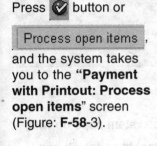 and you are taken to **"Payment with Printout: Display Overview"** screen (Figure: **F-58**-4).

Step-5

Press 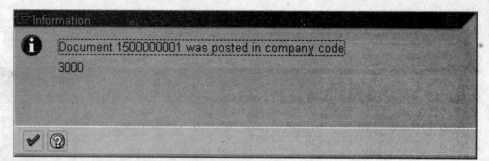, and the systems posts the document (Figure: **F-58**-5).

Figure: **F-58**-5

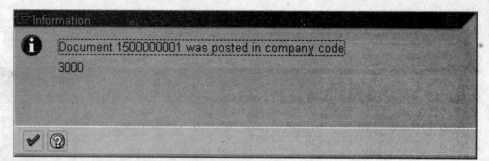

> Document 1500000001 was posted in company code 3000

Step –6

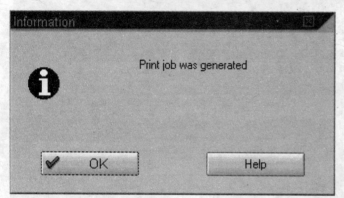

> Print job was generated

Press and the system pops-up with the "**Information**" that the print job has been generated (Figure: **F-58**-6).

Figure: **F-58**-6

=== **End of Transaction** ===

Step-A

Use *Transaction Code: SP02* or *Menu: System > Own spool requests.* You will be taken to "*Output Controller: List of Spool Requests*" screen (Figure: **F-58-SP02**-1).

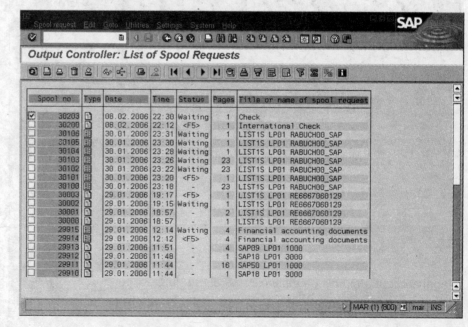

Figure: **F-58-SP02**-1

Step-B

Select the relevant *spool number* and press 🔲 to preview the check (Figure: **F-58-SP02**-2 & 3).

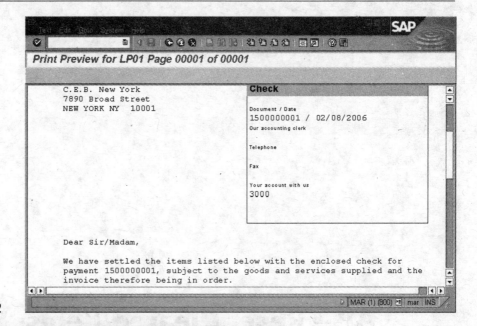

Figure: F-58-SP02-2

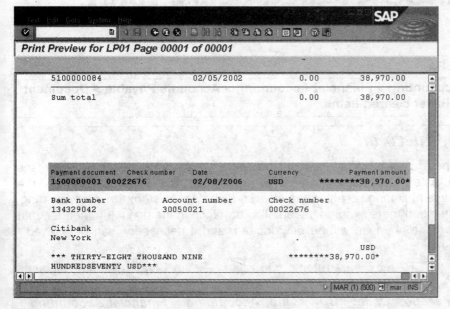

Figure: F-58-SP02-2

Step-C

Press ⬅️ , and from "***Output Controller: List of Spool Requests***" screen (Figure: **F-58-SP02**-1), press 🖨️ for printing the check.

8

AP – Reset Cleared Items: FBRA

Transaction Code	FBRA
Menu	Accounting > Financial Accounting > Accounts Payable > Document > Reset cleared items

Business Process Overview

There may be instances where in you may need to reset the cleared items. When reset, SAP reverses the payment documents created earlier during an earlier payment (automatic or manual) and the items will become 'open' again. During resetting the cleared items, the system removes 'clearing' information from the line items. If there is some 'reversal' information in the document header, that will also be removed. All these changes will be duly logged, and if necessary, can be viewed / displayed in 'change' documents.

This transaction is same as " Reset Cleared Items (G/L) " or " Reset Cleared Items (Accounts Receivable)".

- For G/L: Use *Transaction Code: FBRA Menu: Accounting > Financial Accounting > General Ledger > Document > Reset cleared items.*
- For AR: Use *Transaction Code: FBRA Menu: Accounting > Financial Accounting > Accounts Receivable > Document > Reset cleared items.*

Transaction Steps

Step-1

Access the transaction either by the transaction code or menu, and you will be taken to "**Reset Cleared Items**" screen (Figure: **FBRA**-1).

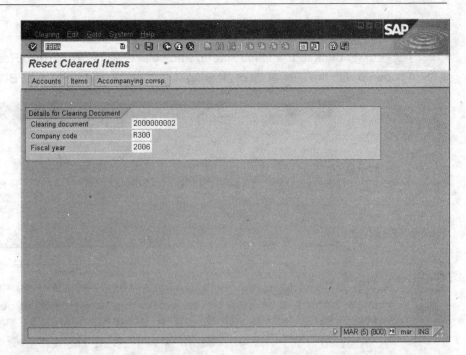

Figure: **FBRA**-1

Enter the details in <u>Details for Clearing Document</u>, as outlined below:

1. **Clearing Document (M):** Enter the clearing document number, which needs to be reset.
2. **Company Code (M):** Enter the Company Code to which the document had been posted to.
3. **Fiscal year (M):** Enter the Fiscal Year in which the document had been posted.

 Before the document is reset, it is a good practice to display the line items to make sure that this is the same clearing document that you want to reset.

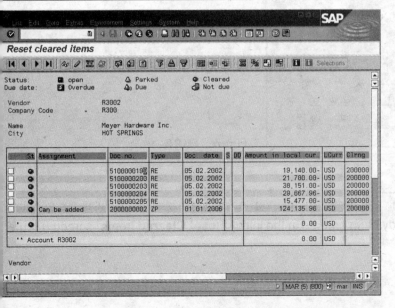

Figure: **FBRA**-2

Step-2

Press Items , and you will be taken to **"Reset cleared Items"** screen with the all the line items for the particular document displayed (Figure: **FBRA**-2).

Step-3

Press 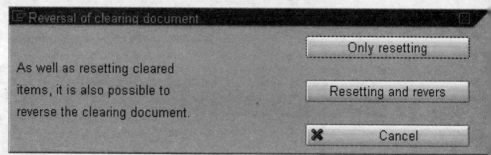 to go back to the initial screen and select Menu **"Clearing>Reset cleared items"**. The system pops-up with the "Reversal of clearing document" screen (Figure: **FBRA**-3).

Figure: **FBRA**-3

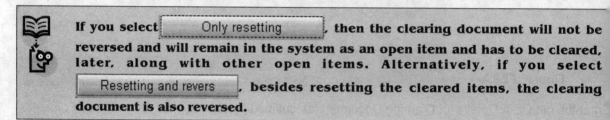

If you select [Only resetting], then the clearing document will not be reversed and will remain in the system as an open item and has to be cleared, later, along with other open items. Alternatively, if you select [Resetting and revers], besides resetting the cleared items, the clearing document is also reversed.

Step-4

Press [Only resetting] to reset the cleared items, the reset confirmation is shown in the pop-up "**Information**" screen (Figure: **FBRA**-4).

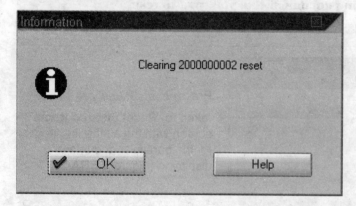

Figure: **FBRA**-4

Step-5

To demonstrate how [Resetting and revers] works; let us start all over from the beginning. Assume that the details have already been entered in the initial "**Reset Cleared Items**" screen (Figure: **FBRA**-5).

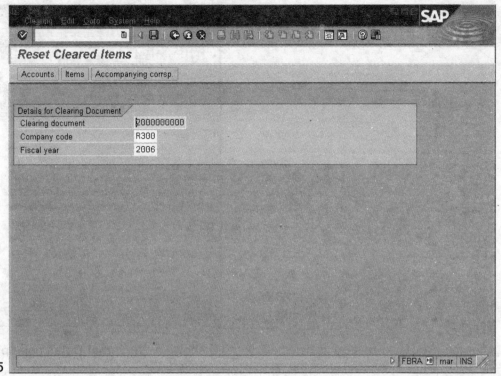

Figure: **FBRA**-5

Step-6

Press | ⬅ to go back to the initial screen and select "*Menu: Clearing>Reset cleared items*". The system pops-up with the "*Reversal of clearing document*" screen (Figure: **FBRA**-6).

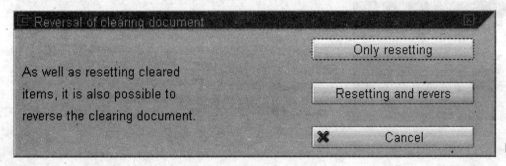

Figure: **FBRA**-6

Step-7

Press | Resetting and revers | to reset the cleared items and to reverse the clearing document. The system now pops-up **"Reason for Reversal"** screen (Figure: **FBRA**-7), from which a '*reversal reason*' needs to be selected.

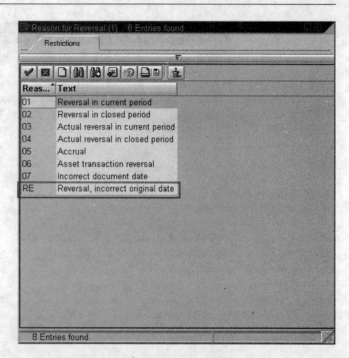

Figure: **FBRA**-7

Step-8

After the '***Reversal reason'*** is selected, you are shown a **"Reversal Data"** pop-up screen (Figure: **FBRA**-8) where in you can enter the corrections required.

Enter:

1. **Posting date (M):** Enter the correct posting date if you have selected "RE" as the reversal reason.
2. **Posting period(M):** Enter the posting period.

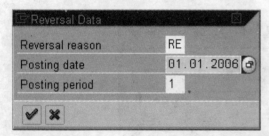

Figure: **FBRA**-8

Step-9

Press , and you will get the confirmation as to reset and reversal. (Figure: **FBRA**-9 & 10).

Figure: **FBRA**-9

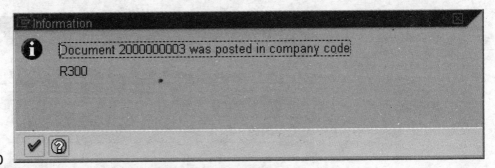

Figure: **FBRA**-10

══════════════════╡ End of Transaction ╞══════════════════

To check the reset/reversal information, let us do the following:

Step-A

Use *Transaction code: FK10N*, enter "**Vendor account balance**" screen and double click on the relevant period for "**Vendor Line Item Display**" screen (Figure: **FBRA- FK10N** -1) showing the original clearing document posting).

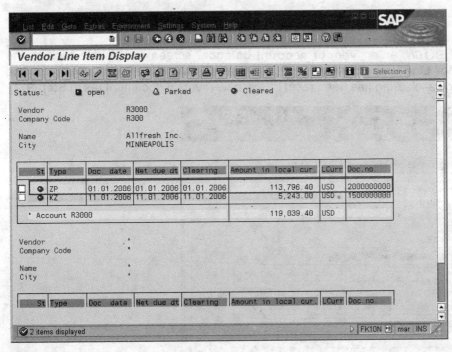

Figure:
FBRA- FK10N -1

Step-B

Use *Transaction code: FB03* and display (Figure: **FBRA- FB03**-2) the document #2000000003 which has reset & reversed the earlier clearing document #2000000000 making the line item as 'open'.

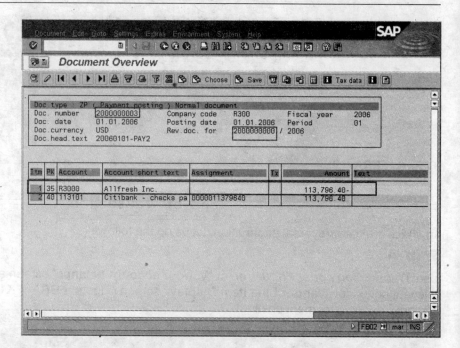

Figure: **FBRA- FB03**-2

Step-C

Use *Transaction code: FK10N*, enter "**Vendor account balance**" screen and double click on the relevant period for "**Vendor Line Item Display**" screen (Figure: **FBRA- FK10N** -3) showing the line item balance after the original clearing has been reset by the new reversal document (as in **Step-9**).

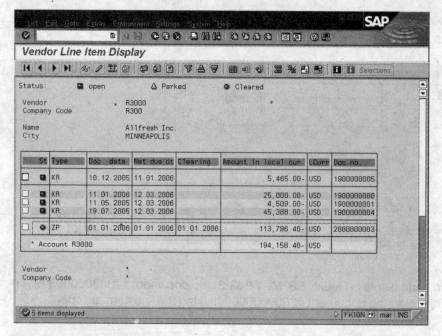

Figure: **FBRA- FK10N** -3

9

AP – Change Payment document: FB02

Transaction Code	FB02
Menu	Accounting > Financial Accounting > Accounts Payable > Document > Change

Business Process Overview

For a variety of reasons, there could be situations where you may want to change a payment document. As in line with SAP's document principle, every document change is duly logged by the system as to who made the change, in which fields and when the change was made. Remember, NOT all the fields can be changed once document has been posted in the system. Certain details like explanatory text or assignment etc can be changed. Any other change, which will affect the 'integrity' of the transaction or document, can only be amended by posting another document, which may be like a document reversal.

This transaction is same as "**Change G/L Document**" or "**Change Invoice/Credit memo**".

Transaction Steps

Step-1

Access the transaction either by the transaction code or menu, and you will be taken to "**Change Document: Initial Screen**" screen (Figure: **FB02**-1).

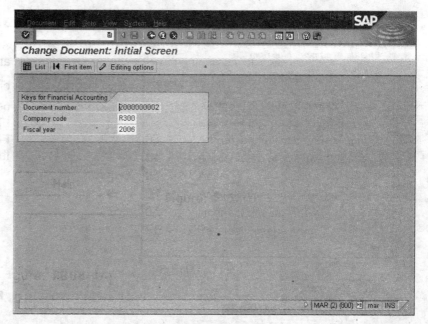

Figure: **FB02**-1

Enter the details as outlined below:

1. **Document Number (M):** Enter the document number, which needs to be changed.
2. **Company Code (M):** Enter the Company Code to which the document had been posted to.
3. **Fiscal year (M):** Enter the Fiscal Year in which the document had been posted.

 If the document number is not known, you may use the 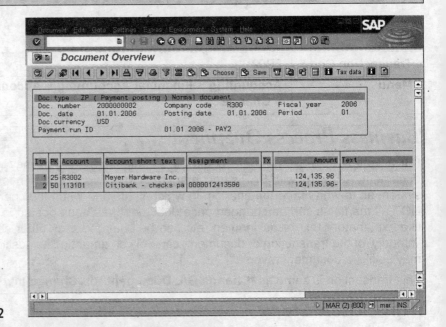 **List to list the documents from where you can pick-up the relevant document for changing.**

Step-2

Click , and you will be taken to "**Document Overview**" screen (Figure: **FB02**-2).

Figure: **FB02**-2

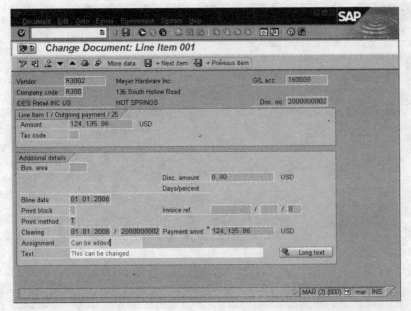

Figure: **FB02**-3

Step-3

Select the line to be changed and double click on the same or click on 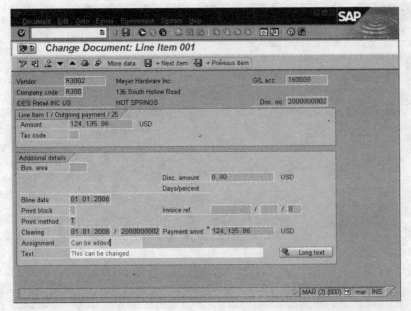 icon. You are now in "**Change document: Line Item 001**" screen (Figure: **FB02**-3). Make the changes in the fields, which are ready for change (not greyed out).

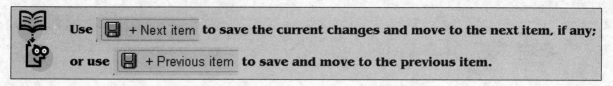

Use 💾 + Next item **to save the current changes and move to the next item, if any;**

or use 💾 + Previous item **to save and move to the previous item.**

Step-4

Use 💾 the changes. If you display the document now, the document overview should show the changes done (Figure: **FB02**-4).

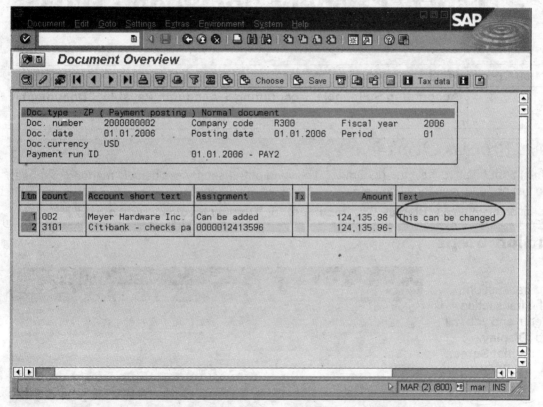

Figure:
FB02-4

10

AP – Display Payment document: FB03

Transaction Code	FB03
Menu	Accounting > Financial Accounting > Accounts Payable > Document > Display

Business Process Overview

Display document helps to view the document. This kind of transactions is usually mapped to those users who just need to view the document without making any change.

This transaction is same as "**Display G/L Document**" or "**Display Invoice/Credit memo**".

Transaction Steps

Step-1

Access the transaction either by the transaction code or menu, and you will be taken to "**Display Document: Initial Screen**" screen (Figure: **FB03**-1).

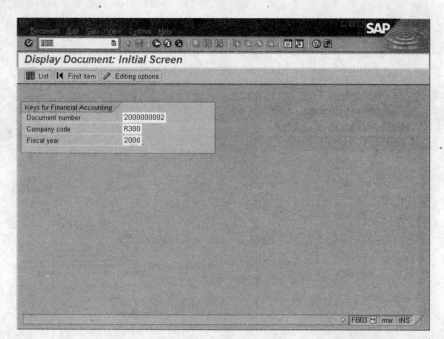

Figure: **FB03**-1

Enter the details as outlined below:

1. **Document Number (M):** Enter the document number, which needs to be displayed.

2. **Company Code (M):** Enter the Company Code to which the document had been posted to.

3. **Fiscal year (M):** Enter the Fiscal Year in which the document had been posted.

If the document number is not known, you may use the List **to list the documents from where you can pick-up the relevant document for display.**

Step-2

Click 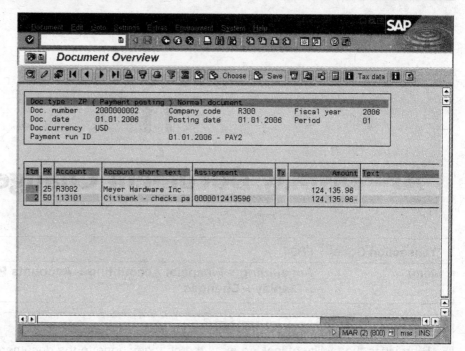, and you will be taken to **"Document Overview"** screen (Figure: **FB03**-2).

Document Overview

```
Doc type : ZP ( Payment posting ) Normal document
Doc. number    2000000002    Company code    R300      Fiscal year    2006
Doc. date      01.01.2006    Posting date    01.01.2006  Period         01
Doc.currency   USD
Payment run ID               01.01.2006 - PAY2
```

Itm	PK	Account	Account short text	Assignment	Tx	Amount	Text
1	25	R3002	Meyer Hardware Inc.			124,135.96	
2	50	113101	Citibank - checks pa	0000012413596		124,135.96-	

Figure: **FB03**-2

Select the line to be display the details and double click on the same or click on icon. Repeat the action for other line items as well.

11

AP– Display Document Changes: FB04

Transaction Code	FB04
Menu	Accounting > Financial Accounting > Accounts Payable > Document > Display > Changes

Business Process Overview

SAP provides the facility of looking at all the changes done to the documents to find out who had changed and what had been the changes made. The system tracks all the changes by logging the details and by generating change documents. The details logged include, at the field level, what was the original content, what is the changed one and who made the change and what time the change has been made. The functionality exists to display the changes made to (a) a particular field or (b) a document or (c) several documents.

This transaction is convenient and handy to look for the details with drill-down option to look at the field values, which had changed. It is possible to display the changes from a point of time by specifying the date (and time); and is also possible to look at changes made to '*sensitive fields*' and or the changes made to the '*company code area*'.

Transaction Steps

Step-1

Access the transaction either by the transaction code or menu, and you will be taken to **"Display Changes: Initial Screen"** screen (Figure: **FB04**-1).

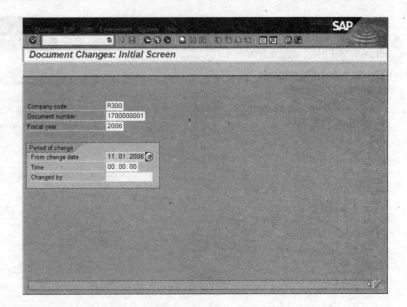

Figure: **FB04**-1

Enter the details as outlined below:

1. **Company Code (M):** Enter the Company Code to which the document had been posted to.
2. **Document Number (M):** Enter the document number, for which the changes need to be displayed.
3. **Fiscal year (M):** Enter the Fiscal Year in which the document had been posted.

Under Period of change:

4. **From change date (O):** Enter a date if you want to display changes from that date, or leave this as blank to display all the changes.
5. **Time (O):** Enter the time.
6. **Changed by (O):** Enter a user name if you need to display changes made by that user, or leave this as blank.

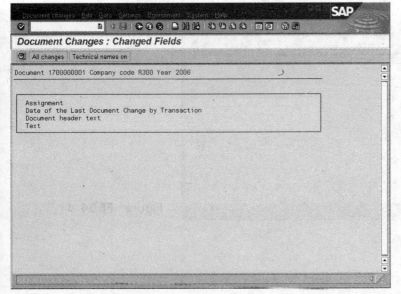

Step-2

Click ⊘ , and you will be taken to "**Document Changes: Changed Fields**" screen (Figure: **FB04**-2).

Figure: **FB04**-2

Step-3

Press All changes from
**"Document Changes:
Overview"** screen
(Figure: **FB04**-3), to look
at all the changes.

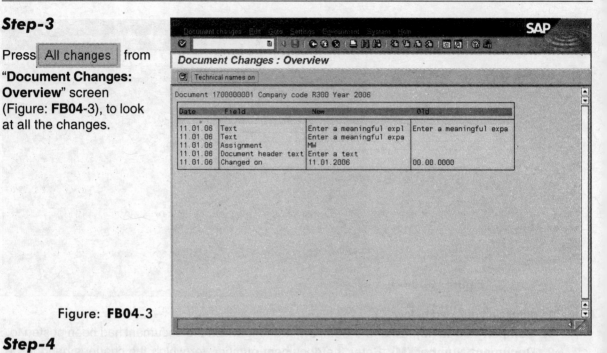

Figure: **FB04**-3

Step-4

Press Technical names on to toggle between field names and the regular display in **"Document
Changes: Overview"** screen (Figure: **FB04**-4).

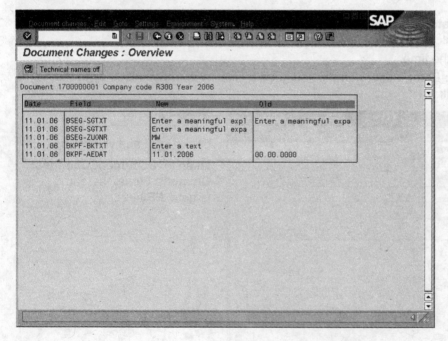

Figure: **FB04**-4

Step-5

Select a filed and press 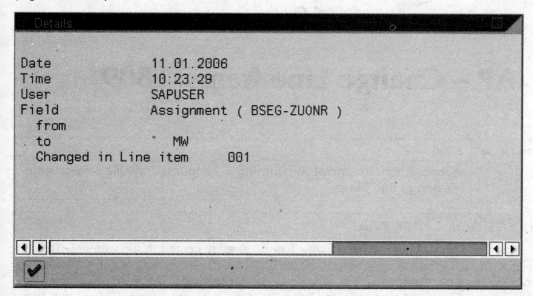 to display the changes and you can see the details in "**Details**" screen (Figure: **FB04**-5).

```
Details                                                    o

Date               11.01.2006
Time               10:23:29
User               SAPUSER
Field              Assignment ( BSEG-ZUONR )
  from
  to                  MW
  Changed in Line item      001
```

Figure:
FB04-5

12

AP – Change Line Items: FB09

Transaction Code	FB09
Menu	Accounting > Financial Accounting > Accounts Payable > Document > Change line items

Business Process Overview

It may some times be necessary to change the line items already posted to a document. Though 'change document' function can also be used to accomplish the same requirement, this transaction helps to directly zero in on a particular line item and to make changes. Again, 'change' does not mean that you can change each and everything in the line item. It is obvious that SAP will not allow you to change the posting date, amount, account etc in the document as this will violate the basic document principle of maintaining the document integrity. Instead, SAP allows changing 'certain' items, which will not compromise the document's integrity but will provide you with the options of changing or adding more information. Normally, one of the editable fields will be the 'text' relating to the line item in question. You may also be allowed to change the 'assignment'.

Transaction Steps

Step-1

Access the transaction either by the transaction code or by the menu and you will be taken to "**Change Line Items**" Screen (Figure: **FB09**-1).

Figure: **FB09**-1

Under Document details:

1. **Document number (M):** Enter the document number, which needs to be changed.

If document number is not known, use 🔳 **List** **option to find the relevant document (See Step-1a).**

2. **Company code (M):** Enter the relevant company code.
3. **Fiscal year (M):** Enter the relevant fiscal year to which the document has been posted to.

Under Item number:

4. **Line item (O):** Enter the line number to change.

Under Only line items for:

5. Check the relevant check box (es), if necessary.

Step-2

Press 🗹 and you are taken to the relevant line item in "**Change line items Line Item 001**" screen (Figure: **FB09**-2).

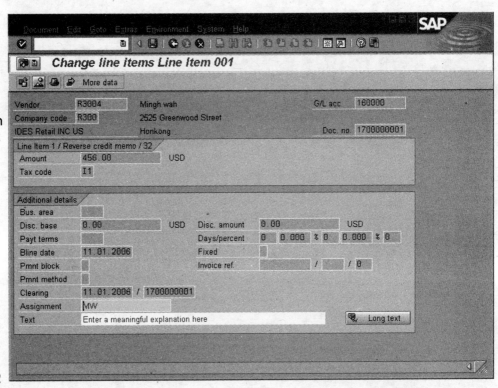

Figure: **FB09**-2

Under Additional details:

1. **Assignment (O):** Enter the desired assignment.
2. **Text (O):** Enter a meaningful description.

Note that when you change the line item(s) in an already posted document, not all the fields are editable. The fields, which are greyed out, cannot be changed. This is again, in line with the SAP's document principle, which is well known for maintaining the document integrity by not allowing changes to the already posted document. The fields, which can be changed, are normally in the white background; the cursor will be at the beginning of one of those editable fields. Even where you are able to edit or change the fields, the field content changes will be duly logged with the time/date and the user who has made the changes along with the changed contents. *Transaction Code FB04* will enable you to display such changes.

Step-3

Press 🖫 to save the changes.

13

AP – Display / Change Vendor Line Items: FBL1N

Transaction Code	FBL1N
Menu	Accounting > Financial Accounting > Account Payable > Account > Display / Change line items

Business Process Overview

As the functionality with the display document / line item, SAP provides to display the account of a vendor. You may select to display a single vendor account in a company code or multiple accounts in multiple company codes. Again, you may select to display only the open items in an account or accounts or cleared items. You may also display all the items in the account(s). Besides display, you may select a particular line item and change some of the fields relating to that line item.

Possible that you are not satisfied with the displayed data: you may resort to some **statistical analysis** and classification of the displayed date. Go and strategize for **ABC classification**, for example. With the default display, you may not be able to display all the columns on the screen and may need to scroll horizontally, to look at a particular column, which sometimes could be time-consuming, if not painful! Customize the layout and you will have a crisp and concise display that fits the window and you have all the columns you wanted.

Transaction Steps

Step-1

Access the transaction either by the transaction code or by the menu and you will be taken to "**Vendor Line Item Display**" Screen (Figure: **FBL1N**-1).

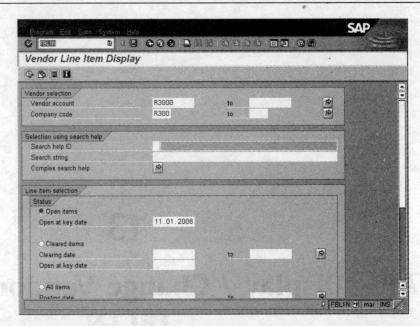

Figure: **FBL1N**-1

Under <u>Vendor Selection</u>:

1. **Vendor account (M):** Enter the vendor account (s), the line items of which needs to be displayed or changed.
2. **Company code (M):** Enter the relevant company code(s).

Under <u>Selection using search help</u>

3. Use any of the search criterion.

Under <u>Line Item selection</u>:

4. **Open items (O):** Select the radio button to display the open items only.
5. **Open at key date (O):** Enter date to restrict the display of open items as on a particular date.
6. **Cleared items (O):** Select the radio button to display the cleared items only.
7. **Clearing date (O):** Enter a single clearing date or a range of dates to enable the system to display all the cleared items based on this date(s).
8. **Open at key date (O):** Enter date to restrict the display of open items as on a particular date.
9. **All items (O):** Select this option to display both the open and cleared items.
10. **Posting date (O)**: Enter the posting date(s)to restrict the selection of items.

It is necessary that you select one of the three options:

1. **Open items**
2. **Cleared items**
3. **All items**

Step-2

Press and you are taken to the relevant line item in **"Vendor Line Item Display"** screen (Figure: **FBL1N**-2).

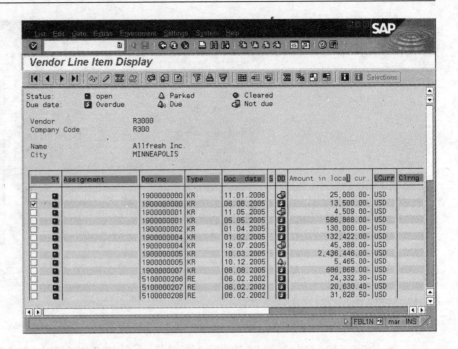

Figure: **FBL1N**-2

Step-3

Select a line item by checking the check box against the line and press 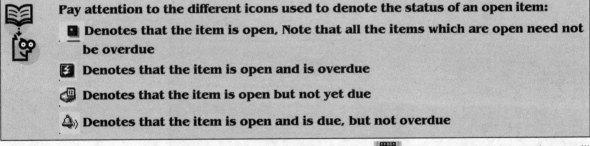 to change the line item displayed.

> **Pay attention to the different icons used to denote the status of an open item:**
>
> ■ **Denotes that the item is open. Note that all the items which are open need not be overdue**
>
> ▣ **Denotes that the item is open and is overdue**
>
> ▤ **Denotes that the item is open but not yet due**
>
> △﹚ **Denotes that the item is open and is due, but not overdue**

To make the display concise with only relevant columns, press ▦ button to customize and you will be presented with the "**Change layout**" screen (Figure: **FBL1N**-3).

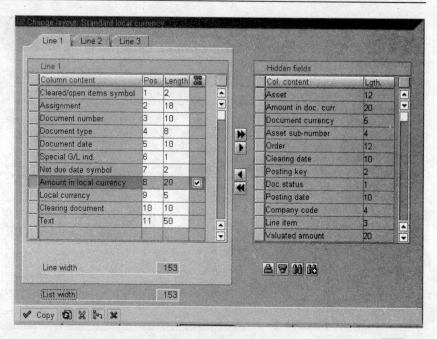

Figure: **FBL1N**-3

a. Select the row(s) to be deleted from the **Column content** pane on the left, and click ✂ .

b. To add new fields (columns), select the row in the **Column content** pane.

c. Select the row(s) from the **hidden fields** pane (Figure: **FBL1N**-4).

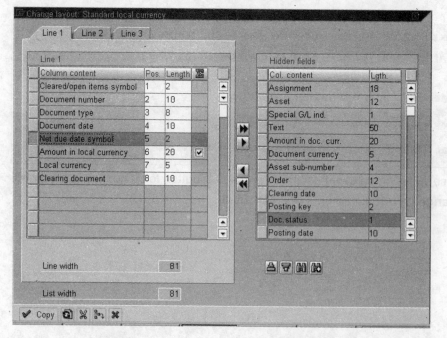

Figure: **FBL1N**-4

d. Press ◀ to add a single filed or column to the **Column content** pane. For multiple addition, press ◀◀ . To move the fields back to **hidden fields** pane, press ▶ or ▶▶ (Figure: **FBL1N**-5).

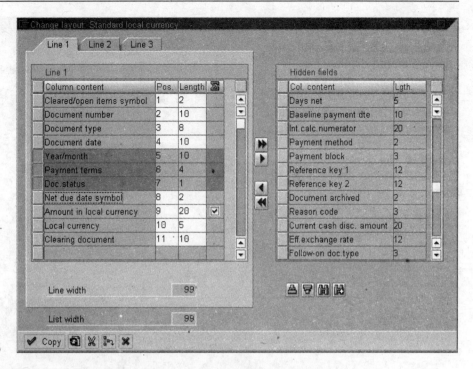

Figure: **FBL1N**-5

e. The newly added columns will appear above the row selected in (b) above.

f. When completed press ✔ Copy .

The display with the new lay out is shown in Figure: **FBL1N**-6. Note how concise is the display with only the relevant fields (others are hidden).

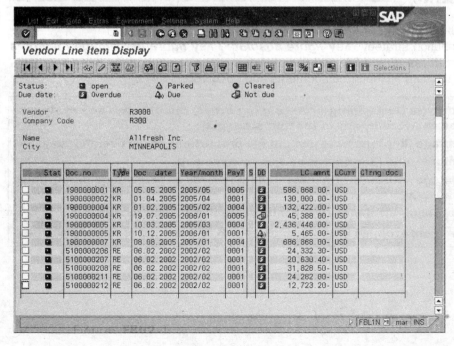

Figure: **FBL1N**-6

Step-4

You may also do some statistical analysis on the display. For example, an **ABC analysis**. Select a **ratio column**, by placing the cursor on the column heading (say **Amount in local cur.**). Now, use **Menu: Go to ->ABC analysis.** The system brings up the "**ABC Analysis Strategy**" screen (Figure: **FBL1N**-7).

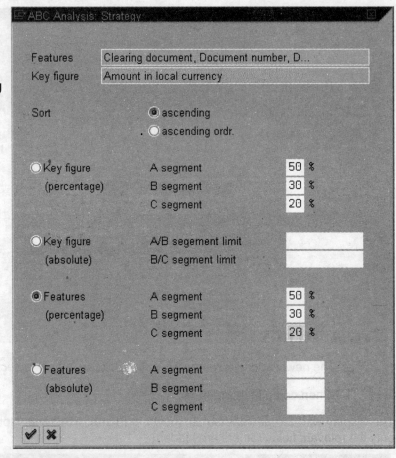

Figure: **FBL1N**-7

1. Select a sorting, **ascending or descending.**
2. Select the distribution strategy (**key figure absolute / key figure percentage / features percentage / features absolute**), and give the distribution to each of the three segments (A, B and C). Take care all the three segments add up to 100.

The system sorts (in Descending or Ascending order) the data by the **key figure.** The data can be analyzed by any of the four strategies:

1. As a percentage (key figures as percentage proportions of the overall total)
2. As an absolute value (key figures as absolute values)
3. As a percentage - attributes (number of data records as percentage proportions of the overall total)
4. As absolute value –attributes (using a fixed number of data records)

The data records are grouped into 3 segments A, B & C and the results displayed.

Step-6

Press 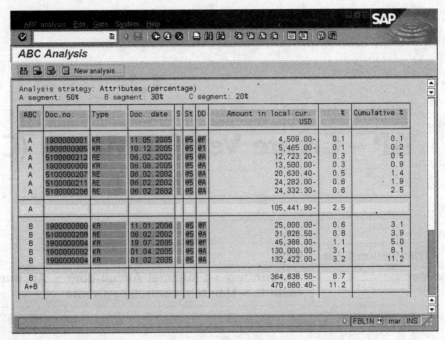 and the system displays the "**ABC Analysis**" screen (Figure: FBL1N-8).

Figure: **FBL1N-8**

14

AP – Create Vendor Master (Centrally): XK01

Transaction Code	XK01
Menu	Accounting > Financial Accounting > Accounts Payable > Master records > Maintain centrally > Create

Business Process Overview

Vendor master record controls how business transactions are carried out in the system for vendor related activities and accounts payables. The control is carried out through various specifications maintained in the master record, like: terms of payment, payment details, bank details, purchasing information, tax details, account information, control data etc. Vendor masters are used not only in the accounting area, but are also used in *material management*.

Vendor master's data is classified into *three* sections:

1. **General data**: this is common across the company codes and purchasing organizations of a company.
2. **Purchasing data**: the information relating to the purchasing organization(s) like quotations, purchase orders, invoice related information etc.
3. **Accounting data**: includes payment terms, dunning data, interest indicators, bank details, payment methods, tax codes, reconciliation accounts etc.

SAP recommends creation of vendor master in two ways:

1. *Centralized* master creation.
2. *Decentralized* master creation.

When Materials Management has been implemented, vendor master creation and maintenance can be carried out:

1. Separately for the **company code** area (Use *Transaction Code: FK01 or Menu: Accounting > Financial Accounting > Accounts Payable > Master records > Create*) / purchasing organization.
2. Centrally for both the company code and purchasing organization.

Since this is an inter-disciplinary activity, depending upon the policies of the company the masters can be created by adopting any one of the methods below:

1. Purchasing & Accounting departments maintain the general data jointly, but the specific details on purchasing or accounting are maintained individually.
2. Entire master is managed centrally.

Transaction Steps

Step-1

Access the transaction either by the transaction code or by the menu and you will be taken to "**Create Vendor: Initial Screen**" Screen (Figure: **XK01**-1).

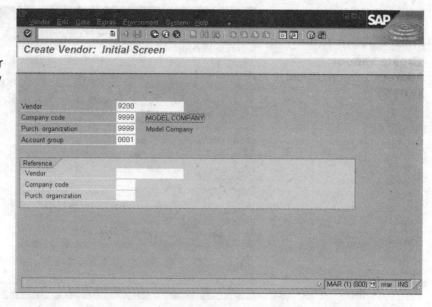

Figure: **XK01**-1

Enter the details:

1. **Vendor (M):** Enter the number of the vendor, if numbering is external. Else, the system will provide a number when the master is saved.

 The master record numbering is based on the account group to which the vendor will belong. If the numbering has been defined as 'external', then you need to provide a number, with in the number range defined earlier. If the vendor group is associated with 'internal numbering', system allocates the next number from the number range.

2. **Company code (M):** Enter the company code in which the vendor needs to be created.
3. **Purch. Organization (M):** Select the purchasing organization defined for the company code.
4. **Account group (M):** Enter the account group to which this new vendor will belong.

 Vendor account group decides how the master record is structured and controlled. You need different account groups for facilitating various partner functions, and to differentiate whether the vendor is a "regular" or "one-time".

Under Reference:

1. **Vendor (O):** Enter the vendor number .
2. **Company code (O):** Enter the company code.
3. **Purch. Organization (O):** Enter the purchasing organization.

 Helpful if a similar master is to be created by referring to an already existing master record in a particular company code. Remember, it is only the common attributes like account group, purchasing organization etc are copied and not the address data etc. The system will issue a warning if you try to reference a vendor but create in a different account group, but you can still continue!

Step-2

Press to go to the 'Create Vendor: Address' screen (Figure: XK01-2).

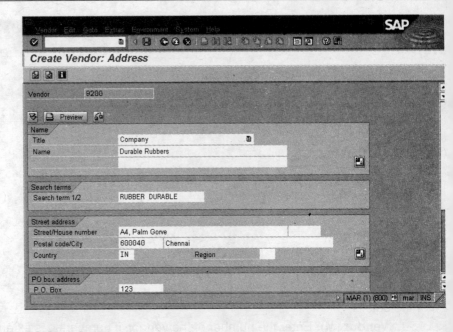

Figure: **XK01**-2

Enter the details:

1. **Title (M):** Select from the drop-down list, to indicate whether the vendor is a **natural person** (Mr / Ms) or a **legal entity** (Company).

2. **Name (M):** Enter the name of the vendor (Very generous, up to 4 lines maximum!).

3. **Search Term 1/2 (M):** Enter a meaningful search term to help system retrieve the vendor when a selection is warranted.

> **Two search terms can be entered here. All the search terms are stored as UPPER case letters.**

Under <u>Street and Address</u> block: ·

1. **Street/House Number (O):** This will be part of the address of the vendor. Enter the details.

2. **Postal code (O):** Enter the postal or zip code.

3. **City (M):** Enter the name of the city or town or place.

4. **Country (M):** Select from the 2-digit country code.

5. **P. O Box (O):** If available.

6. **Language (O):** The language code is defaulted from the log-on. Change, if necessary.

7. **Telephone (O):** Enter the telephone numbers. You may use "-" to indicate ending number (Example: 2472367-9).

Step-3

Press 📄 icon to go to the **"Create Vendor: Control"** screen (Figure: **XK01**-3).

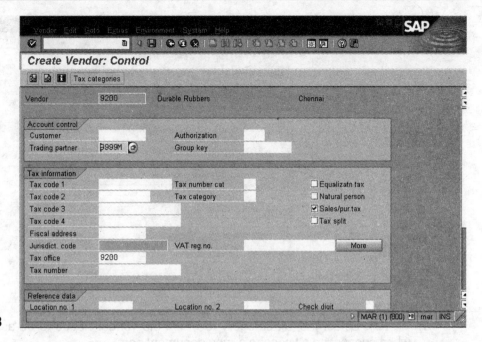

Figure: **XK01**-3

Under <u>Account control</u> block:

1. **Customer (O):** Enter the Customer account number of this vendor if he is defined as a Customer also.

> **This customer number is used in payment/dunning programs to clear the open items. To offset between customer and vendor balances, you need to make sure that (a) customer number is entered in vendor's master record and vendor number is entered in the customer master record and (b) the field *'clrg with vendor'* in the customer master and *'clrg. with customer'* in vendor master should have been selected.**

2. **Trading Partner (O):** Enter the Company ID (standard for the whole group). This is used in elimination functions in consolidation.

Under <u>Tax information</u> block:

3. **Tax Category (O):** Tax category of the vendor.

4. **Natural Person (O):** Check the box, if vendor is not a 'company' (Whether natural person or legal entity. Should be used in conjunction with the field 'Tax number cat').

5. **Sales/Pur tax (O):** Liable for Sales / Purchase tax? If yes, then tick the check box.

6. **Jurisdict. code (O):** Mandatory in US (Code represents the city to which the goods will be supplied).

7. **VAT reg. no.** (O): Enter VAT registration number (If Value Added Tax, is applicable. If an entry is made, make sure to press *"More"* to add additional details).

Step-4

Press | Tax categories | icon to go to the "**Create Vendor: Tax Categories**" screen (Figure: **XK01**-4) and maintain the necessary Tax Codes.

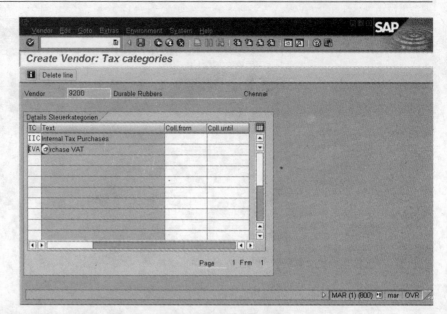

Figure: **XK01**-4

Under <u>Details</u>:

1. **TC (O):** Select the tax category to which the vendor needs to be assigned. This is used when suggesting a tax code during document entry.

Step-5

Press ⬅ to go back and press 📄 icon to go to the "**Create Vendor: Payment transactions**" screen (Figure: **XK01**-5), and enter the details as outlined.

Figure: **XK01**-5

1. **Ctry (O):** Select the country code (2-character country identifier) from the drop-down list.
2. **Bank key (O):** Unique identifier for the vendor's bank (Nine-digit bank key). Before doing this, this bank should have been defined in the **Bank Directory**. Once done, the bank key can be selected using the pop up "**Bank Address**" (Figure: **XK01**-6).

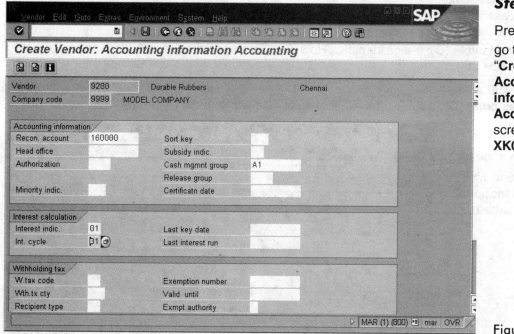

Figure: XK01-6

3. **Bank account (O):** Enter the account number maintained at this bank. The bank details are necessary for automatic payments.

Under Payment Transactions block:

1. **Alternate payee (O):** Enter the Vendor number to whom the automatic payments should be made. Valid only when payments are NOT to be made to the Vendor to whom your company owes the payables.

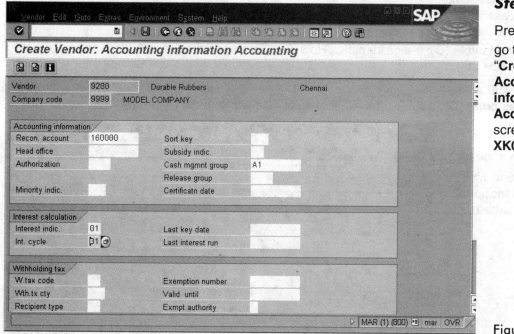

Figure: XK01-7

Step-6

Press 📋 icon to go to the **"Create Vendor: Accounting information Accounting"** screen (Figure: **XK01**-7).

Under Accounting Information block:

1. **Recon. account (M):** Enter the G/L account code.

Reconciliation account is a G/L account, which will be updated in parallel whenever postings are made to the sub-ledger of the vendor. For special G/L transactions like down payment, bill of exchange etc this account is replaced by another account: the special G/L indicator selected during transaction postings triggers this.

2. Head office (O): Enter the master record account number of the HO.

 Valid only when the vendor created is a branch of HO. When entered, all the postings you make are posted to HO account but the branch code is updated in the line items.

3. Sort Key (O): 3-character key (cost center, document date etc), from the drop-down list. This is the lay-out key for 'allocation' field in the document line item.

4. Cash mgmnt group (M): Select from the drop-down list.

 Also called the *'planning group'*, this is the point of integration between AP/AP & TR. Customer cash management groups begin with a letter *'K'* (R3-customers abroad, R5-high risk customers etc) and Vendor groups with *'E'* (E2-vendor abroad, E4-major vendors etc).

Under Interest Calculation block:

5. Interest indic. (O): Select the 2-character identifier, from the drop-down list, if interest is to be calculated on this account.

6. Interest cycle (O): 2-digit identifier. How often interest is calculated? (01-monthly, 02-every 2 months etc).

Under Withholding Tax block:

7. W tax code (O): If subject to withholding tax, select from the drop-down list.

Step-6

Press [icon] icon to go to the "**Create Vendor: Payment transactions Accounting**" screen (Figure: XK01-8).

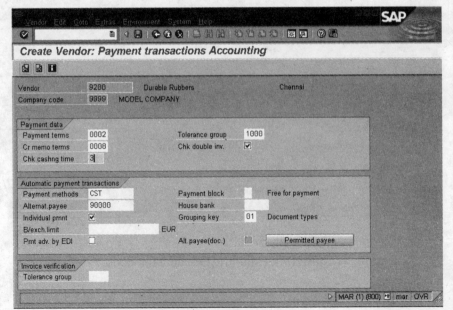

Figure: **XK01**-8

Under Payment data:

1. **Payment terms (O):** Select from the drop-down values, the **Payment terms** decided for this vendor. Payment terms provides the information on credit period, discount period and discount percentage.
2. **Tolerance group (O):** Select from the drop-down list. **Tolerance group** (unique with in company code) affects the processing of discounts, and the payment difference during an under/over payment.
3. **Cr memo terms (O):** 3 digit key, from the drop-down list.
4. **Check double inv (O):** Tick to prevent double invoicing.

Best practice is to tick this check box. At the time of entry, both the incoming invoices and credit memos are checked for duplication.

5. **Check cashing time (O):** Enter the number of days, it will take for the vendor to encash the check sent by you as a payment.

The days entered in *'check cashing time'* field, is taken into account when the system calculates the value date for check payment, during an automatic payment transaction. The value date is calculated by adding these days to the posting date. This is the actual date of cash outflow from your company code. The information is stored in the respective line item.

Under Automatic Payment transactions:

6. **Payment methods (O):** Make a selection from the pop-up screen (**C**-Check, **T**-Bank transfer etc).

***Payment methods* are used in automatic payment transactions. Payment method can also be entered in the line items; if mentioned both in the line items and masters then line item entry has the priority.**

7. **Payment block (O):** Leave it blank for not blocking the payments. Select a 'block' indicator to block the payments.
8. **Alternate payee (O):** Enter a vendor, if payments are to be sent to some one other than this vendor.
9. **House Bank (O):** Select from the drop-down list. If an entry is made here, then the payments will ALWAYS be made from this bank, and any other bank entry in the automatic payment programme selection will be ignored.
10. **Individual payment (O):** Check this, to pay individual open items separately (without grouping all the open items for the vendor).
11. **Grouping key (O):** Select a grouping rule, by which some of the vendor's open items will be grouped for payment for use in an automatic payment program. Useful, when all the items need not be grouped together for payment.

Under Invoice verification:

12. **Tolerance group (O):** Enter a tolerance group, which needs to be used during invoice verification. Used in Logistics Invoice Verification (LIV).

For the *tolerance group,* you may define: (a) how much the actual value of an invoice can vary (over or under) from the expected value of the invoice, which can still be accepted by the system for processing and (b) whether there will be a provision to reduce the invoices automatically. Remember, only one tolerance group can be assigned to a vendor in one company code.

Step-7

Press 🔲 icon to go to the "**Create Vendor: Correspondence Accounting**" screen (Figure: **XK01**-8) and enter the details.

Figure: **XK01**-8

Create Vendor: Correspondence Accounting

| Vendor | 9200 | Durable Rubbers | Chennai |
| Company code | 9999 | MODEL COMPANY | |

Dunning data

Dunn.procedure	0001	Dunning block	
Dunn.recipient	90000	Legal dunn.proc.	
Last dunned		Dunning level	
Dunning clerk	D1	Grouping key	VT

Dunning areas

Correspondence

Local process	☐	Acct statement	
Acctg clerk			
Acct w/ vendor			
Clerk at vendor			
Act.clk tel.no.			
Clerk's fax			
Clrk's internet			

Under Dunning data:

1. **Dunning procedure (O):** Select a dunning procedure to use in automatic dunning program.

 A dunning procedure is a 4-character key used in dunning program, containing the information as to how the vendors/customers are dunned (reminded). The dunning procedure determines, among other things, the dunning frequency / dunning interval, minimum number of days in arrears for an open item to be selected for dunning, grace periods, number of dunning levels to be used, what are all the transactions to be included for dunning etc. You can use as many dunning procedures as you need. The dunning procedure is entered in the master record of the vendor or customer.

2. **Dunning block (O):** Enter a 'block key' if you need to block this account from dunning.
3. **Dunning recipient (O):** Enter the business partner who will receive the dunning notices on behalf of this vendor.
4. **Dunning clerk (O):** Enter the clerk who is responsible for dunning this vendor. The name of the clerk will be printed on the dunning notices.
5. **Grouping key (O):** Select a grouping key, when you want group certain items to a single dunning notice.

Step-8

Press 🔲 icon to go to the "**Create Vendor: Purchasing data**" screen (Figure: **XK01**-9).

Figure: **XK01**-9

Under <u>Conditions:</u>

1. **Order currency (M):** Select from the drop-down values.
2. **Terms of paymnt (O):** Select the appropriate payment terms for this vendor.
3. **Incoterms (O):** Select the relevant terms (terms as approved by International Chamber of Commerce (CIF, FOB etc)), and maintain the 2nd part of the Incoterms as well.
4. **Minimum order value (O):** Enter the minimum value for which a PO needs to be issued.

Under <u>Sales data:</u>

5. **Salesperson (O):** Enter the name of the sales person at the vendor's office.

Step-9

Scroll down to see the other details in "**Create Vendor: Purchasing data**" screen (Figure: **XK01**-10).

Figure: **XK01**-10

Under <u>Control data</u>:

6. **GR-based inv.verify (O):** Tick the check-box, if desired.

 Best practice is to tick this check box *GR-based inv.verify.*. This will allow for *goods-receipt-based invoice verification* for a purchase order item or invoice item.

7. **Automatic Purchase Order (O):** Tick the check box, if desired. Allows automatic creation of POs from **purchase requisitions** if the requisition has been assigned to a vendor.

8. **Shipping conditions (O):** Enter the shipping conditions, for delivery of the goods, agreed with the vendor.

 The *shipping conditions* are defined according to the requirements of your company, and you can specify this condition in the master record of customer / vendor. The *shipping point* proposed by the system, for outbound deliveries, is determined based on the shipping condition defined, the loading point and the relevant plant. In case of out bound deliveries, the shipping condition helps in determining the route based on the combination of country / geographical region / ship-to-party / transportation group.

Under <u>Default material</u>:

9. **Purchasing group (O):** Select the purchasing group that is responsible for purchasing from a group of vendors.

10. **Confirmation control (O):** Select from the drop-down values (Which confirmation is expected: PO? Order acknowledgment or Shipping notice?).

Step-10

Press 🔲 icon to go to the **"Create Vendor: Partner functions"** screen (Figure: **XK01**-11).

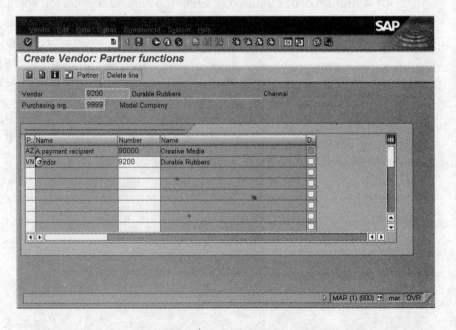

Figure: **XK01**-11

Partner function (O): Select from the drop down list, and enter the vendor number to create the relevant partner functions.

Step-11

Press ![icon] icon and when you reach the last screen Press [Yes] (Figure: **XK01**-11). Or

Press ![icon] (Figure: **XK01**-12) and you get the confirmation as to the creation of the vendor with the vendor number displayed.

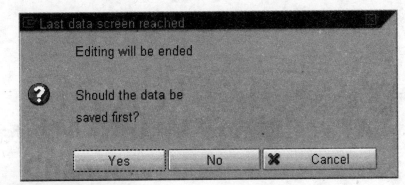

Figure: **XK01**-11

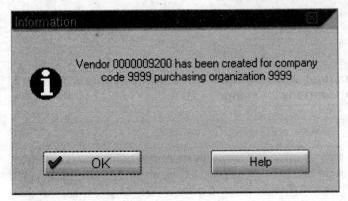

Figure: **XK01**-12

Step-12

Press [✔ OK] to exit the transaction.

15

AP – Change Vendor Master (Centrally): XK02

Transaction Code	XK02
Menu	Accounting > Financial Accounting > Accounts Payable > Master records > Maintain centrally > Change

Business Process Overview

As in the creation, Vendor master records can be changed centrally or at the company code area alone. When done centrally you may edit the details relating to purchasing organization besides the general data and company code area. As dealt in *Transaction Code: XK01*, one can look at the details in the various sections, and change the required ones. For facilitating, easy navigation to the desired are the initial screen itself provides for changing all or select area of:

1. **General data**
   a. Address
   b. Control
   c. Payment transactions
2. **Company code data**
   a. Accounting info
   b. Payment transactions
   c. Correspondence
3. **Withholding tax**
   a. Purchase organization data
   b. Purchasing data
   c. Partner functions

Use *Transaction Code: FK02 (Menu: Accounting > Financial Accounting > Accounts Payable > Master records > Maintain centrally > Change* to change the vendor master in the **company code area** alone.

Transaction Steps

Step-1

Access the transaction either by the transaction code or by the menu and you will be taken to "**Change Vendor: Initial Screen**" Screen (Figure: **XK02**-1).

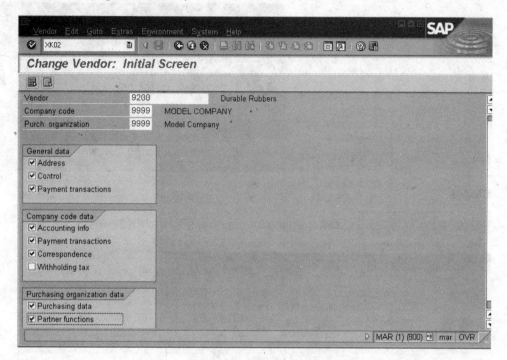

Figure: **XK02**-1

1. Select the sections where the changes need to done. Press 🗒 to select all.

Step-2

Press 📀 to go to the '**Change Vendor: Address**' screen, and enter / change the details as required.

Alternatively, press 📄 icon to go to the next screen or 📄 to go back to the previous screen (Please refer to the various sections in *Transaction code: XK01*).

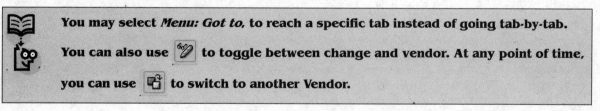

You may select *Menu: Got to*, to reach a specific tab instead of going tab-by-tab.

You can also use 🖉 to toggle between change and vendor. At any point of time, you can use 🗗 to switch to another Vendor.

Step-3

When all the changes have been made, or when you reach the last screen (Figure: **XK02**-2), press,

Yes to save the changes (Figure: **XK02**-3),

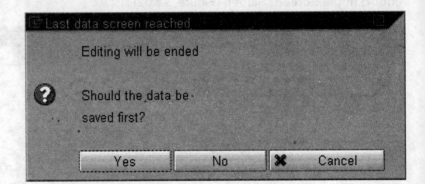

Figure: **XK02**-2

Step-4

Press ✔ OK to exit from the transaction (Figure: **XK02**-3).

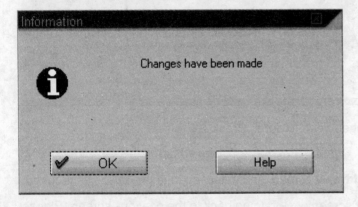

Figure: **XK02**-3

16

AP – Display Vendor Master (Centrally): XK03

Transaction Code	XK03
Menu	Accounting > Financial Accounting > Accounts Payable > Master records > Maintain centrally > Display

Business Process Overview

As in the creation, Vendor master records can be displayed centrally or at the company code area alone. When done centrally you may display the details relating to purchasing organization / partner functions besides the general data and company code area. As dealt in *Transaction Code: XK01/ XK02*, one can look at the details in the various sections, and display the required ones. For facilitating, easy navigation to the desired area the initial screen itself provides for displaying all or select area of:

1. **General data**
   a. Address
   b. Control
   c. Payment transactions
2. **Company code data**
   a. Accounting info
   b. Payment transactions
   c. Correspondence
   d. Withholding tax
3. **Purchase organization data**
   a. Purchasing data
   b. Partner functions

Use *Transaction Code: FK03 (Menu: Accounting > Financial Accounting > Accounts Payable > Master records > Maintain centrally > Display* to display the customer master in the **company code area** alone.

Transaction Steps

Step-1

Access the transaction either by the transaction code or by the menu and you will be taken to "**Display Vendor: Initial Screen**" Screen (Figure: **XK03**-1).

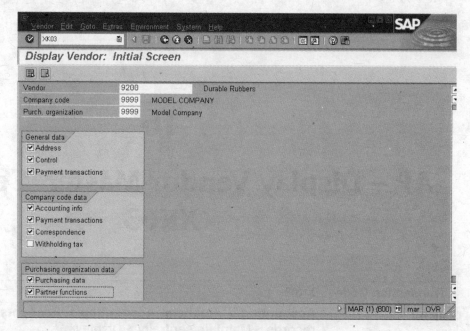

Figure: **XK03**-1

1. Select the sections where the data needs to be displayed. Press 📄 to select all.

Step-2

Press ✅ to go to the **next** screen, and look for the details as required, Alternatively, press 📄 icon to go to the next screen or 🖰 to go back to the previous screen (Please refer to the various sections in **Transaction code: XK01.**

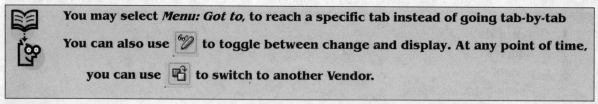

You may select *Menu: Got to,* to reach a specific tab instead of going tab-by-tab You can also use ✏️ to toggle between change and display. At any point of time, you can use 🖰 to switch to another Vendor.

Step-3

When you reach the last screen, press, ⌷ Yes ⌷ to exit the display (Figure: **XK03**-3).

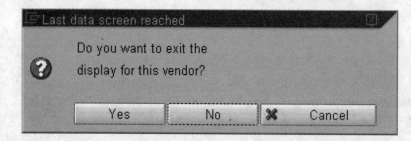

Figure: **XK03**-2

17

AP – Create Vendor Master (Company code area): FK01

Transaction Code	FK01
Menu	Accounting > Financial Accounting > Accounts Payable > Master records > Create

Business Process Overview

Vendor master record controls how business transactions are carried out in the system for vendor related activities and accounts payables. The control is carried out through various specifications maintained in the master record, like: terms of payment, payment details, bank details, purchasing information, tax details, account information, control data etc. Vendor masters are used not only in the accounting area, but also in material management.

When Vendor master's data are created in the accounting view, **purchasing information** will not be created but the other two sections will be maintained:

1. **General data**: this is common across the company codes and purchasing organizations of a company.
2. **Accounting data**: includes:
   i. Payment terms
   ii. Dunning data
   iii. Interest indicators
   iv. Bank details
   v. Payment methods
   vi. Tax codes
   vii. Reconciliation accounts

Even here, the Purchasing & Accounting departments can maintain the general data jointly, but the specific details on accounting can be maintained by the accounting people.

Transaction Steps

Step-1

Access the transaction either by the transaction code or by the menu, and you will be taken to "**Create Vendor: Initial Screen**" Screen (Figure: **FK01**-1).

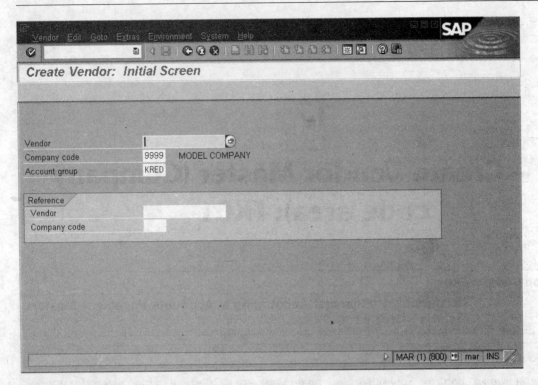

Figure:
FK01-1

Enter the details:

1. **Vendor (M):** Enter the number of the vendor, if numbering is **external**. Else, the system will provide a number when the master is saved.

> **The master record numbering is based on the account group to which the vendor will belong. If the numbering has been defined as 'external', then you need to provide a number, within the number range defined earlier. If the vendor group is associated with 'internal numbering', system allocates the next number from the number range.**

2. **Company code (M):** Enter the company code in which the vendor needs to be created.
3. **Account group (M):** Enter the account group to which this new vendor will belong.

> *Vendor account group* **decides how the master record is structured and controlled. You need different account groups for facilitating various partner functions, and to differentiate whether the vendor is a "regular" or "one-time". The system comes with a number of vendor groups (Figure: FK01-2), which you can use as such. Or, if necessary, you may create your own vendor groups.**

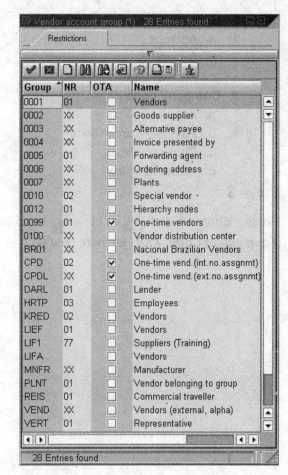

Figure: **FK01**-2

Under <u>Reference:</u>

1. **Vendor (O):** Enter the vendor number .
2. **Company code (O):** Enter the company code.

Helpful if a similar master is to be created by referring to an already existing master record in a particular company code. Remember, it is only the common attributes like account group, purchasing organization etc are copied and not the address data etc. The system will issue a warning if you try to reference a vendor but create in a different account group; but you can still continue!

Between *Transaction code: XK01* and *FK01*, the essential difference is that no purchasing related information would be maintained if you are using *FK01*. That is why *Purch. Organization* and Reference-> *Purch. Organization* fields are not available for entry in the initial screen.

Step-2

Press "***Enter***" or ![icon] to go to other sections. The data pertaining to the following sections can only be maintained using this *Transaction Code: FK01*.

1. **General data**
   a. Address
   b. Control
   c. Payment transactions
2. **Company code data**
   a. Accounting info
   b. Payment transactions
   c. Correspondence
   d. Withholding tax

Step-3

Press, "***Enter***" or click ✅ or click 🔲 to go to other screens till the last screen is reached. (Refer ***Transaction Code: XK01*** for more details).

18

AP – Block / Unblock Vendor (Centrally): XK05

Transaction Code	XK05
Menu	Accounting > Financial Accounting > Accounts Payable > Master records > Maintain Centrally > Block/unblock

Business Process Overview

Blocking is necessary when you do not want to post any more to an account. SAP allows blocking the Vendor either (1) *centrally* (possible only when SAP's MM component has been integrated) or (2) in the *company code area* alone. When a Vendor is blocked centrally, the system prevents both order processing and account posting; but a block in the company code area prevents only further postings. When blocked centrally, you set the block for one or all the **purchasing organizations** besides company code areas.

Again, you have the flexibility of (a) blocking a Vendor in *all the company codes* or (b) in *selected company codes*. Before blocking, you need to ensure that there are no open items in the account, else you will not be able to process and clear these items.

You may also want to block a Vendor from making **automatic payments** or **manual payments** and for blocking the dunning. To block a Vendor for payment or dunning program, necessary *'dunning block'* key (in Correspondence section of the Vendor master) or *'payment block'* key (in payment transaction section of the Vendor master) needs to be entered. Even though both the payment and dunning program will select the open items for payment / dunning during open item determination, the system will not create a payment or dunning notice.

You need to use:

- **Transaction Code: *FK05***   For blocking the account in company code are, from posting alone

At any time you want to **unblock**, just remove the 'check' against the check boxes in the respective transactions or remove the block key(s) from the master record of the concerned Vendor.

Transaction Steps

Step-1

Access the transaction either by the transaction code or by the menu, and you are taken to the **"Block/ unblock Vendor: Initial Screen"** (Figure: XK05-1).

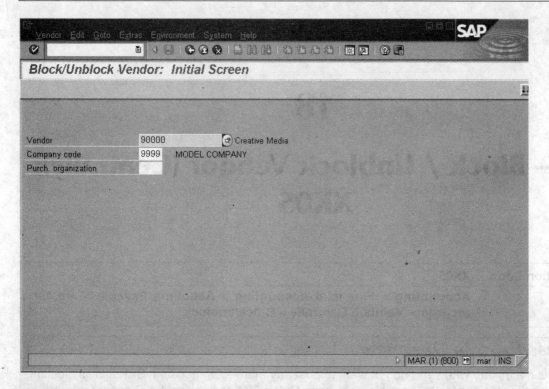

Figure:
XK05-1

Enter the selection details:

1. **Vendor (M):** Enter the Vendor number which needs to be blocked or unblocked.
2. **Company code (O):** Enter the company code, where you need to block or unblock.

 If the company code is not entered, it is only possible to block / unblock in all the company codes! Else, you have both the options like blocking in the already entered company code and or all the company codes.

Under Block for quality reasons:

3. Select the **function that needs to be blocked**, like total block, blocking the source determination etc.

 The block for quality reasons is valid only when Quality Management (QM) in procurement is active for those materials.

Step-2

Press enter . Now you are in **"Block/unblock Vendor: Details Accounting"** screen (Figure: **XK05**-2).

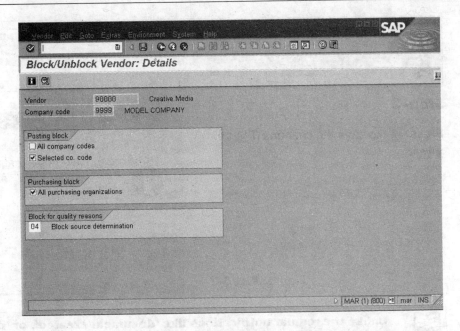

Figure: XK05-2

You have the option of pressing to see the account details (takes you to the master data).

Under <u>Posting block</u>:

1. **All company codes (O):** Check this check box if you wish to block the Vendor in all the applicable company codes.

2. **Selected company code (O):** Check this check box, if you wish to block the Vendor only form the company code which you entered in **Step-1** (This field will be available for input only when the company code is entered in the previous screen).

> You need to block a Vendor before marking the Vendor master record for 'deletion'. Note to block the account only when there are no open items; else you will not be able to clear these items.
>
> If you are using a Vendor only as 'alternate dunning recipient' then it is necessary that you block this Vendor to prevent any posting to be made to this account.

3. **Purchasing Organization (O):** Enter the Purchasing Organization in which the blocking needs to be done.

> If the *Purchasing organization* is not entered in the initial screen, the block indicator is set for all the purchasing areas. If you maintain the relevant information in the screen initially, the Vendor is blocked in the specified purchasing organization area, but you have the option to block in all other purchasing organizations as well.

Under <u>Block for quality reasons</u>:

4. Select the **function that needs to be blocked**, like total block, blocking the source determination etc.

Uncheck the checkbox, to unblock the Vendor, in the relevant area(s)!

Step-3

Press to save the changes (Figure: **XK05**-3).

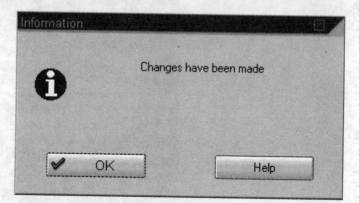

Figure: **XK05**-3

 Unlike the regular notifications like 'document created', or 'document posted' etc, here the system does not 'explicitly' inform that the account has been blocked / unblocked. Instead, you get the information that 'changes have been made' only!

 Use the *Transaction Code: FK05 or Menu: Accounting > Financial Accounting > Accounts Payable > Master records > Block/unblock* for blocking or unblocking at the company code level.

=========== **End of Transaction** ===========

Step-A

Use *Transaction XK02*, and select *Company Code data: Payment transactions*. You will be in "Change Vendor: Payment transaction accounting" screen (Figure: **XK05-XK02**-1), where you can set the payment block from the drop down list.

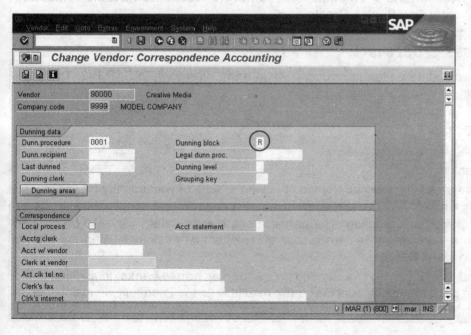

Figure: **XK05-XK02**-1

Step-B

Use *Transaction XK02*, and select *Company Code data: Correspondence*. You will be in " **Change Vendor: Correspondence Accounting**" screen (Figure: **XK05-XK02**-2), where you can set the *dunning block* from the drop down list.

Figure: **XK05-XK02**-2

19

AP– Create Bank Master: FI01

Transaction Code	FI01
Menu	**Accounting > Financial Accounting > Accounts Payable > Master records > Bank > Create**

Business Process Overview

You need to create bank related information, centrally in **bank directory**, in SAP R/3. The bank master data will contain, among other things:

1. Control data
2. Correspondence data
3. SWIFT data

You may create the bank directory by:

1. Importing the bank details obtained from the banking system of your country (in ASCII text) using a program **RFBVALL_0** or
2. Manually by using this transaction (The partner bank master details can also be created whenever you are creating a master record of a vendor or customer using the **Menu: Environment -> Bank Data**).

The banks used by you in your banking transactions are known as **house banks**. In addition to the house banks, you also need to maintain **partner bank** details which will normally be maintained in the master records of customer/vendor.

Transaction Steps

Step-1

Access the transaction either by the transaction code or by the menu and you will be taken to "**Create Bank: Initial Screen**" Screen (Figure: **FI01**-1).

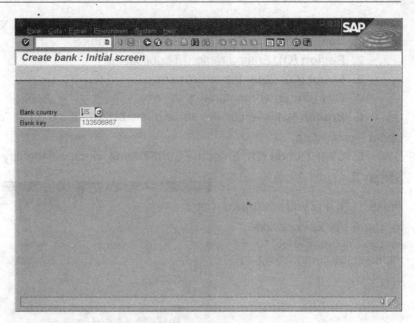

Figure: **FI01**-1

1. **Bank country (M):** Select the country where the bank is to be created.
2. **Bank key (M):** Enter the bank key. This country specific bank key uniquely identifies a bank.

 You should have configured the details relating to bank key in customization. Bank keys are configured to be unique with some country specific *check rules* defined. The check rule, for example, will check whether the bank key defined is of an appropriate length (say bank key in US needs to be 9 digits).

Step-2

Press 🗸 and you are taken to "*Create Bank: Detail screen*" (Figure: **FI01**-2).

Figure: **FI01**-2

Under Address:

1. **Bank name (M):** Enter the name of the bank.
2. **Region (O):** Enter a region, if applicable.
3. **Street (O):** Enter the street name.
4. **City (O):** Enter the name of the city.
5. **Branch (O):** Mention the name of the branch of the bank.

Under Control data:

6. **SWIFT code (O):** Enter the SWIFT code which will identify a bank internationally.

Step-3

Press and you are taken to "***Bank US: xxxxxxxxx***" screen (Figure: **FI01**-3) to maintain the communication details.

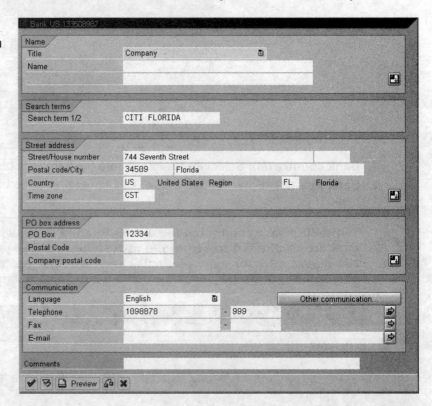

Figure: **FI01**-3

Enter the details:

1. **Title (M):** Select from the drop-down list, to indicate whether the vendor is a natural person (Mr/Ms) or a legal entity (Company).
2. **Name (O):** Enter the name of the bank.
3. **Search Term 1/2 (M):** Enter a meaningful search term to help system retrieve the bank when a selection is warranted.

> **Two search terms can be entered here. All the search terms are stored as UPPER case letters.**

Under Street and Address block:

1. **Street/House Number (O):** This will be part of the address of the bank. Enter the details.

2. **Postal code (O):** Enter the postal or zip code.
3. **City (M):** Enter the name of the city or town or place.
4. **Country (M):** Select from the 2-digit country code.
5. **P. O Box (O):** If available.
6. **Language (O):** The language code is defaulted from the log-on. Change, if necessary.
7. **Telephone (O):** Enter the telephone numbers. You may use "-" to indicate ending number (Example: 2472367-9).

Step-4

Press ✔ and you are taken to the initial screen. Press 🖫 to save the bank data. Note the display on the status bar at the bottom of the screen. (Figure: **FI01**-4).

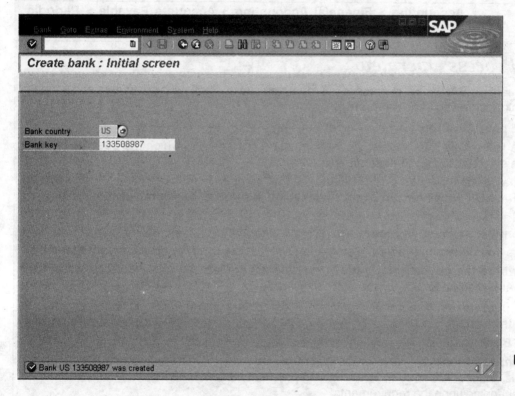

Figure: **FI01**-4

20

AP/AR – Automatic Payments: F110

Transaction Code	F110
Menu	Accounting > Financial Accounting > Accounts Payable > Periodic Processing >Payments

Business Process Overview

Automatic payments in SAP, helps to process payment transactions both with customers and vendors. AR/AP/TR/Bank Accounting uses **payment program**.

The **automatic payment program** helps in determining:

- **What is to be paid?** To do this, you specify rules according to which the open items to be paid are selected and grouped for payment.
- **When payment is carried out?** The due date of the open items determines when payment is carried out. However, you can specify the **payment deadline** in more detail via configuration.
- **To whom the payment is made?** You specify the payee.
- **How the payment is made?** You determine rules that are used to select a **payment method**.
- **From where the payment is made?** You determine rules that are used to select a bank and a bank account for the payment.

Before you are ready to run the automatic payment program, the following should have been defined / configured in the system:

- *House Bank* and the corresponding bank accounts.
- *Payment Methods* to be used for the company code. SAP comes with pre-defined payment methods, both for AR and AP. The following payment methods are available for you to select from depending upon the requirements:
  - ➤ **Accounts payable**
    - o Check (S) / Transfer / Postal Giro transfer / Bill of exchange
  - ➤ **Accounts Receivable**
    - o Bank collection / Bank direct debit / Refund by check / Refund by bank transfer / BE payment request
- *Bank Chain* defined, if necessary. Bank chains are used to make payment via more than one bank, for example via the correspondence banks of the house bank, the recipient bank, or the intermediary banks. You can define up to three banks.
- *Payment Forms* defined. SAP delivers standard forms, which can be modified, or new forms can be created for use.

A. *Payment program configuration settings*

Using the *Transaction Code* **FBZP**, the configuration settings for automatic payment program needs to be defined in the system before you start the actual payment program (transaction code **F110**)

- **Company code specifications** (Transaction code: **OBVU**)
  - ➢ Sending CoCode – if A is making payments on behalf of B, then B is the sending company code. Else, sending is considered as the paying CoCode.
  - ➢ Paying CoCode (responsible for processing outgoing payments).
  - ➢ Tolerance days
- **Paying company code specifications** (Transaction code: **OBVU**)
  - ➢ Minimum amounts for incoming and outgoing payments.
  - ➢ Forms for payment advice and EDI
  - ➢ Bill of Exchange parameters
- **Payment methods /country** (Transaction code: **OBVCU**)
  - ➢ Payment Method for outgoing/incoming
  - ➢ Payment method classification
  - ➢ Master data requirements
  - ➢ Posting details – document types
  - ➢ Payment medium details - Print programs
  - ➢ Permitted currencies (leave blank to allow all currencies)
- **Payment methods / company code** (Transaction code: **OBVU**)
  - ➢ For each payment method and CoCode define:
    - o Minimum / maximum payment amounts
    - o Whether payment abroad or FC is allowed
    - o Payment media
    - o Bank optimization
- **Bank Determination** (Transaction code: **OBVCU**)
  - ➢ Ranking order
    - o Per payment method:
      - ❑ Which bank should be used first, second etc
      - ❑ Currency
      - ❑ Bill of Exchange
  - ➢ Bank accounts
  - ➢ Available amounts
    - o Per house bank and payment method combination:
      - ❑ Offset a/c for sub-ledger posting
      - ❑ Available funds in each bank
      - ❑ Clearing accounts for Bill of Exchange
  - ➢ Value date
  - ➢ Charges
- **House Bank** (Transaction code: **FI12**)

B. *Executing the payment run*

- Maintain Payment Parameters

  To start with, you need to maintain the parameters required like date of execution of payment run, payment run identifier etc. Once this is done, you need to specify what should be the posting date of these payments, the document date up to which the program should consider the items, the paying company code, payment methods to be considered, what will be the next posting date, is there certain accounts which need to be excluded from the run etc. The payment run, then needs to be scheduled either immediately or at a specified time/date.

- Payment proposal

  The system creates a payment proposal, based on the payment parameters maintained.

  The **Open item selection** is based on the following sequence:

  ➢ **Due date** is determined via the baseline date and the terms of payment for each of the line item.

  ➢ Program calculates the **cash discount period** and **due date for the net payment.**

  ➢ **Grace periods** are then added to this due date.

  ➢ Specify which special G/L accounts are to be included.

  ➢ For each payment run, specify the next payment run so that the system will determine whether to include an item during the current run or for the future one.

  ➢ **Blocking** an item.

  The payment proposal can be displayed for further processing, the **log** can be checked to see the system messages, and the exception list generated for further evaluation.

- Edit the payment proposal

  With the payment proposal available, you can now edit the proposal to:

  ➢ Change house bank, from what was maintained earlier.

  ➢ Change payment method, if necessary.

  ➢ Change payment due date so as to relax or restrict certain open items.

  ➢ Block / unblock line items.

- Payment run

  After the payment proposal has been edited, you can run the **payment program** that creates the payment documents and prepares the data for printing the forms or creating the tape or disk. Before printing the forms, check the logs to determine that the payment program run was successful.

- Print run

  Payment medium programs use the data prepared by the payment program to create forms (payment advice, EDI accompanying sheet) or files for the data media.

  Variants for print programs need to be defined:

  ➢ Per payment method per country -> assign a print program.

  ➢ To run the print program ->at least 1 variant per print program per payment method.

  Payment medium workbench: A tool used to configure and create **payment media** sent by organizations to their house banks. This generic tool will gradually phase out the classic payment medium programs (RFFO*) due to the range of advantages that it provides.

Transaction Steps

Step-1

Access the transaction either by the transaction code or menu, and you will be taken to "**Automatic Payment Transactions: Status**" screen (Figure: **F110**-1).

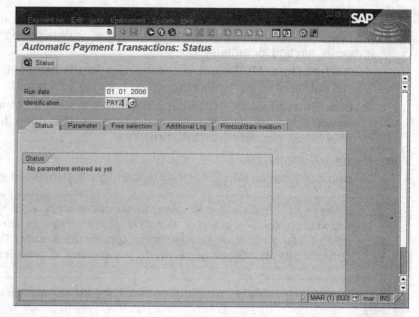

Figure: **F110**-1

Maintain the details as indicated below:

    i. Run Date (M): Enter the payment program run date. This can be the posting date as well.

    ii. Identifier (M): Enter a meaningful identifier which can, later, identify this payment run.

Please note that the message in the '*status*' tab:

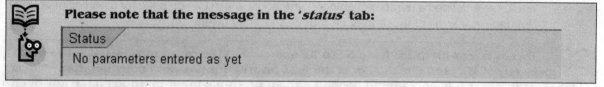

Step-2

Press [Parameter] tab and to reach "**Automatic Payment Transactions: Parameters**" screen (Figure: **F110**-2).

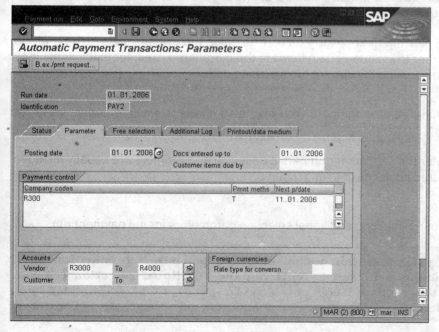

Figure: **F110**-2

You will be maintaining the parameters required for the payment run, in this section. The payment program takes into account the inputs maintained here, to determine the open items to paid and bring out the proposal run and for further processing.

1. **Posting Date (M):** Enter the posting date for the payments. The G/L will be updated with this date for all the payments (defaults from the *'run date'*).
2. **Doc. Entered up to (M):** Enter a date. The system takes into account all the documents posted up to this date for determining the payable open items, and documents after this date will be ignored during the current run.

Under <u>Payment Control</u> window:

3. **Company codes (M):** Enter the company code(s) involved in the current payment run.

> If there is more than one company code entered, the company codes should be separated by a 'comma'. Do *NOT* leave a space after the 'comma'. *Example:* R300,R310. In case of a range of company codes, enter the first and the last company codes within brackets, separated by a comma. *Example:* (R300,R400).

> In case of multiple company codes, they all should be in the same country.

4. **Pmnt meths (M):** Select the payment methods to be used for the current payment run. You would have defined a number of payment methods, which can be used for a particular country. Not necessarily, all of these may be required for the current run.

> The *payment methods* have be to be selected in the order of priority. If the order is, say "CTD", the Check(C) has the first priority for payment consideration, "*Bank Transfer*" (T) is considered second and so on (if payment methods have not been defined either in the line item or master record).

5. **Next p/date (M):** Enter the next posting date. This helps the system while arriving at the open items as whether to include certain items in the current run itself, for these items may become overdue considering the current run's posting date.

Under <u>Accounts</u> window:

6. **Vendor (O):** Enter the Vendor numbers. You may also chose to exclude certain vendors; enter the details in the selection screen by clicking on ⇨.
7. **Customer (O):** Enter the Customer numbers if necessary. Customers are usually included when they have a credit balance in their accounts.

Step-3

Press ▢ Free selection ▢ tab for maintaining additional selection parameters for the payment run.

> You may want to exclude certain documents from open item determination. This kind of restriction is achieved by entering the additional selection criteria (maximum 3) in this section. Fields of tables LFA1, LFB1, KNA1, BSEG, BKPF and KNB1 are used here.

Step-4

Press   Additional Log   tab and enter the details in "**Automatic Payment Transactions: Additional Log**" Screen (Figure: **F110**-3).

 If you need additional details, in the log, you need to maintain certain details in this tab. The system helps you to call for additional processing logic of various steps viz., due date determination, payment method selection etc by entering the required vendor/customer number against each of these options.

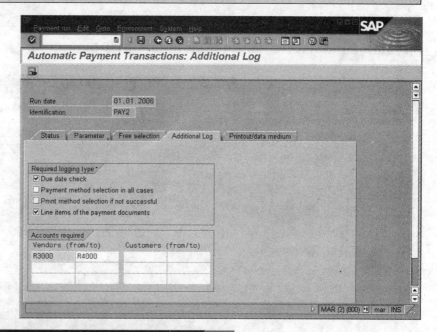

Figure: **F110**-3

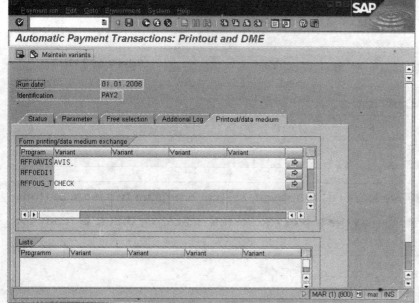

Figure: **F110**-3A

Step-5

Press

  Printout/data medium   tab

to go to "**Automatic Payment Transactions: Printout and DME**" screen (Figure: **F110**-3A) and enter the variant(s) for Form printing / data medium exchange. At least one variant needs to be entered per program.

Step-6

Save the settings (Figure: **F110**-4)

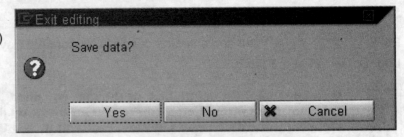

Figure: **F110**-4

System takes you back to the "**Automatic Payments: Status**" screen (Figure: **F110**-5).

Step-7

Press the | Status | tab for current status (Figure: **F110**-5).

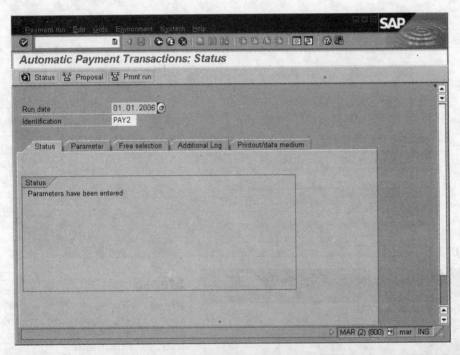

Figure: **F110**-5

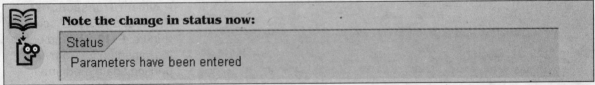

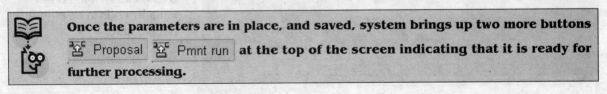

Step-7

Press the 🔧 Proposal button for creating the payment proposal. On the pop-up screen (Figure: **F110-**6), you have the option of starting the proposal immediately or schedule it later.

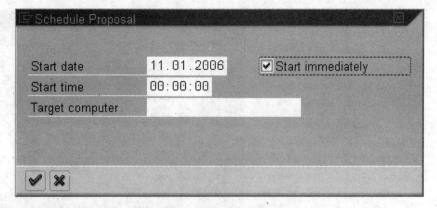

Figure: **F110**-6

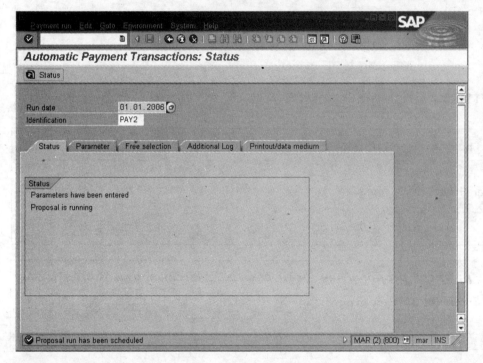

Step-8

Press ✔ after scheduling and the system starts running the proposal (Figure: **F110**-7).

Figure: **F110**-7

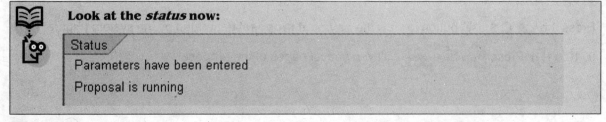

Look at the *status* now:

Status
  Parameters have been entered
  Proposal is running

Step-9

Press 🔄 Status a couple times to refresh the screen (Figure: **F110**-8).

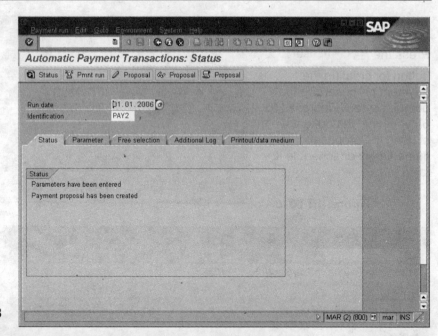

Figure: **F110**-8

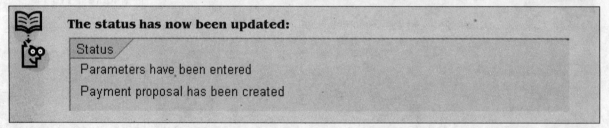

The status has now been updated:

Status

Parameters have been entered

Payment proposal has been created

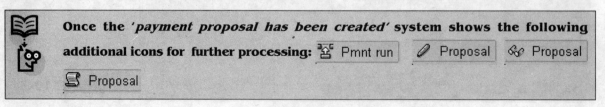

Once the *'payment proposal has been created'* system shows the following additional icons for further processing: Pmnt run   Proposal   Proposal

Proposal

Step-10

Press the Proposal button to view the **payment proposal** generated by the system (Figure: **F110**-9, 10 &11)). Press Next page till you see all pages of the proposal.

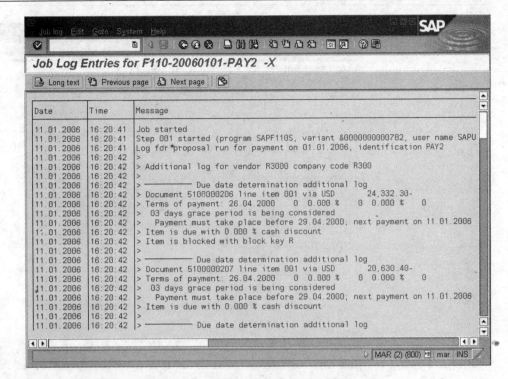

Figure: **F110**-9

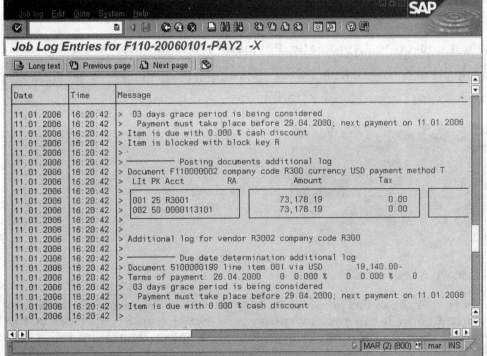

Figure: **F110**-10

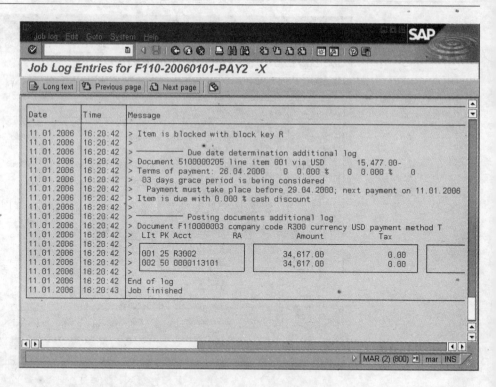

Figure: **F110**-11

Now that you have seen the **proposal list**, you may want to **edit the proposal.**

Step-11

Press the ⬅ button and go to "**Automatic Payment Transactions: Status**" screen.

Press ✎ Proposal to edit the payment proposal. As soon as you press the ✎ Proposal button, system pops – up the following screen (Figure: **F110**-12).

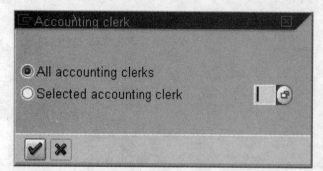

Figure: **F110**-12

 If you want to edit the entire proposal, select 'All accounting clerks' radio button in the above figure. If the second option is selected, you need to select the 'accounting clerk' from the drop-down list to edit proposal items relevant to that particular clerk.

Step-12

Press ✔ and you are taken to the "**Edit Payment proposal: Payments**" screen (Figure: **F110**-13). The screen displays rows where payments as well as exceptions are shown. Both a normal row as well as an exception row can be edited.

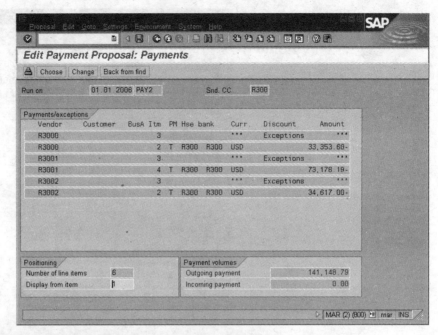

Figure: **F110**-13

Step-13

Place the cursor on the item to be changed (*the 5th line- Vendor R3002-was selected*) and press `Choose`, to display the details of the selected line item. You are now taken to "**Edit Payment Proposal: Open Items**" screen (Figure: **F110**-14). If a payment is '*blocked*' the letter "*R*" appears against that item.

Figure: **F110**-14

Step-14

Double-click on a line (*document number 5100000200*, for example) to change the line item and the system pops-up "**Change Line Item**" screen (Figure: **F110**-15) Now, you can remove the '*payment block*' or *change the cash discount* details. In the example provided below, the '*payment block*' was removed (Figure: **F110**-16).

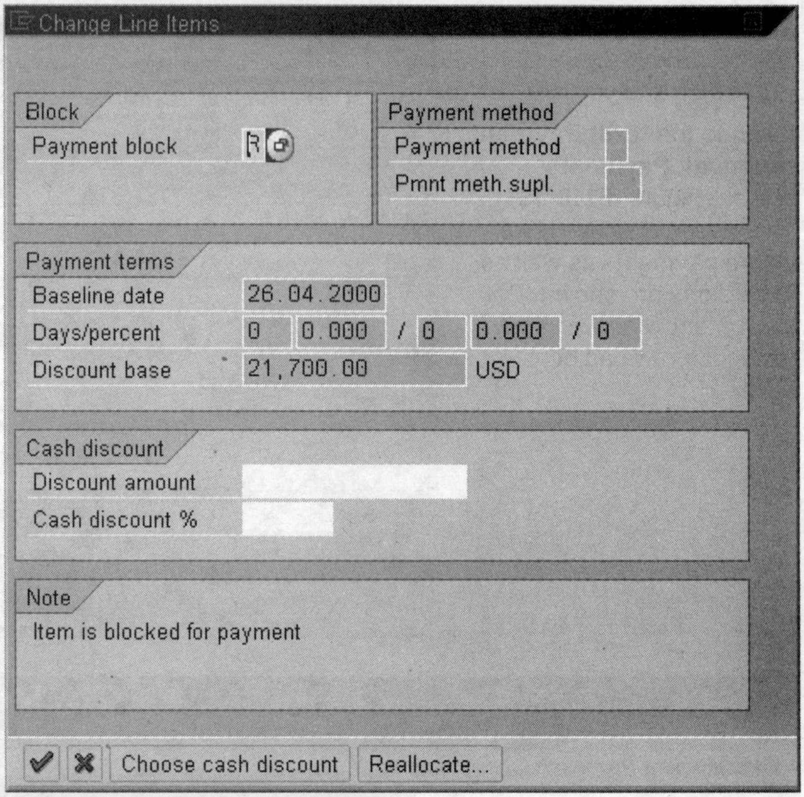

Change Line Items

Block

Payment block   R

Payment method

Payment method

Pmnt meth.supl.

Payment terms

Baseline date   26.04.2000

Days/percent   0   0.000 / 0   0.000 / 0

Discount base   21,700.00   USD

Cash discount

Discount amount

Cash discount %

Note

Item is blocked for payment

Choose cash discount   Reallocate...

Figure: **F110**-15

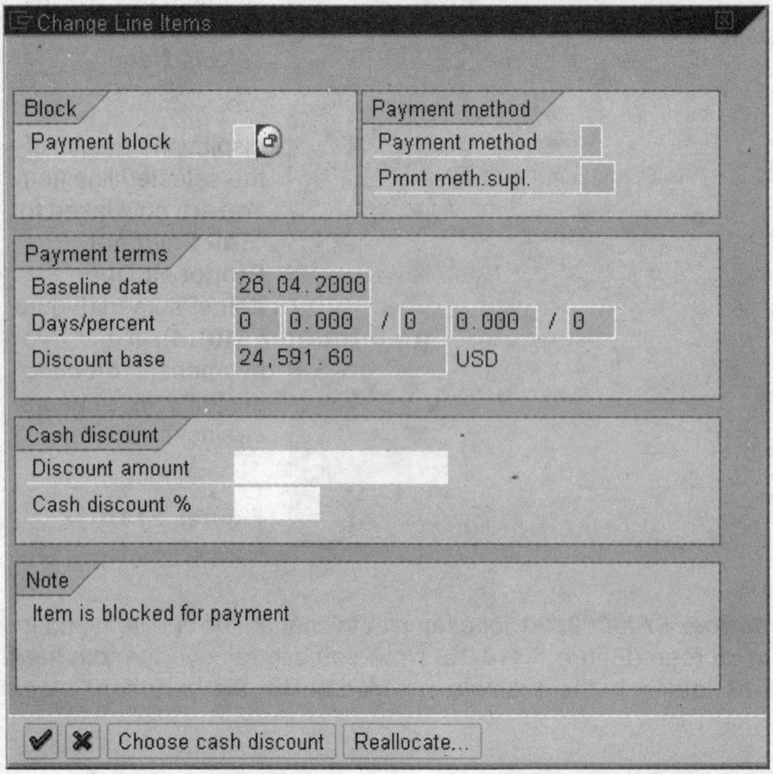

Change Line Items

Block

Payment block

Payment method

Payment method

Pmnt meth.supl.

Payment terms

Baseline date   26.04.2000

Days/percent   0   0.000 / 0   0.000 / 0

Discount base   24,591.60   USD

Cash discount

Discount amount

Cash discount %

Note

Item is blocked for payment

Choose cash discount   Reallocate...

Figure: **F110**-16

Step-15

Press on the *"Change Line Item"* screen to go back to **"Edit Payment Proposal: Open Items"** screen (Figure: F110-17).

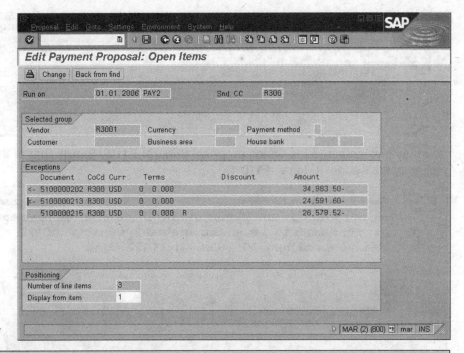

Figure: **F110**-17

All the changed / edited open items will be displayed in a different color (blue, in the example) with a "< -" mark in front of the line item indicating that this item has been edited. You may also notice that the payment block represented by "R" no longer appears against these now un-blocked items.

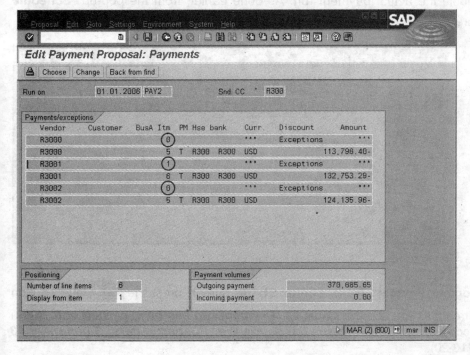

Step-16

When all the exceptions have been suitably edited, the edited proposal is displayed in (Figure: **F110**-18).

Figure: **F110**-18

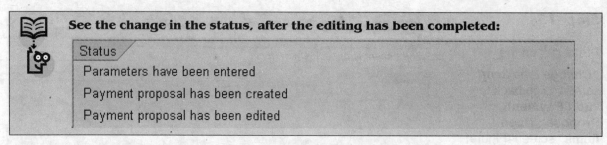

See the change in the status, after the editing has been completed:

> Status
>
> Parameters have been entered
>
> Payment proposal has been created
>
> Payment proposal has been edited

You may now compare the edited proposal (Figure: **F110**-18) with that of the original one proposed earlier by the system (Figure: **F110**-13):

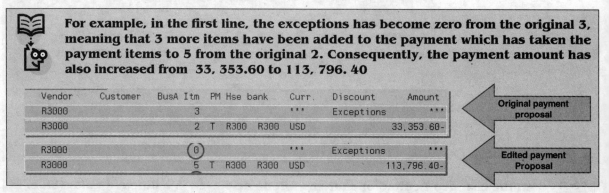

For example, in the first line, the exceptions has become zero from the original 3, meaning that 3 more items have been added to the payment which has taken the payment items to 5 from the original 2. Consequently, the payment amount has also increased from 33, 353.60 to 113, 796. 40

Vendor	Customer	BusA	Itm	PM	Hse	bank	Curr.	Discount	Amount	
R3000			3				***	Exceptions	***	Original payment proposal
R3000			2	T	R300	R300	USD		33,353.60-	
R3000			(0)				***	Exceptions	***	Edited payment Proposal
R3000			5	T	R300	R300	USD		113,796.40-	

Step-17

Press the 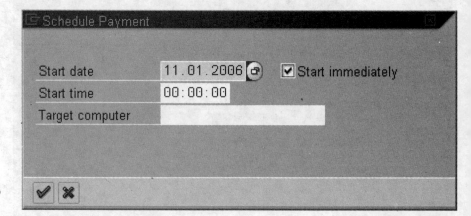 button and go to "**Automatic Payment Transactions: Status**" Screen. Press

⌖ Pmnt run to schedule the actual payment run. As done earlier, from the pop-up "**Schedule Payment**" screen (Figure: F110-19) either it can be started immediately or scheduled for later.

> ⌂ Schedule Payment
>
> Start date   11.01.2006 ⌐   ☑ Start immediately
> Start time   00:00:00
> Target computer
>
> ✔ ✖

Figure: F110-19

Step-18

Press ✔ and on "**Automatic Payment Transactions: Status**" screen, press the ⌂ Status button a couple of times to refresh, till you see the status as "*Payment run has been carried out*". When the payment run is successful, you will also see the details like "*Posting orders: 3 generated, 3 completed*" (Figure: **F110**-20).

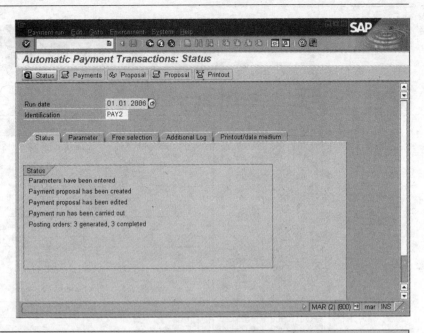

Figure: **F110**-20

Look at the *status* now:

Status
Parameters have been entered
Payment proposal has been created
Payment proposal has been edited
Payment run has been carried out
Posting orders: 3 generated, 3 completed

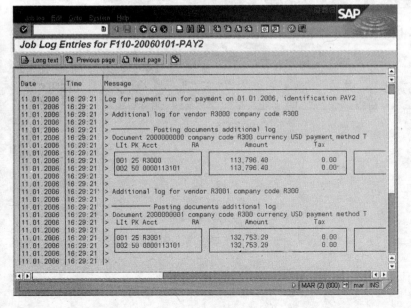

Figure: **F110**-21

Step-19

From "**Automatic Payment Transactions: Status**" screen, you can also view the final log (Figure: F**110**-21 & 22) pertaining to the completed payment run.

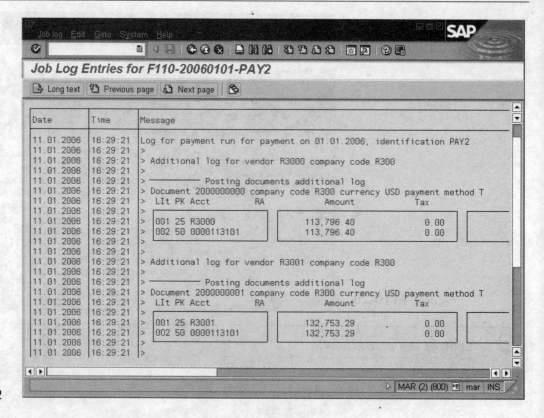

Figure:
F110-22

Step-20

Select the *Menu "Edit >Payments >Display"*, click ✔ in the "**List Variant**" screen (Figure: **F110**-23) and go to "**Display Payment Run: Payments**" screen (Figure: **F110**-24).

Figure:
F110-23

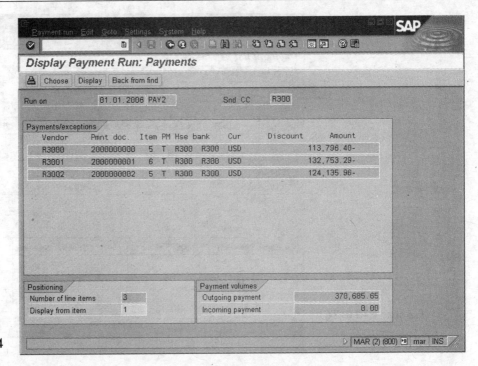

Figure: **F110**-24

Step-21

Go back to "**Automatic Payment Transactions: Status**" Screen by pressing 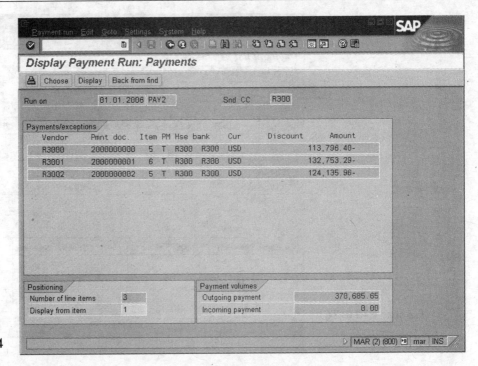. Select *Menu: "Edit >Payments> Exception list"* to display the "**Payment List**" screen (Figure: **F110**-25 & 26).

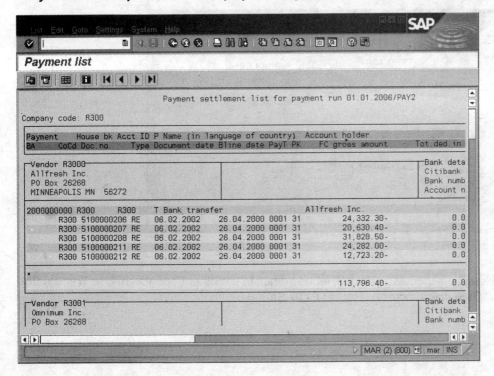

Figure: **F110**-25

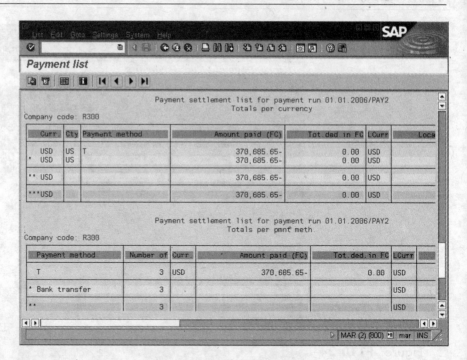

Figure: **F110**-26

Step-22

Go back to "**Automatic Payment Transactions: Status**" screen; press the 🖨 Printout button to print the payment list. On the 'pop-up' screen "**Schedule Print**" (Figure: **F110**-26) maintain the necessary details including '**job name**' which will easily identify this print job from the '**spool request**'.

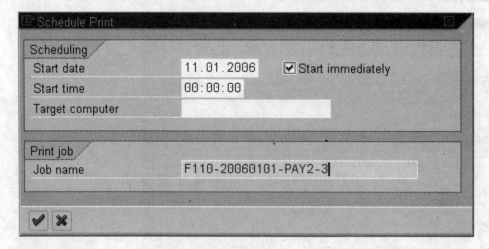

Figure: **F110**-26

Step-23

Since we need to look at the scheduled print job, let us branch to the other transaction. Use **Transaction Code: SMX** to go to "**Own Jobs**" screen (Figure: **F110-SMX**-1).

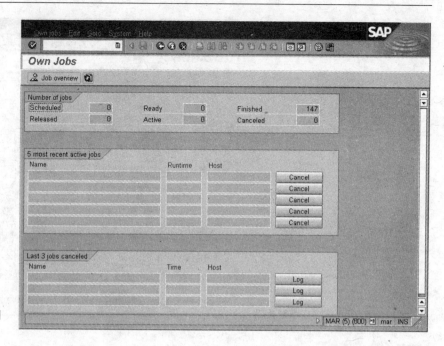

Figure: **F110-SMX**-1

Step-24

Click on 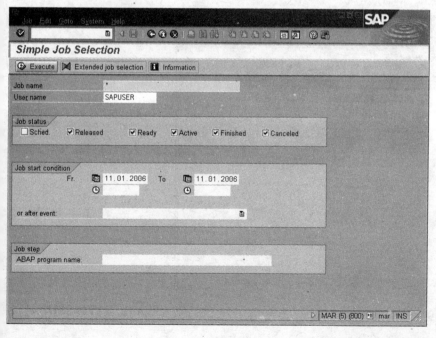 to take you to **"Simple Job Selection"** screen (Figure: **F110-SMX**-2).

Figure: **F110-SMX**-2

Step-25

Press Execute to enter the **"Job Overview screen"** (Figure: **F110-SMX**-3).

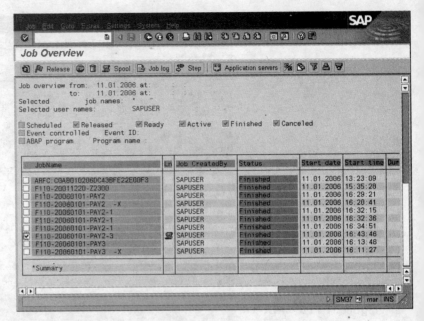

Figure: **F110-SMX**-3

Step-26

Check the relevant "***Job Name***", when the job has been "***Finished***", and press Spool . This will take you to "***Output Controller: List of Spool Requests***" screen (Figure: **F110-SMX**-4).

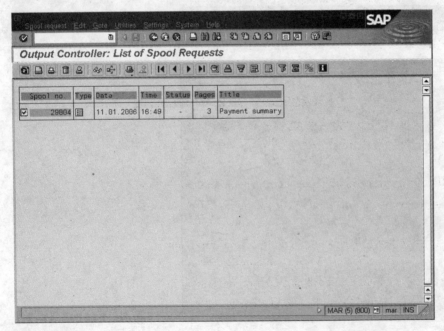

Figure: **F110-SMX**-4

Step-27

Select the relevant "***Spool no.***" and click to display the details (Figure: **F110-SMX**-5) from where the same can be printed.

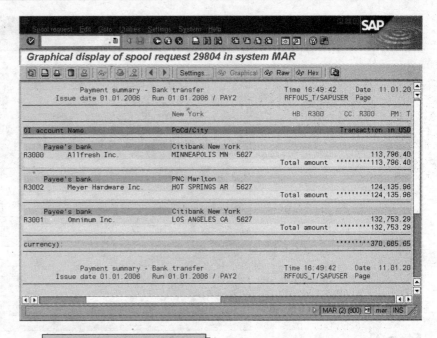

Figure: **F110-SMX**-5

End of Transaction

However, to check how the payment run updates the masters and ledger accounts we need to go little further, as detailed below:

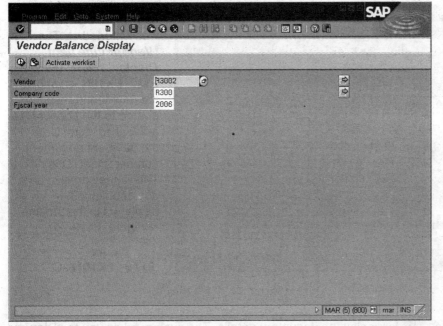

Step-A

Use Transaction Code **FK10N,** and you will be taken to **"Vendor Balance Display"** screen (Figure: **F110- FK10N** -A).

Figure:
F110- FK10N -A

Step-B

Enter the **Vendor, Company code & Fiscal year** and press *F8*, and you are taken to **"Vendor Balance Display"** screen (Figure: **F110- FK10N** -B). You can view the period-wise balances for the vendor selected and also the cumulative balance.

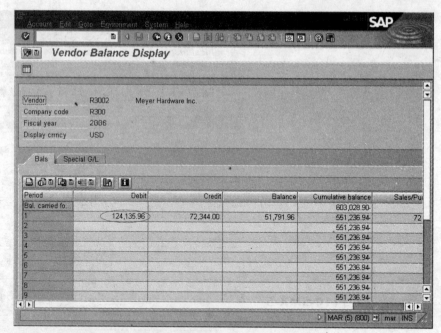

Figure: **F110- FK10N** -B

Step-C

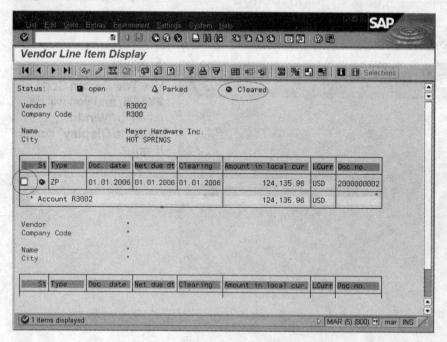

Double Click on the *'debit'* column against the relevant posting period line (in our example the payment run was in period 1). The "*Vendor Line Item Display*" screen (Figure: **F110- FK10N** -C) shows the payment transaction posted to the account as a '*cleared'* item. Note the payment document number under "Doc.no". This is the same document number displayed in the 3rd line in Figure: **F110**-24).

Figure:
F110- FK10N -C

Step-D

Select the line item and press ⚙ to display the document details. The system takes you to "**Display document: Line Item 001**" screen (Figure: **F110- FK10N** -D). *Note the baseline date, payment method, clearing date, document number, and amount, which have been updated automatically by the payment run program*.

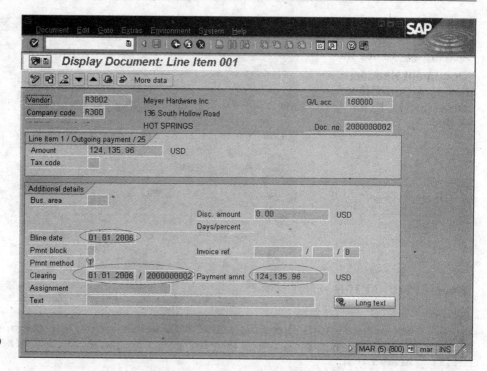

Figure:
F110- FK10N -D

Step-E

Click on 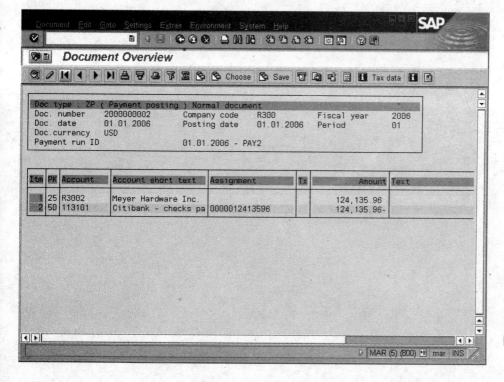 to see the **"Document Overview"** screen (Figure: **F110- FK10N** –E).

Figure:
F110- FK10N –E

Step-F

Click on to see the
**"Document Header:
Company Code R300"**
screen (Figure: **F110-FK10N** –F).

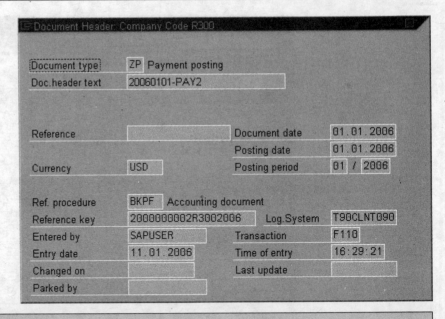

Document type	ZP Payment posting
Doc.header text	20060101-PAY2

Reference		Document date	01.01.2006
		Posting date	01.01.2006
Currency	USD	Posting period	01 / 2006
Ref. procedure	BKPF Accounting document		
Reference key	2000000002R3002006	Log.System	T90CLNT090
Entered by	SAPUSER	Transaction	F110
Entry date	11.01.2006	Time of entry	16:29:21
Changed on		Last update	
Parked by			

Figure: **F110- FK10N** –E

> The screen shows the details like document type used in the posting of the items by the payment program. It also identifies the payment run (*PAY2*) in the document header test.

FI - AR
Accounts
Receivable

1

AR - Easy Access: FDMN

Transaction Code	FDMN

Transaction Overview

The **Transaction FDMN** provides you with all the necessary transactions under FI-AR (Accounts Receivable) for document entry, account analysis, master creation, credit management, archiving, periodic processing and reporting. As in any other 'Easy Access' menu, this menu also groups these transactions conveniently into:

- Document entry
- Account
- Credit management
- Reporting
- Information system
- Document
- Master records
- Periodic processing
- Withholding tax
- Environment

As a single point ready reference, all the transactions in all the above groups have been expanded and nicely arranged in a table at the end of this transaction.

Transaction Steps

Step-1

Access the transaction either by the transaction code or by the menu, and you will be taken to "**SAP Easy Access Customers**" Screen (Figure: **FDMN**-1).

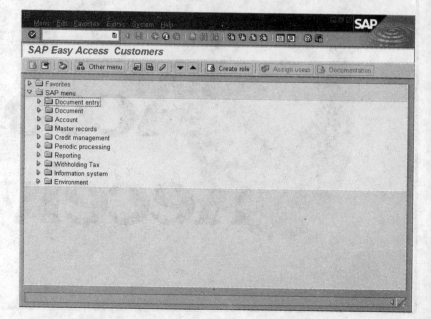

Figure: **FDMN**-1

Step-2

Expand "**Document Entry**" folder to view the transaction codes/menu for **(a) Document entry, (b) Payment advice, (c) Down Payment, (d) Bill of exchange, (e) Other and (f) Reference documents** (Figure: **FDMN**-2).

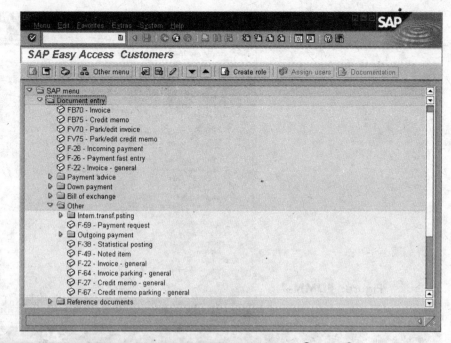

Figure: **FDMN**-2

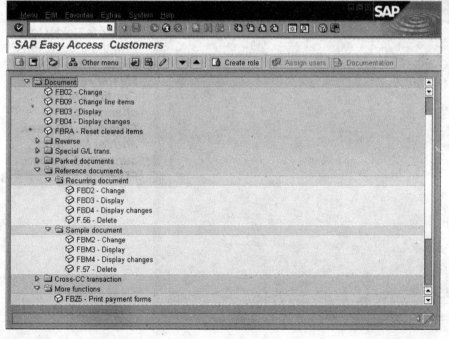

Figure: **FDMN**-3

Step-3

Expand "**Document**" folder to view the transaction codes/menu for **(a) Document, (b) Reverse, (c) Spl G/L trans., (d) Parked documents, (e) Reference documents-Recurring document, Sample document, (f) Cross company code transactions and (g) More functions** (Figure: **FDMN**-3).

Step-4

Expand "**Account**" folder to view the transaction codes/menu for **(a) Account, (b) Correspondence and (c) Assignment** (Figure: **FDMN**-4).

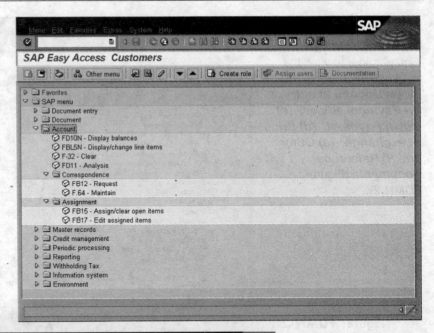

Figure: **FDMN**-4

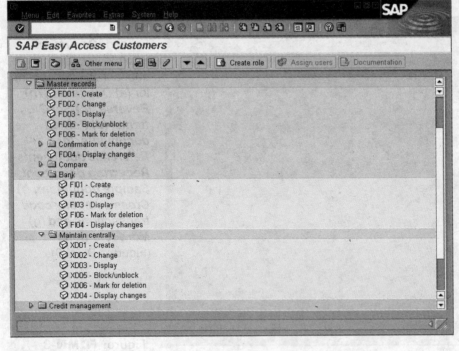

Figure: **FDMN**-5

Step-5

Expand *"Master Records"* folder to view the transaction codes/menu for *(a) Master records, (b) Confirmation of change, (c) Compare, (d) Bank and (e) Maintain centrally* (Figure: **FDMN**-5).

Step-6

Expand *"Credit management"* folder to view the transaction codes/menu for *(a) Exceptions, (b) Sales and distribution docs, (c) Account, (d) Item, (e) Master data (f) Credit management info system and (g) Tools* (Figure: **FDMN**-6).

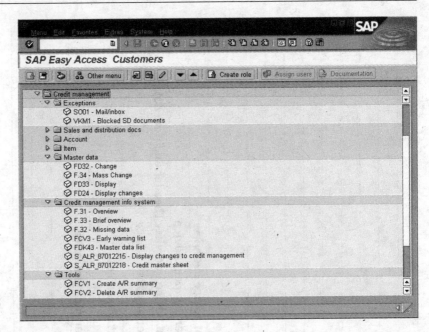

Figure: **FDMN**-6

Step-7

Expand *"Periodic Processing"* folder to view the transaction codes/menu for (a) *Schedule manager, Dunning, Multi-level dunning of bill of exchange requests, (b) Interest calculation-Arrears interest, Balance interest, Payments, Automatic clearing, (c) Print correspondence, (d) Recurring entries, (e) Bill of exchange processing-General, (f) Payment cards (g) Archiving and (h) Closing* (Figure: FDMN-7).

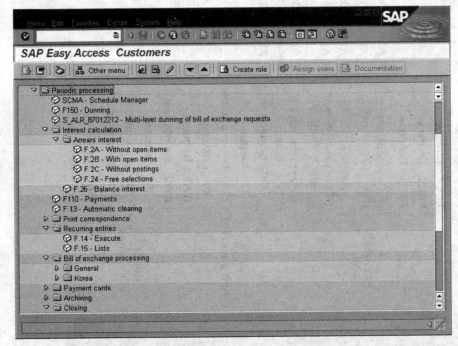

Figure: **FDMN**-7

The entire transactions under *FDMN* are tabulated on the following pages for your ready reference:

Document entry			
FB70 - Invoice			
FB75 - Credit memo			
FV70 - Park/edit invoice			
FV75 - Park/edit credit memo			
FB15 - Incoming payment			
F-26 - Payment fast entry			
F-26 - Payment fast entry			
Payment advice	FBE1 - Create		
	FBE2 - Change		
	FBE3 - Display		
	FBE6 - Delete		
	Payment advice overview	S_ALR_87012201 - Payment advice overview	
		S_ALR_87012200 - Customer payment advice	
	Payment advice overview (header and item data)	S_ALR_87012203 - Payment advice overview (header and item data)	
		S_ALR_87012202 - Customer payment advice	
	Payment advice notes: Reorganization	S_ALR_87012205 - Payment advice notes: Reorganization	
		S_ALR_87012204 - Customer reorganization	
Down payment	F-37 - Request		
	F-29 - Down payment		
	F-39 - Clearing		
Bill of exchange	FBW1 - Request		
	FBW2 - By request		
	F-36 - Payment		
	F-33 - Discounting		
	F-34 - Collection		
	F-35 - Forfeiting		
	F-20 - Reverse contingent liability		

- **Document**
  - FB02 - Change
  - FB09 - Change line items
  - FB03 - Display
  - FB04 - Display changes
  - FBRA - Reset cleared items
  - **Reverse**
    - FB08 - Individual reversal
    - F.80 - Mass reversal
    - F-23 - Reverse bill of exchange request'
    - F-19 - Reverse statistical posting
    - F-25 - Reverse check/bill of exchange
  - **Special G/L trans.**
  - **Parked**
    - FBV0 - Post/delete
- **Reference documents**
  - FKMT - Account assignment model
  - FBD1 - Recurring document
  - F-01 - Sample document
- **Other**
  - FBW5 - Check/bill of exchange
  - **Intern.transf.psting**
    - F-21 - Without clearing
    - F-30 - With clearing
  - F-59 - Payment request
  - **Outgoing payment**
    - F-38 - Statistical posting
    - F-49 - Noted item
    - F-22 - Invoice - general
    - F-64 - Invoice parking - general
    - F-27 - Credit memo - general
    - F-67 - Credit memo parking - general

Account			
documents	FV70 - One-Screen Transaction for Posting/Deleting		
	FBV2 - Change		
	FV70 - One-Screen Transaction for Changes		
	FBV3 - Display		
	FBV4 - Change header		
	FBV5 - Display changes		
	FBV6 - Refuse		
Reference documents	Recurring document	FBD2 - Change	
		FBD3 - Display	
		FBD4 - Display changes	
		F.56 - Delete	
	Sample document	FBM2 - Change	
		FBM3 - Display	
		FBM4 - Display changes	
		F.57 - Delete	
Cross-CC transaction	FBU2 - Change		
	FBU3 - Display		
	FBU8 - Reverse		
More functions	FBZ5 - Print payment forms		
FD10N - Display balances			
FBL5N - Display/change line items			
F-32 - Clear			
FD11 - Analysis			
Correspondence	FB12 - Request		
	F.64 - Maintain		

Master records

- **Assignment**
  - FB15 - Assign/clear open items
  - FB17 - Edit assigned items
- FD01 - Create
- FD02 - Change
- FD03 - Display
- FD05 - Block/unblock
- FD06 - Mark for deletion
- **Confirmation of change**
  - FD08 - Single
  - FD09 - List
- FD04 - Display changes
- **Compare**
  - F.2D - Sales - accounting
  - Company codes
  - FD15 - Send
  - FD16 - Receive
- **Bank**
  - FI01 - Create
  - FI02 - Change
  - FI03 - Display
  - FI06 - Mark for deletion
  - FI04 - Display changes
- **Maintain centrally**
  - XD01 - Create
  - XD02 - Change
  - XD03 - Display
  - XD05 - Block/unblock
  - XD06 - Mark for deletion
- **Exceptions**
  - SO01 - Mail/inbox
  - VKM1 - Blocked SD documents

Credit Management		
Sales and distribution docs	VKM2 - Released	
	VKM4 - All	
	VKM3 - Sales document	
	VKM5 - Delivery	
	V.01 - Incomplete SD Documents	
	VA14L - Sales and distrib. Documents blocked for delivery	
	VL06 - Deliveries	
	VF05 - Billling documents	
Account	FD10N - Display balances	
	FD11 - Analysis	
Item	FBL5 - Display	
	FBL6 - Change	
Master data	FD32 - Change	
	F.34 - Mass Change	
	FD33 - Display	
	FD24 - Display changes	
Credit management info system	F.31 - Overview	
	F.33 - Brief overview	
	F.32 - Missing data	
	FCV3 - Early warning list	
	FDK43 - Master data list	
	S_ALR_87012215 - Display changes to credit management	
	S_ALR_87012218 - Credit master sheet	
Tools	FCV1 - Create A/R summary	

- **Periodic processing**
  - FCV2 - Delete A/R summary
  - F.28 - Reset credit limit
  - SCMA - Schedule Manager
  - F150 - Dunning
  - S_ALR_87012212 - Multi-level dunning of bill of exchange requests
  - **Interest Calculation**
    - **Arrears interest**
      - F.2A - Without open items
      - F.2B - With open items
      - F.2C - Without postings
      - F.24 - Free selections
    - F.26 - Balance interest
  - F110 - Payments
  - F.13 - Automatic clearing
  - **Print correspondence**
    - F.61 - As per requests
    - F.63 - Delete requests
    - F.27 - Periodic account statements
    - F.62 - Internal documents
    - **Standard letters**
      - SO10 - Enter text
      - F.65 - Issue letters
      - F.17 - Print letters
    - **Balance confirmation**
      - F.1B - Create index
      - F.1A - Group customers

- **Recurring entries**
  - F.14 - Execute
  - F.15 - Lists
- **Bill of exchange processing**
  - General
    - S_ALR_87012208 - Bill of exchange list
    - S_ALR_87012209 - Extended bill of exchange list with List viewer
    - S_ALR_87012211 - Maintain bill of exchange liability
  - Korea
    - FCC1 - Settle
    - FCC2 - Repeat settlement
    - FCC4 - Display logs
    - FCC3 - Delete logs
    - FBRC - Reset cleared items
    - FCCR - Standard reports
- **Payment cards**
- **Archiving**
  - F48A - Documents
  - F64A - Transaction figures
  - FCAA - Checks
  - F56A - Customers
  - F61A - Banks
- **Closing**
  - Check/count
    - F.03 - Comparison
    - F.2E - Reconcile affiliated companies
    - F.17 - Balance confirmation: Print
    - F.1B - Balance confirmation: Create index
    - F.1A - Balance confirmation: Group customers
  - Valuate
    - F107 - Further valuations
    - F.05 - Open items in foreign currency
    - F103 - Receivables transfer posting (gross)
    - F104 - Reserve for bad debt (gross)

- FJA4 - Inflation adjustment of open items in foreign currency
- FJA5 - Inflation adjustment of open receivables in local currency
- Regroup
  - F101 - Receivables/payables
- Document
  - All accounts
    - From balance audit trail data
      - S_ALR_87012187 - Extract for the accumulated historical balance audit trail
      - S_ALR_87012188 - Account balance from accumulated historical balance audit trail
      - S_ALR_87012189 - Historical balance audit trail by alternative account number
    - S_ALR_87012190 - Open item account balance audit trail from the document
  - Open item accounts
    - From balance audit trail
      - S_ALR_87012191 - Extract for accumulated open item balance audit trail
      - S_ALR_87012192 - Acct balance from accumulated open item balance audit trail
      - S_ALR_87012193 - Open item balance audit trail by alternative account number
- Carry forward
  - F.07 - Balances
- Withholding Tax
  - S_P00_07000134 - Generic withholding tax reporting
- Information system
  - Reports for Accounts Receivable Accounting
    - Customer Balances
      - S_ALR_87012167 - Accounts Receivable Information System
      - S_ALR_87012172 - Customer Balances in Local Currency.
      - S_ALR_87012186 - Customer Sales
      - S_ALR_87012169 - Transaction Figures: Account Balance
      - S_ALR_87012170 - Transaction Figures: Special Sales

Customers: Items	S_ALR_87012171 - Transaction Figures: Sales
	S_ALR_87012168 - Due Date Analysis for Open Items
	S_ALR_87012173 - List of Customer Open Items for Printing
	S_ALR_87012175 - Open Items - Customer Due Date Forecast
	S_ALR_87012176 - Customer Evaluation with OI Sorted List
	S_ALR_87012177 - Customer Payment History
	S_ALR_87012178 - Customer Open Item Analysis by Balance of Overdue Items
	S_ALR_87012198 - List of Cleared Customer Items for Printing
	S_ALR_87012199 - List Of Down Payments Open On Key Date - Customers
Master Data	S_ALR_87012179 - Customer List
	S_ALR_87012180 - Address List
	S_ALR_87012182 - Display Changes to Customers
	S_ALR_87012183 - Display/Confirm Critical Customer Changes
	S_ALR_87012195 - Customer Master Data Comparison
Configure	OBAN - Specify data volume
	OBAJ - Select evaluations
	F.29 - Create evaluations
Tools	F.30 - Display evaluations
	FQUD - Query for accounts receivable
User parameters	FB07 - Control totals
	FB00 - Editing options
Current settings	S_BCE_68000174 - Enter exchange rates
	S_ALR_87003642 - Open and close posting periods
	S_ALR_87001486 - Available amounts for the payment program
	S_ALR_87001320 - Enter interest rates
	S_ALR_87001487 - Bank selection for payment program
Environment	

- S_ALR_87002510 - Enter time interest terms
- S_ALR_87002678 - Enter reference interest values
- S_ALR_87003149 - Maintain worklist for displaying open items
- S_ALR_87003131 - Maintain worklist for displaying balances
- S_ALR_87001405 - Define failed payment transactions (bills of exchange)
- Check information
  - Display
    - FCH1 - For check
    - FCH2 - For payment document
    - FCHN - Check register
  - Change
    - FCH4 - Renumber
    - FCH7 - Reprint check
    - FCH6 - Additional info/cash
    - FCHR - Online cashed checks
    - FCHT - Assignment to payment
  - Create
    - FCH5 - Manual checks
  - Void
    - FCH3 - Unused checks
    - FCH9 - Issued checks
    - FCH8 - Cancel payment
  - Delete
    - FCHD - For payment run
    - FCHF - Manual checks
    - FCHE - Voided checks
    - FCHG - Reset data
  - FCHX - External data transfer

	FBWARI0EA - FI Internet: Customer line items
	FNETSCA2 - Customer: Change address
	FNETSCB1 - Customer: Create bank details
	FNETSCB2 - Customer: Change bank details
	FNETSCB6 - Customer: Delete bank details
Internet functions	FB16EA - Assign items
FXMN - Additional components	

2

AR - Post Incoming Payments: FB15

Transaction Code	FB15
Menu	Accounting > Financial Accounting > Account Receivable > Document entry > Incoming payment > Post

Business Process Overview

The clearing functions in SAP support processing of incoming payments from the business partners. *Incoming payments*, from customers, are usually for clearing their invoices as against the incoming payments from vendors, which could be for a business transaction like refund from vendor.

The clearing can be done (1) manually or (2) automatically using SAP's clearing program.

Under *manual clearing*, you will select the open items, based on the incoming payment, so that the selected open items are cleared. In cases like refunds from a vendor or transactions involving bank sub accounts and clearing accounts etc, you will resort to manual clearing. When cleared, the system flags these line items as 'cleared', creates a clearing document and enters the clearing document number and clearing date in these open items. Besides the clearing document, the system may also generate additional documents in cases like partial or residual processing, and for posting the loss / gain to the assigned G/L account.

The transaction is same as *Transaction Code: F-06, Menu: Accounting > Financial Accounting > G/L > Document entry > Incoming payment > Post.*

Transaction Steps

Step-1

Access the transaction either by the transaction code or menu, and you will be taken to "**Post Incoming Payments: Header Data**" screen (Figure: **FB15**-1).

Figure: **FB15**-1

Enter the details as outlined below:

1. **Document Date (M):** Enter the date of the document. (This can never be later than the 'Posting Date').

2. **Posting Date (M):** Enter the posting date.

3. **Company Code (M):** If this is the first occasion, a particular company is posted to, then you may need to enter the company Code. For all the subsequent transactions of the day, the same Company Code is defaulted.

4. **(Document) Type (M)** is defaulted to "**DZ**" when we selected the *Transaction: FB15* which relates to manual incoming payments.

Remember, SAP comes delivered with several document types, used in G/L, customer, vendor postings etc, like:

    AB General Documents

    SA   All G/L documents

    DR   Customer Invoice

    DG   Customer Cr memo

    DZ   Customer Payment

    KG   Vendor Cr memo

    KZ   Vendor Payment

    KR   Vendor Invoice

You may use *Transaction: OBA7* to define a new document type, or use *Transaction: OBAB* to rename an existing document type.

Posting Period (M) is defaulted from the posting date entered in the document. You may need to change this if you want the posting period to correspond to any other period like a 'special period'.

5. **Currency/rate (M):** The Company Code currency is defaulted; if required you may enter another currency to post the document.

In the Bank data area:

6. **Account (M):** Select the G/L account (Bank) to which the incoming payment is to be posted.

7. **Amount (M):** Enter the amount of the incoming payment.

8. You may also enter the **Value date (O)**, if it is going to be different from that of the posting date.

9. **Text (O):** Maintain some explanatory text which will possibly identify this payment.

10. **Business Area(O):** if business area accounting is active, enter the relevant business area to where this payment should be updated.

In the Open Item Selection block of the screen:

11. **Account (M):** Enter the Customer account from whom the payment is being received.

12. **Account type (M):** Select 'D' from the drop-down list.

13. **Standard O/Is (M):** Select the check-box so that the system considers the standard open items only.

14. **Automatic Search (O):** If this check box is selected, the system is going to search for open items which will match the payment amount entered in (7).

Step-2

Press button or

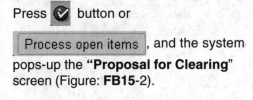 , and the system pops-up the **"Proposal for Clearing"** screen (Figure: **FB15**-2).

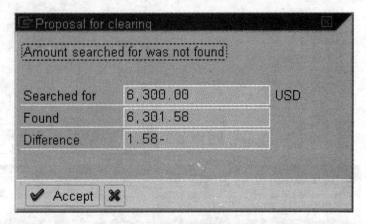

Figure: **FB15**-2

📖 **Note that the system was unable to find an exact match to clear the open item with the incoming payment amount entered, and is proposing to you to accept it for further processing. Either you can accept or go back to Step-1 and change the amount to match the open item amount selected by the system.**

Step-3

Press ✔ Accept , and the system takes you to the **Post Incoming Payments: Process Open Items"** screen (Figure: **FB15**-3).You can see from the screen that the system has actually assigned the line item with 6301.58 against the incoming payment of 6300. So, the 'Not assigned' amount is shown as 1.58, which needs to be effectively dealt with for putting through the transaction. If this has been due to an error, you may correct it by entering the correct amount by going back to screen Figure: **FB15**-1.

The *payment difference* can be treated the way it is configured in the system. If the difference is within the tolerance limit, defined in the system using the *tolerance groups* (defined at the company code level), the cash discount is adjusted or the system automatically posts the difference to a gain/loss account. When the payment difference exceeds the limits of defined tolerance, then the incoming amount may be processed as a *partial payment* (the original open item is not cleared, but the incoming payment is posted with a reference to that invoice) or the difference is posted as the *residual item* (the original open item is cleared and a new open item created by the system for the difference amount) in the system.

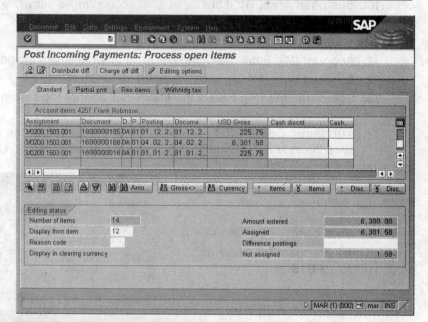

Figure: **FB15**-3

Post Incoming Payments: Display Overview

Figure: **FB15**-4

Step-4

Press Charge off diff. and the system takes you to "**Post Incoming Payments: Display Overview**" screen (Figure: **FB15**-4) where you can post the difference amount of 1.58 and charge it off to square the transaction.

Under Other line item:
1. **PstKy (M):** Enter the posting key (debit) to charge off the difference.
2. **Account (M)**: Enter the relevant G/L account.

Step-5

Press ✅ button and you are taken to "**Post Incoming Payments: Add G/L account item**" screen (Figure: **FB15**-5).

Figure: **FB15**-5

Under <u>Item2/ Debit entry / 40</u>:
1. **Amount (M):** Enter the amount to be charged-off (in our example 1.58).
2. **Value date (M):** Enter the value date.
3. **Text (M)**: Enter an explanation.

Step-6

Press 🖼 to display the line items, which will be posted. You are now taken to "**Post Incoming Payments: Display Overview**" screen (Figure: **FB15**-6) where you can see both credits and debits are equal leaving a zero balance, indicating that you can now post the document.

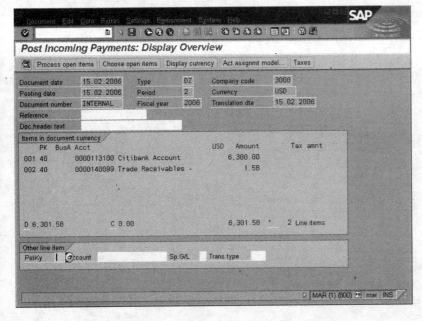

Figure: **FB15**-6

Step-8

Press 🖫 button to post (Figure: **FB15-8**).

Figure: **FB15**-8

> **Information**
>
> ℹ️ Document 1400000000 was posted in company code 3000
>
> [✔ OK]   [Help]

3

AR-Document, Mass Reversal: F.80

Transaction Code	F.80
Menu	Accounting > Financial Accounting > Accounts Receivable > Document > Reverse > Mass reversal

Business Process Overview

Reversal is necessary when you want to correct a document, which has already been posted to in the system. As SAP does not allow you to change the document once it is posted; corrections are to be made by reversing the original posting and posting a new document or by making additional postings.

Mass reversal of documents is a time saving transaction enabling you to reverse any number of documents, should there be a requirement for doing the same in one ,go. But, as in any other transaction, you are provided with the options like (1) test run, to look at the documents proposed by the system for reversal before actual reversal (2) looking at each of the documents by drilling down further. Also, it makes your job easier, by displaying a list of both:

1. Documents that can be reversed
2. Documents that can not be reversed

The other options are:

- Reverse documents posted on a particular posting date or dates
- Reverse documents relating to certain document types
- Reverse documents belonging to a specific fiscal year
- Reverse known document numbers or range of numbers

Transaction Steps

Step-1

Access the transaction either by the transaction code or by the menu and you will be taken to "**Mass Reversal of Documents: Initial Screen**" (Figure: **F.80**-1).

Figure: **F.80**-1

Enter the following details, to enable the system to bring out the documents which would be reversed. Always ensure that you maintain adequate selection parameters to retrieve only the necessary data, so as not to load the system unduly:

1. **Company code (O)**: Enter the company code(s).
2. **Document number (O)**: Enter the document number range to restrict the data selection, if required.
3. **Fiscal year (O):** Enter the fiscal year(s).

Under <u>General selection</u>:

4. **Document type (O)**: Enter the document type(s) if you need to restrict to certain types of documents.
5. **Posting date (O):** Enter the date(s).

Under <u>Reverse posting details</u>:

1. **Reason for reversal (M):** Select a reason for reversing the documents.
2. **Posting date (O):** Enter the posting date the reversal documents to bear.
3. **Posting period (O):** Enter the posting period, if you want the reversed documents to be posted to a specific period than the current period.
4. **Test run (O):** Always a good practice to tick this so as to have a look at the documents to be reversed, before actually carrying out the reversals.

Step-2

Press '**F8**' or ⊕ , and the system will bring up the documents in "**Mass reversal of Documents: Log Test run**" screen (Figure: **F.80**-2).

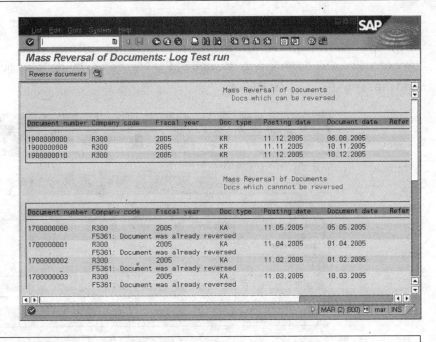

Figure: **F.80**-2

 The system brings up a proposal displaying:
- **Documents which can be reversed**
- **Documents which can not be reversed**

You may need to spend time looking at the information carefully before deciding to reverse the documents enmass, to avoid problems at a later stage. If necessary, select a document and press to look at the details before deciding.

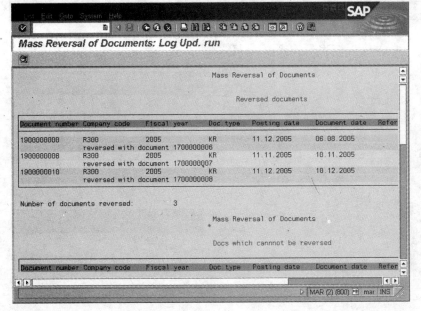

Figure: **F.80**-3

Step-3

Once you are ready to reverse all the documents displayed under "**Docs which can be reversed**" section of the display, press

Reverse documents and the system reverses all those documents and shows the details under " **Reversed documents**" section on the "**Mass Reversal of Documents: Log Upd. run**" screen (Figure: **F.80**-3).

   1. **Reversal Reason (M):** Enter a reversal reason, selecting from the drop-down list.

Step-4

You can also drill down further to look at the line items, by double clicking a line or selecting a line and pressing 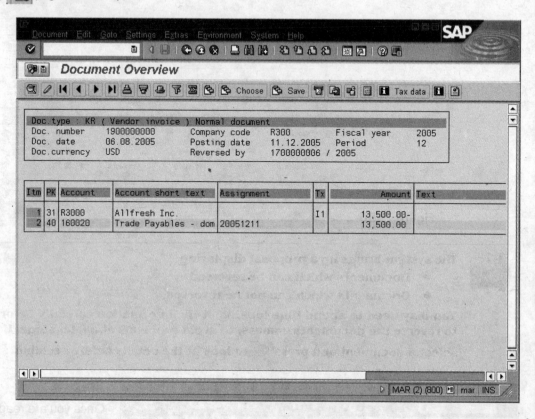(Figure: **F.80**-4).

Figure:
F.80-4

4

AR - Post Customer Invoice: FB70

Transaction Code	FB70
Menu	Accounting > Financial Accounting > Accounts Receivable > Document entry > Invoice

Business Process Overview

Use this transaction to post the invoices directly, and also credit memo, using the G/L invoice entry screens.

As in any document posting, you need to make sure that the amount posted goes to the correct G/L / Customer accounts, tax is properly calculated by selecting the appropriate tax codes suggested by the system or correcting the same when necessary, ensuring that the posting is done to the relevant posting period. These precautions will obviate the needs for a correction at a later stage by posting a reversal or additional document.

The document needs to be entered using the correct template by selecting the same form the initial screen.

Transaction Steps

Step-1

Access the transaction either by the transaction code or menu, and you will be taken to "**Enter Customer Invoice**" screen (Figure: **FB70**-1).

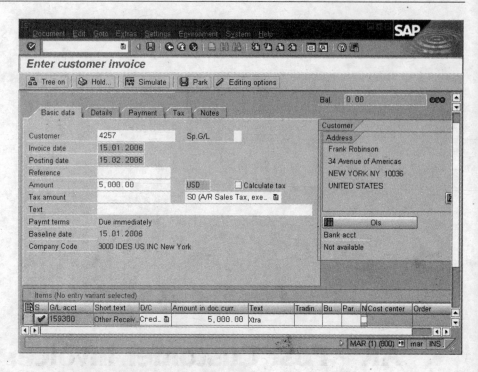

Figure: **FB70**-1

Under Basic data tab, enter the details as outlined below:

1. **Customer (M):** Enter the customer number.
2. **Document Date (M):** Enter the date of the document. (This can never be later than the 'Posting Date'). This is the date of original document like invoice etc.
3. **Posting Date (M):** Enter the posting date. This can be different from the document date.
4. **Currency/rate (M):** The Company Code currency is defaulted; if required you may enter another currency to post the document.
5. **Reference (O):** Enter a reference, if any.
6. **Tax amount (O):** Enter the tax, if it is manually calculated or select from the drop down the applicable tax rate.
7. **Text (O):** Enter an explanatory text.
8. **Company code (M):** Enter or change the company code.

 Company code is defaulted from the user settings. Also, the company code entered for the first transaction will always be defaulted for the subsequent transactions for the day. You can also change the defaulted company code. Use the Menu: Edit > Change the company code or Press 'F7".

In Items:

9. **G/L acct (M):** Enter the relevant G/L account number.
10. **D/C (M):** Select either 'Debit' or 'Credit' as the case may be.
11. **Amount in doc. curr (M):** Enter the amount to be posted.
12. **Tax (O):** Enter the tax code; for all tax relevant accounts, tax code is mandatory.
13. **Value date (O):** Enter a date if the value date is different from the posting date.

14. **Cost Centre (O):** If the G/L account requires a cost center or CO object assignment, then this filed becomes mandatory.

Step-2

Select | Payment | tab in the document header and enter relevant information if any (Figure: **FB70**-2).

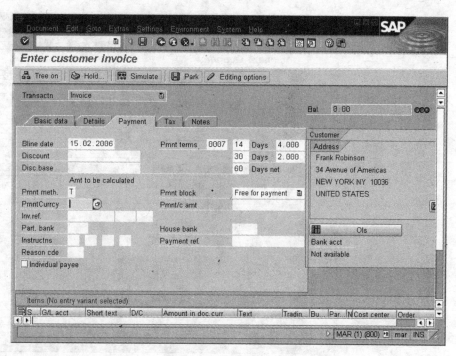

Figure: **FB70**-2

1. **Blinedate (O):** Enter the baseline date, if different from the posting date.
2. **Pmnt terms (O):** Enter or change the payment terms.
3. **Pmnt method (O):** Enter or change the payment method.

 Use the other tabs like *"Details", "Tax" or "Notes"* to maintain the relevant information or to change the default entries proposed by the system like the payment terms or tax code etc.

Step-3

When all the line items have been entered, press .

 The total debit amount must equal the total credit amount and the indicator light must be green ⭕⭕⭕ . Correct any warning or error messages displayed at the bottom left of the screen (Status bar). Warning messages appear in yellow ⭕⭕⭕ and must be noted, corrected if necessary. To ignore the warning and to proceed further, press the enter key. Error messages appear in red ⭕⭕⭕ and must be corrected before the document can be posted.

Step-4

Click on 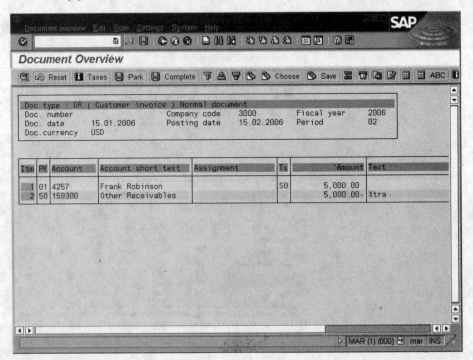 Simulate to view how the document will look like, in respect of all the entries. At this point, the system also displays the system-generated postings (like, tax etc) and displays the same along with the line items entered by you, in the "**Document Overview**" screen (Figure: **FB70**-4).

Figure: **FB70**-4

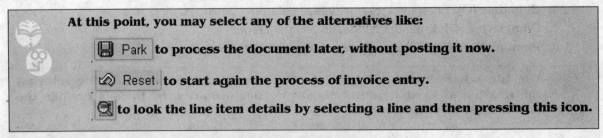

At this point, you may select any of the alternatives like:

Park to process the document later, without posting it now.

Reset to start again the process of invoice entry.

to look the line item details by selecting a line and then pressing this icon.

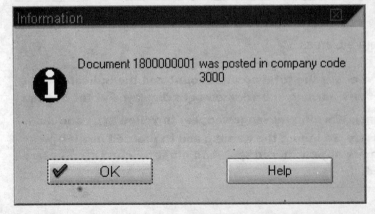

Step-5

When completed, Press 💾 to post the document (Figure: **FB70**-5).

Figure: **FB70**-5

5

AR - Display Customer Master Changes: FD04

Transaction Code	FD04
Menu	Accounting > Financial Accounting > Accounts Receivable > Master records > Display Changes

Business Process Overview

SAP provides the facility of looking at all the changes done to the master records to find out who had changed and what had been the changes made. The system tracks all the changes by logging the details and by generating change documents. The details logged include, at the field level, what was the original content, what is the changed one and who made the change and what time the change has been made. The functionality exists to display the changes made to (a) a particular field or (b) a master record or (c) several master records.

This transaction is convenient and handy to look for the details with drill-down option to look at the field values, which had changed. It is possible to display the changes from a point of time by specifying the date (and time); and is also possible to look at changes made to '**sensitive fields**' and or the changes made to the '**company code area**'.

The same function can also be executed from master records using **Menu: Environment > Field changes or Environment > Account changes.**

For displaying changes made to several master records, use the **Menu: Accounts Receivable > Periodic processing > Info system > Report selection > Adequacy and documentation > Master data > Changes >Display changes to customers** and execute the program **RFDABL00.**

Transaction Steps

Step-1

Access the transaction either by the transaction code or by the menu, and you will reach, "**Customer Account Changes: Initial Screen**" (Figure: **FD04**-1).

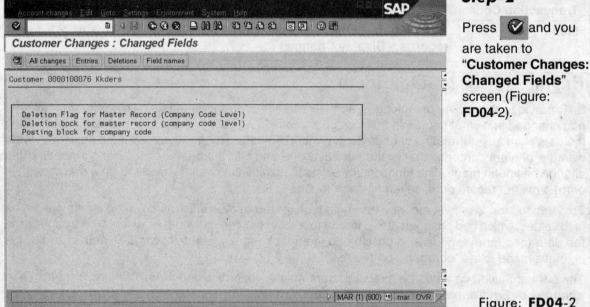

Figure: **FD04**-1

Step-2

Press and you are taken to **"Customer Changes: Changed Fields"** screen (Figure: **FD04**-2).

Figure: **FD04**-2

Step-3

Press Field names to toggle between field names and the regular display in **"Customer Changes: Changed Fields"** screen (Figure: **FD04**-3).

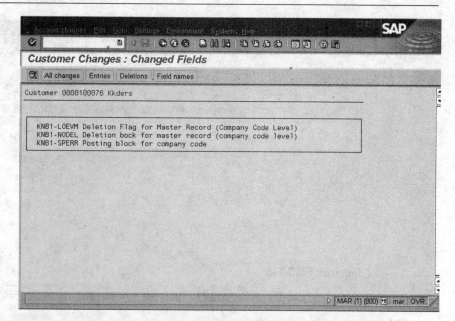

Figure: **FD04**-3

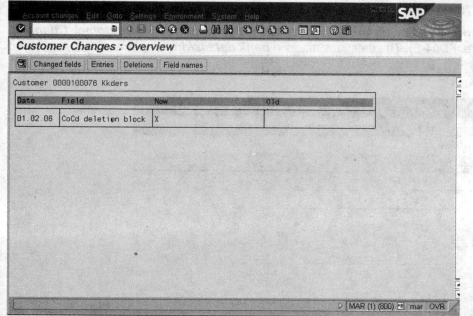

Figure: **FD04**-4

Step-4

Select a filed and press to display the changes, and you can see the details in "**Customer Changes: Overview**" screen (Figure: **FD04**-4).

Step-5

Press All changes from "**Customer Changes: Changed Fields**" screen (Figure: **FD04**-2), to look at all the changes in "**Customer Changes: Overview**" screen (Figure: **FD04**-5).

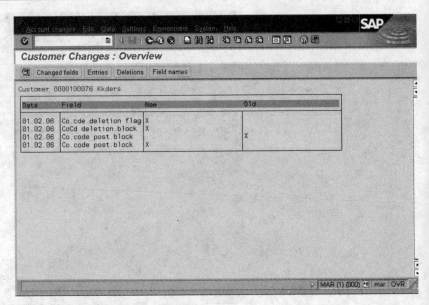

Figure: **FD04**-5

Step-5

Press [Entries] from "**Customer Changes: Changed Fields**" screen (Figure: **FD04**-2), to look at values entered *in bank details or dunning area*, which will be displayed in "*Customer Changes: Entries*" screen (Figure: **FD04**-6). The deletions made in *bank details/dunning area* can be displayed by pressing [Deletions].

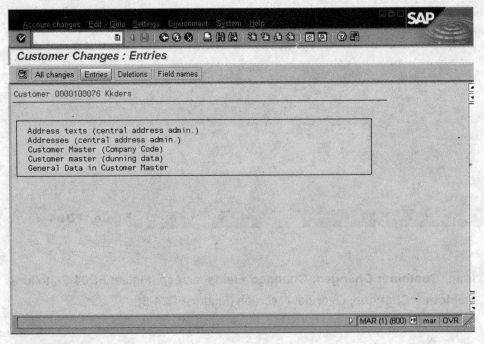

Figure: **FD04**-6

Step-6

Press 🔙 to exit the transaction.

6

AR - Delete Reference Document: F.57

Transaction Code	F.57
Menu	Accounting > Financial Accounting > Accounts Receivable > Documents > Reference documents > Sample document > Delete

Business Process Overview

A *reference document* is used to transfer the data to a new document, which is being posted to. While doing so, you have the flexibility to:

1. Transfer all the contents from the reference document (source) to the new document (target) with out making any changes.
2. Transfer the contents and change in the target document.

The reference document can be an (1) *accounting document* or (2) *sample document*. Accounting documents, by very nature of the term, update the transactions in contrast to the *sample documents*, which are never posted to. But the advantage of using a sample document, as a reference document, is you can always enhance or change them unlike the other. All the sample documents defined in the system takes the number range interval of *X2*.

Transaction Steps

Step-1

Access the transaction either by the transaction code or by the menu, and you are taken to the **"Delete Reference Documents"** (Figure: **F.57**-1).

Figure: **F.57**-1

Enter the selection details:

1. **Company codes (O):** Enter the company code(s) from which the reference document(s) need to be deleted.
2. **Company code (O):** Enter the reference document number(s) to be deleted.
3. **Fiscal year (O):** Enter the fiscal year(s).
4. **Reference document type (O):** Select from the drop down list to specify which type of reference documents need to be deleted (Figure: **F.57**-2).

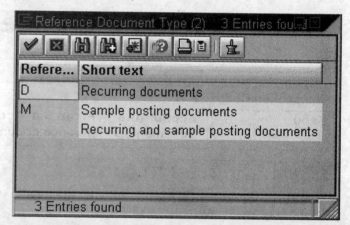

Refere...	Short text
D	Recurring documents
M	Sample posting documents
	Recurring and sample posting documents

3 Entries found

Figure: **F.57**-2

5. **Test run (O):** Check the check box to look at the documents before actually deleting.

Best practice is to have this check box checked, to ensure that you are deleting only the documents, which you surely want to delete.

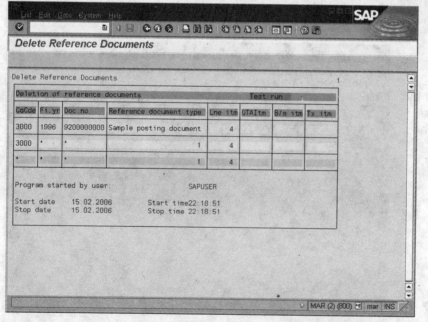

Figure: **F.57**-3

Step-2

Press 🔄. Now you are in **"Delete Reference Documents"** screen (Figure: **F.57**-3).

Step-3

Once you are sure that you want to delete the documents proposed in the Test run , press 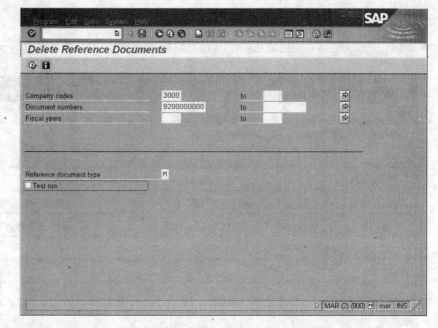 to reach the initial screen and uncheck the "Test run" (Figure: **F.57**-4).

Figure: **F.57**-4

Step-4

Press 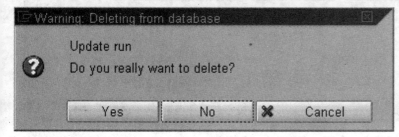 to delete all the reference documents proposed earlier by the system in **Step-2.** The system pops up a warning/confirmation screen (Figure: **F.57**-5).

Warning: Deleting from database

Update run
Do you really want to delete?

Yes   No   Cancel

Figure: **F.57**-5

Step-5

Press Yes to delete (Figure: **F.57**-6).

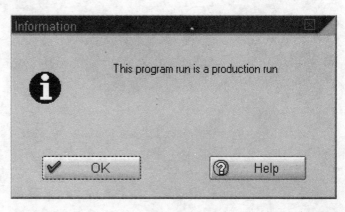

Information

This program run is a production run

OK   Help

Figure: **F.57**-6

Step-5

Press ✓ OK and the system displays the results of the Update run (Figure: **F.57**-7).

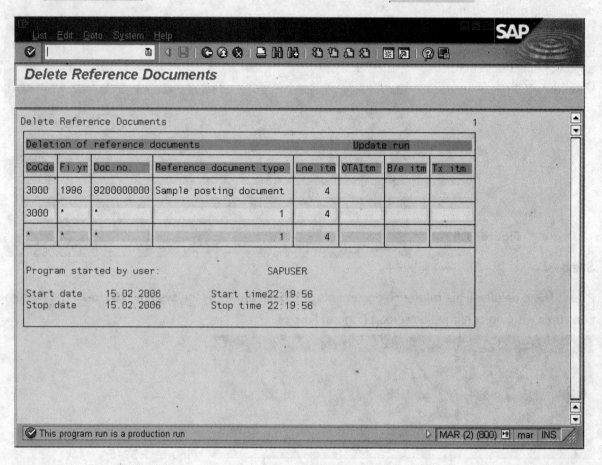

Figure: **F.57**-7

7

AR - Refuse Parked Documents: FBV6

Transaction Code	FBV6
Menu	Accounting > Financial Accounting > Account Receivable > Document > Parked documents > Refuse

Business Process Overview

SAP provides functionality called "**Parking of Documents**" which can store incomplete documents in the system. These can later on be called upon for completion and posting. While doing so, the system does not carry out the mandatory validity checking (no automatic postings or no balance checks) as in other cases when a document is entered. As a result, the transaction figures (account balances) are not updated. This is true in case of all financial transactions except in the area of TR-CM (Cash management) where parked documents will update the transactions.

The data entered, even if not posted, in a parked document can be used for evaluations (unlike in '**hold documents'**). However, it is to be noted that **substitution** functionality cannot be used with document parking, as substitution is activated only upon transaction processing.

Parking of documents can be used to park data relating to customers, vendors or assets (acquisition only). When a cross company code document is parked, only one document is created in the initial company code; when this parked document is posted all other document relevant for other company codes will also be created.

The added advantage is that a document parked by an accounting clerk can be called upon for completion by some one else. The parked documents can be displayed individually or as a list from where the required document can be selected for completion and posting. The **refuse parked document** functionality helps to reject posting parked document(s).

Transaction Steps

Step-1

Access the transaction either by the transaction code or by the menu, and you will be taken to "**Reject Parked Document: Initial Screen**" (Figure: **FBV6**-1). The system brings up the last parked document. Else, enter the **company code, document number & fiscal yea**r in the initial screen.

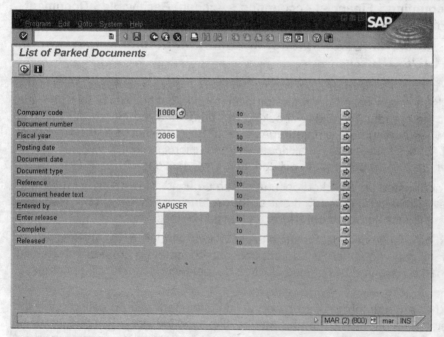

Figure: **FBV6**-1

Step-1a

If you are unsure about the document number,

press List to enter a selection screen (Figure: **FBV6**-2), and maintain the necessary parameters for retrieving the document. Press *F8* and you will be taken to the initial screen (Figure: **FBV6**-1).

Figure: **FBV6**-2

Step-1b

Press ⊕ from the initial screen and you are taken to **"Refuse Parked Documents: List"** (Figure: **FBV6**-3).

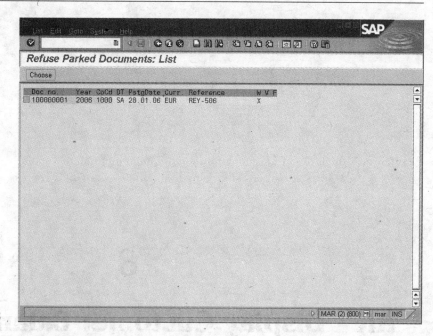

Figure: **FBV6**-3

Select a document from the list, press Choose and press ✓; the system will take you to the initial screen shown in **Step-1**.

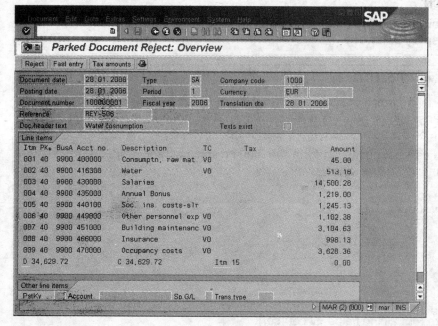

Figure: **FBV6**-4

Step-2

Press ✓ from the initial screen and you are taken to *"Parked Document Reject: Overview"* screen (Figure: **FBV6**-4).

Press Reject to reject the parked document and you will be taken back to the initial screen in **Step-1**.

8

AR - Display Customer Balance: FD10N

Transaction Code	FD10N
Menu	Accounting > Financial Accounting > Accounts Receivable > Accounts > Display balances

Business Process Overview

Display customer balance, is a useful transaction from where you can look at the customer's sub-ledger to view all the transactions, period-wise. You will be able, not only to look at the regular AR related transactions but also the special G/L transactions from the ledger.

The 'line-item' report, which can be, accessed form the initial display screen helps to understand the status of various line items:

- Open items
- Open items, but not yet due
- Open due items
- Open overdue items
- Cleared items
- Parked items

By selecting an item, you can further drill down to see the documents. You may also use the 'Change' function to change a line item (not all the fields, of course!).

Transaction Steps

Step-1

Access the transaction either by the transaction code or by the menu, and you are provided with **"Customer Balance Display"** (Figure: **FD10N**-1).

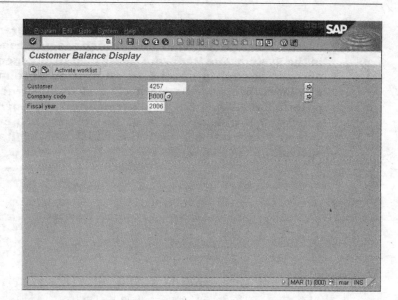

Figure: **FD10N**-1

Enter the following details:

1. **Customer (M):** Enter the customer number.
2. **Company code (M):** Enter the company code.
3. **Fiscal year (M):** Enter the fiscal year for which you want to display the balances.

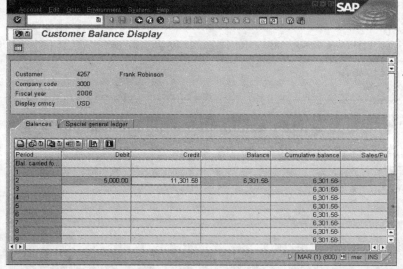

Figure: **FD10N**-2

Step-2

Press ⊕ and you will be taken to "**Customer Balance Display**" Screen (Figure: **FD10N**-2).

By default you will be taken to | Balances | tab, which will display the account balance of normal items, other than the "*Special G/L Transactions*". This 'sub-ledger' display is arranged in such a way to show the balances period-wise, for debit, credit, balance and cumulative balance. The 'balance' shows the balance for the period and the cumulative balance shows the balance up to this period.

You may switch to | Special general ledger | tab to view the details relating to special G/L transactions for the customer.

Down payments, down payment requests, guarantees, bill of exchanges etc are some of the special G/L items, which are processed as 'special G/L transactions' in the system. The items are processed using special procedures in AR, AP & G/L, and are posted to special reconciliation accounts. These transactions will be displayed/processed separately and the user needs to specify in the selection criteria if he/she needs to process or display such items. In all the cases where a special G/L transaction is to be posted, a special G/L indicator needs to be selected during that transaction which will facilitate selecting a particular type of special G/L transaction:

```
A          Down payment
B          Bill of exchange receivable
C          IS-RE Rent deposit
D          Prepaid Transportation Expense
E          Reserve for bad debt
F          Down payment request
G          Guarantee
H          Security deposit
I          BR: Vendor Operation
J          IS-RE Advance payment request
K          IS-RE adv.pymt.operating costs
L          Letter of Credit
M          Serv.charge adv.payt
P          Payment request
Q          Bill of exchange residual risk
R          Bill of exchange pmnt request
S          Check/bill of exchange
T          Down payment
U          IS-RE Ad.pymt.sales-based rent
W          Bill of exchange receivable
Z          Interest receivable
```

Step-3

Position the cursor on a period-row and press [img] (or **"F2"**) to call upon the line item report and the details are displayed in ***Customer Line Item Display*** screen (Figure: FD10N-3).

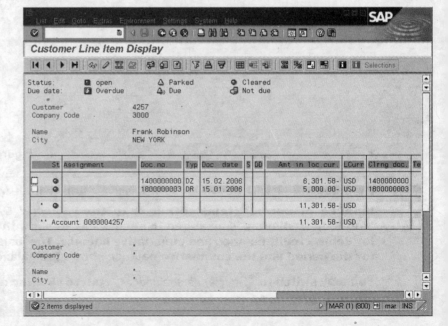

Figure: **FD10N-3**

You may select any line item and double-click on the same to drill down to the document. You may also use ✎ for changing a line item (certain information). The display shows the various items, duly marked by various icons to denote which are all:

■ open	△ Parked	● Cleared
⚡ Overdue	🔔 Due	🔲 Not due

9

AR – Customer Account Analysis: FD11

Transaction Code	FD11
Menu	Accounting > Financial Accounting > Accounts Receivable > Accounts > Analysis

Business Process Overview

Customer account analysis transaction enables you to analyze a customer's account relating to:

- Account balance
- Special G/L transactions
- Sales figures
- Open items (net & discount)
- Deductions / Interests

From the initial selection screen, you can either use a customer number to enter the transaction for details or you can activate a *work list*, if you have already defined one. The transaction offers a one-stop facility of looking at almost all the transactions of the customer including the line items, open items (both net and discount) etc, besides displaying the period-wise sales including sales in the special periods.

Transaction Steps

Step-1

Access the transaction either by the transaction code or by the menu, and you are provided with **"Customer: Initial Screen Account Analysis"** (Figure: **FD11**-1).

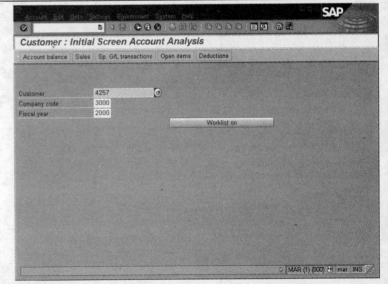

Figure: **FD11**-1

Enter the following details:
1. **Customer (M):** Enter the customer number.
2. **Company code (M):** Enter the company code.
3. **Fiscal year (M):** Enter the fiscal year for which you want to display the balances.

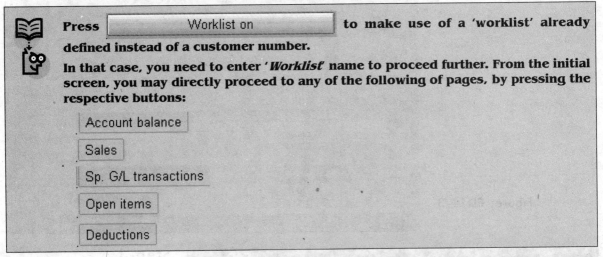

Press [Worklist on] **to make use of a 'worklist' already defined instead of a customer number.**

In that case, you need to enter 'Worklist' name to proceed further. From the initial screen, you may directly proceed to any of the following of pages, by pressing the respective buttons:

[Account balance]

[Sales]

[Sp. G/L transactions]

[Open items]

[Deductions]

Step-2

Press ⊘ and you will be taken to "**4257/3000: Account Balance Account Analysis**" Screen (Figure: **FD11**-2), which displays the posting period-wise debits, credits, balance and cumulative balance for the account, in [Acct bal.] tab.

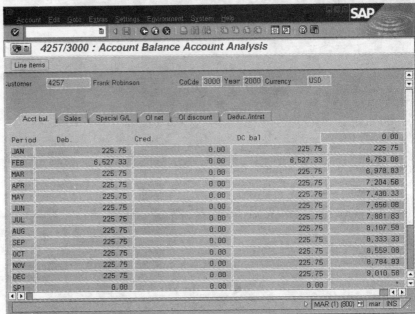

Figure: **FD11**-2

By default you will be taken to [Balances] tab, which will display the account balance of normal items, other than the "**Special G/L Transactions**". This 'sub-ledger' display is arranged in such a way to show the balances period-wise, for debit, credit, balance and cumulative balance. The 'balance' shows the balance for the period and the 'cumulative balance' shows the balance up to this period.

You may switch to [Special general ledger] tab to view the details relating to special G/L transactions for the customer.

Step-3

Press Sales tab (or "**F6**") to view the '*sales*' details. (Figure: **FD11**-3).

Figure: **FD11**-3

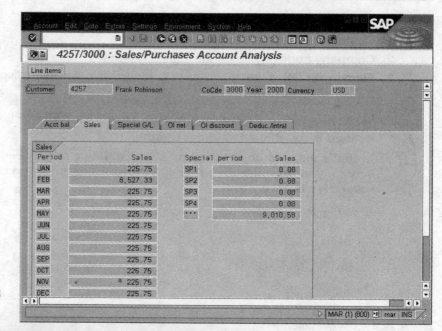

Step-3

Press Special G/L tab (or "**F7**") to view the '*special G/L transaction*' details. (Figure: **FD11**-4).

Figure: **FD11**-4

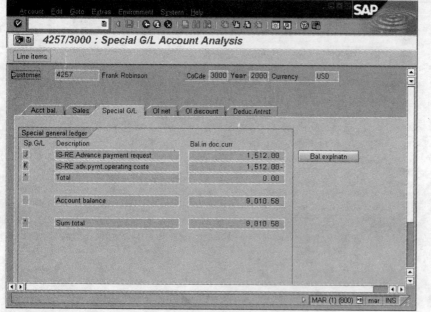

Step-4

Press Bal.explnatn to know whether the balance shown for special G/L transactions relate only to the current period or are there any carry forward balance? (Figure: **FD11**-5).

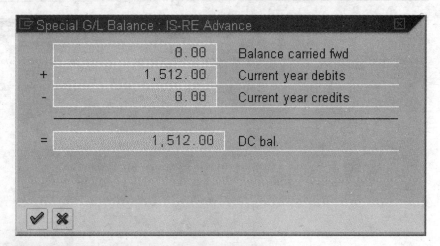

Figure: **FD11**-5

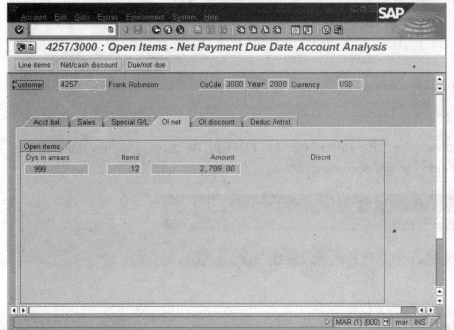

Figure: **FD11**-6

Step-5

Press ☐ OI net ☐ tab (or "**Shift+F9**") to view the '*Open items (net)*' details. (Figure: **FD11**-6).

The screen displays the open items, broken down into number of days in arrears and number of line items falling under each of these 'days in arrears' buckets. You can also further analyze, by pressing

☐ Due/not due ☐ to break the open items into *due items* and *not-due items*.

Step-6

Press ☐ Deduc./intrst ☐ tab (or "**Shift+F8**") to view the '*deductions/interest*' details. (Figure: **FD11**-7).

Besides displaying the interest/deduction information, the screen also displays, for the customer, the total receivable for the company code selected as well as for the corporate group.

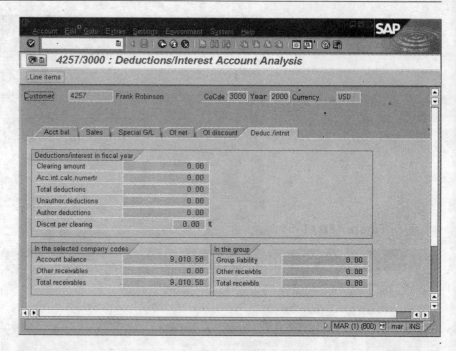

Figure: **FD11**-7

Step-7

Press Line items tab to view the '***Line items***" (Figure: **FD11**-8). As usual, you may drill down, by selecting a line item, further to see the document details.

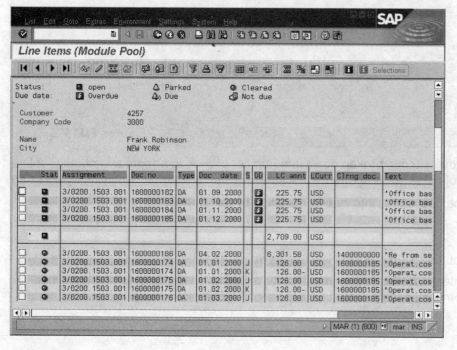

Figure: **FD11**-8

10

AR – Assign / Clear Open Items: FB15

Transaction Code	FB15
Menu	Accounting > Financial Accounting > Account Receivable > Account > Assignment > Assign/clear open items

Business Process Overview

The clearing functions in SAP support processing open items with that incoming payments and adjustments from the business partners. Incoming payments, from customers, are usually for clearing their invoices as against the incoming payments from vendors, which could be for a business transaction like refund from vendor.

This transaction helps in assigning and/or clearing several open items from a single screen. The graphical user interface helps you to look at both the debit and credit items, in two different blocks of the screen; and provides the facility of selecting multiple items from each of these blocks for further processing like assignment and/or clearing. It is also possible to re-set multiple assigned items from the same screen with a single click.

As in individual manual clearing, you will select both debit and credit items, so as to clear the open item(s). When cleared, the system flags these line items as 'cleared', creates a clearing document and enters the clearing document number and clearing date in these open items.

Transaction Steps

Step-1

Access the transaction either by the transaction code or menu, and you will be taken to "**Assignment of Open Items: Customer 4257/ Company Code 3000**" screen (Figure: **FB15**-1).

Figure: **FB15**-1

Step-2

Search for the items you
need to clear. Select the
debit(s) and credit(s)
form the debit and credit
blocks, by selecting the
respective rows (Figure:
FB15-2).The selected
rows will be highlighted
in dark yellow colour.

Figure: **FB15**-2

Step-3

Press 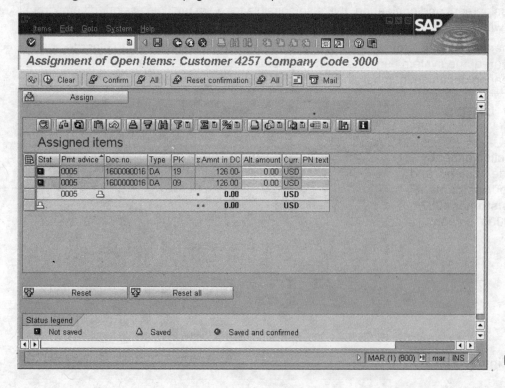 Assign The selected rows in the earlier screen are now moved down to
the "***Assigned items***" block (Figure: **FB15**-3).

Figure: **FB15**-3

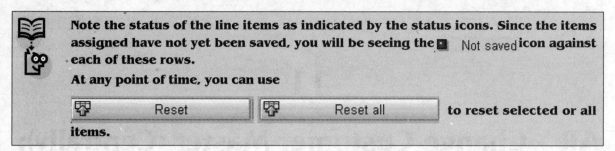

Note the status of the line items as indicated by the status icons. Since the items assigned have not yet been saved, you will be seeing the ■ Not saved icon against each of these rows.

At any point of time, you can use

Reset   Reset all   **to reset selected or all items.**

Step-4

Press Confirm /**F7** to confirm selected items or All / **F8** or simply press Clear / **F6** to confirm all the items in the "***Assigned items***" window (Figure: **FB15**-4). Note the change in the status to ⊘ Saved and confirmed. The system clears the assigned items and posts the payment advice number.

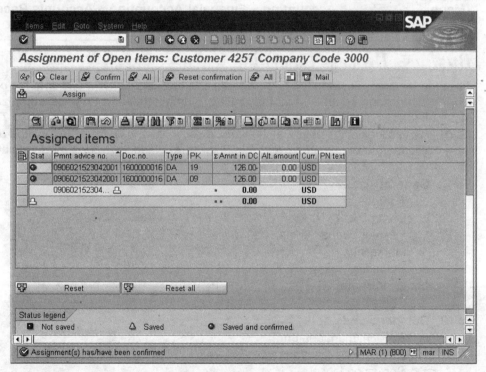

Figure: **FB15**-4

11

AR - Change Customer Master (Centrally): XD02

Transaction Code	XD02
Menu	Accounting > Financial Accounting > Accounts Receivable > Master records > Maintain centrally > Change

Business Process Overview

As in the creation, Customer master records can be changed centrally or at the company code area alone. When done centrally, you may edit the details relating to sales organization, division and distribution channel besides the general data and company code area. As in **Transaction Code: XD01**, one can look at the details in the various sections, and change the required ones. For facilitating easy navigation to the desired area, the initial screen itself provides for changing all or select area of:

1. **General data**
   a. Address
   b. Control data
   c. Payment transactions
   d. Marketing
   e. Unloading points
   f. Export data
   g. Contact persons
2. **Company code data**
   a. Account management
   b. Payment transactions
   c. Correspondence
   d. Insurance
3. **Sales area data**
   a. Sales
   b. Shipping
   c. Billing document
   d. Partner functions

Use **Transaction Code: FD02 (Menu: Accounting > Financial Accounting > Accounts Receivable > Master records > Maintain centrally > Change** to change the customer master in the **company code area** alone.

Transaction Steps

Step-1

Access the transaction either by the transaction code or by the menu, and you are provided with an initial pop-up "**Change Customer: Initial Screen**" (Figure: **XD02**-1).

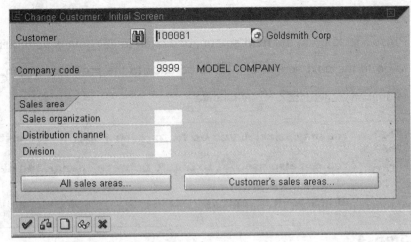

Figure: **XD02**-1

Enter the following details:

1. **Customer (O):** Enter the customer number.
2. **Company code (M):** Enter the company code.

Under <u>Sales area</u> block:

1. **Sales organization (O):** Enter the sales organization, which you want to change.
2. **Distribution channel (O):** Enter the distribution channel.
3. **Division (O):** Enter the division.

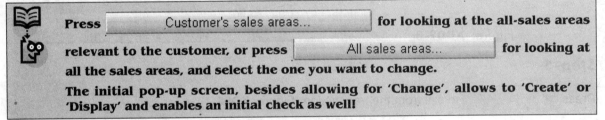

Press [Customer's sales areas...] **for looking at the all-sales areas relevant to the customer, or press** [All sales areas...] **for looking at all the sales areas, and select the one you want to change.**

The initial pop-up screen, besides allowing for 'Change', allows to 'Create' or 'Display' and enables an initial check as well!

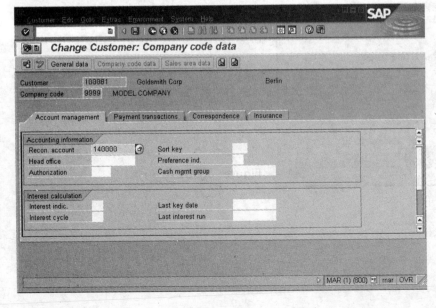

Figure: **XD02**-2

Step-2

Press ✔ and you will be taken to "**Change Customer: Company code data**" Screen (Figure: **XD02**-2).

Step-3

Press to go to the **next** screen, and change the details as required. Alternatively, press 🔁 icon to go to the next screen or 💾 to go back to the previous screen. You may also toggle between

| Company code data | | General data | .

> You may select *Menu: Go to,* to reach a specific tab instead of going tab-by-tab.
>
> You can also use 🖉 to toggle between change and display.
>
> At any point of time, you can use 🖳 to switch to another customer.

Step-4

When you press exit, the system prompts to save (Figure: **XD02**-3). Press | Yes | to save the changes.

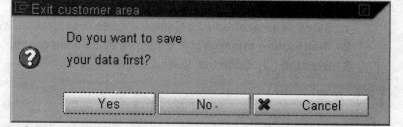

Figure: **XD02**-3

Step-5

Press | ✔ OK | to exit from the transaction (Figure: **XD02**-4).

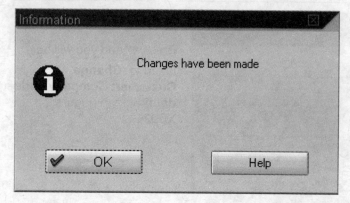

Figure: **XD02**-4

12

AR – Display Customer Master (Centrally): XD03

Transaction Code	XD03
Menu	Accounting > Financial Accounting > Accounts Receivable > Master records > Maintain centrally > Display

Business Process Overview

As in the creation, Customer master records can be displayed centrally or at the company code area alone. When done centrally, you may display the details relating to sales organization, division and distribution channel besides the general data and company code area. As dealt in *Transaction Code: XD02*, one can look at the details in the various sections, and change the required ones. For facilitating, easy navigation to the desired area the initial screen itself provides for displaying all or select area of:

1. **General data**
   a. Address
   b. Control data
   c. Payment transactions
   d. Marketing
   e. Unloading points
   f. Export data
   g. Contact persons
2. **Company code data**
   a. Account management
   b. Payment transactions
   c. Correspondence
   d. Insurance
3. **Sales area data**
   a. Sales
   b. Shipping
   c. Billing document
   d. Partner functions

Use *Transaction Code: FD03 (Menu: Accounting > Financial Accounting > Accounts Receivable > Master records > Maintain centrally > Display* to display the customer master in the **company code area** alone.

Transaction Steps

Step-1

Access the transaction either by the transaction code or by the menu, and you are provided with a initial pop- up "**Display Customer: Initial Screen**" (Figure: XD03-1).

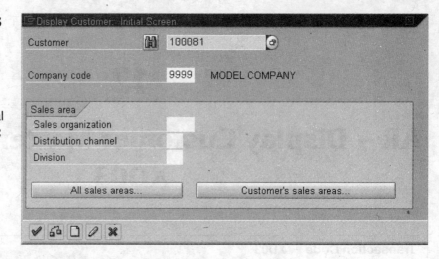

Figure: **XD03**-1

Enter the following details:

1. **Customer (O):** Enter the customer number.
2. **Company code (M):** Enter the company code.

Under Sales area block:

1. **Sales organization (O):** Enter the sales organization.
2. **Distribution channel (O):** Enter the distribution channel.
3. **Division (O):** Enter the division.

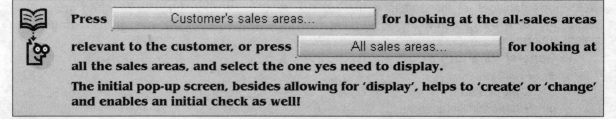

Press ⎨ Customer's sales areas... ⎬ for looking at the all-sales areas relevant to the customer, or press ⎨ All sales areas... ⎬ for looking at all the sales areas, and select the one yes need to display.

The initial pop-up screen, besides allowing for 'display', helps to 'create' or 'change' and enables an initial check as well!

Step-2

Press ✔ and you will be taken to "**Change Customer: Company code data**" Screen (Figure: XD03-2).

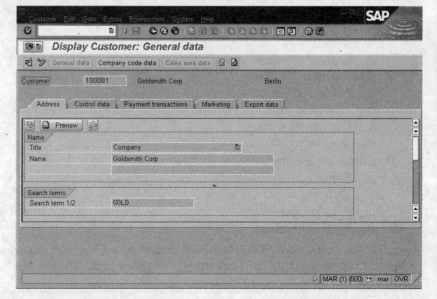

Figure: **XD03**-2

Step-3

Press to go to the **next** screen, and look for the details as required. Alternatively, press 🔲 icon to go to the next screen or 🔲 to go back to the previous screen. You may also toggle between

| Company code data | General data |

You may select *Menu: Go to*, to reach a specific tab instead of going tab-by-tab.

You can also use 🖊 to toggle between change and display.

At any point of time, you can use 🔲 to switch to another customer.

Step-4

When you reach the last screen, press, | Yes | to exit the display (Figure: **XD03**-4).

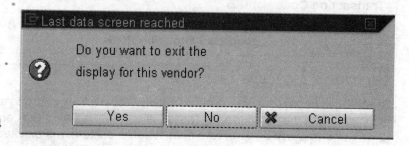

Figure: **XD03**-4

13

AR - Block / Unblock Customer (Company code area): FD05

Transaction Code	FD05
Menu	Accounting > Financial Accounting > Accounts Receivable > Master records > Block/unblock

Business Process Overview

Blocking is necessary when you do not want to post any more to an account. SAP allows blocking the customer either (1) *centrally* (possible only when SAP's SD component has been integrated) or (2) in the *company code area* alone. When a customer is blocked centrally, the system prevents both order processing and account posting; but a block in the company code area prevents only further postings. When blocked centrally, you may set the block for a variety of situations like:

- Order block
- Delivery block
- Invoicing block
- Posting block

Again, you have the flexibility of (a) blocking a customer in *all the company codes* or (b) in *selected company codes*. Before blocking, you need to ensure that there are no open items in the account, else you will not be able to process and clear these items.

You may also want to block a customer from making payments and for blocking the dunning. To block a customer for payment or dunning program, necessary *'dunning block'* key (in Correspondence section of the customer master) or *'payment block'* key (in payment transaction section of the customer master) needs to be entered. Even though both the payment and dunning program will select the open items for payment / dunning during open item determination, the system will not create a payment or dunning notice.

You need to use:

- **Transaction Code: XD05** for blocking the account centrally, from order processing and posting

At any time you want to **unblock**, just remove the 'check' against the check boxes in the respective transactions or remove the block key(s) from the master record of the concerned customer.

Transaction Steps

Step-1

Access the transaction either by the transaction code or by the menu, and you are taken to the **"Block/unblock customer: Initial Screen"** (Figure: FD05-1).

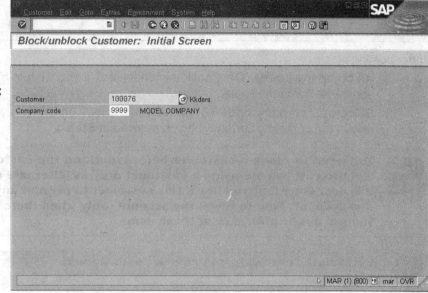

Figure: **FD05**-1

Enter the selection details:

1. **Customer (M):** Enter the customer number which needs to be blocked or unblocked.
2. **Company code (O):** Enter the company code.

If the company code is not entered, it is only possible to block / unblock in all the company codes.

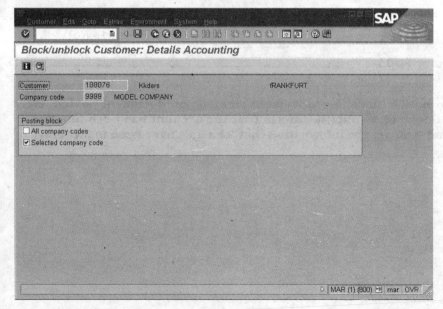

Step-2

Press enter ![enter icon]. Now you are in **"Block/unblock Customer: Details Accounting"** screen (Figure: FD05-2).

Figure: **FD05**-2

You have the option of pressing to see the account details (takes you to the master data).

Under <u>posting block</u>:

1. **All company codes (O):** Check this check box if you wish to block the customer in all the applicable company codes.
2. **Selected company code (O):** Check this check box, if you wish to block the customer only in the company code which you entered in **Step-1**.

 You need to block a customer before marking the customer master record for 'deletion'. If you are using a customer only as 'alternate dunning recipient' then it is necessary that you block this customer to prevent any posting to be made to this account. Note to block the account, only when there are no open items; else you will not be able to clear these items.

 Uncheck the checkbox, to unblock the customer!

Step-3

Press to save the changes (Figure: **FD05**-3).

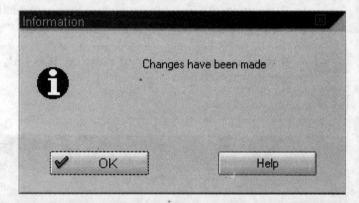

Figure: **FD05**-3

 Unlike the regular notifications like 'document created', or 'document posted' etc, here the system does not 'explicitly' inform that the account has been blocked / unblocked. Instead, you get the information that 'changes have been made' only!

14

AR - Block / Unblock Customer (Centrally): XD05

Transaction Code	XD05
Menu	Accounting > Financial Accounting > Accounts Receivable > Master records > Maintain Centrally > Block/unblock

Business Process Overview

Blocking is necessary when you do not want to post any more to an account. SAP allows blocking the customer either (1) *centrally* (possible only when SAP's SD component has been integrated) or (2) in the *company code area* alone. When a customer is blocked centrally, the system prevents both order processing and account posting; but a block in the company code area prevents only further postings. When blocked centrally, you may set the block for a variety of situations like:

- Order block
- Delivery block
- Invoicing block
- Posting block

Again, you have the flexibility of (a) blocking a customer in *all the company codes* or (b) in *selected company codes*. Before blocking, you need to ensure that there are no open items in the account, else you will not be able to process and clear these items.

You may also want to block a customer from making payments and for blocking the dunning. To block a customer for payment or dunning program, necessary *'dunning block'* key (in Correspondence section of the customer master) or *'payment block'* key (in payment transaction section of the customer master) needs to be entered. Even though both the payment and dunning program will select the open items for payment / dunning during open item determination, the system will not create a payment or dunning notice.

You need to use:

- **Transaction Code: FD05** for blocking the account in company code area, from posting alone

At any time you want to **unblock**, just remove the 'check' against the check boxes in the respective transactions or remove the block key(s) from the master record of the concerned customer.

Transaction Steps

Step-1

Access the transaction either by the transaction code or by the menu, and you are taken to the **"Block/unblock Customer: Initial Screen"** (Figure: **XD05**-1).

Figure: **XD05**-1

Enter the selection details:

1. **Customer (M):** Enter the customer number which needs to be blocked or unblocked.
2. **Company code (O):** Enter the company code, where you need to block.

> **If the company code is not entered, it is possible to block / unblock in all the company codes!**

3. **Sales Organization (O):** Enter the Sales Organization in which the blocking needs to be done.
4. **Distribution channel (O):** Enter the distribution Channel.
5. **Division (O):** Enter the sales division.

> **If the sales organization related information is not entered in the initial screen, the block indicator is not set for the related organization for this customer, and you will be able to block the customer centrally in all sales areas. If you maintain the relevant information in the screen initially, the customer is blocked in the specified sales area, and you have the option to block in all other sales area as well.**
>
> Use Sales areas   Sales areas by customer   buttons to find and select the sales areas.

Step-2

Press enter ✅ . Now you are in **"Block/unblock Customer: Details Accounting"** screen (Figure: **XD05**-2).

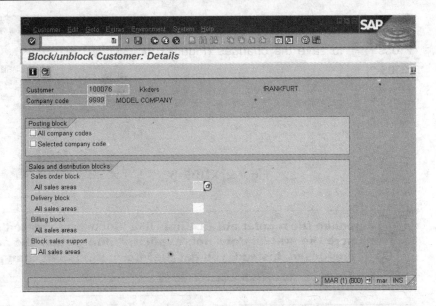

Figure: **XD05**-2

 You have the option of pressing to see the account details (takes you to the master data).

Under <u>posting block</u>:

1. **All company codes (O):** Check this check box if you wish to block the customer in all the applicable company codes.

2. **Selected company code (O):** Check this check box, if you wish to block the customer only in the company code which you entered in **Step-1** (This field will be available for input only when the company code is entered in the previous screen).

> **You need to block a customer before marking the customer master record for 'deletion'. If you are using a customer only as 'alternate dunning recipient' then it is necessary that you block this customer to prevent any posting to be made to this account. Note to block the account, only when there are no open items; else you will not be able to clear these items.**

Under <u>Sales and Distribution blocks</u>, you have the option of selecting the type of block required in each of the below mentioned areas, besides the central block in all sales area:

1. **Sales order block (O):** Select from the drop down list, what type of sales order block is required.

2. **Delivery block (O):** Select the type of block required for blocking the order..

3. **Billing block (O):** Enter what kind of billing block is desired.

4. **All sales area (O):** When checked, the customer is blocked in all sales areas.

> **Uncheck the checkbox, to unblock the customer, in the relevant area(s)!**

Step-3

Press to save the changes (Figure: XD05-3).

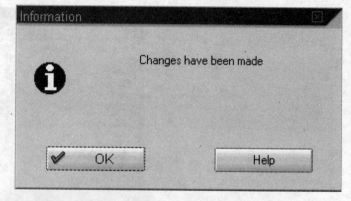

Figure: **XD05**-3

Unlike the regular notifications like 'document created', or 'document posted' etc, here the system does not 'explicitly' inform that the account has been blocked / unblocked. Instead, you get the information that 'changes have been made' only!

End of Transaction

Let us verify the '**payment / dunning block**' for the customer:

Step-A

Use **Transaction XD02**, and select `Payment transactions` tab in " **Change Customer: Company code data**" screen (Figure: **XD05-XD02**-1), where you can set the payment block from the drop down list. Note that a payment block indicator '**A**' has been entered in the payment block field in the above example.

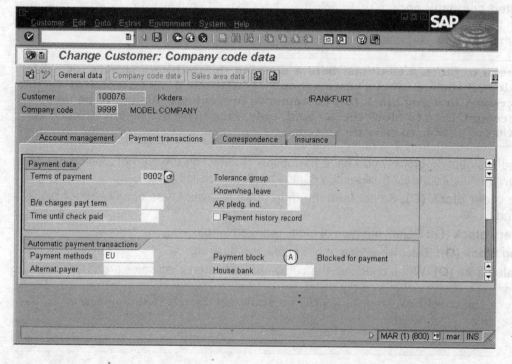

Figure: **XD05-XD02**-1

Step-B

Use **Transaction XD02**, and select | Correspondence | tab in " **Change Customer: Company code data**" screen (Figure: **XD05-XD02**-2), where you can set the **dunning block** from the drop down list.

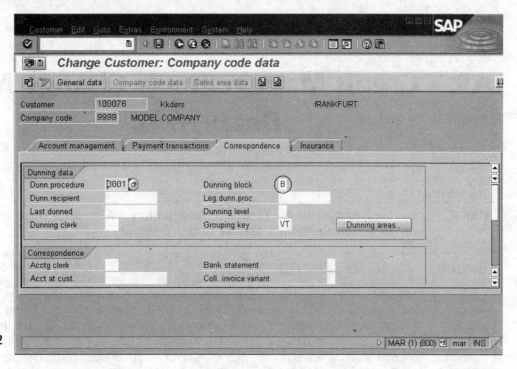

Figure:
XD05-XD02-2

Note that the dunning block key '**B**' has been inserted in the field 'Dunning block'.

15

AR – Credit Management: Change Master Data: FD32

Transaction Code	FD32
Menu	Accounting > Financial Accounting > Accounts Receivable > Credit Management > Master data > Change

Business Process Overview

Credit management helps the companies to manage their receivables in such a way that the bad debt occurrence is eliminated or minimized. Credit management enables defining credit limits to individual customers and credit-related decision-making, whether to advance further credit to a customer or group of customers based on certain information and analysis available from the system. It also helps to undertake different policies for different groups of customers depending upon their **risk profile** to differentiate and decide from a high-risk customer from the others. When SAP SD is in place, together with FI /AR component, SAP enables credit management by:

a. Specifying **automatic credit checks** based on a variety of criteria. You can specify at which critical points in the SD cycle (for example, order entry, delivery, goods issue etc) the system carries out these checks.

b. Enabling e-mail communication of all critical credit information to the key people concerned in credit decision so that they can review each of these situations to decide whether or not extend further credit.

As in case of any automated process like dunning, payment etc, credit management in SAP requires certain pre-requisites to be defined before hand:

a. Customer master data is created both in SD & FI.

b. Credit data (maximum limit per credit control area as well as the total for all areas, in the control data screen) for the customer has been created.

Credit limits and **Credit exposure** are managed at both **credit control area** and customer level. Each customer is attached to a specific credit control area, as each company code is attached to a credit control area. The appropriate credit limits are defined in the customer master record (the currency in the master record can be different than that of the currency of the credit control area). Individual credit limits are maintained for each of the credit control area and an over all credit limit is also maintained for all the credit control areas put together. Credit limit can also be assigned to a group of customers.

- Example: Customer XYZ has been given an over-all limit of 100, 000 USD, with a maximum individual limit of 70, 000 USD. Individual limit under Credit Control Area "A" is 30, 000 USD and 70, 000 USD for Credit Control Area "B".

c.   Credit control area has been defined and assigned to company code

Credit Control Area is the central organization, which controls how the credit management is handled for the company code(s), which are attached to this area. Each credit control area should have a currency defined. If the credit control area takes care of more than one company code with different company code currencies, then the receivables are converted into the currency of the credit control area.

- One credit control area is sufficient for all the company codes if credit control/risk management is centralized. A customer dealing with more than one company code, then, will have a combined limit.
- If credit management is decentralized, then you need to define different credit control areas to different company codes. A customer dealing with more than one company code, then, will have a separate limit in each of the company codes.

d.   *Risk categories* have been defined and assigned to customers.

e.   *Credit groups* (document credit group) for document types have been defined. **Document credit groups** combine order types and delivery types for credit control.

f.   Defined, in SD, at what of time (when order is received or when a delivery is made etc) the credit check should happen.

The *Credit management process* starts when a sales order is entered in SD. Imagine this results in exceeding the credit limit defined for the customer. Now:

a.   System creates three comparison total considering (1) Open receivables, (2) Sales order values, value of goods to be delivered, and billing document value from SD and (3) Special G/L transactions (e.g. down payments and bills of exchange).

b.   Based on (a) above the system throws an (1) Error message, and prevents from saving the order or (2) Warning message, and the system does not prevent saving, but order is blocked.

c.   **Credit representative**, using the **Information Functions** (SD information system, FI information system, credit overview, credit master list, early warning list, oldest open item, last payment, customer master, account analysis etc), process this blocked order either (1) from the blocked SD documents list or (2) the mail box, and releases the order, if necessary.

d.   Delivery is created, billing document generated and posted, A/R updated.

e.   Customer pays the invoice, A/R is posted.

Credit check is defined for any VALID combination of the following:

1.   Credit Control Area
2.   Risk Category
3.   Document Credit Group

The credit check can be (1) Static or (2) Dynamic:

1.   **Static Credit Check**

   Under 'static' credit check, the system calculates the **credit exposure** of a particular customer as the total of:

   a.   Open order (delivery not yet done)
   b.   Open delivery (value of deliveries yet to be invoiced)
   c.   Open billing documents (not transferred to accounting)

d.   Open items (AR item not yet settled by the customer).

Customer's credit exposure is not to exceed the established limit.

2. **Dynamic Credit Check with Credit horizon**

The "dynamic" check is split into two parts:

a.   Static limit: Total of open items, open billing, and open delivery values.

b.   Dynamic limit: Open order value. The value of all un-delivered and partially delivered orders, totaled and stored on a time-scale in future (10 days, 1 wk etc) – **horizon date**.

During the dynamic check, the system will ignore all orders beyond the horizon date. The sum total of static and dynamic limits should not exceed the credit limit established for the customer.

Transaction Steps

Step-1

Access the transaction either by the transaction code or by the menu and you will be taken to "**Customer Credit Management Change: Initial Screen**" Screen (Figure: **FD32**-1).

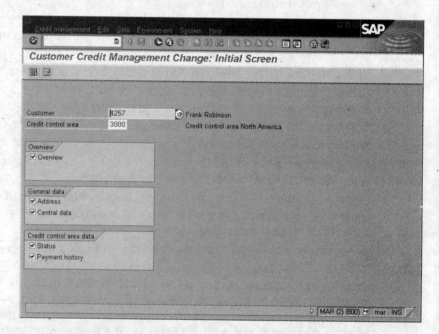

Figure: **FD32**-1

Select, by checking the check box, the area(s) you want to edit/change:

1. **Overview (O)**
2. General Data:
   a. **Address (O)**
   b. **General data (O)**
3. Credit control data:
   a. **Status (O)**
   b. **Payment history (O)**

To select all, just press ▣ icon.

Step-2

Press "Enter" or click ✅ to go to "**Customer Credit Management Change: Overview**" screen (Figure: FD32-2).

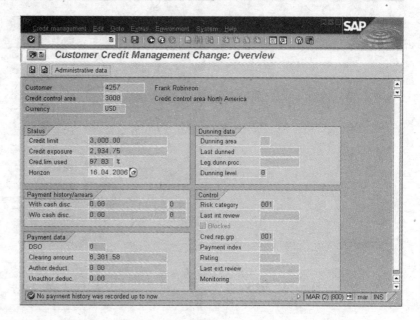

Figure: FD32-2

The overview screen provides a glimpse of the customer credit under:

- **Status**

  The status area provides information like:

  o Credit limit assigned to the customer.

  o Credit exposure, as of now.

  o Credit limit utilized by the customer.

  o Horizon (O): Change the date, id required.

> **Horizon or credit horizon date is used by the system to decide what are all items, which need to be taken into account while arriving at the credit exposure. When a dynamic credit check is carried out, the system does not take in to account the sales/billing documents beyond this horizon date.**

- **Payment history/arrears**

  Payment history provides the information like the payments (with or with out discount) made and the arrears, if any.

- **Payment data**

- **Dunning data**

  The details like when the customer was dunned last, what is/was the dunning area used for dunning, what was the last dunning level etc.

- **Control**

  All the control parameters, for credit management, like risk category, credit management group etc are displayed here.

Step-3

Press "Enter" or click ✅ or click 🖫 to go to" ***Customer Credit Management Change: Address***" screen (Figure: **FD32**-3).

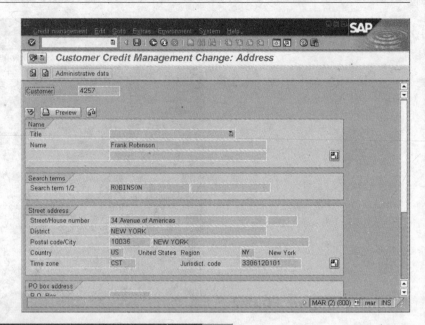

Figure: **FD32**-3

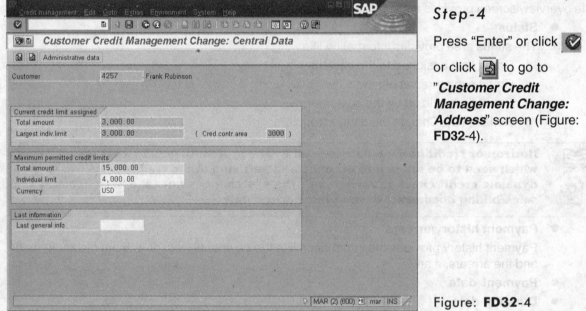

Step-4

Press "Enter" or click

or click to go to
"*Customer Credit
Management Change:
Address*" screen (Figure:
FD32-4).

Figure: **FD32**-4

Current <u>Credit limit assigned</u>:

1. **Total amount:** Displays the total credit limit assigned, as of now.
2. **Largest Individual limit:** Displays the maximum limit allowed, right now. This limit is allowed
   in the credit control area mentioned with in brackets in the same line (credit control area;
   3000 in the displayed screen).

Under <u>Maximum permitted credit limits</u>:

3. **Total amount (M):** Change the credit limit to reflect the limit allowed for all the credit control
   area put together.

4. **Individual limit (M)**: Change to increase or decrease the maximum limit the customer can receive in any of the credit control areas. In the screen displayed, (2) will later change to 4,000 from the initial 3, 000.

5. **Currency (O)**: Change if you need different currency.

You may use different currencies for different credit control areas. Besides, you may also use yet another different *currency* for the total limit managed in (3) above. All these currencies can be different from that of the local (company code) currency. Irrespective of the transaction currencies, the credit limits are updated using the currencies mentioned in the credit control areas and in the total limit area, and are updated accordingly.

Credit limit is managed, per customer per credit control area. You define the credit limit by setting up the individual limits in each of the credit control areas, if the customer falls under different credit control areas. You also define a central credit limit, in the customer master, which will be the maximum for all the credit control areas put together.

The credit limit for a particular credit control area is defined in "Credit limit data" area in Customer Credit Management Change: Status (Figure: FD32-6) and the screen Customer Credit Management Change: Central Data (Figure: FD32-4) displays the credit limits for all the credit control areas together: the "Maximum permitted credit limits" portion of the screen shows the total credit limit, in all the credit control areas, for the customer. It also shows the maximum allowed individual limit in any of the credit control area at any point of time.

Let us look at an illustration:

A customer, XYZ, is serviced by three credit control areas namely CCA1, CCA2 & CC3. You may decide, in total, that the customer should be given a credit limit of INR 500, 000. You may also decide that the customer will have a maximum of INR 250, 000 as the maximum individual limit in any of the credit control areas. You further decide that this customer should have credit limit as detailed below:

Credit control area	Maximum Credit Limit (INR)
CCA1	100, 000
CCA2	250, 000 Largest Individual Limit
CCA3	150, 000
	500, 000 Total Credit Limit

Graphically, you can depict the credit limits as in Figure: FD32-5:

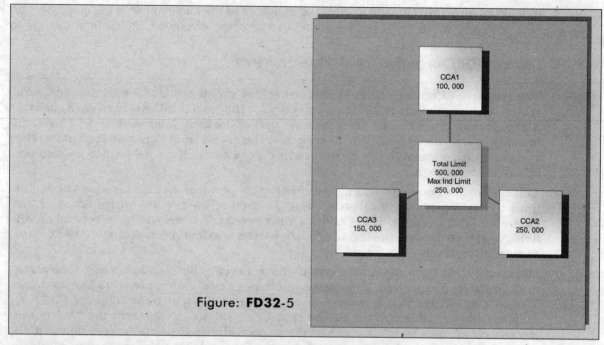

Figure: **FD32**-5

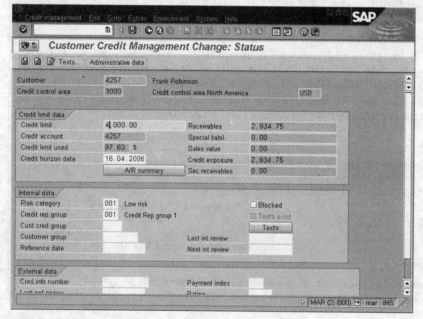

Figure: **FD32**-6

Step-5

Press "***Enter***" or click or click to go to" ***Customer Credit Management Change: Status*** screen (Figure: **FD32**-6).

Under <u>Credit limit data:</u>

1. **Credit limit (M):** Enter or change the credit limit for this controlling area. If the customer is not receiving credit limits in other credit control areas, then this limit could be the same as that of Individual Limit defined in "Maximum permitted credit limits" in Figure: **FD32**-4 above.

2. **Credit limit used:** This is the percentage of credit limit utilization by the customer (97.83% with respect to the original credit limit of 3, 000 (now changed to 4, 000) and with the receivable balance of 2, 934.75).

Under <u>Internal data:</u>

   3. **Risk category (O):** Enter or change a risk category, from the drop down list (Figure: FD32-7).

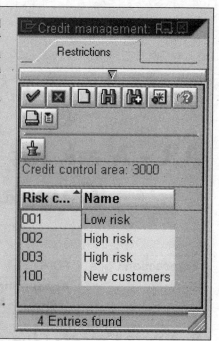

> ***Risk category*** allows defining the risks associated with doing business with customers; by categorising the risks into low, medium or high etc. Customers are grouped and associated with a risk category so as to monitor them effectively. Once assigned with the risk category, this informs the system what kind of checks need to be carried out when activating the credit management related functions for processing sales orders.

Figure: **FD32-7**

---

   4. **Credit rep group(O):** Enter or change a the group.

> ***Credit representative group*** is an employee group associated with the credit management functions of the company code. This group identifier will be transferred in to the order and is used as a selection parameter for evaluations/release.

Step-5

Press [💾].

16

AR – Mark for Deletion, Customer Master (Company code area): FD06

Transaction Code	FD06
Menu	Accounting > Financial Accounting > Accounts Receivable > Master records > Mark for Deletion

Business Process Overview

When you no longer need certain master records, you may wish to delete and archive them. Before processing, first of all you need to ensure that these accounts do not have any transaction figures in the system (transactions should have already been archived), and that the accounts have been **marked for deletion** in the master records. Before marking an account, the same should have been blocked.

The steps are:

1. Block the accounts from posting.
2. Mark the accounts for deletion.
3. Delete the master records from the system.
4. Archive the master records.

As in blocking, you can mark the accounts for deletion by setting the '*deletion flag*' (1) in all the company codes or (2) in selected company codes. Also, you can set the 'deletion flag' (a) centrally or in the (b) company code area alone. When set centrally, all the master data relating both to the **company code area** as well as the **sales area** is marked for deletion. During the next archiving run, the system deletes these accounts and archives. However, it is to be remembered that 'marking for deletion' with out blocking an account will not prevent you from posting to that account.

Use **Transaction Code: XD06** to mark the accounts centrally. You may also access the same transaction using **Menu: Accounting > Financial Accounting > Accounts Receivable > Master records > Maintain centrally > Mark for Deletion.**

The **deletion flag** can be removed any time, before the master record is physically deleted from the system.

Transaction Steps

Step-1

Access the transaction either by the transaction code or by the menu, and you are taken to the **"Flag for Deletion Customer: Initial Screen"** (Figure: **FD06**-1).

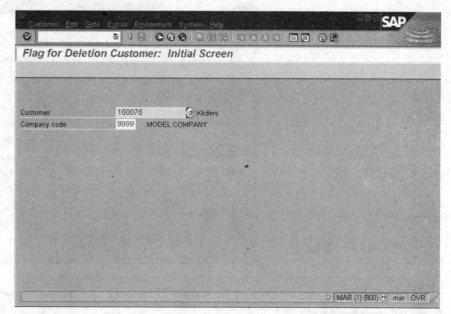

Figure: **FD06**-1

Enter the selection details:

1. **Customer (M):** Enter the customer number which needs to be flagged for deletion.
2. **Company code (O):** Enter the company code.

> **If the company code is not entered, it is possible to 'mark for deletion' in all the company codes.**

> **Use *Transaction Code: XD06* (*Menu: Accounting > Financial Accounting > Accounts Receivable > Master records > Maintain centrally > Mark for Deletion*) to 'mark' a customer centrally. When entering the transaction, you may need to maintain details, besides customer & company code, like sales organization, sales area and distribution channel and sales division. Else, the 'deletion flag' will not be set for that organization for the customer.**

Step-2

Press enter ✅ . Now you are in **"Flag for Deletion Customer: Details Accounting"** screen (Figure: **FD06**-2).

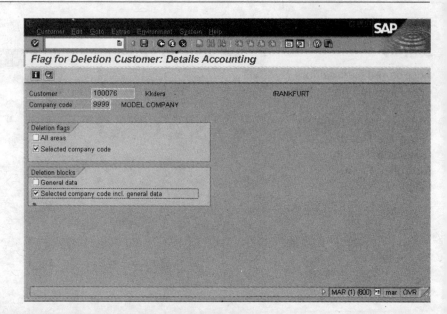

Figure: **FD06**-2

 You have the option of pressing ⬜ to see the account details (takes you to the master data).

Under <u>Deletion flags block</u>:

1. **All areas (O):** Check this check box if you wish to 'mark ' the customer in all the applicable company codes and in all sales area, for deletion.
2. **Selected company code (O):** Check this check box, if you wish to 'mark' the customer for deletion only form the company code which you entered in **Step-1**.

 You need to block a customer before marking the customer master record for 'deletion'. This will ensure that the customer account is not posted with any new transactions. Note that you may just 'mark' an account even if it is not ' blocked'; but the problem is that the system will continue allowing posting in this account, even after marking, but with a warning message every time you are trying to post the account.

 Uncheck the check box, any time, to remove the 'deletion flag'.

Under <u>Deletion block</u>:

1. **General data (O):** If this is checked, system will 'block' deleting the general data for the customer, but will allow to delete the company code specific data.
2. **Selected company code incl. general data (O):** This is inclusive of (1) above. If checked, you will not be able to delete the company code specific data as well as the general data.

The marked area(s) with the deletion block, for this particular customer, will be deleted when you rum the 'archiving' program next time.

Step-3

Press to save the changes (Figure: **FD06**-3).

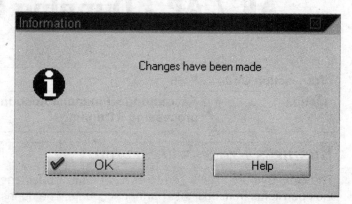

Figure: FD06-3

17

AR / AP - Dunning Program: F150

Transaction Code	F150
Menu	**Accounting > Financial Accounting > Accounts Receivable > Periodic processing > Dunning**

Business Process Overview

The SAP System allows you to dun ("remind") business partners automatically. The system duns the open items from business partner accounts. The dunning program selects the overdue open items, determines the dunning level of the account in question, and creates a dunning notice. It then saves the dunning data determined for the items and accounts affected. You can use the dunning program to dun both customers and vendors. It may be necessary to dun a vendor in case of debit balance as a result of a credit memo.

Dunning is administered through a ***Dunning Program,*** which uses **Dunning Key** (to limit the dunning level per item), **Dunning Procedure** and **Dunning Area** (if dunning is not done at company code level).

Dunning Procedure controls:
- Dunning Interval / frequency.
- Grace days / minimum days in arrear.
- Number of Dunning levels (at least one level) —one level dunning procedures are known as 'payment reminders'.
- Transactions to be dunned.
- Interest to be calculated on the overdue items.
- Known or negotiated leave, if any, which needs to be considered in selecting the overdue items.
- Company code data like (a) Is dunning per dunning area? (b) Is dunning per dunning level? (c) Reference Company code (d) Dunning Company code etc.
- Dunning forms / media to be selected for the dunning run.

Dunning Area is optional, and is required only if dunning is not done at company code level. The Dunning area can correspond to a sales division, sales organization etc.

The **Dunning Process** involves three major steps:
1. Maintaining the parameters for the dunning run.
2. Creating / editing the dunning proposal generated by the system .
3. Printing dunning notices.

1. Dunning Parameter

As the first step in dunning, you need to maintain certain parameters, which will identify the current dunning run. Entering the date of execution and the dunning run identifier is the starting point, after which you will continue to maintain other parameters like:

i.   Dunning date to be printed on the notice.

ii.   Document posted up to.

iii. Company Code.

iv.   Account restrictions (optional).

Now, you can save the parameters and display the log generated (to see if there were any errors), dunning list (list of accounts and items) and some dunning statistics (blocked accounts / items etc).

2. Dunning Proposal

Once scheduled, the dunning program prepares the dunning proposal as described below:

a.   Program determines which accounts to dun:

    i.   System checks the fields **Dunn.procedure** and **Last dunned** in the customer master record to determine whether the arrears date or the date of the last dunning run lies far enough back in the past.

    ii.   Checks whether the account is blocked for dunning according to the **Dunning block** field in the customer master record.

    iii. Program processes all open items, relating to the accounts thus released in (ii) above, that were posted to this account on or before the date entered in the field **Documents posted up to**.

    iv.   Program checks all the open items, as released in (iii) above, in an account to decide:

- Is the item blocked?
- Is overdue according to the date of issue, the base date, the payment conditions, and the number of grace days granted?

    v.   Program then proceeds to process all open items thus released, in (iv):

- How many days the item is overdue?
- Which dunning level for a particular open item?

    vi.   Program determines the highest dunning level for the account based on (v) above. The highest dunning level determined is stored in the master record of the account when you print the letters. This dunning level determines the dunning text and a special dunning form, if defined.

    vii. Program then proceeds to check each account:

- Does the customer / vendor has a debit balance with regard to all open overdue items selected?
- Is the total amount to be dunned and the percentage of all open items more than the minimum amount and percentage defined in the dunning procedure?
- Is the dunning level for the account or the overdue items higher than it was for the last dunning run? If not, are there new open items to be dunned (with a previous dunning level of 0)? If not, does the dunning procedure for this level specify that dunning be repeated?

b.   Program creates the dunning proposal list.

  c. Edit dunning proposal.

     i. You can edit the Dunning Proposal so as to:

- Raise or lower the dunning level of an item.
- Block an item from being dunned.
- Block an account for the current dunning run or remove the block.
- Block an account in the master record for dunning or remove the block.
- Block a document for dunning or remove the block.

    ii. You can view the sample print out, to ascertain how the printed notice would look like. (maximum 10 notices can be seen in the screen).

   iii. You may also display logs to see the changes made in the editing earlier, as a confirmation of what you wanted to change in the system generated proposal earlier. If necessary, you can go back and change the proposal.

3. Print dunning notices

You can use a single form or multiple forms, which will have different text, based on the dunning levels. There may also be a requirement to use a completely different form for **'legal dunning'**. Once the print option is activated, the program prints the notices, and the dunning related information like the dunning level, last dunned etc are updated in the customer / vendor masters. SAP provides the option to optically archive the notices as the system prints the dunning notices. There is also a provision to re-start the printing if the same is interrupted before complete printing.

Transaction Steps

Step-1

Access the transaction either by the transaction code or menu, and you will be taken to **"Dunning"** screen (Figure: **F150**-1).

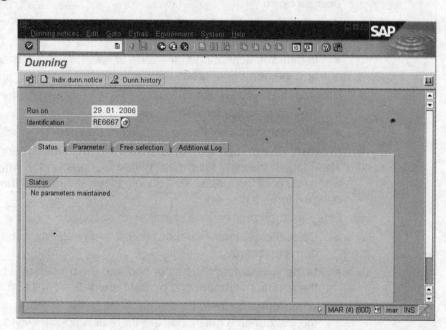

Figure: **F150**-1

Step-2

Enter the details for identifying the dunning run:

1. **Run on (M):** Enter the date of the dunning run.
2. **Identification (M):** Enter an unique identifier which will identify the current run.

Note, "No parameters maintained" in Status tab.

Step-3

In Parameter tab, enter the relevant parameters, which will help the dunning program to determine the overdue items to be dunned. (Figure: **F150**-2).

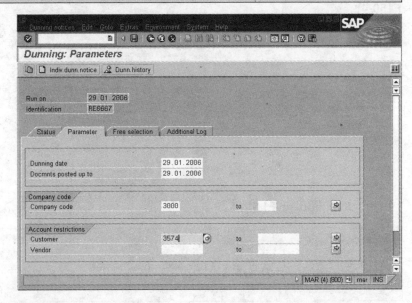

Figure: **F150**-2

1. **Dunning date (M):** Enter the date of dunning, which needs to be updated on the documents, including the dunning notices.
2. **Docmnts posted up to(M):** Enter the date up to which the system will look for the overdue and dunnable items.
3. **Company code (M):** Enter the company code (s) for which the dunning is done.

Under, Account restrictions:

4.**Customer (O):** Enter the customers to whom the dunning is relevant. For all the customers to be considered, leave the field(s) blank

Step-4

Press 💾 to save the parameters and to return to the initial screen (Figure: **F150**-3).

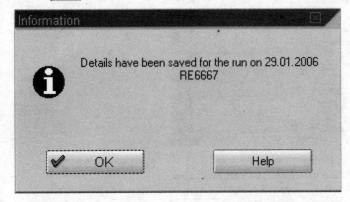

Figure: **F150**-3

Step-5

Press Status tab to see the current status (Figure: **F150**-4).

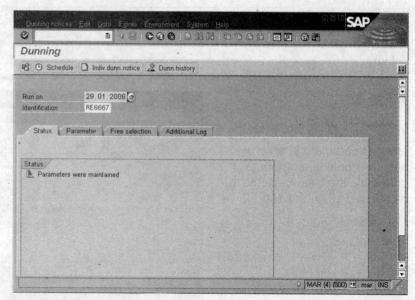

Figure: **F150**-4

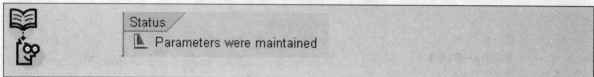

Step-6

Press ⊕ Schedule to schedule the dunning run, and the system pops up " **Schedule Selection and Print**" screen (Figure: **F150**-5).

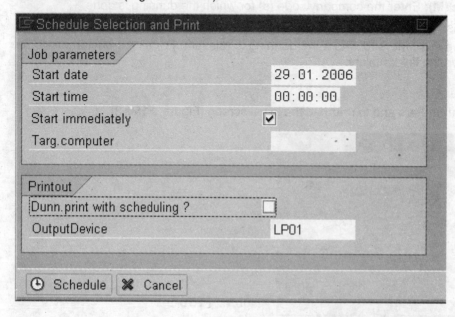

Figure: **F150**-5

Step-7

Under the Job parameters, you may schedule it immediately or later and press
⏰ Schedule . The system pops up the "Information" (Figure: **F150**-6).

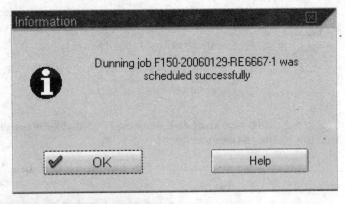

Figure: **F150**-6

Step-8

Press ✓ OK and see the status (Figure: **F150**-7).

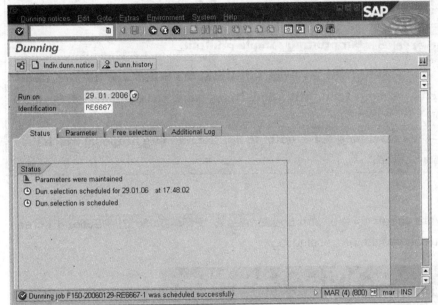

Figure: **F150**-7

Step-9

Press ✓ a few times till you see the change in the status (Figure: **F150**-8).

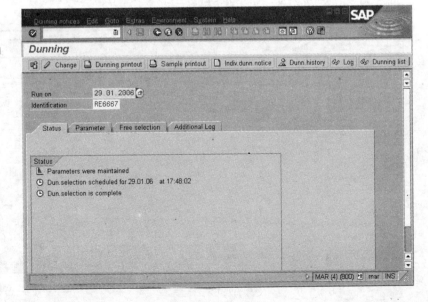

Figure: **F150**-8

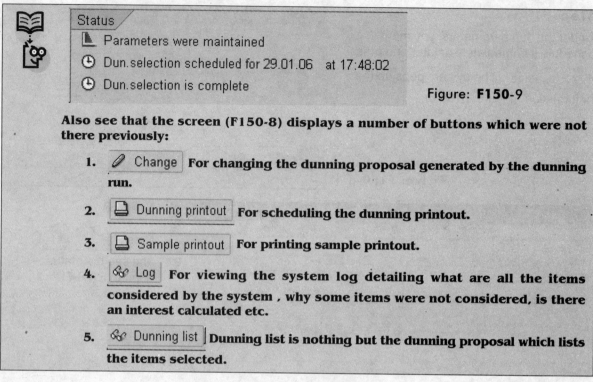

Status

🔖 Parameters were maintained

🕐 Dun.selection scheduled for 29.01.06   at 17:48:02

🕐 Dun.selection is complete

Figure: **F150**-9

Also see that the screen (F150-8) displays a number of buttons which were not there previously:

1. 🖉 Change **For changing the dunning proposal generated by the dunning run.**

2. 🗐 Dunning printout **For scheduling the dunning printout.**

3. 🗐 Sample printout **For printing sample printout.**

4. 𝒢 Log **For viewing the system log detailing what are all the items considered by the system , why some items were not considered, is there an interest calculated etc.**

5. 𝒢 Dunning list **Dunning list is nothing but the dunning proposal which lists the items selected.**

Step-10

Press 𝒢 Log and you are taken to the *Job Log Entries for F150-20060129-RE6667-1* screen (Figure: **F150**-10), where you can see the processing log.

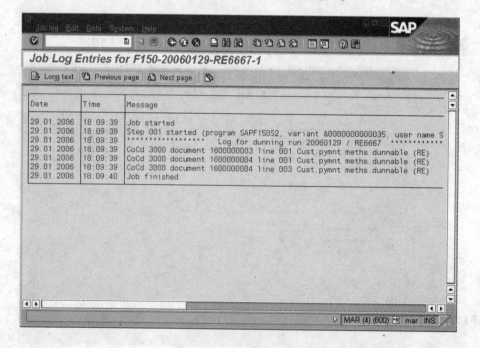

Figure: **F150**-10

Step-11

Press  to go to the initial screen. Press ⟨Dunning list⟩, the system pops up the "**Dunning List Variant**" screen (Figure: **F150**-11).

Figure: **F150**-11

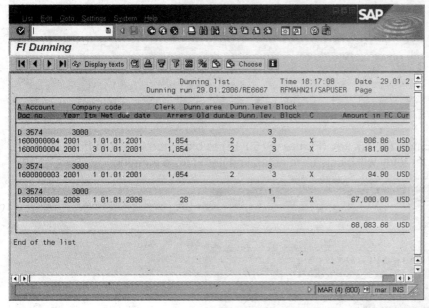

Step-12

Press ✓ to view the dunning list (dunning proposal) generated by the system. The details are shown in "**FI Dunning**" screen (Figure: **F150**-12).

Figure: **F150**-12

Step-13

Press  to go to the initial screen. Now by pressing ⟨Change⟩, you can change the dunning proposal from the "**FI Dunning screen**" (Figure: **F150**-13).

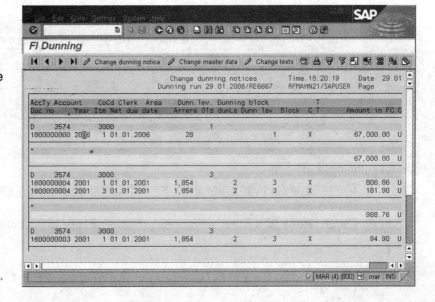

Figure: **F150**-13

Step-14

Select the relevant line item and press

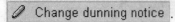
✎ Change dunning notice .

The system pops up **"Change Dunning Notice"** screen (Figure: **F150**-14).

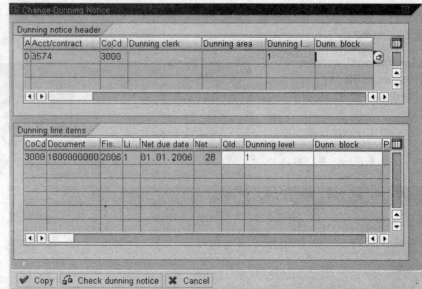

Figure: **F150**-14

Under <u>Dunning Notice Header</u>:

1. **Dunn. Block (O):** Enter a <u>block key</u> (Figure: **F150**-15) to block the line item from dunning. Blocking at the header level will block all selected line items from dunning.

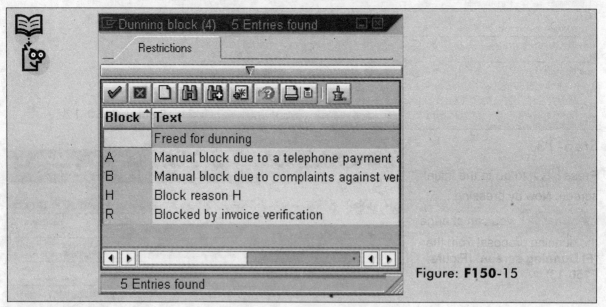

Figure: **F150**-15

Under <u>Dunning Line Items</u>

2. **Dunning level (O):** Enter a different dunning level, if required, than the one proposed by the system.

3. **Dunn. Block (O):** Enter a <u>block key</u> (Figure: **F150**-15) to block the **line item** from dunning.

Step-15

Press ✔ Copy and go back to **FI Dunning screen"** (Figure: **F150**-13).

Step-16

Press

 Change master data

to go to "**Change Customer: Company code data**" screen (Figure: **F150**-16). You may change the "***Dunning data***" if required.

Figure: **F150**-16

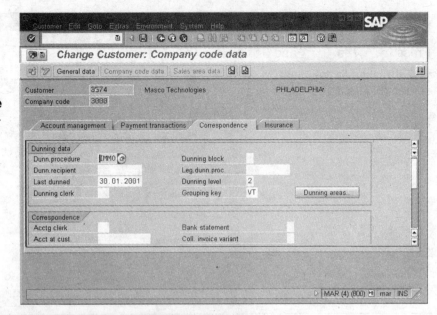

Step-17

Press 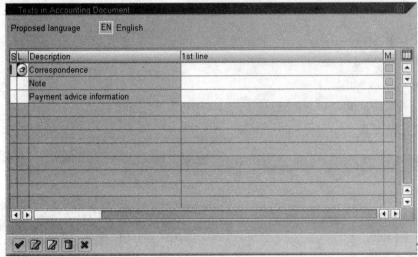. And, go back to "**FI Dunning**" screen (Figure: **F150**-13). Press

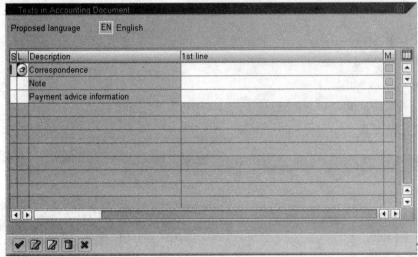 Change texts. The system pops up "**Texts in Accounting Document**" screen (Figure: **F150**-17).

Figure: **F150**-17

Step-18

After making changes, if any, press 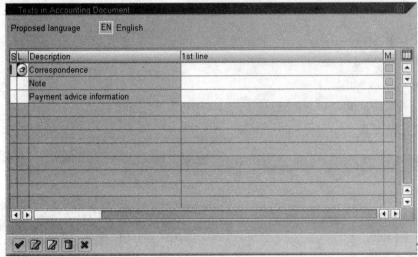 to go back to "**FI Dunning**" screen (Figure: **F150**-13).

Press 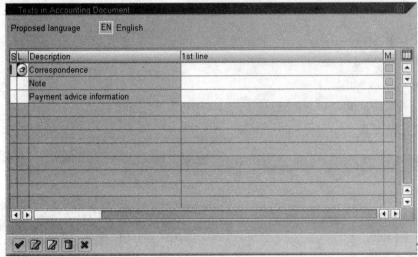 and <u>confirm</u> to save the changes (Figure: **F150**-18).

Figure: **F150**-18

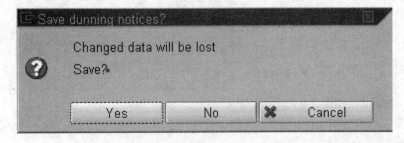

Step-19

Press 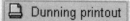 and you are taken to the initial screen (Figure: **F150**-19).

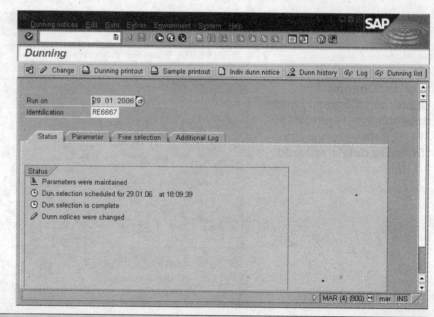

Figure: **F150**-19

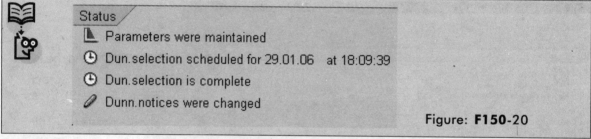

Status

- Parameters were maintained
- Dun. selection scheduled for 29.01.06   at 18:09:39
- Dun. selection is complete
- Dunn. notices were changed

Figure: **F150**-20

Step-20

Press

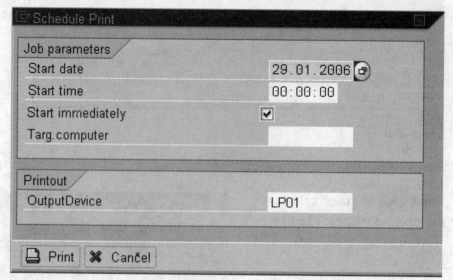

Dunning printout

on the initial screen (Figure: **F150**-19), and schedule the dunning print run. The system pops up **"Schedule Print"** screen (Figure: **F150**-20).

Figure: **F150**-20

Maintain the Job Parameters.

Step-21

Press 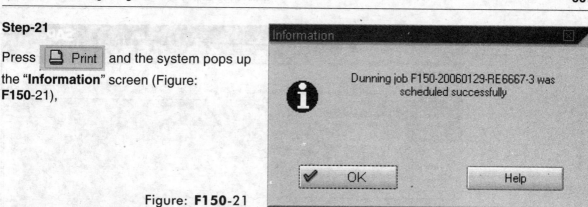 Print and the system pops up the "**Information**" screen (Figure: **F150**-21),

Figure: **F150**-21

Step-22

Press ✔ OK , and you can see the changed status in the initial screen (Figure: **F150**-22).

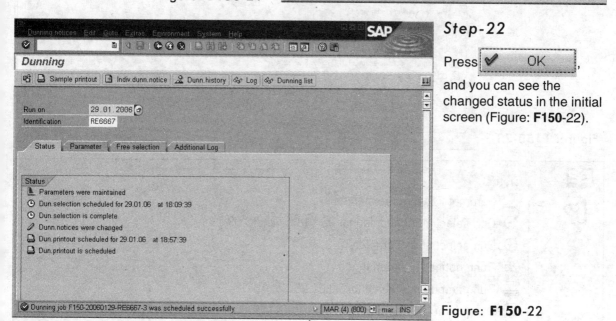

Figure: **F150**-22

You no longer see ✐ Change **button. You also additionally see** 🖨 Sample printout **button.**

Step-23

Press ✅ a few times till you see the change in the status (Figure: **F150**-23).

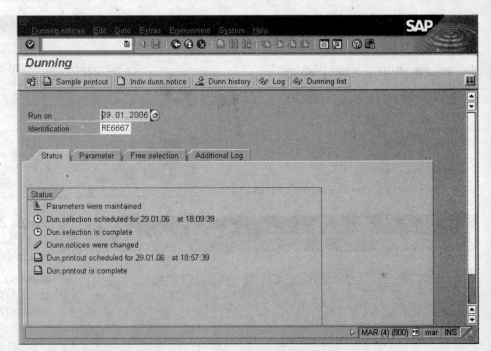

Figure: **F150**-23

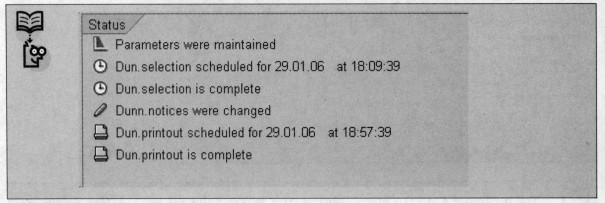

Step-24

Press **Sample printout** to view the dunning notice generated by the system. On the pop up "**Schedule Sample Printout**" screen, maintain the required Job parameters (Figure: **F150**-25).

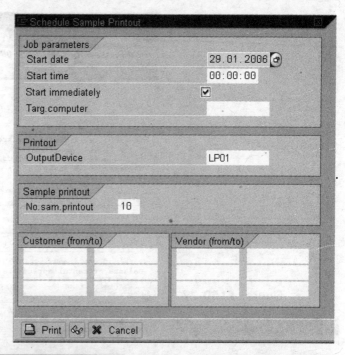

Figure: **F150**-25

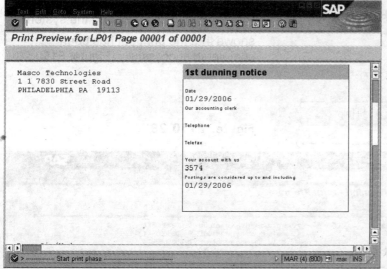

Figure: **F150**-26

Step-25

Press to view the notice before actually printing. The system displays the dunning notice generated for the first item for the first customer (Figure: **F150**-26 & 27).

Alternatively, you may press 🖶 Print **straight away without looking at the notices. In this case you will see the print status in "FI Dunning – Print Program" screen (Figure: F150-29).**

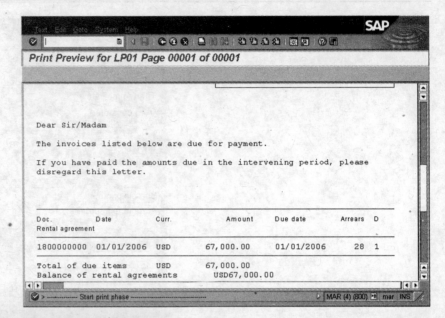

Print Preview for LP01 Page 00001 of 00001

Dear Sir/Madam

The invoices listed below are due for payment.

If you have paid the amounts due in the intervening period, please disregard this letter.

Doc.	Date	Curr.	Amount	Due date	Arrears	D
Rental agreement						
1800000000	01/01/2006	USD	67,000.00	01/01/2006	28	1
Total of due items		USD	67,000.00			
Balance of rental agreements			USD67,000.00			

> ----- Start print phase -----   ▷ MAR (4) (800) ▣ mar INS

Figure: F150-27

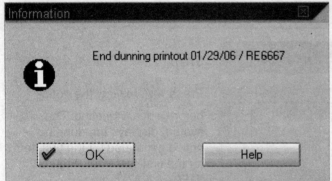

Information

End dunning printout 01/29/06 / RE6667

OK   Help

Step-26

Press 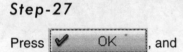 a few times and the system shows that the print out has been completed successfully (Figure: **F150**-28).

Figure: F150-28

Step-27

Press [✔ OK], and you can see the print status in **"FI Dunning – Print Program"** screen (Figure: **F150**-29).

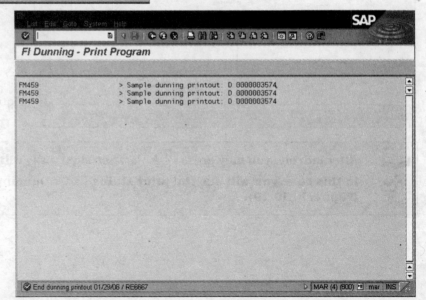

FI Dunning - Print Program

FM459	> Sample dunning printout: D 0000003574
FM459	> Sample dunning printout: D 0000003574
FM459	> Sample dunning printout: D 0000003574

End dunning printout 01/29/06 / RE6667   ▷ MAR (4) (800) ▣ mar INS

Figure: F150-29

Step-28

Select Menu: **Go to > Dunning statistics**, to view the dunning statistics relating to the current dunning run (Figure: **F150**-30).

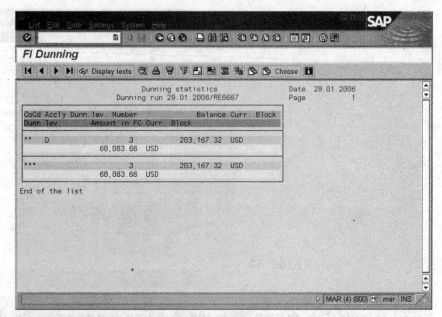

Figure: **F150**-30

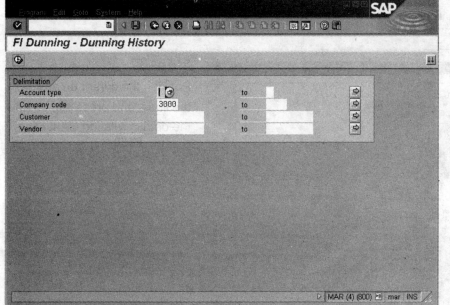

Step-29

From the initial screen, (Figure: **F150**-23),

press 🔦 Dunn.history

to view the history of dunning. The system takes you to "**FI Dunning –Dunning History**" screen (Figure: **F150**-31).

Figure: **F150**-31

Step-30

Maintain the details (you may limit the selection to the current company code / customers or leave the selection blank to bring all the history) and press 🕒, the system takes you to "**FI Dunning – Dunning History**" screen (Figure: **F150**-32).

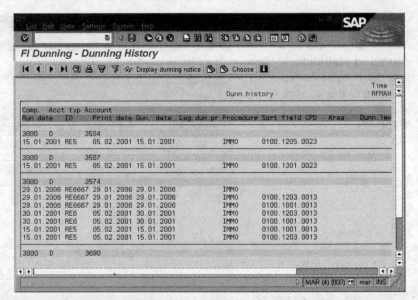

Figure: **F150**-32

 From this screen also the dunning notices can be displayed, by pressing
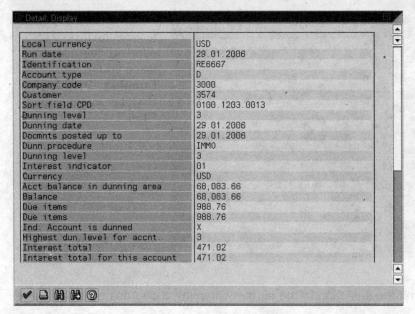

Step-31

Position the cursor on any of the lines, and press 🔍 to view the details relating to that line (Figure: **F150**-33).

Figure: **F150**-33

Step-32

Press ✓ to go out of the pop-up to Figure: **F150**-32, from where press 🔙 thrice (!) to exit the transaction.

End of Transaction

It is time to check how the system has updated the relevant master records with the results of the dunning run. Remember, dunning details are maintained in the customer master from where the system picks up the dunning procedure, when the account was last dun etc.

Step-A

Use **Transaction Code: FD03** to view the customer master record. When you enter the code, system pops up "Display Customer: Initial Screen" (Figure: **F150-FD03**-1).

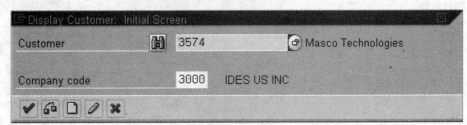

Figure:
F150-FD03-1

Step-B

Press to go to "**Display Customer: Company code data**" (Figure: **F150-FD03**-2). Select the

Correspondence tab to view the details under <u>Dunning data</u> block.

The system has updated the 'Last dunned date' field with the date of the above dunning run. The 'Dunning level' has also been updated (the highest dunning level used by the program during the last run is updated here irrespective of the fact that some of the line items would have fallen under a lower dunning level). When you dun again this customer, the system will take into account these information for determining whether to dun a item or not, and if to dun, what should be the next dunning level to be used.

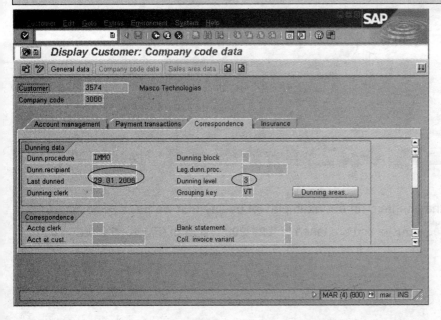

Figure: **F150-FD03**-2

Step-C

Use *Transaction Code:*
FD11 to view the documents
relating to the customer.
When you enter the code,
system pops up "**Customer:**
Initial Screen Account
Analysis" (Figure: **F150-**
FD11-1).

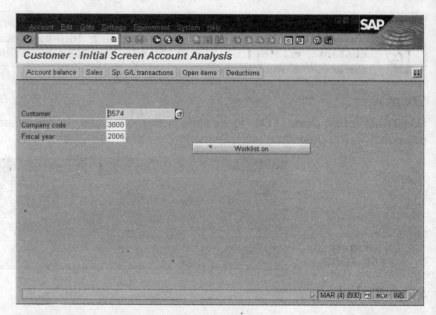

Figure: **F150-FD11**-1

Step-D

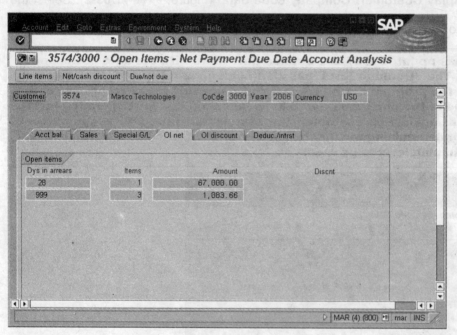

Press Open items to
view the documents.
When you enter the
code, system pops up
" **3574/3000: Open**
Items – Net Payment
Due Date Account
Analysis " (Figure:
F150-FD11-2).

Figure: **F150-FD11**-2

Step-E

Place the cursor on any of the line item (in our example, let us say that we have selected 2nd line
item, 1,083.66) and press Line items . You are taken to "**999-9999**" screen (Figure: **F150-FD11**-3).

The number "999-9999" denotes the days in arrears for that particular line item(s).

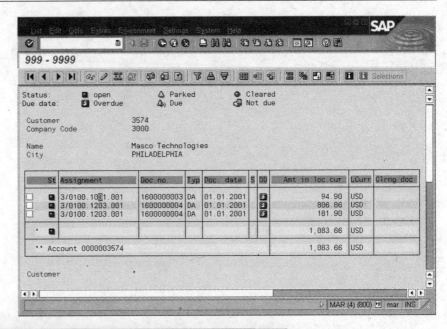

Figure: **F150-FD11**-3

Step-F

Select the 'tick box' against the line item

and press . You are taken to **"Display Document: Line Item 001"** screen (Figure: **F150-FD11**-4).

Figure: **F150-FD11**-4

> **Note the dunning level updated for this document (3). Remember, this has been the level (highest) updated in the customer master record for the customer. So, when there are multiple open overdue items considered for dunning, the system always duns the customer at the highest level and the same is updated accordingly in the master record!**
>
> Last dunned   29.01.2006   3

FI - AA
Asset
Accounting

1

AA - Easy Access: ASMN

Transaction Code	ASMN

Transaction Overview

As in with any other easy access menu, Transaction **ASMN**, helps you to access all the important transactions related to asset accounting from a single screen conveniently arranged from the functional view point. ASMN groups the various transactions into:

- Posting
- Asset
- Periodic processing
- Information system
- Environment

Needless to say, all these transactions have been grouped in a more convenient, easy-to-locate table at the end of the transaction, which I am sure you will find as a ready reckoner.

Transaction Steps

Step-1

Access the transaction either by the transaction code or by the menu, and you will be taken to "**SAP Easy Access Asset Accounting**" Screen (Figure: **ASMN**-1).

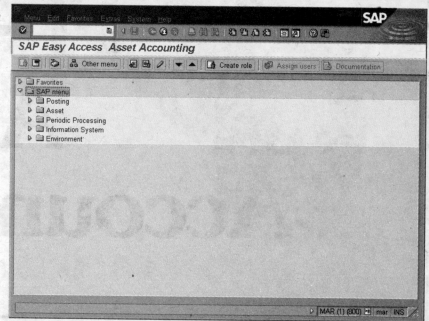

Figure: **ASMN**-1

Step-2

Expand "*Posting*" folder to view the transaction codes/menu for *(a) Acquisition, (b) Capitalize asset under construction, (c) Transfer, (d) Retirement, (e) Manual value correction (f) Edit document (g) Reverse document* (Figure: ASMN-2).

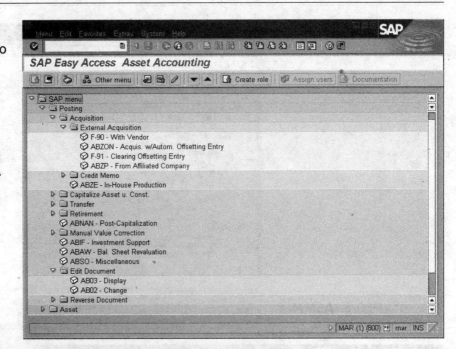

Figure: **ASMN**-2

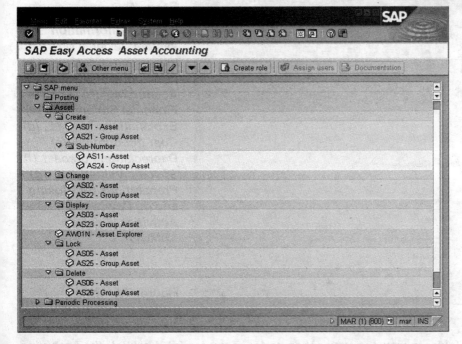

Step-3

Expand "*Asset*" folder to view the transaction codes/menu for *(a) Create, (b)Change, (c)Display, (d) Lock and (e) Delete* (Figure: ASMN-3).

Figure: **ASMN**-3

Step-4

Expand "*Periodic processing* folder to view the transaction codes/menu for *(a) Schedule Manager, (b) Revaluation for the Balance sheet and (c) Year end closing*(Figure: ASMN-4).

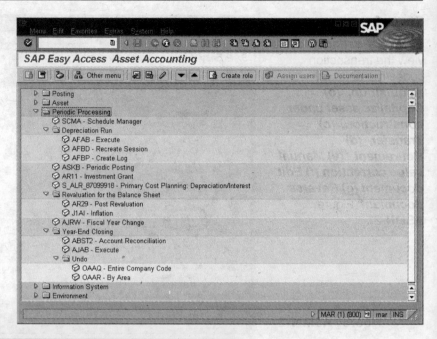

Figure: **ASMN**-4

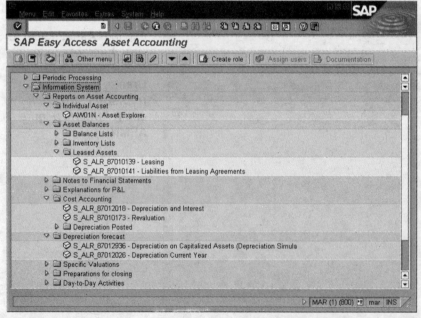

Figure: **ASMN**-5

Step-5

Expand *"Information system"* folder to view the transaction codes/menu for *(a) Reports on Asset Accounting, (b) Notes to Financial Statements, (c) Explanations for P&L, (d) Cost Accounting, (e) Depreciation Forecast, (f) Specific Valuations, (g) Preparations for Closing and (h) Day-to-day Activities* (Figure: ASMN-5).

Step-6

Expand *"Environment"* folder to view the transaction codes/menu for *(a) Worklist, (b) Archiving, (c) Problem Analysis and (d) Current Settings* (Figure: ASMN-6).

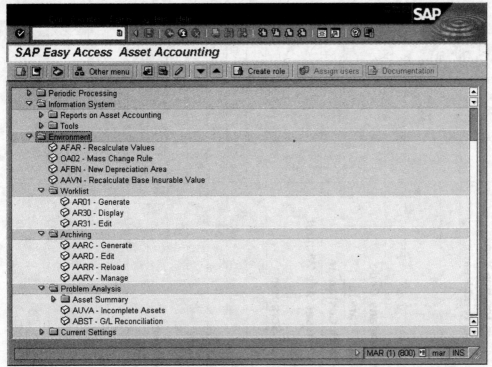

Figure: **ASMN**-6

Posting

- **Acquisition**
  - **External Acquisition**
    - F-90 - With Vendor
    - ABZON - Acquis. w/ Autom. Offsetting Entry
    - F-91 - Clearing Offsetting Entry
    - ABZP - From Affiliated Company
  - **Credit memo**
    - ABGL - ... in Invoice Year
    - ABGF - ... in Next Year
  - ABZE - In-House Production
- **Capitalize Asset u. Const.**
  - AIAB - Distribute
  - AIBU - Settle
- **Transfer**
  - ABUMN - Transfer within Company Code
  - ABT1N - Intercompany Asset Transfer
- **Retirement**
  - **Retirement w/ Revenue**
    - F-92 - With Customer
    - ABAON - Asset Sale Without Customer
  - ABAVN - Asset Retirement by Scrapping
  - ABNE - Subsequent Revenue
  - ABNK - Subsequent Costs
  - ABNAN - Post-Capitalization
- **Manual Value Correction**
  - ABZU - Write-Up
  - ABMA - Manual Depreciation
  - ABAA - Unplanned Depreciation
  - ABMR - Transfer of Reserves
- ABIF - Investment Support
- ABAW - Bal. Sheet Revaluation
- ABSO - Miscellaneous
- **Edit Document**
  - AB03 - Display
  - AB02 - Change
- **Reverse**
  - AIST - Capitalize Asset u. Const.

Asset

- **Document**
  - AB08 - Other Asset Document
- **Create**
  - AS01 - Asset
  - AS21 - Group Asset
  - **Sub-Number**
    - AS11 - Asset
    - AS24 - Group Asset
- **Change**
  - AS02 - Asset
  - AS22 - Group Asset
- **Display**
  - AS03 - Asset
  - AS23 - Group Asset
- **AW01N - Asset Explorer**
- **Lock**
  - AS05 - Asset
  - AS25 - Group Asset
- **Delete**
  - AS06 - Asset
  - AS26 - Group Asset

Periodic Processing

- **SCMA - Schedule Manager**
- **Depreciation Run**
  - AFAB - Execute
  - AFBD - Recreate Session
  - AFBP - Create Log
- **ASKB - Periodic Posting**
- **AR11 - Investment Grant**
- **S_ALR_87099918 - Primary Cost Planning: Depreciation/Interest**
- **Revaluation for the Balance Sheet**
  - AR29 - Post Revaluation
  - J1AI - Inflation
- **AJRW - Fiscal Year Change**
  - ABST2 - Account Reconciliation
- **Year-End Closing**
  - AJAB - Execute
  - **Undo**
    - OAAQ - Entire Company Code
    - OAAR - By Area

Information System
└─ Reports on Asset Accounting
   ├─ Individual Asset
   │ └─ AW01N - Asset Explorer
   └─ Asset Balances
      ├─ Balance Lists
      │ └─ Asset Balances
      │   ├─ S_ALR_87011963 - ... by Asset Number
      │   ├─ S_ALR_87011964 - ... by Asset Class
      │   ├─ S_ALR_87011965 - ... by Business Area
      │   ├─ S_ALR_87011966 - ... by Cost Center
      │   ├─ S_ALR_87011967 - ... by Plant
      │   ├─ S_ALR_87011968 - ... by Location
      │   ├─ S_ALR_87011969 - ... by Asset Super Number
      │   ├─ S_ALR_87011970 - ... by Worklist
      │   ├─ S_ALR_87010125 - Sample for address data for an asset
      │   ├─ S_ALR_87010127 - Real Estate and Similar Rights
      │   ├─ S_ALR_87010129 - Transportation Equipment
      │   └─ S_ALR_87011978 - Asset Balances for Group Assets
      └─ Inventory Lists
         └─ Physical Inventory List
            ├─ S_ALR_87011979 - ... by Cost Center
            ├─ S_ALR_87011980 - ... by Location
            ├─ S_ALR_87011981 - ... by Asset Class
            ├─ S_ALR_87011982 - ... by Plant
            └─ S_ALR_87010137 - Bar Codes

- **Leased Assets**
  - S_ALR_87010139 - Leasing
- **Notes to Financial Statements**
  - **International**
    - S_ALR_87010141 - Liabilities from Leasing Agreements
    - S_ALR_87011990 - Asset History Sheet
    - S_ALR_87011992 - Liabilities from Leasing Agreements
    - S_ALR_87011994 - Asset Balances
  - **Country Specifics**
- **Explanations for P&L**
  - **International**
    - **Depreciation**
      - S_ALR_87012004 - Total Depreciation
      - S_ALR_87012006 - Ordinary Depreciation
      - S_ALR_87012007 - Special Depreciation
      - S_ALR_87012008 - Unplanned Depreciation
      - S_ALR_87012009 - Transfer of Reserves
      - S_ALR_87012011 - Write-Ups
      - S_ALR_87012013 - Depreciation Comparison
      - S_ALR_87012015 - Manual Depreciation
  - **Country Specifics**
    - S_ALR_87012018 - Depreciation and Interest
    - S_ALR_87010173 - Revaluation
- **Cost Accounting**
  - **Depreciation Posted**
    - S_P99_41000192 - Posted depreciation by asset and posting period
    - S_ALR_87010175 - Posted depreciation, related to cost centers
- **Depreciation forecast**
  - S_ALR_87012936 - Depreciation on Capitalized Assets (Depreciation Simulation)
  - S_ALR_87012026 - Depreciation Current Year

Specific Valuations
- International
  - S_ALR_87012028 - Net Worth Valuation
  - S_ALR_87012030 - Insurance Values
- Country Specifics

Preparations for closing
- International
  - S_ALR_87012033 - Gain for transfer of reserves
  - S_ALR_87012035 - Depreciation Current Year
  - S_ALR_87012037 - Changes to Asset Master Records
  - S_ALR_87012039 - Asset Transactions
  - S_ALR_87012041 - Asset Portfolio (Current Book Values)
  - S_ALR_87012043 - G/L Account Balances
- Country Specifics

Day-to-Day Activities
- International
  - S_ALR_87012048 - Asset transactions
  - S_ALR_87012050 - Asset Acquisitions
  - S_ALR_87012052 - Asset Retirements
  - S_ALR_87012054 - Intracompany Asset Transfers
  - S_ALR_87012056 - Directory of Unposted Assets
  - S_ALR_87012058 - List of Origins of Asset Debits
  - S_ALR_87012060 - List of Origins by Cost Elements
- Country Specifics

Taxes
- International
  - S_ALR_87012064 - Total Depreciation
- Country Specifics

History
- S_ALR_87012075 - Asset History

Tools

ARQ0 - Ad Hoc Reports

OAV7 - Simulation Versions

- OAVI - Sort Variants
- OAW3 - Currency Translation Methods
- ARAL - Application Log
- AFAR - Recalculate Values
- OA02 - Mass Change Rule
- AFBN - New Depreciation Area
- AAVN - Recalculate Base Insurable Value
- Worklist
  - AR01 - Generate
  - AR30 - Display
  - AR31 - Edit
- Archiving
  - AARC - Generate
  - AARD - Edit
  - AARR - Reload
  - AARV - Manage
- Asset Summary
  - AUN0 - All Subject Areas
  - AUN1 - Postings
  - AUN2 - Value Determination
  - AUN3 - Posted Values
  - AUN4 - Legacy Data
  - AUN5 - Account Allocation
  - AUN6 - Insurance
  - AUN7 - Leasing
  - AUN8 - Investment Support
  - AUN9 - Screen Layout
  - AUN10 - Fiscal Year
  - AUN11 - Intercompany Transfer
- Problem Analysis
  - AUVA - Incomplete Assets
  - ABST - G/L Reconciliation
  - S_ALR_87008998 - Define Substitution (Master
- Environment

	Data)
	S_ALR_87009207 - Change Asset Classes
	S_ALR_87009182 - Maintain Index Series
	S_ALR_87009086 - Task Customizing for Workflow Control
	S_ALR_87009162 - Define Specifications for Depreciation Posting Runs
	S_ALR_87009161 - Define Unit-of-Production Depreciation
Current Settings	S_ALR_87009144 - Define Maximum Base Values
	S_ALR_87009145 - Define Asset-Specific Base Value Percentages
	S_ALR_87009140 - Define Time-Dependent Period Control
	S_ALR_87009141 - Generate Period Controls
	S_ALR_87009120 - Define Sort Variants
	S_ALR_87009113 - Define Simulation Versions
	S_ALR_87009111 - Maintain Currency Translation Methods
	S_ALR_87009081 - Cancel Year-End Closing

2

AA - Asset Acquisition with Automatic Offsetting Entry: ABZON

Transaction Code	ABZON
Menu	Accounting > Financial Accounting > Asset Accounting > Posting > Acquisition > External Acquisition > Acquis. w/Autom. Offsetting entry

Business Process Overview

Asset Acquisition can be through:

1. **External acquisition through purchase**

   External acquisition of assets will primarily from vendors, who are either your business partners or third parties. It can also be from your affiliated companies (use *Transaction Code: ABZP*). The external asset acquisition can be through different routes:

   - The asset can be posted in MM module.
   - The asset can be created in FI-AA with automatic clearing of the offsetting entry (Transaction Code: ABZON). This can be achieved either of the following ways:

     i.   The posting is made initially in FI-AP and the clearing account cleared when the posting is made to the asset (FI-AA).

     ii. Post the asset with the automatic offsetting entry(FI-AA), then clear the clearing account through a credit posting by an incoming invoice (FI-AP).
   - When not integrated with FI-AP, acquire the asset in FI-AA with an automatic offsetting entry without referencing to a Purchase Requisition (PR). This kind of acquisition is necessary when:

     i.   You have not yet received the invoice or

     ii. When the invoice has already been posted in FI-AP.
   - When integrated with FI-AP, acquire the asset in FI-AA using an incoming invoice but without a reference to a Purchase Order PO).

2. **In-house production**

3. **Subsequent acquisition**

   When the asset /vendor accounts are posted, the system updates the corresponding G/L accounts (FI-AP & FI-AA) through the proper account determinations. SAP uses various kinds of transaction types to distinguish the different transactions. During acquisition the system makes the following entries in the asset master data:

- Date of initial acquisition / period & year of acquisition.
- Capitalization date of the asset.
- Start date for ordinary depreciation (start date is determined from the asset value date/period/year of acquisition).
- Vendor is automatically entered in the "origin".

Transaction Steps

Step-1

Use the transaction code or access the function through the menu. You will be taken to *"Enter Asset Transaction: Acquis. w/Autom. Offsetting Entry"* (Figure: **ABZON**-1).

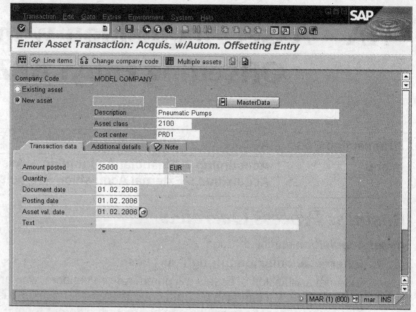

Figure: **ABZON**-1

1. Select **Existing asset or New asset**.
   For the new asset:
2. **Description (M):** Enter the description for the asset.
3. **Asset class (M):** Select the asset class form the drop down list.

Asset class, in SAP, is the basis for classifying an asset based on business and legal requirements. It is essentially a grouping of assets having certain common characteristics. The asset class can be:

- **Buildings**
- **Technical assets**
- **Financial assets**
- **Leased assets**
- **AuC (assets under construction)**
- **Low value assets**

Each asset class will have certain control parameters. You can also define the default values for each of the asset class, for depreciation calculation and other master data. Each asset in the system needs to be associated with an asset class. An *asset class catalog* contains all the asset classes in an enterprise and hence valid across the client. Since an asset class is valid across the client, most of the characteristics of the asset class are defined at the client level; however there are certain characteristics (like the depreciation key, for example), which can be defined at the chart of depreciation level.

Under Transaction data tab:

4. **Amount posted (M):** Enter the acquisition amount to be posted to the asset.
5. **Document date (M):** Enter the document date.
6. **Posting date (M):** Enter the posting date for the document.
7. **Asset val. Date (M):** Enter the date for asset valuation.

 The *asset value date* will be the start date for depreciation for the asset. The planned depreciation is calculated by the system based on this depreciation start date and the selected depreciation term for that asset. Be careful with the posting date and asset value date. Both these dates need to be in the same fiscal year.

Step-1a

You may press

[icon] MasterData to branch into "***Create Asset***" screen to maintain master data information (Figure: **ABZON**-1a).

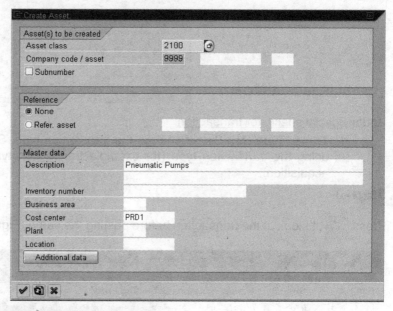

Figure: **ABZON**-1a

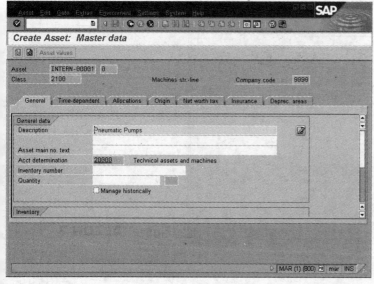

Step-1b

Press Additional data and you will be taken to the " ***Create Asset: Master data***" screen to maintain master data information (Figure: **ABZON**-1b).

Figure: **ABZON**-1b

Step-2

Press Additional details tab
to enter details like the
transaction type, reference etc
(Figure: **ABZON**-2).

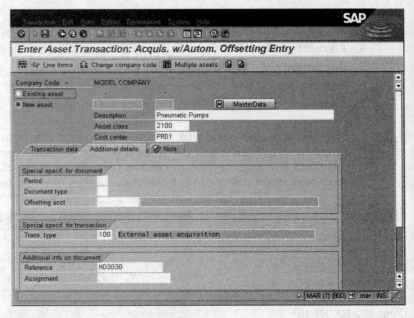

Figure: **ABZON**-2

Under Special specif. for transaction:

1. **Trans. Type (M):** Select/change the transaction type. SAP identifies an asset transaction using the transaction type (for example transaction type 100 is used for external asset acquisition).

Step-3

Press 🔲 , to look at the transaction before posting the same (Figure: **ABZON**-3).

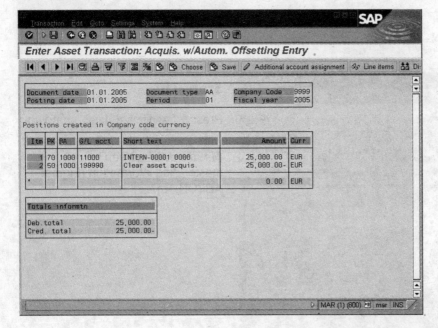

Figure: **ABZON**-3

Step-4

Look at the line items proposed by the document. If necessary, select a line and drill down further to see the details. When completed, press 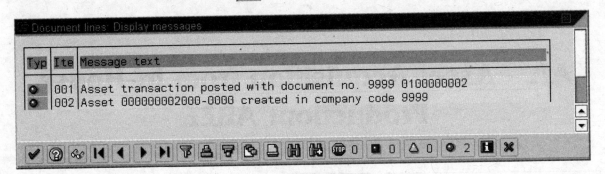 to post the document (Figure: **ABZON**-4).

Figure: **ABZON**-4

AA - Asset Acquisition with Automatic Offsetting Entry: ABZON

Step-2

Look at the items proposed by the document. If necessary, select a line and drill down further to see the details. When completed, press [icon] to post the document. (route: ABZON-4).

3

AA - Asset Acquisition from In-House Production: ABZE

Transaction Code	ABZE
Menu	Accounting > Financial Accounting > Asset Accounting > Posting > Acquisition > In-House Production

Business Process Overview

In-House Asset Acquisition is primarily the capitalization of goods/services produced by your company. The costs associated with the complete or partial production of the goods/services from within the company needs to be capitalized into separate asset(s). Usually, the capitalization is done as under:

1. Create an order/project (in **Investment Management**) to capture the production costs associated with the goods/services produced in-house.
2. Settle the order/project to an **AuC (Asst under Construction)**.
3. Distribute/Settle the AuC so created in to new asset(s).

You will be using the **transaction type 110** for asset acquisition from in-house production

Transaction Steps

Step-1

Use the transaction code or access the function through the menu. You will be taken to **"Acquisition from in-house production: Initial Screen"** (Figure: **ABZE**-1).

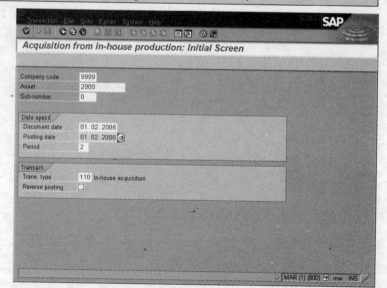

Figure: **ABZE**-1

Enter:

1. **Company code (M):** Enter the relevant company code.
2. **Asset number (M):** Enter the asset number.
3. **Sub-number (O):** Enter the sub-number. By default system proposes the sub number as '0".

Under Date Specif.:

4. **Document date (M):** Enter the document date.
5. **Posting date (M):** Enter the posting date for the document.
6. **Period (M):** Enter or change the period.

Under Transact:

7. **Trans. type (M):** Select an asset transaction type from the drop down values. System updates the assets/accounts based on the transaction type selected. Select:
   - **Transaction type 110** for In-House Acquisition.

Transaction type **identifies the nature of asset transaction (acquisition or transfer or retirement) so as to specify what is that updated, among (a) Depreciation area, (b) Value field and (c) Asset accounts (in B/S). The following are some of the common transaction types used:**

- **100   Asset Acquisition – Purchase**
- **110   Asset Acquisition – In-House Production**
- **200   Asset Retirement – Scrapping**
- **210   Asset Retirement – Sale**

Every transaction type is grouped into a *Transaction type group (10 -> Acquisition)* **which characterizes the various transaction types (for example, transaction types 100 & 110) with in that group. The system makes it possible to limit the transaction type groups that can be associated with certain asset classes.**

The transaction type is extensively used in most of the asset reports, including the asset history sheet, to display the various asset transactions differentiated by the transaction types. SAP comes with a numerous transaction types which will take care of almost all your requirement. However, should there be a specific case, you may also create your own transaction type which will certainly be remote!

Step-2

Press ✅ to enter other details in the "***Create Asset Transaction: In-house acquisition***" screen (Figure: **ABZE**-2).

Figure: **ABZE**-2

Maintain necessary values in "***Posting data***" area (including offsetting account details).

Figure: **ABZE**-3

Step-3

Press Dep. areas ... and the system pos-up "***Overview of Posted Areas***" (Figure: **ABZE**-3) Close the pop-up to go back to the initial screen.

Step-4

Press Display document
to look at the transaction
before posting the same
(Figure: **ABZE**-4).

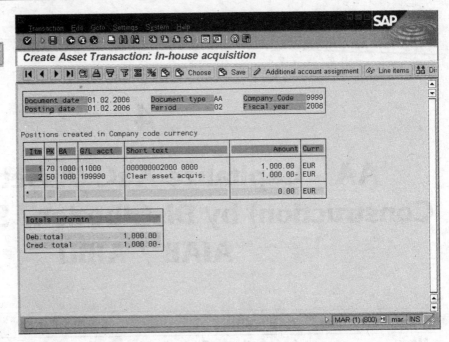

Create Asset Transaction: In-house acquisition

| Document date | 01.02.2006 | Document type | AA | Company Code | 9999 |
| Posting date | 01.02.2006 | Period | 02 | Fiscal year | 2006 |

Positions created in Company code currency

Itm	PK	BA	G/L acct	Short text	Amount	Curr
1	70	1000	11000	000000002000 0000	1,000.00	EUR
2	50	1000	199990	Clear asset acquis.	1,000.00-	EUR
*					0.00	EUR

Totals informtn	
Deb.total	1,000.00
Cred. total	1,000.00-

Figure: **ABZE**-4

Step-5

Look at the line items proposed by the document. If necessary, select a line and drill down further to
see the details. When completed, press 🖫 to post the document (Figure: **ABZE**-5).

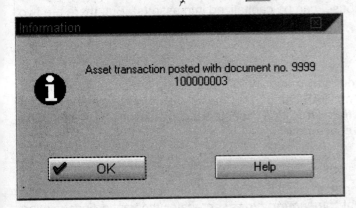

Information

ℹ Asset transaction posted with document no. 9999
100000003

OK   Help

Figure: **ABZE**-5

4

AA – Capitalize AuC (Asset under Construction) by Distribution/ Settlement: AIAB / AIBU

Transaction Code	AIAB / AIBU
Menu	Accounting > Financial Accounting > Asset Accounting > Posting > Capitalize Asset u. Const. > Distribute / Settle

Business Process Overview

The goods and/or services produced, in-house, can be capitalized into asset(s). But, there are two distinct phases during this process:

1. Construction phase
2. Utilization phase

The construction phase is one in which you start producing or assembling the asset which is not yet ready for putting into economic utilization. SAP categorizes these kinds of assets into a special asset class called "*Assets under Construction*" (*AuC*). An asset under construction can be managed in two ways, as regard the asset master is concerned:

1. As a "normal" asset.
2. As an asset with 'line item management'.

Later on, the AuC is capitalized and transferred to regular asset(s), by distribution/settlement. While doing so, the system with the help of different *transaction types* segregates the transactions relating to the current year with that of the previous years. The capitalization can be:

1. Lump sum capitalization.
2. With line item settlement (when capitalized using line item settlement, it is not necessary that you need to settle (a) all the line items and (b) 100 % in a particular line item).

In case of integration with SAP-IM (**Investment Management**), capital investments can be managed as AuC by:

- Collecting the production costs associated to an order/project.
- Settling the collected costs to an AuC.
- Capitalizing the AuC into new assets by distribution/settlement.

Transaction Steps

Step-1

Use the transaction code or access the function through the menu. You will be taken to **"Settlement AuC: Initial Screen"** (Figure: **AIAB**-1).

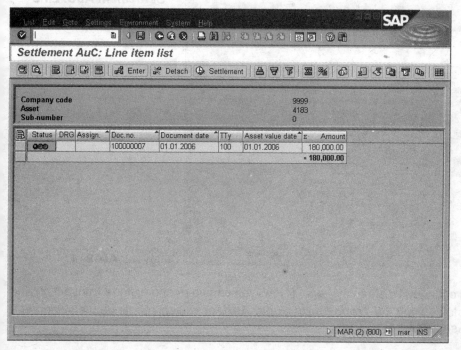

Figure: **AIAB**-1

Enter:

1. **Company code (M):** Enter the company code.
2. **Asset (M):** Enter the asst number.
3. **Sub number (O):** Enter the asset sub number, if any.

Under Settings:

4. **Layout (M):** Select the one proposed by the system, unless you have a reason to select another.

Step-2

Press ![icon] and you are taken to **"Settlement AuC: Line item list"** screen (Figure: **AIAB**-2).

Note that the status button is 'red'.

Figure: **AIAB**-2

Step-3

Press 🔲 Enter and you will be taken to *"Maintain Settlement Rule: Overview"* screen (Figure: **AIAB**-3).

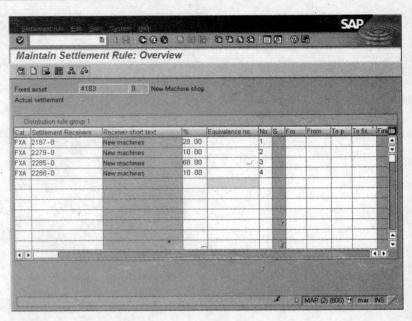

Figure: **AIAB**-3

Under the <u>Distribution rule group1</u>, table:

1. Select a category from the drop-down list.
2. Select the settlement receivers (new machines/assets).
3. Under %, enter the percentage each of the new assets should receive from AuC.

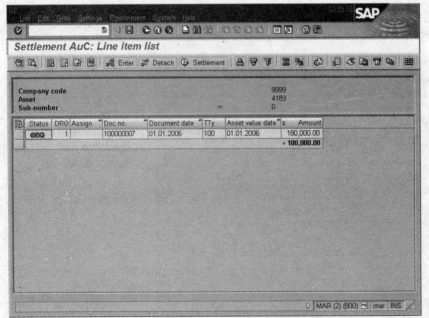

Figure: **AIAB**-4

Step-4

Press 🔙 to go to *"Settlement AuC: Line item list"* screen (Figure: **AIAB**-4).

Note that the status has changed to green. 🟢🟢🟢 Now, you can save and exit the transaction and complete the settlement later using the *Transaction Code: AIBU* or you can continue the settlement. Let us continue with the settlement.

Step-5

Press ⊕ Settlement and you will be in the "**AuC Settlement: Initial Screen**" (Figure: **AIBU**-1).

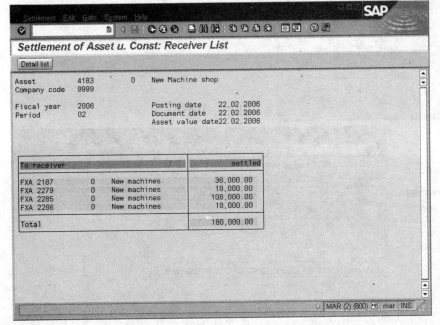

Figure: AIBU-1

Since we reached this screen from the **AIAB** transaction, the system has already filled-up the details for you! Under "Processing option", tick mark both "**Test run**" and "**Detail list**".

Step-6

Press ⊕ Execute and you will be in "**Settlement of Asset u. Const: Receiver List**" screen (Figure: **AIBU**-2).

Figure: **AIBU**-2

Step-7

Now go back by pressing ⊙ and remove the tick mark against "Test run" field (Figure: **AIBU**-3).

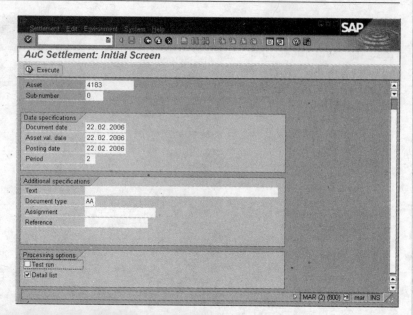

Figure: **AIBU**-3

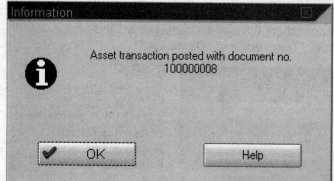

Step-8

Pres 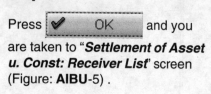 sand the system pops-up the information that the asset transaction has been posted to (Figure: **AIBU**-4).

Figure: **AIBU**-4

Step-9

Press [✔ OK] and you are taken to "***Settlement of Asset u. Const: Receiver List***' screen (Figure: **AIBU**-5) .

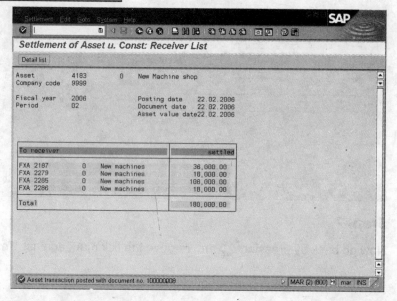

Figure: **AIBU**-5

Step-10

Press Detail list and you will be in "*Settlement of Asset u. Const: Detailed Receiver List*" screen (Figure: **AIBU**-6).

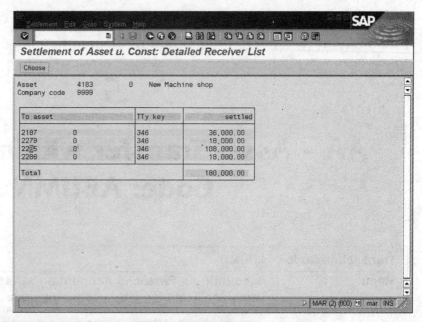

Figure: **AIBU**-6

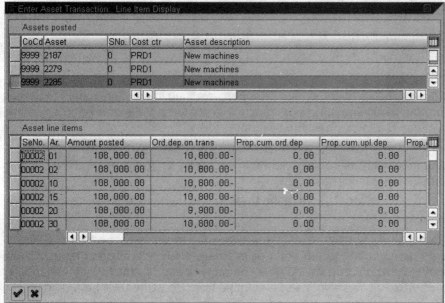

Step-11

Select a line, and press Choose to display the assets/ asset line items posted (Figure: **AIBU**-7).

Figure: **AIBU**-7

5

AA - Asset Transfer within Company Code: ABUMN

Transaction Code	ABUMN
Menu	Accounting > Financial Accounting > Asset Accounting > Posting > Transfer > Transfer within company code

Business Process Overview

Asset transfer is of two types, namely:

1. Inter-company asset transfer
2. Intra-company asset transfer

Inter-company asset transfer is between the company codes, resulting in creation of the new asset in the target company code (the receiving one). The transaction posts the values as per the posting method selected during the transfer. In doing so the system:

- Retires the asset in the source/sending company code by an *asset retirement*.
- Posts acquisition in the new/target company code by an *asset acquisition*, and creates the new asset in the target company code.
- Posts inter-company profit/loss arising out of the transfer.
- Updates FI-G/L automatically.

An inter-company asset transfer is usually necessiated when (a) there is a need for physically changing the location from one company to the other or (b) there is an organization restructuring resulting that the new asset to be attached with the new company code. You may use the standard *transfer variants* supplied by SAP. The selection of a suitable transfer variant will be based on (1) the legal relationship among the company codes and (2) the methods chosen for transferring the asset values.

Inter-company asset transfer can be handled:

- Individually using the normal transaction.
- Collectivily for a number of assets using the 'mass transfer'.

If you need to transfer assets cross-system, you need to use **ALE** functionality.

Intra-company asset transfer is the transfer of an asset with in the same company code. This would have been necessiated by:

- Change in the asset class or business area etc.

- Settlement of an AuC to a new asset.
- Transfer of stock materials into an asset (by posting a GI to an order through MM or settlement of a production order to an asset).
- Splitting an existing asset into one or more new assets.

Transaction Steps

Step-1

Use the transaction code or access the function through the menu. You will be taken to *"Enter Asset Transaction: Transfer with in Company Code"* (Figure: **ABUMN**-1).

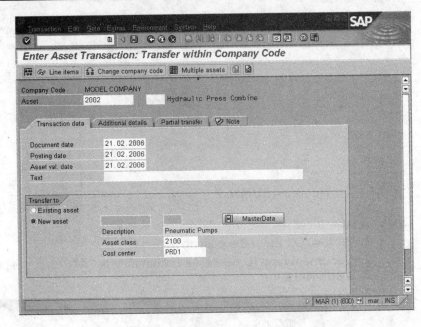

Figure: **ABUMN**-1

Enter:

1. **Asset (M):** Enter the asst number, including a sub number, if any Under Transaction data .
2. **Document date (M):** Enter the document date.
3. **Posting date (M):** Enter the posting date for the document.
4. **Asset val. Date (M):** Enter the date for asset valuation.

Under <u>Transfer to</u>:

5. **Existing asset / New asset (M):** Select either of the options.

If the asset needs to be transferred to an existing one, then select the first option and enter the asset number/sub-number of the existing asset. Else, to transfer to an new asset, select the 'new asset' option and maintain the details like:

- **Description (M)**
- **Asset Class (M)**
- **Cost center (M)**

You may also branch to master data creation by pressing [🗒] MasterData button, for the new asset to be created by the system.

Step-2

Press Additional details tab to maintain additional information (Figure: **ABUMN**-2).

Figure: **ABUMN**-2

Under <u>Special specif. for document:</u>

1. **Period (O):** Enter the posting period.
2. **Document type (O):** Select a document type (**AA**, for asset postings) for the posting (Figure: **ABUMN**-3 & 4).

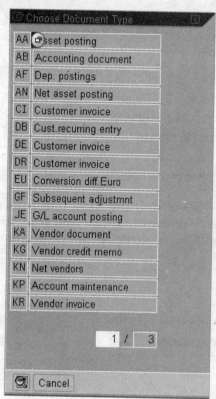

Figure: **ABUMN**-3   Figure: **ABUMN**-4

Under <u>Special specif. for transaction:</u>

3. Transfer variant (O): Select the suitable transfer variant.

Transfer variant **is dependent upon whether the company codes involved are legally dependent or independent. Transfer variants specify (1) how the transferred asset will be valued at the receiving company code and (2) type of transaction (acquisition or transfer) used for the transaction.**

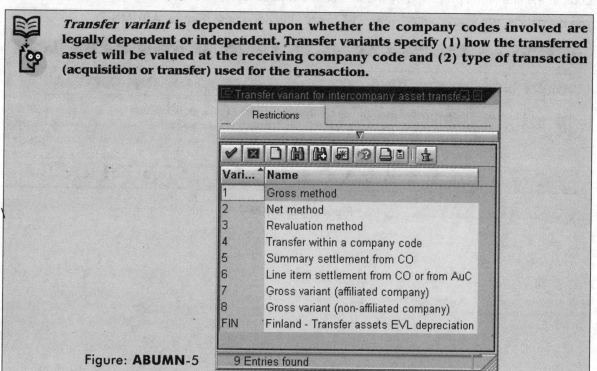

Figure: **ABUMN**-5

Use | Partial transfer | **to maintain details relating to partial transfer.**

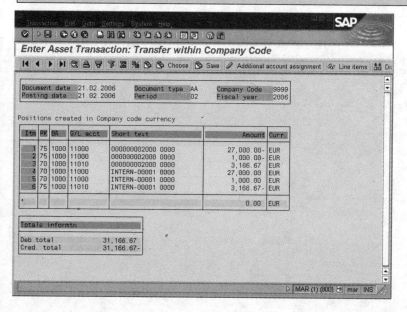

Step-3

Press [icon], to look at the transaction before posting the same (Figure: **ABUMN**-6).

Figure: **ABUMN**-6

Step-4

Look at the line items proposed by the document. If necessary, select a line and drill down further to see the details. When completed, press 🖫 to post the document (Figure: **ABUMN**-7).

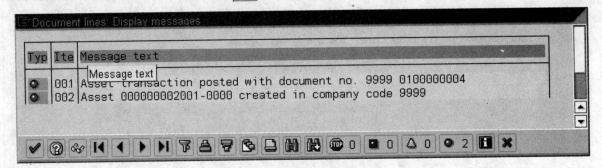

Figure: **ABUMN**-7

6

AA - Asset Sale without Customer: ABAON

Transaction Code	ABAON
Menu	Accounting > Financial Accounting > Asset Accounting > Posting > Retirement > Retirement w/Revenue > Asset sale without customer

Business Process Overview

Asset retirement is an integral part of asset management. You may retire an asset (1) by sale or (2) by scrapping. In case of sales, it can be (1) with revenue or (2) without revenue: again the asset sale can be (1) with the customer or (2) with out customer.

During asset sales transactions, the system removes the *APC (Acquisition and Production Costs)* and also the corresponding accumulated depreciation, then the profit or loss arising out of the sale is recorded in the system. Even, in case of partial retirement or partial sales, the system records the proportionate gain/loss arising out of the transaction. Any tax posting arising out of the transaction is automatically created by the system.

SAP provides various ways of posting retirement in the system, which include:

- **Mass retirement**
- **Asset retirement with revenue**
  - With customer (involving integration with FI-AR)
    - o Debit customer, credit assets
  - Without customer
- **Asset retirement without revenue**
  - With customer
    - o Debit clearing account, credit asset
    - o Debit customer in A/R, credit the clearing account
- **Asset retirement using G/L document posting**

Transaction Steps

Step-1

Use the transaction code or access the function through the menu. You will be taken to *"Enter Asset Transaction: Asset Sale without Customer"* (Figure: **ABAON**-1).

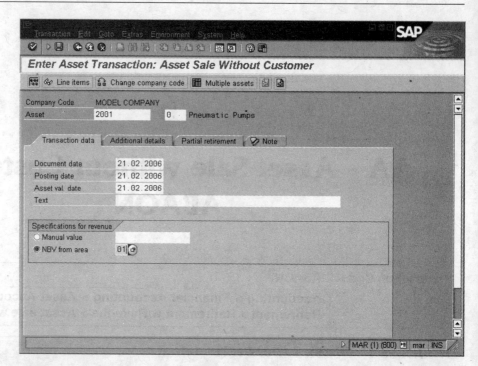

Figure: **ABAON**-1

Enter:

1. **Asset (M):** Enter the asst number, including a sub number , if any Under Transaction data .

2. **Document date (M):** Enter the document date.

3. **Posting date (M):** Enter the posting date for the document.

4. **Asset val. Date (M):** Enter the date for asset valuation.

Under Specifications for revenue:

5. **Manual value / NBV area (M):** Select either of the options.

 If you want give a value, then select the manual value option and enter the amount. Else, select the other option where in the system will calculate the revenue taking into account the net book value (NBV). When 'NBV area' option is selected, note to select the appropriate valuation area (01, 03 etc) from the drop down list.

Select other tabs, if necessary, and enter the details.

The various asset retirement transactions are taken care of by the *transaction types* in the system (Figure: **ABAON**-2).

Look at the various asset retirement transactions starting with '200' which is for retiring an asset without revenue. You will use transaction '210' when an asset is to be retired with revenue. Note to select the transaction which is appropriate for the given situation.

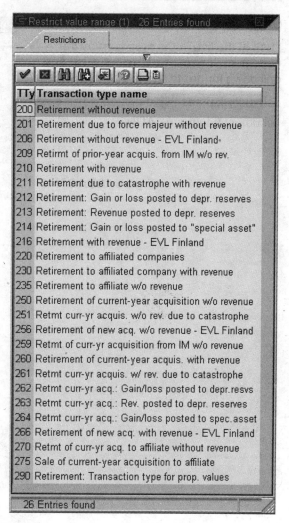

TTy	Transaction type name
200	Retirement without revenue
201	Retirement due to force majeur without revenue
206	Retirement without revenue - EVL Finland
209	Retirmt of prior-year acquis. from IM w/o rev.
210	Retirement with revenue
211	Retirement due to catastrophe with revenue
212	Retirement: Gain or loss posted to depr. reserves
213	Retirement: Revenue posted to depr. reserves
214	Retirement: Gain or loss posted to "special asset"
216	Retirement with revenue - EVL Finland
220	Retirement to affiliated companies
230	Retirement to affiliated company with revenue
235	Retirement to affiliate w/o revenue
250	Retirement of current-year acquisition w/o revenue
251	Retmt curr-yr acquis. w/o rev. due to catastrophe
256	Retirement of new acq. w/o revenue - EVL Finland
259	Retmt of curr-yr acquisition from IM w/o revenue
260	Retirement of current-year acquis. with revenue
261	Retmt curr-yr acquis. w/ rev. due to catastrophe
262	Retmt curr-yr acq.: Gain/loss posted to depr.resvs
263	Retmt curr-yr acq.: Rev. posted to depr. reserves
264	Retmt curr-yr acq.: Gain/loss posted to spec.asset
266	Retirement of new acq. with revenue - EVL Finland
270	Retmt of curr-yr acq. to affiliate without revenue
275	Sale of current-year acquisition to affiliate
290	Retirement: Transaction type for prop. values

Figure: **ABAON**-2

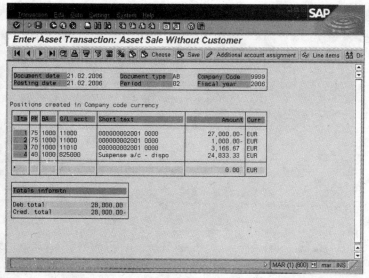

Figure: **ABAON**-3

Step-2

Press [icon], to look at the transaction before posting the same (Figure: **ABAON**-3).

Step-3

Look at the line items proposed by the document. If necessary, select a line and drill down further to see the details. When completed, press 🔘 to post the document (Figure: **ABAON**-4).

Figure: **ABAON**-4

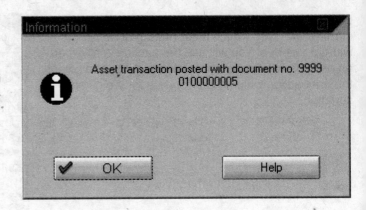

7

AA - Miscellaneous Transactions: ABSO

Transaction Code	ABSO
Menu	Accounting > Financial Accounting > Asset Accounting > Posting > Manual value correction > Miscellaneous

Business Process Overview

Use **manual value corrections** for, manually performing and adjusting:

- Write-Up (Transaction Code: ABZU)
- Manual Depreciation (Transaction Code: ABMA)
- Unplanned Depreciation (Transaction code: ABAA)
- Transfer of Reserves (Transaction Code: ABMR)

The miscellaneous transaction is useful for:

- Posting incidental costs without capitalization

Transaction Steps

Step-1

Use the transaction code or access the function through the menu. You will be taken to **"Miscellaneous Transactions: Initial Screen"** (Figure: **ABSO**-1).

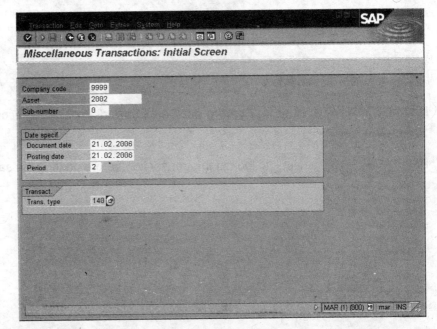

Figure: **ABSO**-1

Enter:

1. **Company code (M):** Enter the relevant company code.
2. **Asset number (M):** Enter the asset number.
3. **Sub-number (O):** Enter the sub-number. By default, system proposes the sub number as '0".

Under Date Specif.:

5. **Document date (M):** Enter the document date.
6. **Posting date (M):** Enter the posting date for the document.
7. **Period (M):** Enter or change the period.

Under Transact:

8. **Trans. type (M):** Select an asset transaction type from the drop down values. System updates the assets/accounts based on the transaction type selected. Select **Transaction type 140** for posting Incidental Costs w/o Capitalization.

Step-2

Press ✓ to enter other details in the "***Create Asset Transaction: Incidental costs without capitalization***" screen (Figure: **ABSO**-2).

Figure: **ABSO**-2

Maintain necessary values in "***Posting data***" area (including offsetting account details).

Step-3

Press Display document , to look at the transaction before posting the same (Figure: **ABSO**-3).

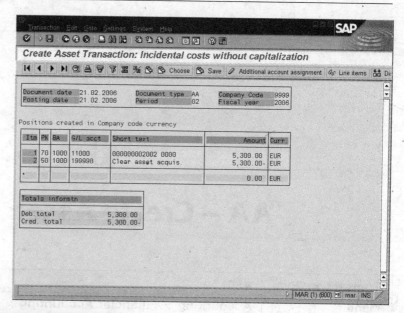

Figure: **ABSO**-3

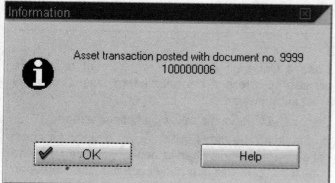

Step-4

Look at the line items proposed by the document. If necessary, select a line and drill down further to see the details. When completed, press 💾 to post the document (Figure: **ABSO**-4).

Figure: **ABSO**-4

8

AA – Create Asset: AS01

Transaction Code	AS01
Menu	Accounting > Financial Accounting > Asset Accounting > Asset > Create

Business Process Overview

An asset can be a **simple asset** or **complex asset**. Depending upon the requirement, assets are maintained with **asset main number** and **asset sub-numbers.** A *complex asset* consists of many sub-assets; each of them identified using an asset sub-number.

Before a master can be created in the system, you need to have the following defined already:

- **Chart of depreciation**: This is the list containing the depreciation areas defined for asset evaluation and reporting. As in a chart of account, a single chart of depreciation can be used by many company codes but the converse is not true (No company code can use more than one chart of depreciation).

- **Asset class:** This is the most important configuration element which decides the type of asset (like land, buildings, furniture & fixtures, equipment, assets under construction, leased assets, low-value assets etc), the document number range, data entry screen lay out for asset master creation, G/L account assignments, depreciation areas, depreciation terms etc. An asset class is defined at the client level and is available to all the company codes of that client.

- **Depreciation area:** A depreciation area decides how and for what purpose an asset is evaluated. A depreciation area can be 'real' or a 'derived one'. You may need to use several depreciation areas for a single asset depending upon the valuation and reporting requirements.

An asset master can be created by copying an existing asset in the same company or another company; it can also be created from the scratch when it is done for the first time. Again, while creating the master, SAP allows to create multiple assets in one go, provided all such assets are similar (having the same **asset class** and all belonging to the same company code).

From Release 4.5, the transaction codes for creating asset master has been changed to AS series instead of the earlier AT series (for example create asset is by AS01 (AT01 earlier), change asset is AS02 (AT02 earlier) and so on. If you are still comfortable with creation of assets using the conventional screen than with the 'tab' feature available now in AS transaction series, you are welcome to do so, but you can not find these transactions under 'ASMN'!

Transaction Steps

Step-1

Use the transaction code or access the function through the menu. You will be taken to "**Create Asset: Initial screen**" (Figure: **AS01**-1).

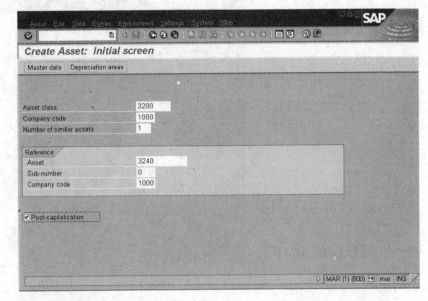

Figure: **AS01**-1

Enter the details:

1. **Asset class (M):** Enter the asset class.
2. **Company code (M):** Enter the company code in which the asset needs to be created.
3. **Number of similar assets (M):** Enter, how many such assets you want to create.

 You have the option of creating multiple, similar assets from this single transaction. Though a number of assets are thus created in a single go, the system still allows you to maintain the individual descriptions and inventory details pertaining to each asset when the data is saved.

 Use this option to create multiple but similar assets, belonging to the *same asset class and company code*. If the asset class is to be different, create the master one-by-one.

Under <u>Reference</u> (if the asset is to be created by referring to an existing asset in the system):

1. **Asset (O):** Enter the asset number which will be used as the reference.
2. **Sub-number (O):** Enter the asset sub-number.
3. **Company code (O):** From which company code the asset is being referenced to.
4. **Post-capitalization (O):** Check this, if you need to post capitalization as well.

Step-2

Press | Master data | to maintain master data or | Depreciation areas | to maintain depreciation areas, if master data have already been maintained, and you are taken to "**Create Asset: Post-capitalization Master Data**" screen (Figure: **AS01**-2).

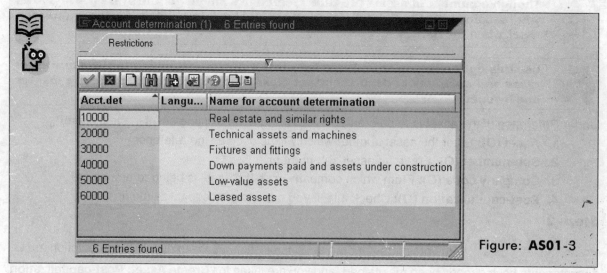

Figure: **AS01**-2

Step-3

In General tab, maintain the following:

1. **Description (M):** Enter the asset description.
2. **Asset main no. text (O):** Provide a meaningful text.
3. **Account determination (M):** This is defaulted from the ***asset class configuration*** (Figure: **AS01**-3).

Acct.det	Langu...	Name for account determination
10000		Real estate and similar rights
20000		Technical assets and machines
30000		Fixtures and fittings
40000		Down payments paid and assets under construction
50000		Low-value assets
60000		Leased assets

6 Entries found

Figure: **AS01**-3

4. **Manage historically (O):** If, you want to manage the asset with its history, then check this indicator.

> **When an asset is managed historically, the system will not allow the asset values and transactions to be re-organized unless you deactivate the asset.**

5. **Quantity (M):** Unit.

Posting information:

6. **Capitalized on (M):** Leave the field to be filled in by the system with the first posting of capitalization of the asset.

Step-4

Press Time-dependent tab (Figure: **AS01**-4), and enter the details as mentioned below:

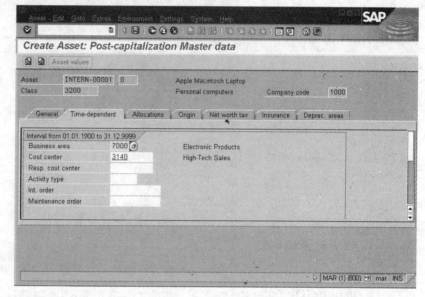

Figure: **AS01**-4

Under Interval from 01.01.1990 to 31.12.9999:

1. **Business area (O):** Select the appropriate business area for the asset.
2. **Cost center (M):** Select the cost centre.
3. **Plant (O):** Assign the asset to a plant.

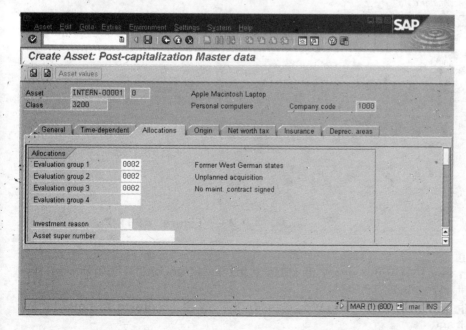

Step-5

Press Allocations tab (Figure: **AS01**-5).

Figure: **AS01**-5

Under <u>Allocations:</u>

1. **Evaluation group1, 2, 3, and 4 (O):** Depending on how you wish to classify the asset. enter a suitable evaluation group.

Step-6

Press ` Origin ` tab
(Figure: **AS01**-6).

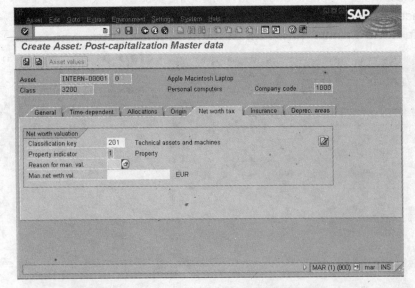

Figure: **AS01**-6

Under <u>Origin:</u>

1. **Vendor (O):** Enter the vendor number from whom the asset has been purchased.
2. **Asset purch new (O):** Check if purchased new.

Step-7

Press ` Net worth tax ` tab, and maintain the details, if applicable for the asset (Figure: **AS01**-7).

Figure: **AS01**-7

Under <u>Net worth valuation:</u>

1. **Classification key (O):** Enter a key to classify the asset according to net worth law requirements, if any.
2. **Property indicator (M):** Enter a key to classify the asset according to property law requirements, if any.

Step-8

Press Insurance tab
(Figure: **AS01**-8).

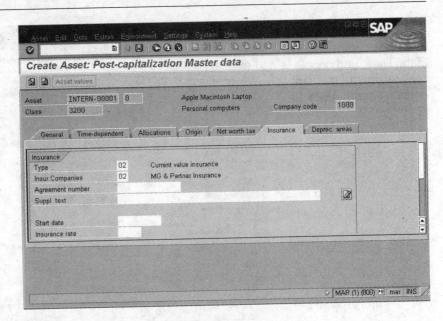

Figure: **AS01**-8

Under Insurance:

1. **Type (O):** Enter the type to determine the insurable value of the asset.
2. **Insur Companies (O):** The insurance company with which the asset has been insured.

Step-9

Press

Deprec. areas tab
(Figure: **AS01**-8).

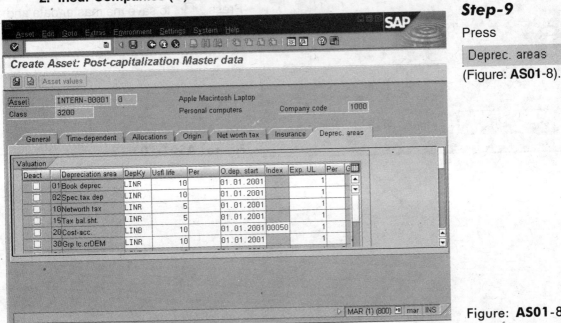

Figure: **AS01**-8

Under Valuation:

1. **Deact (O):** Deactivate the rows which you will not require, by selecting the check-box.
2. **Usfl life (M):** Enter the useful life in years.
3. **O. dep start (M):** Change the default date proposed by the system for start of ordinary depreciation.

Step-9

Place the cursor on any of the lines, and double click to see the relevant details (Figure: **AS01**-9).

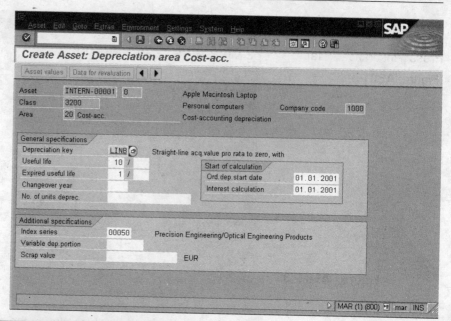

Figure: **AS01**-9

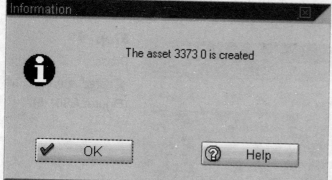

Step-10

Press to save the master data and exit from the transactions (Figure: **AS01**-10).

Figure: **AS01**-10

9

AA - Asset Explorer: AW01N

Transaction Code	AW01N
Menu	Accounting > Financial Accounting > Asset Accounting > Asset > Asset Explorer

Business Process Overview

Asset Explorer, is a handy and convenient single interface transaction helping you to display the asset values, depreciation details etc in a very user friendly way. Gone were the days, where you had to move to different pages, and re-enter the same transaction many a time for displaying the same details of different assets.

Using asset explorer you have the convenience of:

- Moving from one asset number to the other effortlessly
- Displaying asset values, both planned and posted, for any number of depreciation areas from the same page but in various tab pages
- Jumping to the asset master or cost centre master or G/L account master
- Calling up various asset reports
- Currency converted views
- Looking at the various transactions relating to an asset
- Looking up all the values for different fiscal years
- Distinguishing between real and derived depreciation areas with two differentiating symbols
- Displaying depreciation calculation function, and if necessary, recalculation of depreciation

Asset explorer is designed for easy navigation, with the following sections:

1. **Asset values window**

   The top-left area/window is the 'asset values' window, which is in a tree-like structure, expanding to various depreciation areas like 01, 03, 10 etc. By selecting any one of these depreciation areas, you will be able to view the value of an asset in the 'asset value details window'.

2. **Objects related to asset window**

   This is also on the left hand side of the display page, just below the 'asset values window'. With a drill down tree-like structure you will be able to navigate between cost centres and G/L accounts relating to the asset.

3. **Asset value detail window (with tab pages)**

This is the main window on the right, usually occupying most of the page area. Here is where you see the information like company code, asset number selected, fiscal year etc. This window is made of , completely re-sizeable, two components: the top area displaying the asset details and the bottom showing the *asset value/transactions*. The entire bottom area is divided into different tabs which display:

● Planned values
● Posted values
● Comparison
● Parameters

A helpful *'icon legend'* makes your understanding of the items/display easier than ever.

Transaction Steps

Step-1

Use the transaction code or access the function through the menu. You will be taken to "*Asset Explorer*" (Figure: **AW01N**-1).

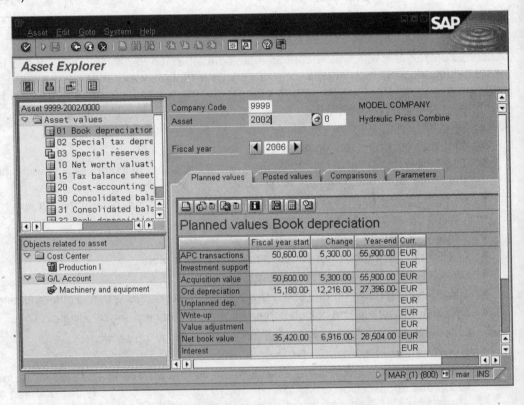

Figure:
AW01N-1

Step-2

Before navigating through the transaction, it will be easier if you understand the different icons and their usage with this transaction. Press [icon] to see the details (Figure: **AW01N**-2).

Familiarize yourself with the various icons, so that you will be able to make effective use of the available functionality and options. Needless to say, these graphic icons really help.

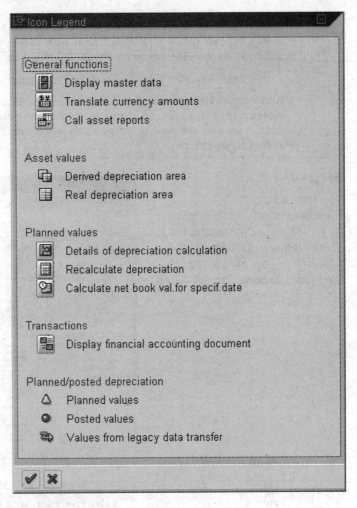

General functions
- Display master data
- Translate currency amounts
- Call asset reports

Asset values
- Derived depreciation area
- Real depreciation area

Planned values
- Details of depreciation calculation
- Recalculate depreciation
- Calculate net book val.for specif.date

Transactions
- Display financial accounting document

Planned/posted depreciation
- Planned values
- Posted values
- Values from legacy data transfer

Figure: **AW01N**-2

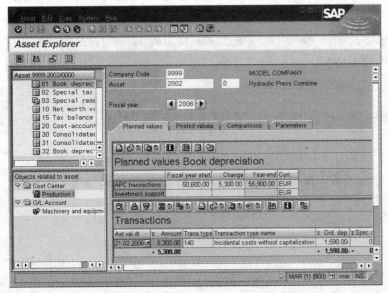

Figure: **AW01N**-3

Step-3

As explained else where, enter the company code, asset and select a fiscal year from the *'Asset value detail* window which is the main window (Figure: **AW01N**-3).

Under the left 'Asset values' window, expand the tree to display all the depreciation areas relevant for the asset just selected/entered for the display. Highlight the desired depreciation area (highlighted row is shown in yellow background), and press the | Planned values | tab in the main window on the right. Now, you will be looking at the planned values of the selected depreciation area with details like year-beginning values, change, year-end values etc. At the bottom *"Transactions"* area, you can view all the transactions associated with this asset for the year already selected at the top.

Step-4

You may adjust the *"Transactions"* area's display by enlarging or decreasing the divider (Figure: **AW01N**-4). This screen has now almost shrunk the *"Transactions"* area.

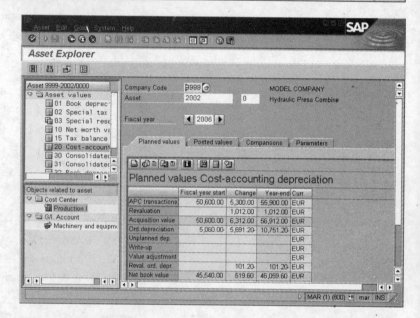

Figure: **AW01N**-4

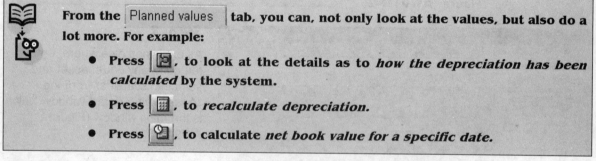

From the | Planned values | tab, you can, not only look at the values, but also do a lot more. For example:

- Press ▣, to look at the details as to *how the depreciation has been calculated* by the system.

- Press ▦, to *recalculate depreciation.*

- Press ▣, to calculate *net book value for a specific date.*

Step-5

Press | Posted values | to display (Figure: **AW01N**-5) the *values posted* for the asset, for the selected depreciation area, for the year (say, 2006).

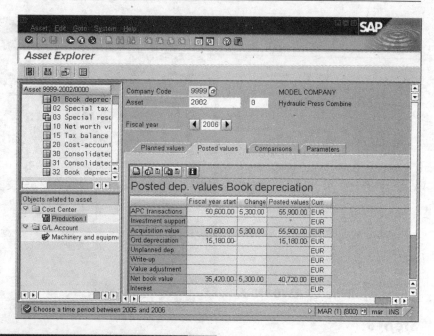

Figure: **AW01N**-5

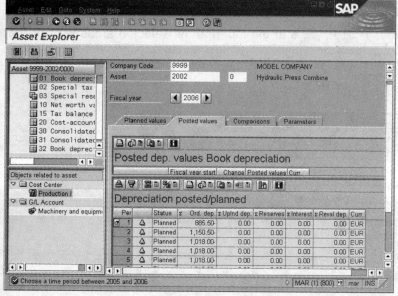

Figure: **AW01N**-6

Step-6

To look at the depreciation posted/planned, restore the **"Transactions"** area by minimizing '**Posted dep. values –Book depreciation**' area (Figure: **AW01N**-6).

Step-7

For looking **fiscal-year wise comparison**, for a single depreciation area, press Comparisons tab, and the system displays the details by selecting the first depreciation area which is marked by <01> (Figure: **AW01N**-7). Please also note that the **fiscal year** at the top is now displaying **from/to** range with the 10 year spread.

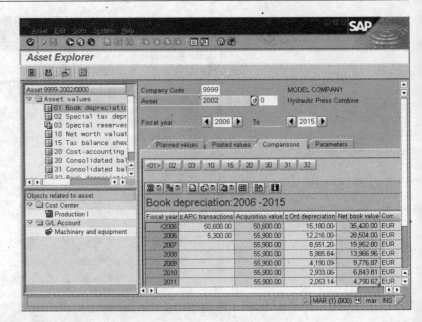

Figure: **AW01N**-7

Step-8

For comparing more than one depreciation area, press the other depreciation area buttons
02 03 10 15 20 30 31 32 at the top, and the selected areas will now be
marked as <01> <02> <03> <10> <15>. You can see the details in "***Comparison of several depreciation areas: 2006-2015***" (Figure: **AW01N**-8).

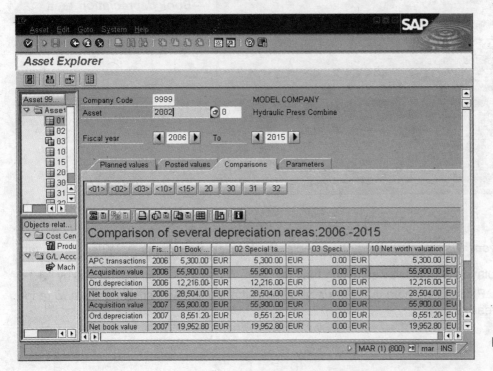

Figure: **AW01N**-8

Step-9

Press [Parameters] tab, to look at the **parameters,** the system is using to arrive at the calculation of depreciation, asset values etc (Figure: **AW01N**-9).

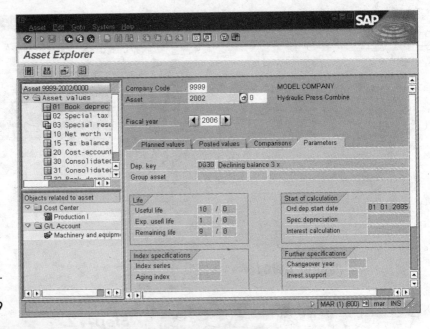

Figure: **AW01N**-9

Step-10

At any point of time, press 💾 to jump to the master record of the asset (Figure: **AW01N**-10).

Figure: **AW01N**-10

Step-11

Press ⬅ to go back, and double-click on 🗐 Production I from the Objects related to asset on the left bottom of the page to view the cost centre details associated with the asset (Figure: **AW01N**-11).

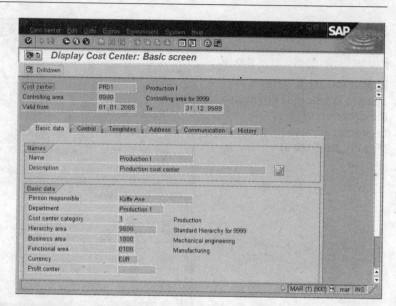

Figure: **AW01N**-11

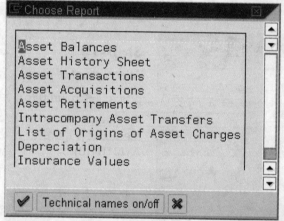

Step-12

Press 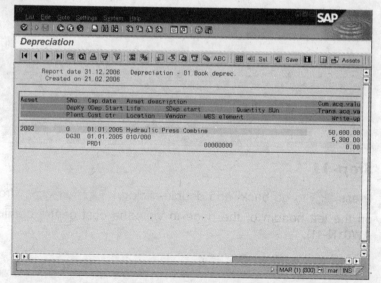 to go back. Press to call up the 'asset reports'. You will receive a pop-up, "**Choose Report**", displaying the various reports (Figure: **AW01N**-12).

Figure: **AW01N**-12

Step-13

Select a report (example:

Depreciation), and press . The system brings up "***Depreciation***" report (Figure: **AW01N**-13).

Figure: **AW01N**-13

Step-14

Press 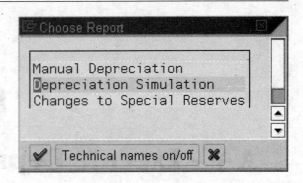 Assets (right corner) for further reports.
You will see a pop-up **"Choose Report"** (Figure: **AW01N**-14).

Figure: **AW01N**-14

Step-15

Select a report (example: **Depreciation Simulation**), and press ✔. The system brings up *"Depreciation Simulation"* report (Figure: **AW01N**-15).

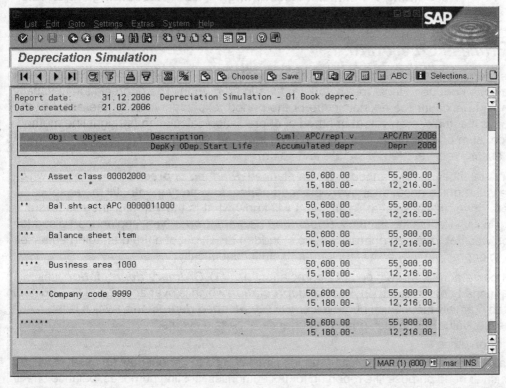

Figure: **AW01N**-15

The utility of Asset Explorer is not limited to what has been mentioned above. Experiment, and explore: Asset Explorer will not disappoint you!

10

AA - Execute Depreciation Run: AFAB

Transaction Code	AFAB
Menu	Accounting > Financial Accounting > Asset Accounting > Periodic Processing > Depreciation Run > Execute

Business Process Overview

Depreciation is the reduction in the book value of an asset due to its usage over time ('decline in economic usefulness') or due to legal framework for taxation reporting. The depreciation is usually calculated taking into account the economic life of the period, expected value of the asset at the end of its economic life (junk/scrap value), method of depreciation calculation (straight line method, declining balance, sum of year digits, double declining etc) and the defined percentage decline in the value of the asset every year (20%, or 15% and so on).

The depreciation can either be (1) planned or (2) un-planned. *Planned depreciation* is the one which brings down the value of the asset after every planned period, say every month, till the asset value is fully depreciated over its life period. By this you will know what is the value of the asset at any point of time in its active life. On the contrary, *unplanned depreciation* is (yes, unplanned!) a sudden happening which was not foreseen (there could be a sudden break out of a fire damaging an asset, and forcing you to depreciate fully as it is no longer useful economically).

In SAP, you will come across three types of depreciation viz., (1) *Ordinary depreciation* which is nothing but the planned depreciation, (2) *Special depreciation* which is over and above the ordinary depreciation, used normally for taxation purposes and (3) *Unplanned depreciation* which is the result of reducing the asset value due to the sudden occurrence of certain events.

1. **Depreciation Area**

   Depreciation Area in SAP is a 2-digit numeric identifier used to denote how an asset is valued for a particular need/purpose like reporting for tax authorities, costing purposes, balance sheet/ P&L purpose etc. The depreciation area contains information like depreciation terms, how depreciation is calculated etc. Many depreciation areas can be defined in the system, which will enable you to manage different types of valuations simultaneously. For each depreciation area, you will be defining the values that need to be managed (like positive or negative book value etc). SAP comes delivered with the depreciation areas like:

   - 01   Book depreciation
   - 02   Special tax depreciation
   - 03   Special reserves
   - 10   Networth valuation

- 15   Tax balance sheet
- 20   cost accounting

Per depreciation area and per company code, you can define how you want the system to post the values: (a) post on-line or post periodically, (b) posting frequency, (c) distribution methods (d) account assignment with regard to CO objects and (e) posting settings. As of Release 4.6 C you can post on-line to FI in one depreciation area only; all other area's values need to be posted periodically in the system. In each of the depreciation area, you will be specifying what type of depreciation / transaction(s) you are managing.

2. **Depreciation Key**

   Depreciation is calculated using the depreciation key and internal calculation key, in the system. *Depreciation keys* are defined at the chart of depreciation level and are uniform across all company codes, which are attached to a particular chart of depreciation. The system contains a number of pre-defined depreciation keys (like LINA, DWG, DG10 etc) with the controls already defined for calculation method and type. A depreciation key can contain multiple internal calculation keys.

3. **Internal Calculation Key**

   Internal calculation keys are the control indicators with in a depreciation key. Together with the depreciation key, these calculation keys help in determining the depreciation amounts. Each internal calculation key contains:

   - Depreciation type (ordinary or unplanned)
   - Depreciation method (straight-line or declining balance or any other)
   - Base value
   - Rate of percentage for depreciation calculation
   - Period control for transactions (acquisition, retirement etc)
   - Change-over rules (in case of declining/double declining methods of calculation)
   - Treatment of depreciation after useful life period

4. **Asset master**

   Each asset master contains the necessary information to calculate the depreciation:

   - Capitalization date / acquisition period
   - Depreciation areas relevant for the asset
   - Depreciation key
   - Useful life / Expired useful life
   - Change over year, if any
   - Scrap value, if any
   - Start date (of ordinary depreciation)

The *depreciation run*, an important periodic processing, takes care of calculating depreciation for the assets and posting the corresponding transactions in both AA and FI. The depreciation calculation is usually done in sessions, and the posting session posts the different depreciation types, interest/revaluation, and also writing-off / allocating special reserves. The depreciation run is recommended to be started with a 'test run' before making it as the "production run" which will update the system. The system provides the facility to re-start a run session should there be problems in the earlier run. The depreciation run needs to be completed per period. During every depreciation run, the system will create summarized posting documents per business area and per account determination; no individual posting documents will be created.

Transaction Steps

Step-1

Use the transaction code or access the function through the menu. You will be taken to "**Depreciation Posting Run**" (Figure: **AFAB**-1).

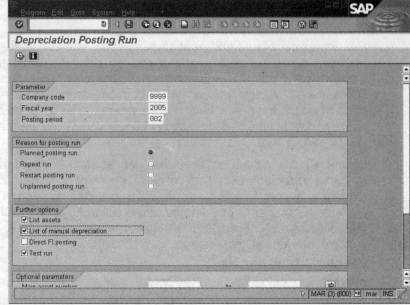

Figure: **AFAB**-1

Enter the details:

1. **Company code (M):** Enter the company code.
2. **Fiscal year (M):** Enter the relevant fiscal year.
3. **Posting period (M):** Enter the period in which the depreciation needs to be posted.

 Unless the earlier depreciation run posting was successful, you will not be able to run the transaction for the next period. And, depreciation run (planned) needs to competed period-by-period.

Under <u>Reason for posting run</u>, select any one of the options:

5. **Planned posting run:** Select this for the regular depreciation run which is usually scheduled at the end of a month, quarter etc. This is selected by default.
6. **Repeat run:** Select the radio button if you want to repeat the depreciation run for additional postings with in the last posting period or to make adjustments at the end of the fiscal year.

 Repeat run is normally used at the end of the fiscal year to carry out posting adjustments or corrections which may arise due to changes in depreciation terms or manual depreciation calculations. However, you can also use this to repeat but with in the same posting period. The 'repeat run' also provides the flexibility to restrict the calculations to specific assets.

7. **Restart posting run:** Select this to restart a previously aborted or not completed depreciation run.

 Restart depreciation run is used only when there has been a problem with the previous run resulting in termination of that run. To make sure that all the steps in a depreciation run is completed with out errors, the system logs the status at every stage of the processing and provides error logs so as to find out the problem. This option of "restart' is not available during the 'test run' mode.

8. **Unplanned posting run:** Use this when you want to skip the normally defined posting cycle (say monthly, half-yearly) etc.

Under <u>Further Options:</u>

9. **List assets (O):** Check to have the list of assets and the amount of depreciation posted for each of the assets.

10. **List of manual depreciation (O):** The system will display a list of manual depreciation at the end of the posting log, which could help your auditors while finalizing the financial statements.

11. **Direct FI posting (O):** If the check box is ticked then the system will <u>not</u> create the 'batch input session' for depreciation posting; instead the FI-G/L is posted directly.

Be careful when checking *"Direct FI posting"* check box, because there will not be an opportunity to correct mistakes, if any, in accounts and account assignments like business area, cost objects etc. Also, there will be no possibility to check and correct postings. Note that if this option is selected during a depreciation run, and if the run is terminated for any reason and needs to be re-started, this has to be kept checked, when re-started.

The system comes with the document type *"AF"* (number range defined as 'external numbering') configured to be used in 'batch input'. Hence, with this default configuration, you will get an error when you to try depreciation posting run by selecting *Direct FI posting*. You can, however, overcome this by not restricting the same in AA customization (Use Transaction OBA7 and remove the tick mark form *'Btch input only'.*

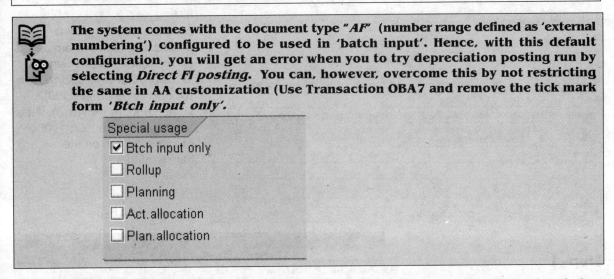

12. **Test run (O):** Select this, to look at what will be posted. Once you are convinced, then uncheck and go ahead with the production run.

Under <u>Optional parameters:</u>

13. **Main asset number (O):** Enter the asset number/number range for selecting the assets for which you need to calculate the depreciation.

Under <u>BDC control:</u>

14. **Session name (O):** Enter or change the batch input name, which will be processed for the postings in FI-G/L/FI-AA.

Step-2

Press "*F8*" or and the system warns you with a pop-up (Figure: **AFAB**-2).

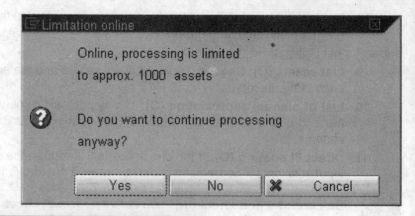

Figure: **AFAB**-2

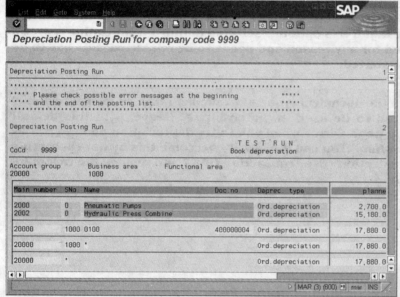

Step-3

When the assets are less than 1, 000 in number, you can press | Yes | and continue with the on-line processing. The system brings up the results of the 'test run' in "***Depreciation Posting Run for company code 9999***" screen (Figure: **AFAB**-3). If the assets are more than 1, 000 process the run on the background.

Figure: **AFAB**-3

Step-4

Press and go back to the initial screen and uncheck the "***Test run***" check box to make the actual production run (Figure: **AFAB**-4).

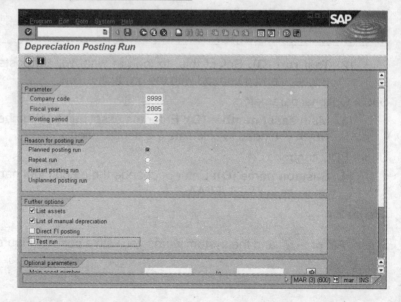

Figure: **AFAB**-4

Step-5

Press "**F8**" or 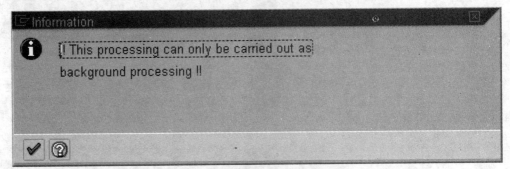 and the system informs you with a pop-up that the depreciation production run can only be executed in the background (Figure: **AFAB**-5) Instead of pressing "**F8**" you may press "**F9**" or execute the transaction using *Menu (Program > Execute in Background)*.

Figure:
AFAB-5

Step-6

Press ✔ and you are taken to "***Background Print Parameters***" screen (Figure: **AFAB**-6) where you need to maintain the necessary parameters like name of the printer (***Output device***), ***Number of pages*** to be printed (all or select pages), ***spool options*** (print immediately, print priority etc), and the ***print settings*** (format, report width etc).

Figure: **AFAB**-6

Step-7

Press ✔ and schedule the job in "***Start Time***" screen (Figure: **AFAB**-7).

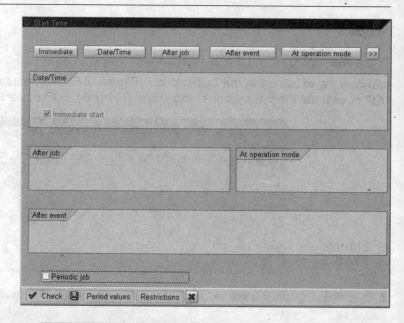

Figure: **AFAB**-7

Press Immediate and you will se the ☑ Immediate start appearing on the screen under Date/
Time block.

 You may also schedule a later date/time by pressing Date/Time **. If you plan
to schedule this job after an already scheduled job, give the details by pressing**
After job **.**

Step-8

Press 💾 and you get the "*Information*" on the background job scheduled (Figure: **AFAB**-8).

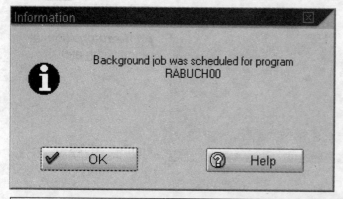

Figure: **AFAB**-8

**The system uses the depreciation-posting program *RABUCH00*, for updating the
asset's values and generating a batch input session for updating FI-G/L. The posting
session posts values in various depreciation areas, interest, revaluation besides
updating special reserves allocations and writing-off, if any. If there are more than
100, 000 assets for depreciation calculation and posting, you need to use a special
program *RAPOST00*.**

Step-9

Use **Transaction Code SM35** and enter "**Batch Input: Session Overview**" screen (Figure: **AFAB**-9).

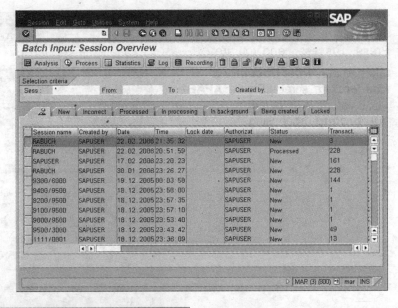

Figure: **AFAB**-9

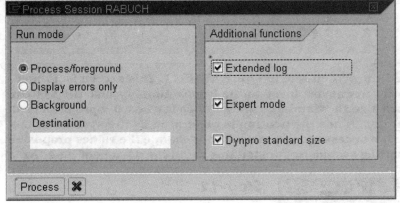

Step-10

Select the batch input session name, which was entered in **Step-1**, and press "**F8**" or ⊕ Process . The system pops-up "**Process Session RABUCH**" (Figure: **AFAB**-10).

Figure: **AFAB**-10

Under <u>Run mode</u>:

1. Select the processing mode (**foreground / background / display error** only).

Under <u>Additional functions</u>:

2. **Extended log (O):** Provides with additional information in the log.
3. **Expert mode (O):** If checked, this will deactivate error message 344 (" Error: Batch input data not available for this screen"). This 'expert mode' works only with interactive batch input processing.
4. **Dynpro standard size (O):** If checked, this will reset the screen size to the standard size which is a pre-requisite for interactive batch input processing.

 If the screen size is not of a standard size, then interactive batch input processing would fail because one or more data input fields may not be available for input in a particular screen (if the screen is smaller than the standard size) or there could be more fields for data entry than the identified number of fields by the program (if the screen size is bigger than the standard). Resetting the screen size during a batch input processing session is also not possible.

Step-11

Press **Process** and you are
taken to the "*Post Document:
Header Data*" screen(Figure: **AFAB**-
11), if you have selected
'*foreground*' processing.

Post Document: Header Data

| Held document | Act assgnmt model... | G/L item fast entry | Post with reference |

Document date	28.02.2005	Type	AF	Company code	9999
Posting date	28.02.2005	Period	02	Currency/rate	EUR
Document number	0400000004			Translation dte	
Reference				Cross-CC no.	
Doc.header text	AFB01200500201-0400000004			Branch number	
				Number of Pages	

Document origin details
Reference procedure
Object key
Logical system

Batch input barcode entry
Document type   Doc. ID

First line item
PstKy 75 Account 0000011010   G/L   Trans.type 501

MAR (3) (800) mar INS

Figure: **AFAB**-11

You could have noticed the screen-size in figure AFAB-11. This screen is 'longer'
than the other standard screens displayed in the transaction because the system
has changed the screen size to 'standard' when the check box Dynpro standard
size is selected in Step-10. Since the posting is generated by the system all the
entries are shown in red. If necessary, you may alter or change the values proposed
by the system. Note that the system has posted this using the document type "AF".

Post Document: Add Asset Item

| | More data | Area values... | Act assgnmt model... | G/L item fast entry | Tax amounts |

G/L account	11010	Accumulated depreciation - machinery and equipme	
Company code	9999	MODEL COMPANY	220
Asset			

Item 1 Credit asset / 75 / 501
Amount   1,350.00   EUR
                          ☐ Calculate tax
                          Bus.place/sectn
Asset val. date   28.02.2005
                                                        ☑ More
Assignment
Text   Long text

Next line item
PstKy 40 Account 0000211100   G/L   Trans.type   New co.code

MAR (3) (800) mar INS

Figure: **AFAB**-12

Step-12

Press "Enter" or press ✅ and the system
takes you to the next screen (Figure:
AFAB-12). Keep on advancing to the next
screen.

When the last screen of the transaction is reached, system pops up with the "**Post Document: Add Asset item**" screen (Figure: **AFAB**-13).

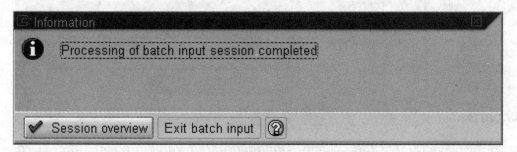

Figure: **AFAB**-13

Step-14

Press ✓ to post and proceed with other transactions. When all the transactions are completed, system pops up with the "*information*" (Figure: **AFAB**-14) to this effect and you have the option of either *(1) going to the session overview (2) or exiting the batch input program.*

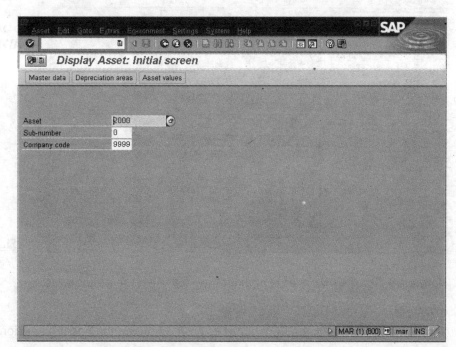

Figure: **AFAB**-14

─────── **End of Transaction** ───────

As in line with our idea of verifying what has been updated by the system and where, let us check how the system has updated the asset values during the depreciation postings.

Step-A

Let us use the **Transaction Code AS03** and you are taken to "**Display Asset: Initial Screen**" (Figure: **AFAB-AS03**-A).

Figure: **AFAB-AS03**-A

Step-B

Press Asset values and you are taken to "***Asset Explorer***" (Figure: **AFAB-AW01N**-B).

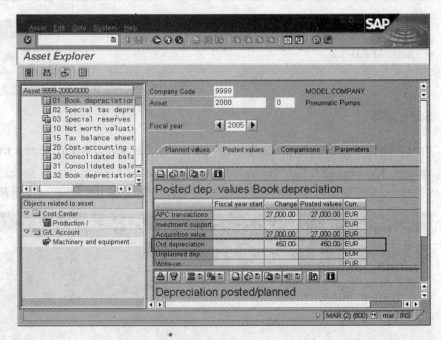

Figure: **AFAB-AW01N**-B

Notice the amount displayed under the column "***Change/Posted values***" against the "***Ord. Depreciation***" row. This denotes the depreciation posted by the system during the depreciation run(s).

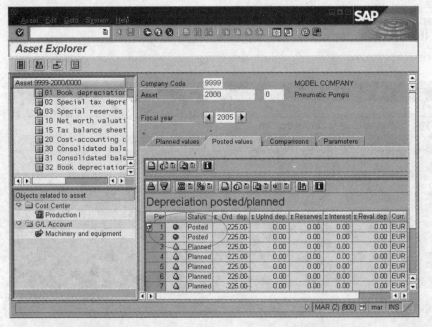

Step-C

Enlarge the right hand side bottom window in the "***Asset Explorer***" to display the "***Depreciation posted/ planned***" (Figure: **AFAB-AW01N**-C).

Figure: **AFAB-AW01N**-C

Note the ⚫ Posted status against the △ Planned status.

Step-D

You can also the check the FI documents created during the posting session by the system.

Use **Transaction Code:**
FB03 and you will be in
the "**Display Document:**
Initial Screen" (Figure:
AFAB-FB03-D). Enter the
details from (Figure:
AFAB-11) i.e. enter the
document number.

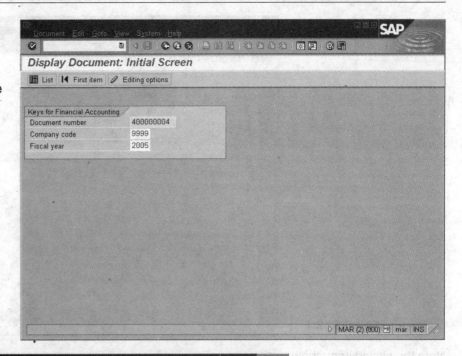

Figure: **AFAB-FB03**-D

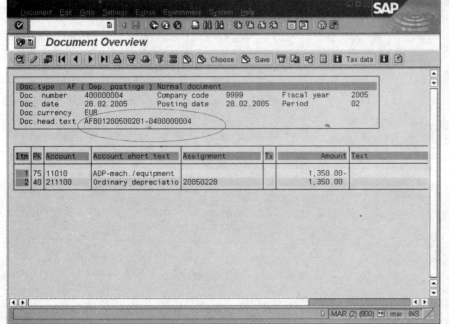

Figure: **AFAB-FB03**-E

Step-E

Press and you will
be in the "**Document**
Overview" (Figure:
AFAB-FB03-E).

Note that the document header entered by the system during the posting run (check with Figure: **AFAB-**
11) in **Step-11**.

Step-F

Press after selecting a line or double click on a line to drill down to "**Display Document: Line**
Item 002" (Figure: **AFAB-FB03**-F).

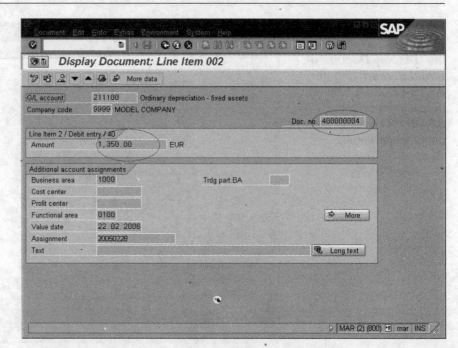

Figure: AFAB-FB03-F

Note the circled item: the amount and the document number.

11

AA – Ad Hoc Reports: ARQ0

Transaction Code	ARQ0
Menu	Accounting > Financial Accounting > Asset Accounting > Information System > Tools > Ad Hoc Reports

Business Process Overview

In Asset Accounting, SAP provides a number of tools, which you can find under the Information system group under Transaction ASMN. The tools include:

- Ad Hoc Reports
- Simulation versions
- Sort variants
- Currency translation methods
- Application log

Ad Hoc Reports are actually **ABAP Queries** defined in the system. Either you can use the existing queries or you can modify and or create your own.

Transaction Steps

Step-1

Use the transaction code or access the function through the menu. You will be taken to **"Query from User Group / SAPQUERY/AM: Initial Screen** (Figure: **ARQ0**-1).

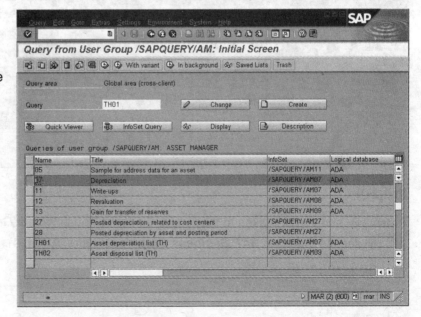

Figure: **ARQ0**-1

Step-2

Select a query from the table and press 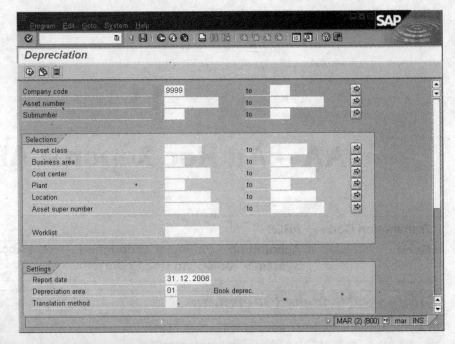; you are taken to the selection screen; in our case **"Depreciation"** screen (Figure: **ARQ0**-2).

Figure: **ARQ0**-2

Step-3

Maintain the necessary selection parameters like *company code, asset number, asset class, business area, cost centre, plan*t etc. Scroll down and maintain *program selections* and also the *output format* (Figure: **ARQ0**-3).

Figure: **ARQ0**-3

Step-4

Press and you are taken to the report. Since we had selected '*Graphics*' as the *output format*, you will see the reports in *SAP Business Graphics* (Figure: **ARQ0**-4).

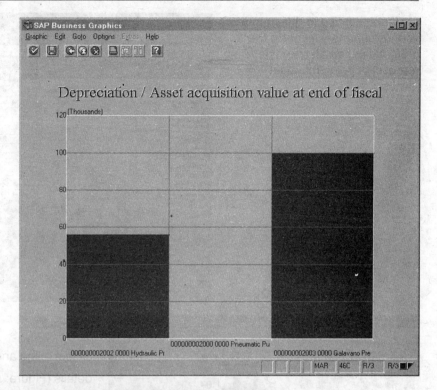

Figure: **ARQ0**-4

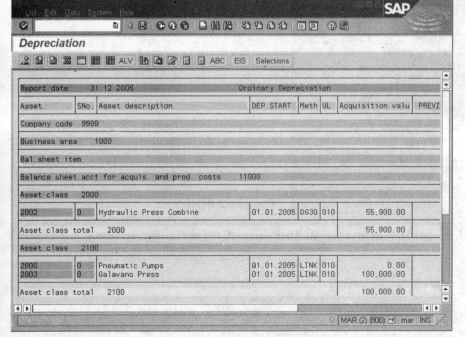

Figure: **ARQ0**-5

Step-5

Press . Now, select '**ABAP List**' as the **output format** and press to view the report (Figure: **ARQ0**-5).

Step-6

Press 🔲 ALV to see the same in ALV format (Figure: **ARQ0**-6).

ALV format helps to drill from the various summary levels to the bottom most detail line. The * represents the summation level(s).

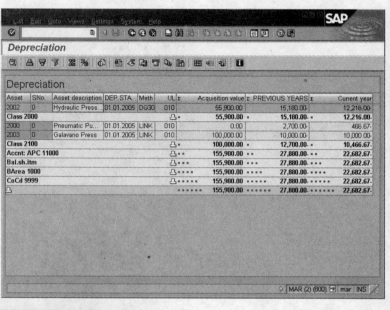

Asset	SNo.	Asset description	DEP.STA.	Meth	UL	Σ	Acquisition value	Σ	PREVIOUS YEARS	Σ	Current year
2002	0	Hydraulic Press...	01.01.2005	DG30	010		55,900.00		15,180.00-		12,216.00-
Class 2000						▣ ▪	55,900.00	▪	15,180.00-	▪	12,216.00-
2000	0	Pneumatic Pu...	01.01.2005	LINK	010		0.00		2,700.00-		466.67-
2003	0	Galavano Press	01.01.2005	LINK	010		100,000.00		10,000.00-		10,000.00-
Class 2100						▣ ▪	100,000.00	▪	12,700.00-	▪	10,466.67-
Accnt: APC 11000						▣ ▪▪	155,900.00	▪▪	27,880.00-	▪▪	22,682.67-
Bal.sh.itm						▣ ▪▪▪	155,900.00	▪▪▪	27,880.00-	▪▪▪	22,682.67-
BArea 1000						▣ ▪▪▪▪	155,900.00	▪▪▪▪	27,880.00-	▪▪▪▪	22,682.67-
CoCd 9999						▣ ▪▪▪▪▪	155,900.00	▪▪▪▪▪	27,880.00-	▪▪▪▪▪	22,682.67-
▣						▪▪▪▪▪▪	155,900.00	▪▪▪▪▪▪	27,880.00-	▪▪▪▪▪▪	22,682.67-

Figure: **ARQ0**-6

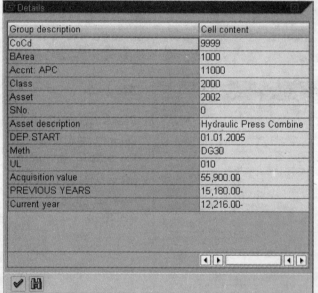

Group description	Cell content
CoCd	9999
BArea	1000
Accnt: APC	11000
Class	2000
Asset	2002
SNo.	0
Asset description	Hydraulic Press Combine
DEP.START	01.01.2005
Meth	DG30
UL	010
Acquisition value	55,900.00
PREVIOUS YEARS	15,180.00-
Current year	12,216.00-

Step-7

Select a line and press [icon] to view the details (Figure: **ARQ0**-7).

Figure: **ARQ0**-7

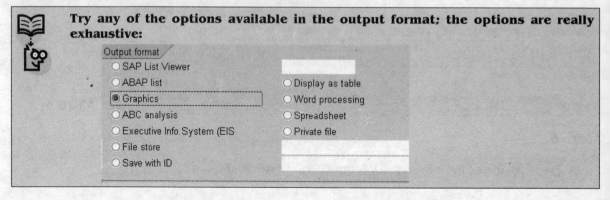

Try any of the options available in the output format; the options are really exhaustive:

Output format
- ○ SAP List Viewer
- ○ ABAP list
- ◉ Graphics
- ○ ABC analysis
- ○ Executive Info System (EIS
- ○ File store
- ○ Save with ID
- ○ Display as table
- ○ Word processing
- ○ Spreadsheet
- ○ Private file

12

AA – Depreciation, Current Year: S_ALR_87012026

Transaction Code	S_ALR_87012026
Menu	Accounting > Financial Accounting > Asset Accounting > Information System > Reports on Asset Accounting > Depreciation Forecast > Depreciation current year

Business Process Overview

The **Information System**, in asset accounting, gives a plethora of reports which are almost exhaustive to cover all your reporting requirements.

There are reports on:

- Individual assets
- Asset balances
- Notes to financial statements
- Explanations for P&L
- Cost accounting
- Depreciation forecast
- Specific valuations
- Preparations for closing
- Day-to-day activities
- Taxes
- Asset history

Under **depreciation forecast**, the system comes with two important reports:

1. Depreciation on capitalized assets (**depreciation simulation**)
2. Depreciation current year

Transaction Steps

Step-1

Use the transaction code or access the function through the menu. You will be taken to *"Depreciation"* (Figure: **S_ALR_87012026**-1). This is the selection screen which helps you to maintain the selection parameters for retrieving the report.

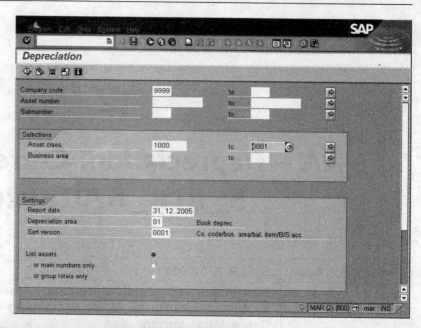

Figure: **S_ALR_87012026**-1

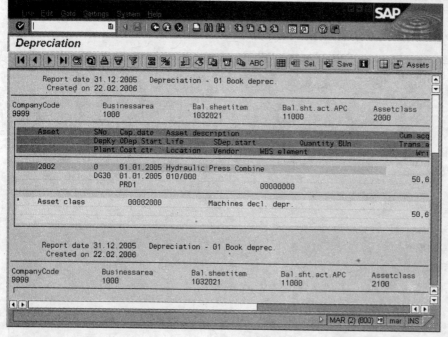

Figure:
S_ALR_87012026-2

Step-2

Maintain the necessary selection parameters like *company code, asset number, asset class, business area, report date, depreciation area* etc.

and press 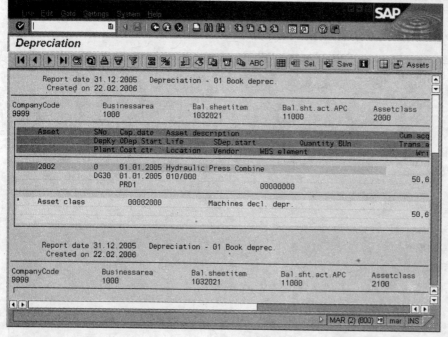 ; the system displays the report per depreciation area (Figure: **S_ALR_87012026**-2 & 3).

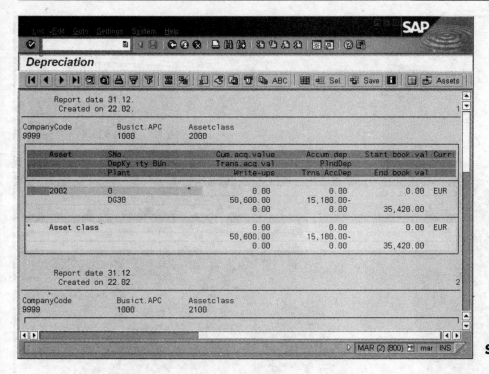

Figure:
S_ALR_87012026-3

Misacellaneous

1

Schedule Manager: SCMA

Transaction Code	SCMA
Menu	Accounting > Financial Accounting > General ledger / Asset Accounting / Accounts Receivable / Accounts Payable > Periodic Processing >Schedule Manager

Business Process Overview

SAP's **Schedule Manager** helps you to organize, execute and monitor complex and repetitive business transactions (like, month end processing) from easy-to-use workspace, which resembles an all-in-one "organizer" kind of utility containing:

1. User Notes window
2. Task Overview window
3. Calendar window
4. Daily Overview window

The *information window* provides with the details of what and how you can achieve, by providing useful information with hyperlinks to processes and steps with in a process. This appears to the left of all other windows. Depending upon the requirement, this can be 'switched-on' or 'switched-off'. After a while, I am sure you may not need this and you will certainly 'switch-off' this pane for you would have mastered the details!

The *task overview window* provides a complete drill-down facility in a tree-structure of all tasks entered and monitored by you. The tasks are grouped into an upper level **task** list, which can be scheduled, released and monitored using the "daily overview" window. Remember, that the tasks maintained in the task overview window needs to be properly scheduled / released for execution: the mere listing of tasks here will not start a transaction or a program or a report.

The *daily overview window* is similar to an appointment column of any organizer, with fully customizable time intervals (in increments of, say, 30 minutes, 45 minutes etc). Ideally, the tasks appearing in the task list in "task overview" window, when scheduled / released, will appear here against the appropriate time slot. By selecting a task here, you can monitor the same using the 'monitor' icon or from the menu. A look at this daily overview window, at the beginning of a day, will remind you of the tasks scheduled for that day. What a nice way of starting your day!

The *Calendar window* is a calendar utility, (what else that can be!) to help you organized better. However, this goes beyond the regular calendar by displaying, in different colours like Yellow / Green, a particular date indicating that the status of tasks scheduled for that day. A green background indicates that every thing is OK, but a yellow indicates that there are some warnings.

The Schedule Manager can be accessed through various screens like the "Easy Access: General Ledger" (**Transaction Code: FSMN**), "Easy Access: Assets Accounting" (**Transaction Code: ASMN**), "Easy Access: Accounts Receivables" (**Transaction Code: FDMN**), "Easy Access: Accounts Payables" (**Transaction Code: FKMN**) etc. In all these places, under **periodic processing**, the first transaction available for execution is the Schedule Manager.

How to use the Schedule Manager?

The Schedule Manager has **three distinct functionalities** built in:

1. **Processes**

    This is the functionality which helps you to define the **task list** (also called as **task group**) and the individual **tasks** (a task is essentially a transaction or a program / report), which are later on scheduled / released and monitored using the special '**monitoring**' function available. Any number of task lists can be created and these lists are shown in a tree format for easy navigation. A task list may contain another task list or a **chain of tasks** within; tasks are grouped into a task list.

    While defining the task itself, you can maintain who is the owner of the task, when this needs to be executed etc. The scheduling of tasks is also possible by simply dragging them into the appropriate time slots in the 'daily overview' window. You may also take the help of '**Job Wizard**' while scheduling. A task, by mere scheduling, is not started automatically unless the same is properly '**released**'. The tasks / task lists defined can be moved in the hierarchy up / down or deleted form a list. The tasks can also be documented using MS-Office Word or Excel etc.

2. **Scenarios**

    The Schedule Manager gives you **three options** for scheduling and monitoring:

    a. Start transaction / program / report online and schedule the jobs (tasks) in the scheduler. Here, you can create or select a new task list in the schedule, enter these in the "daily overview", monitor and control the tasks' execution in the 'monitor'.

    b. Start transaction / program / report online and schedule the jobs (tasks) / job chain (task chain).

        This is similar to (a) above except that you have the option of inserting a 'job chain' defined in "flow definition" into the task list.

    c. Start transactions / reports online, schedule job or job chain, work-list.

        Here, you can also execute and monitor a complete work-list, involving several processing steps with all the step sequences. Besides scheduler, monitor, and flow definition, you can use the "work-list monitor", for monitoring the processing status.

3. **Help Functions**

    Schedule Manager supplements with really useful help functions like (a) **Run time analysis**, (b) **working with variables, (c) releasing jobs** etc.

Step-1

Enter the Transaction code or access the transaction using the menu path. The system will pop up "**Choose Task List**" screen (Figure: **SCMA**-1), asking you to select a task list if it is the first time you are starting the transaction.

Figure: **SCMA**-1

1. **Task list (M):** Select the task list from the available values.

Step-2

When completed, press

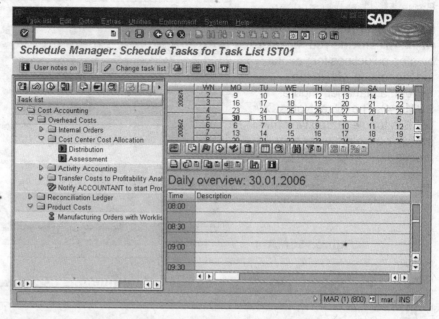

and you will be taken to "**Schedule Manager: Schedule of Tasks for Task List IST01**" screen (Figure: **SCMA**-2).

Figure: **SCMA**-2

Before you start using the schedule manager, you need to familiarize yourself with the numerous icons and what they denote in the schedule manager.

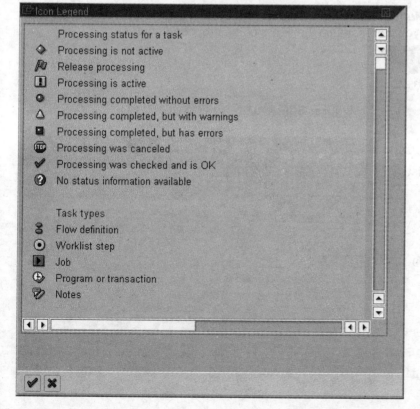

Step-3

Press [image] icon to see the details in "**Icon Legend**" screen (Figure: **SCMA**-3).

Figure: **SCMA**-3

Step-4

Press 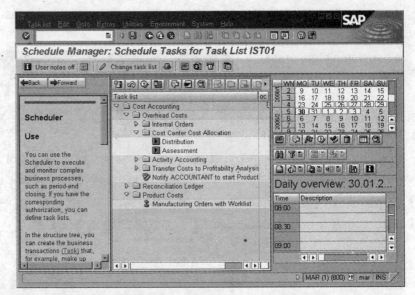 to see the '**user notes**' window which will provide you with step-by-step guidelines for various functionalities with in the Schedule Manager (Figure: **SCMA**-4). The "User Notes Off/on" is a toggle button which will switch 'on' or 'off' whenever it is pressed.

Figure: **SCMA**-4

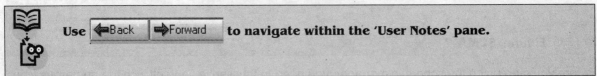

Use 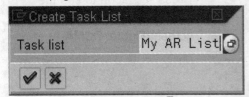 to navigate within the 'User Notes' pane.

Step-5

To add a new task list, use the **Menu: Task List > Create**. The system pops up "**Create Task List**" screen (Figure: **SCMA**-5), where you can maintain the name of the proposed new list.

Figure: **SCMA**-5

1. **Task list (M):** Enter a name for the proposed task list.

Step-6

When completed, press and you are taken to "**New Entries: Details of Added Entries**" screen (Figure: **SCMA**-6). Maintain the details as below:

Figure: **SCMA**-6

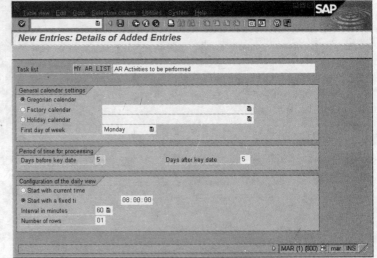

Enter the required details:

Task List (M): Enter a detailed description for the task list.

Under <u>General Calendar settings</u>:

1. Select the appropriate radio button for the type of calendar.

> **For calendar other than "Gregorian", you need to maintain the name of the *factory calendar or holiday calendar*.**

2. **First day of week (M):** Select the first of the week.

Under <u>Period for time processing</u>:

3. **Days before key date (M):** Enter the number of days.

> **The default is 5 days. This means that the Schedule Manger will import log information relating to the tasks or jobs which had taken place in the last 5 days, from today (key date). You are instructing the system *'from which'* date the log information should be made available.**

4. **Days after key date (M):** Enter the number of days.

> **The default is 5 days. This means that the Schedule Manger will keep log information relating to the tasks or jobs which will take place in the future 5 days, from today (key date). You are instructing the system *'up to which'* date the log information should be made available.**

> **Take care to mention the number of days as less as possible. Else, the system performance may be slowed down as the system needs to retrieve all the relevant information pertaining to all the tasks during these time interval.**

Under <u>Configuration of the daily view</u>:

5. Select either '**start with the current time**' or '**start with the fixed time**'. When '**start with the fixed time**' is selected, enter the time.

6. **Interval in time (M):** Enter the interval in minutes, which is convenient to you.

7. **Number of rows (O):** Enter the desired number of rows. If you enter '2', the system provides two rows for each time slot in the 'daily overview'.

Step-7

Press and icons; you will be taken to **"Schedule Manager: change Task List MY AR LIST"** screen (Figure: **SCMA**-7).

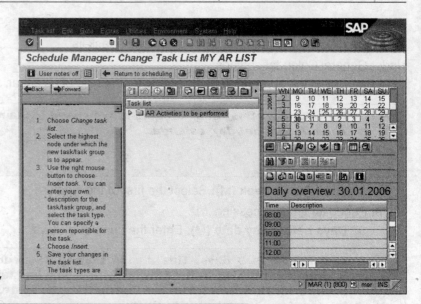

Figure: **SCMA**-7

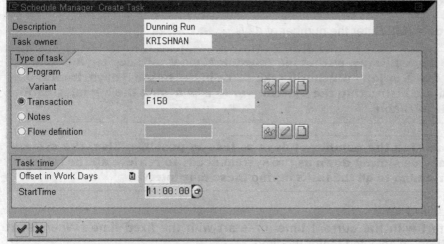

Figure: **SCMA**-8

Step-8

Select the task list's top node and press

to add a new task to the newly defined task list. Enter the details in **"Schedule Manager: Create Task"** screen (Figure: SCMA-8).

In the header:

1. **Description(M):** Enter a description of the task.
2. **Task Owner (M):** Assign the task to one of the users, selected from the drop-down list of users.

In the **Type of task (M):**

3. Select a suitable task and enter the details. The task can be a transaction or program (provide the variant as well), notes or a flow definition (work-flow like).

In the Task time:

4. Select from the drop down, how the duration needs to be arrived at (**M**): either by taking into the working day or by calendar day, and enter the task duration.
5. **Start Time(M):** Enter the start time (Figure: **SCMA**-9).

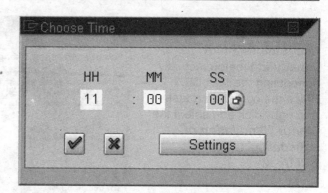

Figure: **SCMA**-9

Step-9

When completed, press 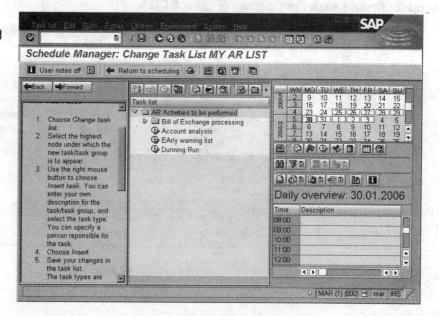 and the task will be added to the task list. Repeat **Step-8** for defining as many tasks as you need.

Step-10

For defining another **task list**, with in the task list originally selected, press . The system pops up **"Schedule Manager: Create Task Group"** screen (Figure: **SCMA**-10).

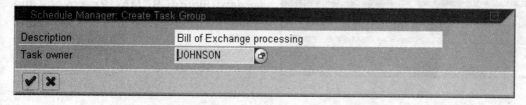

Figure:
SCMA-10

1. **Description (M):** Enter a description for the new task list (also called, **task group**).
2. **Task owner (M):** Select a task owner who will be responsible for this.

Step-11

When completed, press and you are taken to **"Schedule Manager: change Task List MY AR LIST"** screen (Figure: **SCMA**-11), where you can see all the **tasks / task lists** defined. You can re-arrange the tasks /task list, delete if necessary.

Figure: **SCMA**-11

Step-12

Use '**Simulation of scheduling**' before actually scheduling the task list. Place the cursor on a task and right click and select the *Menu: "Simulation of scheduling"* (Figure: SCMA-12).

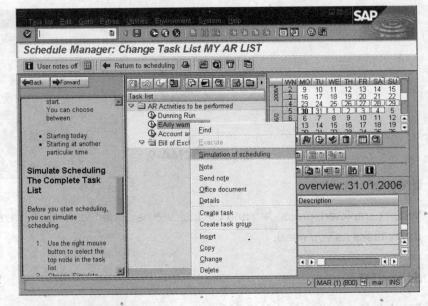

Figure: **SCMA**-12

Step-13

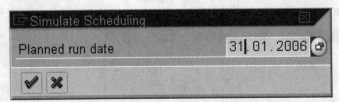

On the pop up "**Simulate of Scheduling**" screen (Figure: **SCMA**-13), change the "**Planned run date**", if necessary.

Figure: **SCMA**-13

Step-14

Press [← Return to scheduling], select the top node of the task list and press [🖫]. The system pops up "**Schedule Task Plan**" screen (Figure: **SCMA**-14).

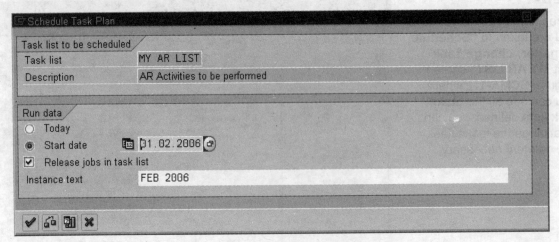

Figure: **SCMA**-14

Under Run data:

1. Select either '**Today**' or "**Start date**" radio button (**M**). Maintain the start date if "Start date' is selected.

2. **Release jobs in task list (O):** Tick to release the jobs.

 Mere definition of a task does not automatically execute that particular transaction or program / report. For the task to be executed, the transaction needs to be released, after it has been properly scheduled.

3. **Instance text (O):** Enter a text which will easily identify this run. Though optional, it is a good practice to enter a meaningful text here.

Step-15

Press 🔲 to see the schedule details in '**Schedule Manager: Schedule Tasks for Task List MY AR LIST**' screen (Figure: **SCMA**-15), change the "**Planned run date**", if necessary.

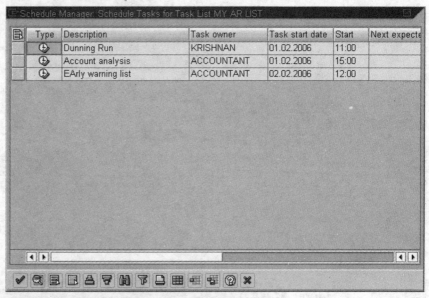

Figure: **SCMA**-15

Step-16

When done, press ✔ and you are taken to **"Schedule Manager: change Task List AR LIST"** screen (Figure: **SCMA**-16), where you can see all the tasks / task lists defined, and scheduled / released.

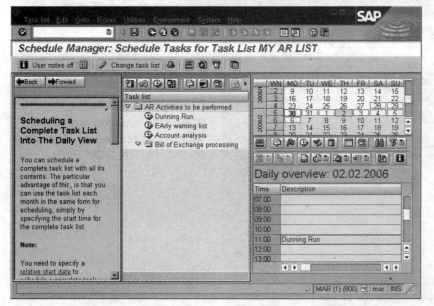

Figure: **SCMA**-16

The calendar display provides you with the information whether 'all-is-well' or not with the scheduling / release of the tasks / jobs. The date on which some transaction or program / report has been scheduled / released will have a yellow back ground, if there is some warning. It should be 'green' for you to proceed further.

You may also use the "job wizard" for creating a job to be processed (Figure: SCMA-17). Use the Menu: *Environment -> Schedule with job wizard* and follow the steps.

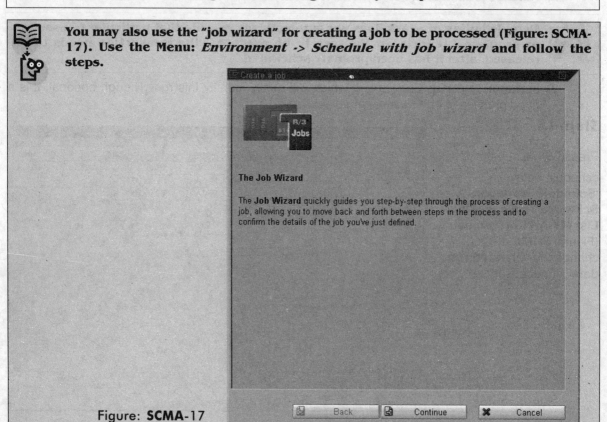

Figure: **SCMA**-17

Step-17

To monitor a task, right click on the task in the 'daily overview' and follow the *Menu: Monitor*.

Alternatively, press 🔲 (Figure: **SCMA**-18) and you are taken to **"Schedule Manager: Monitor"** screen (Figure: **SCMA**-19).

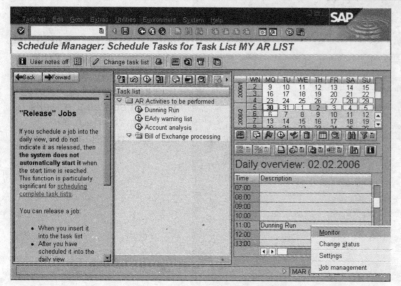

Figure: **SCMA**-18.

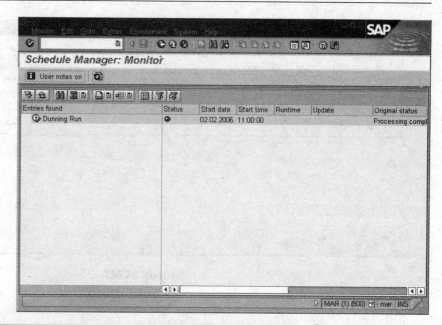

Figure: **SCMA**-19

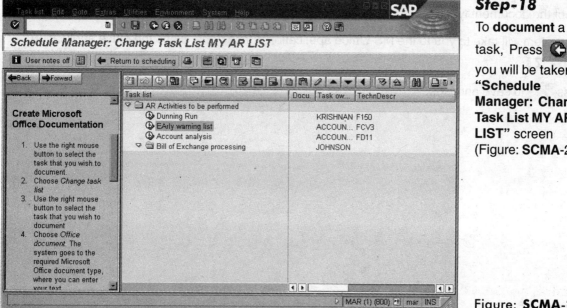

Step-18

To **document** a task, Press ⬅ , you will be taken to **"Schedule Manager: Change Task List MY AR LIST"** screen (Figure: **SCMA**-20).

Figure: **SCMA**-20

Step- 19

Press ✏ Change task list . Select the task for which you want to maintain some documentation.

Press ⬜ icon, the system prompts a pop up **"Select document category"** screen (Figure: **SCMA**-21).

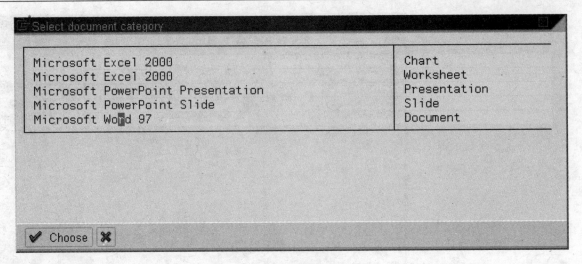

Figure: **SCMA**-21

Step- 20

Select the document type by placing the cursor on a row, and press ✔ Choose .

The system will take to you to the MS-Office application. Once done, close the office application.

Step- 21

Press 🖫 to save and exit.

2

Copy Number Ranges to Fiscal Year: OBH2

Transaction Code	OBH2
Menu	(IMG) Financial Accounting > Financial Accounting Global Settings > Document > Document Number Ranges > Copy to Fiscal Year

Business Process Overview

As already explained else where in the book, SAP follows the 'document' principle to keep up the transaction integrity. Any posting in the system ends when a document is created and, once a document is created it can never be deleted unless the same is archived and stored in another separate storage medium. Each document in SAP is uniquely identified by the combination of (a) document number, (b) company code and (c) fiscal year. The system creates a minimum of one document when a transaction is created / completed. The business process (for example: goods receipt) can also result in more than one document. Not all the transactions, with in the system, will create accounting documents. All the documents are linked together in the system to provide a complete document trail for easy retrieval and drill-down to zero-in on a particular document.

The **number range** for a document type can be defined per fiscal year starting from scratch or an existing list of number ranges can be conveniently copied to another fiscal year. To circumvent creating number ranges every year, you can also define that the number ranges are valid for ever i.e., till year 9999; the only point to be noted here is when the number ranges are defined for eternity (!), the system starts the new number for the current year from the last number utilized for the last year (and not from the first number in the number range) and you may soon run out of the range.

 As usual, the fastest and easiest way to create is to copy, if one already exists! This holds good for creating number ranges for a new fiscal year as well. The function is less time consuming, easy to do and error-free as you are referring to something which has already been defined in the system.

Transaction Steps

Step-1

Access the transaction either by the transaction code or menu, and you will be taken to **"Document Number Ranges: Copy to Fiscal year"** screen (Figure: **OBH2**-1).

Figure: **OBH2**-1

Enter the details as mentioned below.

In <u>General Selections</u>:

1. **Company code (M):** Enter the Company code to which the number ranges need to be copied to another fiscal year. You may also enter a range, if the same is to be copied to a number of company codes in one operation.

2. **Number range number (O):** Remember there could be a number of number ranges, defined in the system, corresponding to various document types. Enter if you need to restrict copying to a select number of number ranges (Example: you may want to copy the number ranges only for 01 and 02). Leave this field blank to copy all.

In <u>Source fiscal year details</u>:

3. **To fiscal year (M):** Enter the fiscal year which needs to be used as the reference for copying. This is the '*from*' fiscal year from where the number ranges would be copied.

In <u>Target fiscal year details</u>:

4. **To fiscal year (M):** Enter the new fiscal year to which the number ranges are to be copied. This is the '**to**' fiscal year.

> **Before a number range can be copied to another fiscal year, the number range should have been defined and available in the system. You can only copy and create if the range has not been already created for the target fiscal year. Else, the system will skip those number ranges, which have already been created for the target year, but will create the rest. You will get the message "can not be added" if 'interval already exists'.**

Step-2

Press 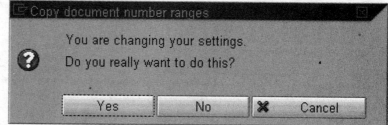 or F8. The system pops-up a confirmation screen **"Copy document number ranges"** (Figure: **OBH2**-2).

Figure: **OBH2**-2

Step-3

Press [Yes] as the confirmation to copy the number ranges for the target fiscal year, and the system will take you to screen **"Document Number Ranges: Copy to Fiscal year"** screen (Figure: **OBH2**-3). You can see the results of copy. Where ever the system has failed to copy a number range, you will see the reason "Interval already exists".

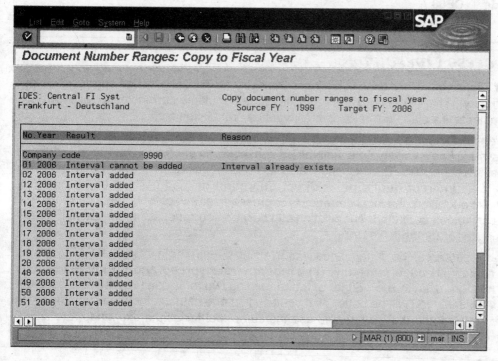

Figure: **OBH2**-3

3

Maintain Currency Exchange Rates: OB08

Transaction Code	OB08
Menu	(IMG) General Settings > Currencies > Enter exchange rates

Business Process Overview

Translation rate or **exchange rate** is used in business transactions involving foreign currencies (other then the local currency). The system provides a facility to use multiple currencies to meet various transaction requirements like planning, valuation, conversion, translation etc.

In SAP, each **currency** is identified using a 3-character alphanumeric **currency code**. Each of these currencies in the system has a validity date maintained in a table. An **exchange rate type** is defined for a combination of two currencies. The exchange rate is defined for pair of currencies. Each exchange rate type can be of an **indirect quotation** or **direct quotation** defined per unit of the currency concerned. In a direct quotation, the local currency is expressed per unit of the foreign currency and vice versa in case of indirect quotation. The relationship between currency pairs and exchange rate type is defined using the **translation factors.**

Exchange rate maintenance can be done manually or by using certain **tools** available. SAP provides three such tools namely **(1) base currency, (2) exchange rate spread and (3) inversion.** The tool 'inversion' is no more used in SAP. Either of the remaining two tools can be used to reduce the maintenance work. Usually, you will be better off if you use just one of these for each exchange rate type. But, there is no hard rule that you should use the same tool for all the exchange rate types: you may use different tools for different types.

Transaction Steps

Step-1

Enter the Transaction code or access the transaction using the menu path, and you will be taken to **"Change View "Currency Exchange Rates": Overview"** screen (Figure: **OB08**-1).

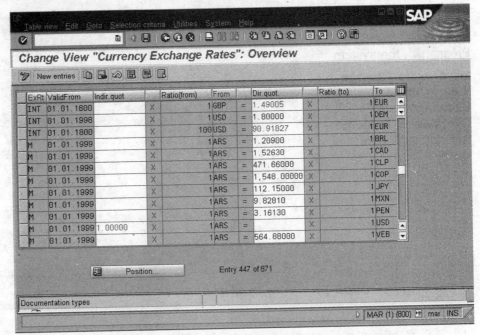

Figure: **OB08**-1

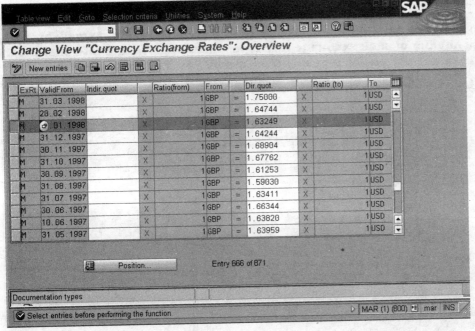

Figure: **OB08**-2

Step-2

To maintain new entries, select the rows to be copied from "**Change View "Currency Exchange Rates":** Overview" screen (Figure: **OB08**-2).

Step-3

Press 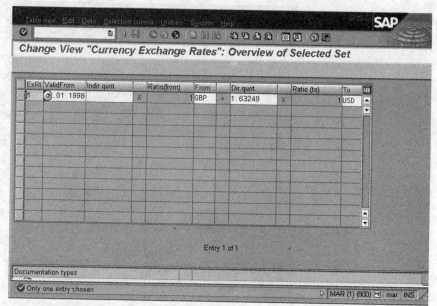, the system takes you to "**Change View "Currency Exchange Rates": Overview of Selected Set**" screen (Figure: **OB08**-3).

Figure: OB08-3

Enter the information as detailed below:

1. **ExRt (M):** Select the **exchange rate type** you need to maintain (Figure: **OB08**-4).

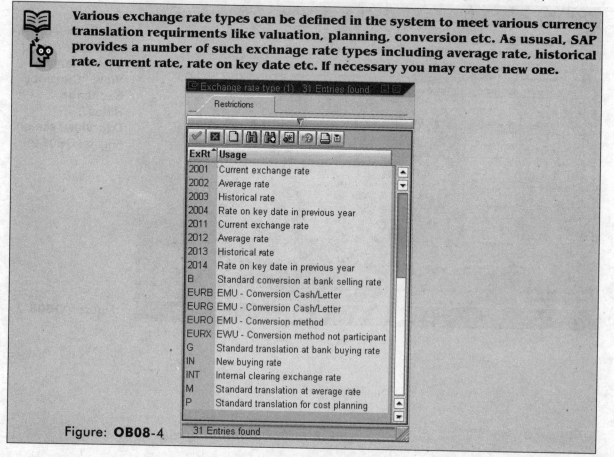

Various exchange rate types can be defined in the system to meet various currency translation requirments like valuation, planning, conversion etc. As ususal, SAP provides a number of such exchnage rate types including average rate, historical rate, current rate, rate on key date etc. If necessary you may create new one.

ExRt	Usage
2001	Current exchange rate
2002	Average rate
2003	Historical rate
2004	Rate on key date in previous year
2011	Current exchange rate
2012	Average rate
2013	Historical rate
2014	Rate on key date in previous year
B	Standard conversion at bank selling rate
EURB	EMU - Conversion Cash/Letter
EURG	EMU - Conversion Cash/Letter
EURO	EMU - Conversion method
EURX	EWU - Conversion method not participant
G	Standard translation at bank buying rate
IN	New buying rate
INT	Internal clearing exchange rate
M	Standard translation at average rate
P	Standard translation for cost planning

31 Entries found

Figure: OB08-4

2. **Valid from (M):** Enter the date from which this rate will come into effect.
3. **Indir quot (O):** Maintain if indirect quotation is required.
4. **Ratio (from) (M):** Number of unit of currency.
5. **Dir quot (M):** Maintain the quotation.
6. **From (M):** Enter the currency.
7. **Ratio (to) (M):** Number of unit of currency (usually 1. Can be 100 or 1000 (JY).
8. **To (M):** Enter the currency.

Use of direct quotation or indirect quotation is decided by the market standard of a country or business requirement. In <u>direct quotation</u>, the local currency is expressed per unit of a foreign currency (if local currency is USD and the foreign currency is EURO, the direct quote is expressed as 1 EURO = 1.0809 USD). In case of <u>indirect quote</u>, the foreign currency is expressed per unit of local currency (1 EURO = 0.9251 USD). For each pair of currencies, you can maintain the direct or indirect quotation in the system. Unless it is required, maintain the exchange rates as direct quotation.

An exchange rate displayed in 'red' in the exchange rate table indicates that indirect quotation has been maintained for that pair of currencies.

Step-4

When completed, press and the values are updated (Figure: **OB08**-5).

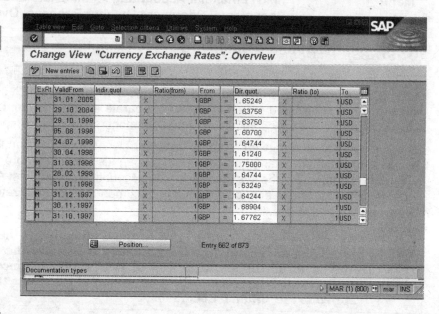

Figure: **OB08**-5

Step-5

When completed, press .

Use the program RFTBFF00 to maintain the exchange rate table automatically by uploading an input file in multicash-format.

4

Maintain Number Ranges for Accounting Documents: FBN1

Transaction Code	FBN1
Menu	(IMG) Financial Accounting > Financial Accounting Global Settings > Document > Document Number Ranges > Overview

Business Process Overview

SAP follows the 'document' principle to keep up the transaction integrity. Any posting in the system ends when a document is created, and once a document is created it can never be deleted unless the same is archived and stored in another separate storage medium. Each document in SAP is uniquely identified by the combination of (a) document number, (b) company code and (c) fiscal year.

The system creates a minimum of one document when a transaction is created / completed. The business process (for example: goods receipt) can also result in more than one document. Not all the transactions, with in the system, will create accounting documents. All the documents are linked together in the system to provide a complete document trail for easy retrieval and drill-down to zero in on a particular document.

 SAP recommends to 'file' the original documents under the number of the processing document. The best practice is to enter the (external) number of the 'original document' in the 'Reference' field of the document created in SAP system. For easy cross-reference, the SAP document number thus created needs to be entered in the 'original document'.

The number range for a document type can be defined per fiscal year or until a fiscal year in future. If defined to last only a fiscal year, then this needs to be defined every year. When number ranges are defined every year, the system starts from the first number in the range for that particular year and this will help in not reaching the upper limit fast.

 If you specify the fiscal year as '9999', then the document number range is valid for ever (well, almost!) and you do not have to do this exercise of maintaining number ranges every fiscal year. But, every year the system starts from the last number used up in the previous year and if a small number range is defined for a document type, you could easily run out of the number range fast.

The document numbers can either be internally assigned by the system or externally input when the same is created. The number ranges can be defined in such a way that system generates the number automatically when a document is created. This is known as *"internal number assignment"*. Under this, the system stores the last number used for a document in the 'current number' field and will bring up the next number when another document is created. If *"external numbering"* is used, the user needs to input a document number every time a document is created in the system. Since user supplies the number every time, the subsequent numbering may not be sequential. Unlike internal numbering, system does not store the 'last' number in the 'current number' field.

Transaction Steps

Step-1

Access the transaction either by the transaction code or menu, and you will be taken to ""**Number Ranges For Accounting Documents**" screen (Figure: **FBN1**-1).

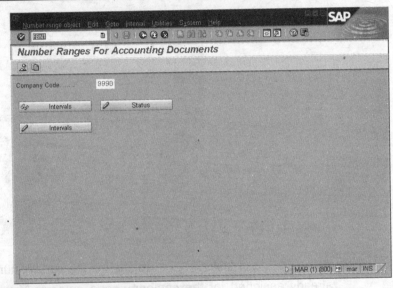

Figure: **FBN1**-1

Step-2

Press the icon to go to "**Number Range Object Overview**" screen that will display the current settings of document number ranges assigned to various documents, company code-wise (Figure: **FBN1**-2).

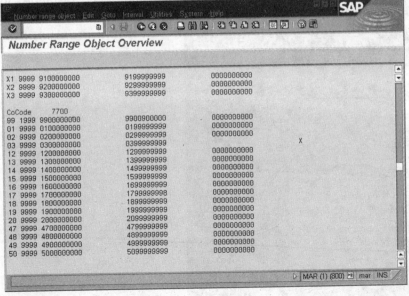

Figure: **FBN1**-2

Step-3

Press the icon to the initial screen. Enter the Company code, for which you want to maintain the number ranges.

There are many options provided by the system form this initial screen:

1. Press ⟨ Intervals ⟩ to display the status of the number ranges assigned for the company code entered. You can see the details of ranges in **"Display Number Range Intervals"** screen (Figure: **FBN1**-3).

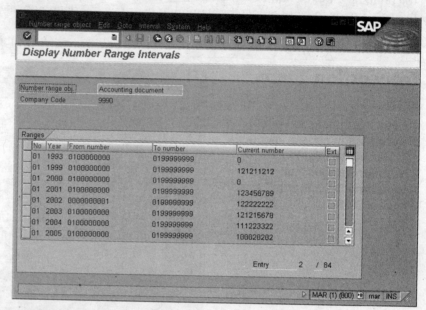

Figure: **FBN1**-3

2. Press ⟨ Status ⟩ to change the current number status of the number ranges already assigned for the company code entered. You can see the details of ranges in **"Maintain Number Range Intervals"** screen (Figure: **FBN1**-4).

Figure: **FBN1**-4

Step-4

Press 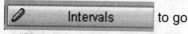 to the initial screen. Enter the Company code, for which you want to maintain the number ranges. Press

Intervals to go

to "**Maintain Number Range Intervals**" screen (Figure: **FBN1**-5), from where you can maintain the details for the company code entered.

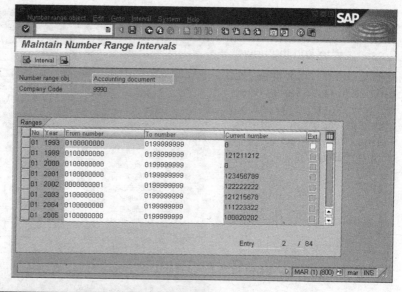

Figure: **FBN1**-5

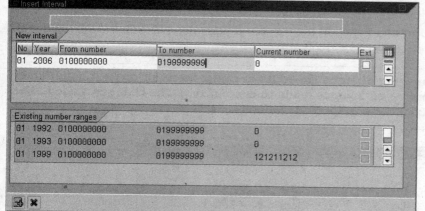

Step-5

Press **Interval** to add a new interval. The system pops-up "**Insert Interval**" screen (Figure: **FBN1**-6).

Figure: **FBN1**-6

Enter the following:

1. **No (M):** Enter the number which identifies a number range interval.
2. **Year (M):** Enter the year for which the new number range is to be added, if the number range is year dependent.
3. **From number (M):** Enter the starting number (10 digits, maximum) for the new range.
4. **To number (M):** Enter the ending number (10 digits, maximum) for the new range.
5. **Current number (O):** Enter the current number to be considered by the system to bring up the next number when the system uses this new number range. When the number range is defined for the first time, leave the field blank.
6. **Ext (O):** Tick the check-box if the numbering is to be 'external'.

 The same number range can be used by different document types, and the external number range can be alpha-numeric!

Step-6

Press to add the new number range so defined. You can see the new range (the last row: No. 01, year 2006...) added in "**Maintain Number Range** Intervals" screen (Figure: **FBN1**-7).

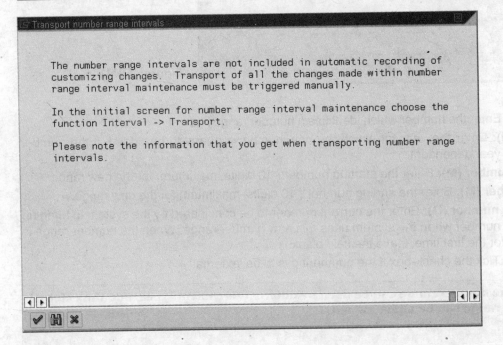

Maintain Number Range Intervals

Number range obj.   Accounting document
Company Code   9990

No	Year	From number	To number	Current number	Ext
01	1999	0100000000	0199999999	121211212	
01	2000	0100000000	0199999999	0	
01	2001	0100000000	0199999999	123456789	
01	2002	0000000001	0199999999	122222222	
01	2003	0100000000	0199999999	121215678	
01	2004	0100000000	0199999999	111223322	
01	2005	0100000000	0199999999	100020202	
01	2006	0100000000	0199999999	0	

Entry   3   / 85

MAR (1) (800)   mar   INS

Figure: **FBN1**-7

Step-7

Use **Menu: Interval > Transport** and transport the number range intervals. See the information on "**Transport number range intervals**" screen (Figure: **FBN1**-8).

> **Unlike other customizing objects, the number range intervals are not included in the automatic recording of changes made to customizing. The changes made to the number ranges need to be transported manually.**

Transport number range intervals

The number range intervals are not included in automatic recording of customizing changes. Transport of all the changes made within number range interval maintenance must be triggered manually.

In the initial screen for number range interval maintenance choose the function Interval -> Transport.

Please note the information that you get when transporting number range intervals.

Figure: **FBN1**-8

5

Maintain Terms of Payment: OBB8

Transaction Code	OBB8
Menu	(IMG) Financial Accounting > Accounts Receivable and Accounts Payable > Business Transactions > Incoming Invoices/Credit Memos > Maintain Terms of Payment

Business Process Overview

Terms of Payment defines the payment terms agreed upon between a vendor and customer, and is made up of:

1. Payment period(s)
2. Cash discount(s)

The payment due date for an item is calculated using the payment terms and the **base line date** for that open item. The terms of payment usually consists of three components: (a) **cash discount percentage** which is available provided the payment is made with in a specified (b) **cash discount period**, if not what is the (c) **net duration of credit allowed** within which the whole amount (with out any discount) is to be paid back.

Typically terms of payment is denominated as:

2%   20,   Net 45

(a)   (b)   (c)

Terms of payment is used in invoices, purchase orders, sales orders etc. SAP utilizes terms of payment information in payment transactions, dunning program and in cash management. In SAP, terms of payment is defined using a 4-letter key in the system and is referred to in the customer or vendor master records. For most of the business transactions, system defaults the terms of payment mentioned in the master record of the customer or vendor; however, the same can be altered during document entry, both at the item level or at the header level.

SAP allows you to enter different payment terms in the same master record: you can enter a term in sales area (say, payment term 0001) which is different from that of another term (say, payment term 0003) maintained in accounting area, or the one entered in purchasing area (say, PUR1) etc. Depending upon the business transaction, which is carried out, system defaults that term relevant to that area (If you are processing a purchase order, system defaults the terms payment PUR1, though there are other terms as well defined in the master).

Step-1

Enter the Transaction code or access the transaction using the menu path, and you will be taken to **"Change View "Terms of Payment": Overview"** screen (Figure: **OBB8**-1).

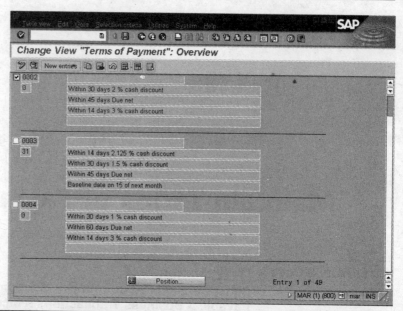

Figure: **OBB8**-1

This is a composite screen, which allows for:

1. 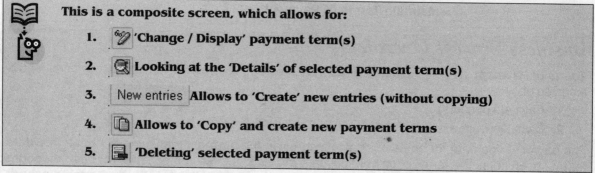 **'Change / Display' payment term(s)**

2. **Looking at the 'Details' of selected payment term(s)**

3. New entries **Allows to 'Create' new entries (without copying)**

4. **Allows to 'Copy' and create new payment terms**

5. **'Deleting' selected payment term(s)**

The display is limited to a few numbers of terms of payments. To see more press

Position... , and enter the details on the pop-up **"Another entry"** screen (Figure: **OBB8**-2).

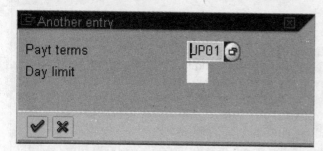

Figure: **OBB8**-2

1. **Payt terms** (M): can be selected by pressing or '*F4*' (Figure: **OBB8**-3).

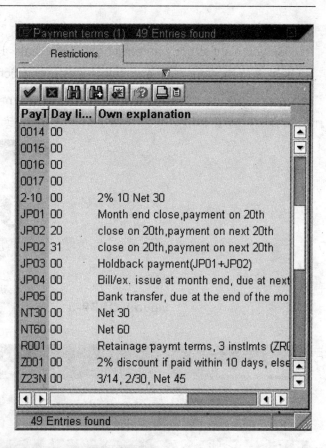

Figure: **OBB8**-3

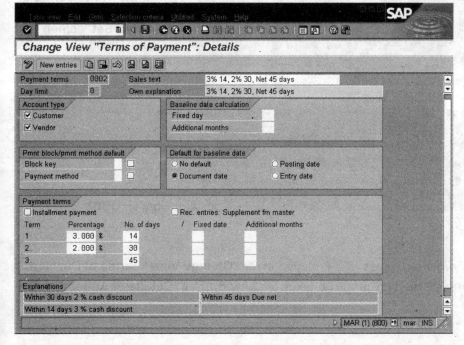

Figure: **OBB8**-4

Step-2

Select the payment terms, for which you want to display/change the details and press

, to go to "**Change View "Terms of Payment": Details**" screen (Figure: OBB8-4).

Step-3

In case you want to copy an existing one to create a new by changing some of the details, you can go back by pressing 🔙 and select the term which you want to copy and then press 📋 or you can press 📋 on "**Change View "Terms of Payment": Details**" screen itself (Figure: **OBB8**-4). The system will pop-up "**Information**" screen (Figure: **OBB8**-5).

Figure: **OBB8**-5

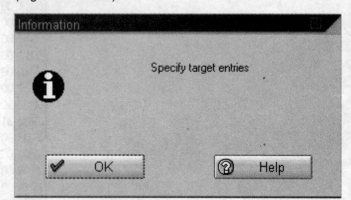

Step-4

Press ✔ OK

and you can change the desired information on "**Change View "Terms of Payment": Details of Selected Set**" screen (Figure: **OBB8**-6).

Figure: **OBB8**-6

Step-5

To *create new terms of payment*, press New entries in the "**Change View "Terms of Payment": Overview**" screen (Figure: **OBB8**-1). You will be taken to "**New Entries: Details of Added Entries**" screen (Figure: **OBB8**-7).

Figure: **OBB8**-7

Maintain the details as mentioned below:

1. **Payment Terms (M):** Enter a name (4-digit alpha numeric) for the new payment term you are creating.

2. **Sales Text (O):** Enter short explanation (30 characters, maximum).

3. **Day Limit (O):** Enter a number between 1 and 31, if you decide that the payment terms needs to depend on the day of a month.

4. **Own Explanation (O):** Give suitable description. Used only when you want the system to display this text in 'Explanations' at the bottom of the screen. Else, leave this as blank.

In <u>Account Type:</u>

5. **Customer (O):** Tick the check-box if this payment term is to be used for A/R.

6. **Vendor (O):** Tick the check-box if this payment term is to be used for A/P.

In <u>Baseline date calculation:</u>

7. **Baseline date calculation (O):** Enter the date if the default baseline date is to be ignored in the calculations. The system will take the date entered here as the baseline date.

8. **Additional months (O):** Enter the number of months, which needs to be added to the baseline date mentioned in (7). The system adds up these two, to arrive at the new baseline date for calculation.

In <u>Pmnt block / pmnt method default:</u>

9. **Payment method (O):** Enter a payment method, which will be tied to this terms of payment. This is in addition to the payment methods already defined in the master record of the customer or vendor.

10. In **<u>Default for the baseline date</u>** (O): Select the appropriate radio button.

In <u>Payment terms:</u>

11. **Installment payment (O):** Tick the check-box if you want the system to break a single line item into various line items with different due dates depending upon the terms of payment. If this indicator is selected, while entering the document in FI, instead of you manually entering several line items, you enter the line item only once and system automatically brings up the other line items depending upon the terms of payment.

12. **Percentage (M):** Enter the discount rate offered.

13. **No. of days(M):** Enter the number days associated with a particular discount rate or net payment.

14. **Fixed date (O):** if you do not want to use the baseline date, enter the day of the month after which the discount is no longer available.

15. **Additional months (O):** Enter the number of months if you want to extend the baseline date month to increase the length of time during which the discount would be still available.

Step-6

Save the entry by pressing ![save icon]. The configured screen will look like the one below (Figure: **OBB8**-8).

Figure: **OBB8**-8

6

Create Bank Master: FI12

Transaction Code	FI12
Menu	(IMG) Financial Accounting > Bank Accounting > Bank Accounts > Define House Banks

Business Process Overview

The system requires details of your bank, the **house bank**, to be entered in the master records of the customer or vendor, the details of which will be used by the automatic payment program to make the payments from this bank. Essentially, you would be entering the bank identifier which will be used by the system to identify the bank and also the account(s) created for the bank for transaction updates.

You need to define the **Bank ID** (5-character alphanumeric key) per company code and is unique within that company code. For each bank you need to maintain country wherein the bank is situated and the bank number or the country specific key.

Besides the Bank ID, you also define the accounts at these banks. Each account at a bank is defined under a **Bank Account.**

Account Id, which is unique per company code per house bank. Take care to name the account properly so as to provide you clear and necessary information by looking at the account name, as you will be referring this account name/identifier in the corresponding G/L master records as well.

Transaction Steps

Step-1

Access the transaction either by the transaction code or by the menu and the system pops up "**Determine Work Area Entry**" Screen (Figure: FI12-1).

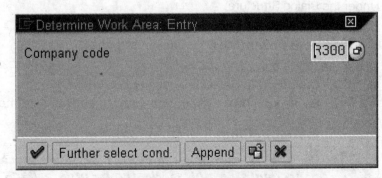

Figure: **FI12**-1

1. **Company code (M):** Enter the company code where you want to create the **house bank.**

Step-2

Press 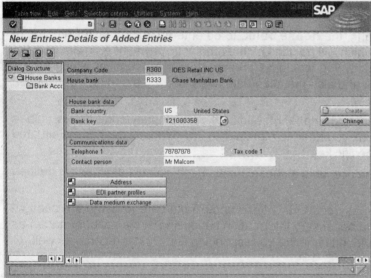 and you are taken to *"**Change View "House Banks": Overview**"* screen (Figure: **FI12**-2).

Figure: **FI12**-2

Step-3

Press New entries and you are taken to *"**New Entries: Details of Added Entries**"* screen (Figure: **FI12**-3).

Figure: **FI12**-3

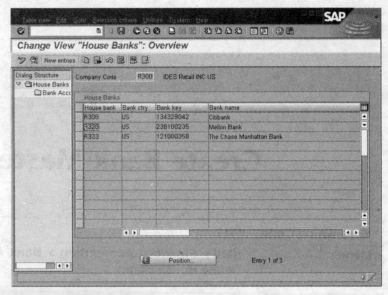

Under the Dialog Structure:

Select House Banks and double click:

  1. **House bank (M):** Enter the house bank id.

Under the House bank data

  2. **Country (M):** Select the country key.

  3. **Bank key (M):** Select the bank if already defined in the bank directory. Or use ☐ Create to define the same.

 Use the *Transaction Code: FI01* or *Menu: Accounting > Financial Accounting > Accounts Payable > Master records > Bank > Create* for creating a bank master.

Under communications data:

    4. Telephone 1(O): Enter the telephone number.

    5. Contact Person (O) : Enter the name of the contact person at the bank.

    6. Press   Address   to maintain the relevant details.

    7. Press   EDI partner profiles   to maintain the EDI (Electronic Data Interface) related information.

    8. Press   Data medium exchange   to maintain the details on DME for data exchange to/from the bank.

Under <u>Control data:</u>

    9. SWIFT code (O): Enter the SWIFT code which will identify a bank internationally.

Step-4

Press 💾 to save to create the house bank. Select "***Bank Account***" from the left hand side <u>dialog structure a</u>nd double click on the same to enter "***New Entries: Details of Added Entries***" screen (Figure: **FI01**-4).

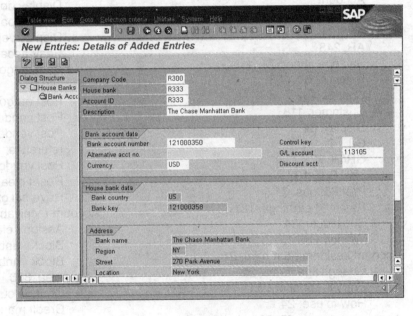

Figure: **FI01**-4

Under <u>Bank account data:</u>

    1. Bank account number (M): Enter a suitable account identifier at the bank.

    2. Alternate acct no. (O): Enter if you need an alternate account number.

    3. Currency (O): Enter the currency in which the account needs to be maintained.

    4. G/L account (M): Enter a G/L account for the account.

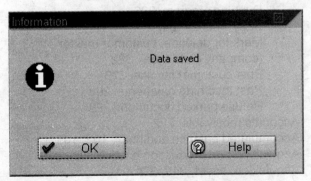

Step-5

Press 💾 to save and create the house bank accounts (Figure: **FI01**-5).

Figure: **FI01**-5

Index